THE EREZ SERIES

RABBI ADIN
EVEN-ISRAEL
STEINSALTZ

A CONCISE GUIDE TO MAHSHAVA

AN OVERVIEW OF JEWISH PHILOSOPHY

A Concise Guide to Mahshava
First edition, 2020

Koren Publishers Jerusalem Ltd.
POB 8531, New Milford, CT 06776-8531, USA
& POB 4044, Jerusalem 91040, Israel

www.korenpub.com

This book was published in cooperation with
the Israeli Institute for Talmudic Publication.

Steinsaltz Center is the parent organization of institutions
established by Rabbi Adin Even-Israel Steinsaltz
POB 45187, Jerusalem 91450 ISRAEL
Telephone: +972 2 646 0900, Fax +972 2 624 9454
www.steinsaltz-center.org

ISBN 978-1-59264-565-7, *hardcover*

Printed and bound in the United States

The Erez Series

Dedicated in loving memory of

Joseph "Erez" Tenenbaum

Whose love of learning, endless curiosity and zest for life
Survived the Destruction
And found full expression in his ultimate return to Zion.

By his son Zisman Tuvia

סדרת ארז

מוקדש לעלוי נשמת

יוסף צבי בן טוביה זיסמן טננבואם
(המכונה ארז)

"אוד מוצל מאש"
שלא נכבה בו אהבת לימוד, סקרנות אין-סופית, ושמחת חיים

ע"י בנו זיסמן טוביה

Contents

Life Cycle

Cycle of the Jewish Year

Torah Concepts

Biographies

Foreword

This book contains an anthology of passages that address profound questions. We focus not only on the content of the passages and descriptions of events, but on responses to questions such as: Why? What is the meaning of this? Much of the material brought here relates to the content of the other books in this series, but this volume also contains a selection of various problems and responses to general questions relating to the nation and the individual, to life, fate, and purpose. Essentially, one will find here a series of meditations and contemplations that are relevant to anyone insofar as he contemplates his own humanity.

The book draws from the writings of many authors that relate, each in their own way, to these essential questions. The array of sources includes works composed since the time of the Sages, beginning approximately in the eighth century, until the twentieth century. One will also find here thoughts and ideas from people who lived more recently, up to the present day. Arguably, one can say that the conceptual and spiritual world of most people up to World War I was similar to that of earlier times, while the modern world we live in can be understood, to a significant extent, as a different conceptual world. It is for this reason that modern writings constitute only a small part of this book.

In addition to longer passages, this volume includes aphorisms and some excerpts from poetry and hymns.

The many topics addressed in this book, which to a degree constitute a review of Jewish thought, are arranged here into three main sections: the Jewish year, the life cycle, and miscellaneous topics. The full list of topics can be found in the detailed table of contents at the front of the book.

At the end of the book there is an appendix that contains short biographies of the many personalities mentioned in the book.

Rabbi Adin Even-Israel Steinsaltz

Introducing the Erez Concise Guides

A Jewish home, at any time or place, cannot be maintained based on the mere identity of its residents as Jews. Whether they conceive of themselves as religious, traditional, or secular, people need to have access to written expression of their tradition through which they can come to know, understand, and "enter" their tradition.

"To enter the tradition" can mean something different for each person. Some are simply curious, others have a particular interest, and there are undoubtedly many Jews who just do not want the worlds of the Jewish spirit to be closed to them. People therefore require bridges and gates to gain access. There is no obligation to use these, but their existence makes it possible for anyone – when that person so desires – to enter, or even to glance within; the way is clear and he or she can do so.

We have thus produced the Erez series which provides different gates by which one can enter the Jewish tradition. Just as it is told about Abraham's tent that it was open from all four directions in order to welcome guests from everywhere, these books allow anyone, whenever he or she feels like it or finds something interesting, to enter into the tradition.

There are thousands of books that cover, in various ways and at different levels, the materials presented here. However, most of them require prior knowledge and no small amount of effort to be understood. In these volumes, we have striven to give anyone who seeks it a paved road into the riches of the Jewish world. More than merely a gate, we hope that these books can be said to offer their readers a "ride" into the tradition. Each person can get off whenever he or she desires and continue traveling when their interest is reawakened.

These volumes contain some of the fundamentals of Judaism. In each of them there are elements that can be considered hors d'oeuvres that can be snacked upon and others that are more comparable to entrees, that require more time for digestion. In either case, the invitation offered by Wisdom in Proverbs (9:5) is relevant: "Come, partake of my bread, and drink of the wine that I have mixed." The books were deliberately designed to be accessible to everyone, whether he or she is highly educated or someone whose source of intellectual stimulation consists in occasionally reading the newspaper. Anyone can enjoy something, whether by means of an occasional taste, or by sitting down to a hearty meal. The way is open and anyone can find the gate appropriate for him or her, without effort.

We have aimed to keep the translation as true to the original Hebrew and Aramaic as possible. As some of these texts are not easy to understand, we have added clarifying comments in square brackets where appropriate. Further explication is appended in notes at the end of certain passages. When we have felt it appropriate to use a transliteration, the term transliterated is first explained and then followed by the transliteration in square brackets. At the end of each book we have provided a glossary of Hebrew terms mentioned in the series. Some of the terms found there may not be found in this book, as we have used the same glossary for all the volumes of the Erez series. *The Reference Guide to the Talmud* has a more extensive glossary as is necessary for that work.

Given the antiquity of the texts collected here, there are many occasions where it was impossible to avoid gendered usage and we have followed the texts themselves in using the male gender as the default.

Each of the volumes in this series stands alone, with only occasional citations connecting them. The first volume, *A Concise Guide to the Torah,* contains the translation of the Torah taken from the *Steinsaltz Humash*; we have abridged the commentary that can be found there. One can take this volume to the synagogue but also peruse it in the comforts of one's home.

The second volume, *A Concise Guide to the Sages,* is an anthology of rabbinic literature, organized by topics. One part includes rabbinic thinking associated with the Torah, while other topics are also addressed: the cycle of the Jewish year, the cycle of life in rabbinic eyes, as well as other topics where a person can find something that fits his or her needs.

The third volume, *A Concise Guide to Mahshava,* addresses spiritual matters. It contains an anthology of non-halakhic literature from the Jewish spiritual tradition: Kabbala, Jewish philosophy, the Musar tradition, and hasidic writings. Here too, the texts are presented in a manner that is accessible to all, in clear English. This volume addresses a broad array of topics: Besides comments and explanations on the Torah, there are sections devoted to the cycle of the Jewish year, the life cycle, and fundamental questions of human life such as parenthood, marriage, and death. There are many other topics addressed in this volume and one can open it at random and find wisdom that touches the soul.

The fourth volume, *A Concise Guide to Halakha,* is a survey of practical *halakha*. It does not delve into the sources of *halakha* and provide an opportunity for intensive study but serves rather as a guidebook to what the *halakha* instructs one to do in various situations. In this way the book offers a summary of the *halakhot* of Shabbat and the holidays, of life cycle events, and of those mitzvot that any Jew is likely to encounter. If one wishes to act in accordance with the *halakha,* he or she will know what to do with the help of this volume. It is written in clear English with a minimum of technical language so that it is accessible to anyone, man, woman, or child. And if he or she decides to act accordingly, may he or she be blessed.

The fifth volume, *Reference Guide to the Talmud,* is a reprint of the work that was issued as a companion to the *Koren Talmud Bavli.* It is an indispensable resource for students of all levels. This fully revised, English-language edition of the *Reference Guide* clearly and concisely explains the Talmud's fundamental structure, concepts, terminology, assumptions, and inner logic; it provides essential historical and biographical information; it includes appendixes, a key to abbreviations, and a comprehensive index.

For improved usability, this completely updated volume has a number of new features: topical organization instead of by Hebrew alphabet, re-edited and revised text to coordinate with the language used in the *Koren Talmud Bavli,* and an index of Hebrew terms to enable one seeking a Hebrew term to locate the relevant entry.

These books are certainly not the entire Torah, but they are beneficial for any Jew to have in his or her home. If one finds something interesting, or is curious about something, these books offer a resource to investigate that topic. Even if one opens one of these volumes by chance, he or she will gain from reading them, both intellectually and spiritually. In short, these are books that it is convenient to have in one's home.

Our thanks are extended to all the people who participated in the project of writing these books, editing them, and finding the sources therein. We likewise would like to thank the publisher, and those first readers who offered helpful criticism and advice, and finally to those good people whose donations made it possible to create these books.

The Editors

Translator's Note

We have aimed to keep the translation as true to the original Hebrew or Aramaic (and in a few cases, Arabic) as possible. Some of these texts are not easy to understand and we have added clarifying comments in square brackets where appropriate. Some further explication is appended in notes at the end of some of the passages. When we have felt it necessary to use a transliteration, the term transliterated is first explained followed by the transliteration in square brackets. In general, we have striven to use gender-neutral language, though given the antiquity of the texts collected here, there are many occasions where it was impossible to avoid gendered usage and we have followed the texts themselves in using the male gender as the default.

We would like to express our gratitude to Feldheim Publishers for their permission to use their translations of the citations from the various writings of Rabbi Samson Raphael Hirsch.

Life Cycle

Pregnancy and Birth

The formation of a human being begins with the act of intercourse from which a fetus is created. The fetus is then gestated, and ultimately born, with a new child coming into the world.

Each of these stages has an element of spirituality which affects the child. The holy intentions that one has during intercourse affect the soul that God entrusts to the couple. During the months of pregnancy, the fetus learns the entire Torah, and when it is born, it is affected by the holiness of the environment into which it enters. In essence, a person's good deeds are like his children; each deed contains the stages of thought, will, and action.

The Moment of Conception

At conception, God entrusts the couple with a soul, which will reside within the child to be born. The baby is accompanied by a spiritual image that corresponds to an image in the upper world. Before a person's death, that spiritual image departs, and this is a sign that he is about to die:

At the moment when a man undertakes to sanctify himself and engage in intercourse with his wife with his holy will, a holy spirit awakens in him, which includes [both] male and female elements, and the Holy One, blessed be He summons the messenger who is appointed over human pregnancies, and deposits with him that spirit, and tells him where to deposit it...The Holy One, blessed be He, infuses into that spirit everything that He infuses, and [the Sages of the mystical Torah] have explained this.

A person is accompanied by a spiritual image in this world, and parallel to this there is an image in the World to Come:

Then a spirit descends, and an image is with it, that which corresponds to its form above. He is created in that image and he walks in this world in that image. This is as it is written: "Surely man walks with an image" (Psalms 39:7). While this image is with the person, he exists with it in this world and in the next world, and the two of them are joined together as one.

Before a person dies his image departs from him:

When a person's time for leaving this world approaches, the evil spirit [that is a result of contact with the physical world] that had clung each day to the elevated image that was given to him comes and takes the image and uses it to rectify itself, and [the elevated image is repaired and] departs, and never again returns to that person. Then one knows that he has been turned away from everything [and is about to die].

(*Zohar* 3:43a)

Further reading: For more on pregnancy and birth, see *A Concise Guide to the Sages*, p. 407; *A Concise Guide to Halakha*, p. 3.

During Pregnancy

The Talmud states that a person learns the entire Torah while in the womb, but when he is about to be born, an angel appears and strikes him on the mouth to make him forget it (*Nidda* 30b). Why does a person need to learn the entire Torah if he will subsequently forget it? It is impossible to understand God's Torah without divine assistance. However, if everyone remembered the Torah he had learned in the womb, he would not be able to receive reward for Torah study. Therefore, he forgets the entire Torah before birth and reacquires it only through hard work.

A person is incapable of understanding the Torah without divine assistance:

This Torah is concealed from the eyes of all living creatures, and humankind in this material world has no possibility to grasp even a tiny iota of it without divine assistance…

The reason that one forgets all the Torah he learned while in the womb:

Behold, if [understanding the Torah] is [solely the result of] an act of the eternal God, there will be no possibility for reward and punishment, since it all will necessarily be decreed by the Creator.[1] Therefore, one is made to forget all the Torah when he comes into the world so that he will subsequently acquire knowledge of the Torah by his own will, through effort, and by choice, with complete awareness.

The benefit of studying Torah in the womb even though it is subsequently forgotten:

The act of learning, the fact that one is taught all of the Torah in his mother's womb, is beneficial, as something of the divine assistance will remain etched within him such that he, with his earthly abilities, will be able to retrieve it…. This is the desired outcome of teaching a person all of the Torah before he comes into the world and then causing him to forget it: So that the matter will come to him through effort and by means of his choice. It is unattainable without divine assistance, but since it remains in his memory, he is able to retrieve it through his labor and effort.

(Rabbi Tzvi Elimelekh Shapira, *Benei Yisaskhar, Sivan* 1:5)

After Birth

From the time of the child's birth, it is incumbent upon the parents to ensure that he is surrounded by holiness. Doing so increases the chances of success in raising him to a life of Torah and the performance of good deeds. Each year on the child's birthday, the parents should reflect on the fact that they have merited tremendously; God has deposited with them a soul inside a body. They should consider the way to educate the child so that he will walk a straight path.

One should see to it that from the time of birth the child is surrounded by holiness:

Another crucial matter with regard to the newborn is that after he comes into the world he should immediately be surrounded by holy matters. It is known that the things that an infant, even one who is one day old, sees and hears have an impact on his development (recently, modern psychology has adopted this age-old insight). Therefore, the infant's being surrounded with holiness brings blessing and success for [his parents] to merit raising him or her to [a life that includes] Torah, marriage, and good deeds.

The merit and joy of raising and educating children:

The main thing [for parents] is to reflect on the greatness of the merit and joy that have come to them because the Holy One, blessed be He, deposited into their hands a soul in a holy body, relying upon them to properly safeguard this precious security by educating and guiding the child in the path that leads up to the House of God.

(Rabbi Menaḥem Mendel Schneerson,
Torat Menaḥem, Hitva'aduyot 5747, part 2, p. 37; 5742, part 4, p. 2190)

Good Deeds Are Called Children

The stages in the formation of the baby, conception, gestation, and birth, correspond to three stages in the formation of good deeds: thought, will, and action. Just as there is anguish involved in childbirth, so too, a person who intends to do a good deed in its entirety is required to exert himself and suffer.

A person's good deeds are called his children:

Observe that which the Sages said: A person's good deeds are called children (*Tanḥuma, Noah* 2). The truth is that they are indeed alike. There are three stages to childbirth prior to the actual emergence of the child: conception, gestation, and birth, and that which happens to a woman occurs likewise to a person serving the Creator, with regard to his progeny, i.e., his good deeds. The same three stages are necessary: first in the concealed realm of thought, then will, and then complete action, and this is the mystery of birth.

The pain of childbirth and the effort of raising children are also aspects of the performance of good deeds:

Therefore, it is like the case of a woman who, when she comes close to giving birth, begins crying out from the pain of the birth contractions. Afterward there is also the pain of raising children. Likewise, much anguish comes to a person before he completes an action for no other purpose than to serve God alone. [With] all this, perhaps [he will succeed].

(Rabbi Zev Wolf of Zhitomir, *Or HaMe'ir, Koraḥ*)

A young hasid approached Rabbi Tzvi Hirsh, son of the Ba'al Shem Tov, and asked him to instruct him in the service of God so that he could reach the level of a saintly person.

Rabbi Tzvi Hirsh said to him: "Certainly you know So-and-So, the wealthy man, whose father was a very wealthy man and left him a great fortune. Once, someone came to him and asked for his advice regarding how to become rich. The wealthy man said to him: 'I have no idea how to become rich; I inherited my wealth from my father. Go and ask another wealthy person, one who became wealthy with his own two hands, and ask him.'"

"I am the same," concluded Rabbi Tzvi Hirsh. "My holy father toiled so that I would be given a lofty soul, and he bequeathed to me his spiritual powers; I did not labor for this. Go to a saintly person who was born to simple people and who reached his level through his own labor and ask him how to do it."

When the soul comes to this world, it is anguished about the fact that it has been dispatched from the world of delight, merriment, and happiness, and placed in this world. Therefore, when a person emerges from his mother's womb he cries, because the soul is crying about its arrival in this world.

(Rabbi Levi Yitzḥak of Berditchev, *Kedushat Levi, Likutim*)

The Giving of a Name

The parents are the ones who choose the name of their newborn child. Occasionally, a person chooses a new name for himself later in life.

A person's name is not only a means of identification; rather, it contains a spiritual meaning. According to the Kabbala, one's name expresses his heavenly roots and the unique mission that has been allocated to him to fulfill in this world.

The Significance of the Name Given by One's Parents

A person's name is linked to his soul. His parents receive a type of prophecy from above in order to give the child the name that is fitting for him.

When a person is born and his father and mother give him the name that they have thought of, this is not random or by chance; rather, the Holy One, blessed be He, puts that name, which is necessary for that soul, into [the parents'] mouths.

(Rabbi Yitzḥak Luria (Arizal), *Sha'ar HaGilgulim*, Introduction 23)

A name expresses an object's spiritual life force, and therefore people are profoundly linked to their names.

An object's name is linked to its essence:

Whatever something is called in the holy tongue is its true name, the name at the root of its essence. For example, an ox [*shor*] in the lower [world] is called this due to the root of its life force above, which contains the three letters *shin-vav-reish*, שו"ר. This is the case with regard to all things…

Even when a child is named after another person, his name fits the root of his soul:

Although we name our children after our ancestors or our relatives, as it says in the Midrash, nevertheless the Ari, may his memory be for life in the World to Come, revealed to us that even those names were not given by chance or by the will of the father and mother. Rather, the Holy One, blessed be He, is the One who places intelligence, wisdom, and knowledge into the heart of the father and mother to give a name that is from the root of the child's soul.

There is a very strong connection between a person and his name:

Because of this, people are extremely connected to their names. The proof of this is that if a person turns away from all of his other affairs and attends to one thing, and he focuses his eyes, heart, and thoughts on that one thing in total concentration... nevertheless, if someone calls him by name, he will immediately disengage from his business and from his thoughts. All this is for the aforementioned reason, because his name is the root of his soul.

(Rabbi Dov Ber of Mezeritch, *Or Torah, Bereshit* 14)

Further reading: For more on how the first man gave names to all the creatures, see *A Concise Guide to the Sages*, p. 5.

One's Name as an Expression of His Mission

Every individual has a mission in this world, and one's name expresses his unique mission. After our patriarch Jacob fulfilled the mission of his name Jacob, he was called "Israel," and was given an additional mission to fulfill in this world.

One's name alludes to the mission that he must fulfill in this world:

One's name is that matter that he was created to rectify; he was named for this. Therefore, evil people [who do not rectify that which they are supposed to rectify during their lifetimes] forget their names in the grave. But Jacob, not only did he rectify that for which he was named, but he merited being called by the name Israel as well [see Genesis 32:29].

A person is engaged in a mission all his days, and he is named for it:

All his days, a person is engaged in his mission, until he fulfills the mission and departs to the upper world. Jacob, who had already rectified that for which he was named, was given another name.

(Rabbi Yehuda Aryeh Leib Alter, *Sefat Emet, Vayishlaḥ* 5657)

One should pray that all those who are called by his name will have these good attributes, and not one of the evil attributes.

(Rabbi Yehuda HeḤasid, *Sefer Ḥasidim*)

Further reading: For the *halakhot* that relate to naming, see *A Concise Guide to Halakha*, pp. 7, 15 (for boys), and p. 30 (for girls).

The Covenant of Circumcision

On the eighth day after the birth of a baby boy, we bring him into the covenant of circumcision. A covenant is a powerful and significant relationship, and the circumcision is a symbol of the unbreakable bond between us and the Holy One, blessed be He. Our patriarch Abraham was the first to be commanded to circumcise himself, and his son, Isaac, was the first to be circumcised when he was eight days old. Since then, the covenant has symbolized our deep connection to God, which is ingrained in our very being.

The Sages explain that the circumcision takes place specifically on the reproductive organ in order to reduce excessive desire. Circumcision is a constant sign on our bodies that reminds us that God shines His face upon us wherever we are. At the time of the circumcision we pray that the child will have a holy soul and will be able to study Torah and observe the mitzvot.

The Reasons for Circumcision

There are mitzvot that we fulfill only because we have faith in God and are certain that if He gave us a particular mitzva it is good to fulfill it. Circumcision is a mitzva that is difficult to comprehend, yet our patriarch Abraham fulfilled it, and we follow in his footsteps, having faith in He who gave the mitzva.

The rabbi[1] said: In fact, our minds have no access whatsoever to divinely mandated actions, and what is more, the mind rejects them, and accepts them only like a sick person agrees to the doctor's orders or medicines. Behold [the commandment of] circumcision, which is far from reason and contains nothing approaching society's laws, yet you see that Abraham fulfilled it with regard to himself, despite the natural difficulty involved, as he was then one hundred years old. He also fulfilled it with regard to his sons as well, and in this way it became a mark of the covenant, so that the Divine would cling to him and his descendants; as God said to him: "I will establish My covenant between Me and you and your descendants after you

1. The Kuzari was written as a dialogue between a rabbi and the Khazar king.

throughout their generations for an eternal covenant, to be your God and for your descendants after you" (Genesis 17:7).

(Rav Yehuda HaLevi, *Kuzari* 3:6–7)

All sons of the Jewish people are righteous when they become members of the people of the Holy One, blessed be He, at circumcision. The covenant is an offering to God; it is as though we are offering up our children when they are eight days old.

Rabbi Abba began and said: "Your people, they are all righteous…" (Isaiah 60:21). This matter was explicated by the Sages: Why is is written "Your people, they are all righteous"? Is all of Israel righteous? There are in fact some people who are liable [for punishment] in Israel, some sinners and some evildoers who transgress the Torah's commandments. Rather, this is what they taught in the mystical teachings: Meritous are Israel, who willingly perform an offering to the Holy One, blessed be He, as they offer up their eight-day-old children [for circumcision] as offerings. When they are circumcised, they enter the good graces of the Holy One, blessed be He, as it is written: "But the righteous is the foundation of the world" (Proverbs 10:25). Since they have entered into this lot of the righteous, they are called righteous.

(*Zohar* 1:93a)

Circumcision does not impair the practical functioning of the reproductive organ but it does reduce excessive desire, and in this manner a man improves his character. The mark of the covenant also distinguishes all who have entered into the covenant from outsiders.

The most important reason for circumcision – reducing excessive desire:

This commandment does not come to fix a deficiency in the design of Creation, but rather to fix a deficiency in [a man's] character. The physical harm caused to that organ is the deliberate goal. Circumcision does not damage any vital function, nor is the ability to have children impaired as a result. But the fervor of sensuality and excessive desire are lessened because of it…. This, in my opinion, is the most important reason for circumcision.

The covenant of circumcision unites all the faithful and distinguishes them from others:

…With regard to circumcision there is, in my opinion, another very important matter, which is that all who are of this worldview, namely [the Jewish people,] the believers in the oneness of God, have a common physical mark, and a person who is not one of them cannot claim that he is one of them when he is an outsider, which is something he may do in order to make a profit or to attack members of the faith. A man would not perform this act [of circumcision] upon himself or upon his children unless it was out of true faith, as this is not a scratch on the leg, nor a burn on the arm, but rather something that is considered extremely difficult.

(Rambam, *Guide of the Perplexed* III:49)

Further reading: For more on circumcision, see *A Concise Guide to the Torah*, pp. 34, 142, 277; *A Concise Guide to the Sages*, p. 144; *A Concise Guide to Halakha*, p. 5.

The Meaning of the Covenant of Circumcision

The mark of the covenant indicates the deep connection between us and the Holy One, blessed be He. Even when we are distant or in a dark place, God is with us and He lights up the darkness for us.

The meaning of the covenant is the connection between our souls and God:

This is the essence of the covenant of circumcision, which is called a covenant, a new [permanent] alliance between two parties who were previously distant. For the body is alienated [from the spiritual], and through this organ, closeness and connection are achieved. In truth, this organ is an exception that teaches us about all the rest: That the spiritual realm is close, but covered in darkness. Therefore, when permission is granted to remove the outer covering from this organ, its inner spiritual aspect is awakened...

The Holy One, blessed be He, is with us always:

The merit of circumcision always accompanies a man... and we should learn from this that the Holy One, blessed be He, walks everywhere with a person who serves God.

(Rabbi Yehuda Aryeh Leib Alter, *Sefat Emet, Lekh Lekha* 5644)

An infant is circumcised when he is eight days old, just like our patriarch Isaac was circumcised at eight days old, and unlike Ishmael son of Abraham, who was circumcised at the age of thirteen. The difference between these two ages represents two different notions of the covenant. Do we enter the covenant out of understanding and consent, or is it a covenant of devotion, which is not limited to one's level of knowledge or understanding?

The connection is formed at a moment when the infant is too young to understand or agree to the act:

Isaac was circumcised at the age of eight days. An eight-day-old infant is not considered to be giving consent [to entering into a covenant with God], and nevertheless he is bound at that point to the Holy One, blessed be He, with an unbreakable bond, as the verse states: "An eternal covenant" (Genesis 17:7).

The connection between us and the Holy One, blessed be He, is not limited to particular levels of understanding or intellect.

When establishing generations of Jews there is no place for a natural approach. The very essence and existence of the Jewish people are supernatural. The entire existence of a Jew, from his conception and birth, is through miracles, without any regard for nature [like Isaac, who was born when his parents were elderly]. The Holy One, blessed be He, said to our patriarch Abraham: True Jewish satisfaction comes only from a child whose birth and beginnings are caused by God, and who, when he is eight days old, at the first opportunity [as before this it is dangerous to circumcise a child], is bound to the Holy One, blessed be He, in an eternal covenant, although he still does not understand and there is no possibility of asking him. The Judaism of such a boy will not be limited by his knowledge or intellect, but will be imbued with devotion.

(Rabbi Menaḥem Mendel Schneerson, *Likutei Siḥot* 1, pp. 20–21)

Further reading: For more on the covenant of circumcision accompanying a man wherever he goes, see the story of King David, *A Concise Guide to the Sages*, p. 145.

What to Do during the Circumcision

When parents circumcise their child they should greatly rejoice, and after the circumcision they should pray for the child, that he will have a holy soul and will be able to study and practice the Torah.

When one brings his son to circumcise him, a great joy will be awakened in his heart, and he shall glorify and praise God for granting him a son and the ability to bring him into the covenant of our patriarch Abraham ... and he shall rejoice with a great joy in his heart, a spiritual joy which entails cleaving to Him, may He be blessed ... and he shall pray to the Lord immediately after the circumcision that He will bestow upon the child a holy soul, [enabling him] to learn, to teach, to keep [the mitzvot], to perform, and to fulfill [the Torah and its commandments]. He shall bless the child, and let others bless him too.

(Rabbi Yeshaya HaLevi Horowitz, *Shenei Luḥot HaBerit, Ḥullin* 43–44)

Rabbi Shalom of Belz was invited to celebrate a circumcision, and he said to the child's father: "Today, your circumcision was completed." The man asked in astonishment: "My circumcision?"

The *tzadik* explained: "Every mitzva must be fulfilled perfectly, in thought, speech, and act. We perform the act of circumcision on an infant, but he does not fulfill the thought aspect of the mitzva, as he does not yet possess understanding. Only when one brings his son into the covenant of our patriarch Abraham does he rectify the thought that was missing at his own circumcision."

Bar Mitzva

At the age of thirteen a boy becomes bar mitzva: He becomes obligated by Torah law to observe the mitzvot. Prior to this, he is educated in the observance of the mitzvot and the study of Torah, but this education is an obligation instituted by the Sages on his parents. The child's Torah obligation begins when he becomes bar mitzva.

From this point onward, a man is accompanied by angels who guard his footsteps. He becomes whole, and is infused with his holy soul. Wise choices made at this age will make it possible for him to walk a straight path all his life.

The Change That Occurs at the Bar Mitzva

From one's bar mitzva onward, two angels accompany the person. When he walks a straight path they rejoice with him, but if he walks a crooked path they abandon him.

The Holy One, blessed be He, does good for mankind, as once one reaches the age of thirteen, He places with him two guardian angels to guard him, one to his right and one to his left. When one walks a straight path, they rejoice with him and encourage him to be happy; they proclaim before him: Give honor to the image of the King. But when he walks a crooked path they mourn for him and distance themselves from him.

(*Zohar* 2:106b)

A person possesses a holy soul, and it begins to bond with him at his circumcision, and even more so when he begins to learn how to keep the mitzvot. Nevertheless, he is infused with the main component at his bar mitzva, when he becomes obligated by Torah law to observe the commandments.

The completion and the primary infusion of the holy soul into a person [transforming him or her into a complete, adult Jew], occurs at thirteen years and one day for a male, and at twelve for a female, and therefore from that time they are obligated by Torah law to observe the commandments, and become liable for punishment for their sins. This holy soul begins to be infused [in the body] when one is educated [at a young age] how to keep the Torah and its commandments, an obligation imposed by the Sages [upon the parents].

(Rabbi Shneur Zalman of Liadi, *Shulḥan Arukh HaRav, Mahadura Batra* 4:2)

A Crossroads

At the time of his bar mitzva, a person stands at a spiritual and psychological crossroads, in which he must choose his or her path. Proper education during this period paves a straight path for one's entire life.

An infant is tainted by the filth of the evil inclination, and his wisdom and understanding are concealed and imperceptible. When the reaches the age of a youth, which is at the beginning of the thirteenth year, and the signs of wisdom and understanding appear, the young person is similar to a person standing at a crossroads ... and if he does not know the particular way to each place, he will stray. So too, when a person reaches the age of thirteen years he stands at a crossroads. He will either go on the path of good to the right, or on the path of evil to the left, and admonishment and rebuke given during that time direct the young person to the good path and save him from the evil. He will then walk all his life along the path that he becomes accustomed to in his youth, and this is what Solomon, in his wisdom, said: "Train the lad in accordance with his way; even when he grows old, he will not turn from it" (Proverbs 22:6).

(Rav Yoseph Gikatilla, *Sefer HaMeshalim* 127)

A Jew came before his rebbe and complained about his son, who had just become bar mitzva but refused to attend the synagogue or say blessings, and he neglected the mitzvot.

His rebbe asked him: "How did your son behave before he became bar mitzva?"

"The same way as he behaves now," the father replied, and added apologetically, "but he was not obligated to keep the mitzot then."

The rebbe answered: "You are mistaken. One does not become a bar mitzva suddenly, in the course of one day. We begin to educate the Jewish child in Torah and mitzvot already from the time of his birth, so that after thirteen years he will be able to behave as a bar mitzva."

Further reading: For more on bar and bat mitzva, their meaning, and how we celebrate them, see *A Concise Guide to Halakha*, p. 36.

Wedding

A man and a woman are two halves of one soul, and those who are fortunate find the other half of their soul and get married. The joy at a wedding is the precursor to the joy of worldwide redemption. One's ancestors who have passed into the World of Truth attend the wedding, and the heavenly bride [the Divine Presence] comes to rejoice with the bride entering the wedding canopy.

Anyone who brings joy to the bride and groom indicates that God has worked a miracle and is responsible for the match. This joy leads the bride to act upon her desire for the groom, and this should inspire everyone to act upon one's soul's yearning for God.

Two Halves

The bride and groom are ideally parts of one soul that have found one another. Only those who have merit succeed in finding their matching soul. When a man does not succeed in doing so, part of that soul is given to another.

All spirits contain [both] male and female [elements]. When they are manifest, they are [both] male and female, and only afterward, [when they descend to this world,] do they go their separate ways. If one has merit, they [the male and female parts] subsequently match up. They are joined together in one union, entirely, in body and soul.... If one merits, he is given his mate, and if not, she is separated from him and given to another.

(*Zohar* 3:43a)

The Importance of Marriage

Redemption will come when all the souls that need to come into this world have descended from the upper world. This is one reason we rejoice at weddings, because they lead to the bringing of children into the world, and thus bring the redemption closer.

The joy of a wedding indicates the approach of the redemption, and this is the allusion in the Talmud: "The son of David will not come until all the souls of the body [in heaven] have been finished [have descended to this world]" (*Yevamot* 62a). This is the joy of a wedding; it is for the souls that will come into this world as a result; this is the union, and through it we come closer to the redemption. For this reason we say in the seven wedding blessings [the blessing of]: "Celebrate greatly...," [alluding to] the building of the Temple, because from this joy, the Temple will be built.

(Rabbi Levi Yitzḥak of Berditchev, *Kedushat Levi, Likutim*)

Further reading: For more on the wedding ceremony, see *A Concise Guide to Halakha*, p. 47.

Who Comes to Rejoice at a Wedding Celebration?

The Song of Songs describes the relationship between a bride and groom, and the Sages explain this as a parable describing the relationship of the Jewish people with their Creator. God is the bridegroom, the beloved, and He searches for His bride, the Jewish people. Every wedding ceremony is attended by the mystical community of Israel that comes from the upper world, and participates in the joy of the bride in this lower world.

One must make the wedding canopy with precious materials in honor of the [heavenly] bride, mentioned in Song of Songs, who attends the celebration of the earthly bride, who symbolizes her. The wedding canopy in which the bride abides is a symbol for the heavenly canopy where the [heavenly] bride is, and it is perfectly beautiful, in a variety of precious shades. For the heavenly and earthly brides are in one image: The former is blessed with seven mystical blessings; seven rivers empty fine oil upon her. The latter is blessed with seven blessings [recited under the canopy] that reflect the seven heavenly blessings.

(Rabbi Yeshaya HaLevi Horowitz, *Shenei Luḥot HaBerit, Sha'ar HaOtiyot, Kedushat HaZivug*)

The *Zohar* describes how God brings the souls of deceased parents from the Garden of Eden in order to rejoice at the weddings of their children. Earlier generations also come to participate in the celebration.

At the time of the wedding, the souls of the ancestors arrive from the World of Truth, as far as three generations back; this is the case for all of Israel, and there are those for whom [souls come from] even [earlier generations].

(Rabbi Yosef Yitzḥak Schneersohn, *Sefer HaMa'amarim Kuntresim* 1:38b)

Further reading: For more on relationships, see p. 179; *A Concise Guide to the Sages*, p. 376.

Bringing Joy to the Bride and Groom

The Sages of the Talmud offer three suggestions as to the significance of bringing joy to the bride and groom (*Berakhot* 6b). Each suggestion relates to a different aspect of a wedding, and their combination reflects the great joy involved: (a) Rejoicing with the bride and groom is like receiving the Torah; (b) it is like bringing a thanks offering; (c) it is like rebuilding one of the destroyed parts of Jerusalem. Each of these represents a way the wedding symbolizes God's interaction with the world.

The joy at a wedding is a recognition of God's command over everything:

The bride and groom are two separate entities, as this one is man and this one is woman, and as such they are completely separate. Their union is from God, may He be blessed, who brings them together… and when one brings joy to the groom, their union is completed, and [this expresses the notion that] it is God who unites the couple. This teaches that all changes in reality, like the fact that they separate into male and female, come from God. This aspect of [bringing joy to the bride and groom is] "as if one had offered a thanks offering" (*Berakhot* 6b) … which exists only to teach that all changes in reality are due to God.[2]

The wedding is the establishment of a new entity by God and is like rebuilding one of the ruins of Jerusalem:

With regard to that which it says [that bringing joy to the bride and groom is considered] "as if one rebuilt one of Jerusalem's ruins" (*Berakhot* 6b), the interpretation is that the union of the bride and groom brings about the completion of the formation of man; because he was previously considered a deficient form, and is now considered a complete form. This is considered like rebuilding the ruins of Jerusalem [the city of God], because this union of the bride and groom is an edifice built by God…

The completion of a person is comparable to the completion of the world:

It says that if he brings joy [to the bride and groom]: "He receives the reward of acquiring the Torah, which was given with five voices" (*Berakhot* 6b)…. The Torah was given with five voices [the word "voice" appears five times in the account of the giving of the Torah (Exodus 19:16–19)]. [The Torah] is the divine order that was given to the world, and it brings completion to the world, as has been explained. Therefore, one who brings joy to the bride and groom is completing the union of the bride and groom, to the point where there is a completed reality, and a person is considered like the entire world… as was explained above that man is a microcosm of the entire world. Likewise, the Torah is a microcosm of the entire world. When one brings joy to the bride and groom, whose union is the completion of a person, who is the entire world, one thereby merits Torah, which is also the completed

---

2. A thanks offering is brought by someone who has escaped an extreme situation, such as traveling at sea or across a desert, or one who has been released from prison or recovered from an illness. The offering expresses the person's recognition that God is present in every situation and in every change in a person's reality.

reality of the entire world, which is why the Torah was given with five voices, as has been explained. This interpretation is unquestionably true and clear to anyone who understands wisdom.

(Maharal, *Tiferet Yisrael* 30)

Dancing before the bride causes her joy and delight, enabling her to reveal her inner desire, and her yearning for her husband. Each and every Jew, and the community of Israel as a whole, is the bride of God. In their spiritual essence they yearn for God, yet they must draw this desire and yearning out of their place of concealment to be revealed.

The heavenly bride is the community of Israel and the divine spark that is within each member of the Jewish people:

The matter of the heavenly bride is well known: It is the community of Israel as a whole [the source of all Jewish souls], and, in particular, it is in the divine spark within each and every Jew. The word bride [*kalla*] derives from *kilayon*, meaning completion or expiration as in: "My soul longs, indeed it expires [*kalta*], for the courtyards of the Lord" (Psalms 84:3). This refers to the natural, essential love that is rooted in every divine spark to be willing to die for the One, because it is indeed a part of the Divine and is drawn to its source…[3]

The desire each person has to connect to God is concealed and needs to be revealed:

But even though one's soul is rooted in the desire and passion to be constantly drawn to the source of its formation, as it says: "The spirit of the sons of man, does it ascend" (Ecclesiastes 3:21)…it is always moving upward…, nevertheless, this [desire] is hidden and enclosed in a person, and is in no way revealed…and this is why the word bride [*kalla*] derives from *kilayon*, as in: "My soul…expires [*kalta*]," as this refers to love that is concealed in the mysterious place in the heart of the Jewish people…

When we dance and rejoice it is possible to reveal that which is concealed:

This is the idea of dancing before the bride: Through dancing before her, we arouse within her a point of connection, bringing it from the concealed to the revealed, and she becomes a kind of receptacle in order to unite with her husband. For through her joy and delight, which we impart to her by

3. That is to say that Jews are prepared to sacrifice their lives to sanctify the name of God because there is a divine spark in each Jew's soul that is drawn to God.

dancing before her, she raises herself up, and that which is blocked inside her is aroused and becomes revealed, her desire for union… and so too with regard to the divine spark in the individual, which is called a bride; through the dance that we perform before it, that which was concealed within it [i.e., the soul's love] is illuminated and revealed.

(Rabbi Dovber Schneuri, *Derushei Ḥatuna* 2, p. 659)

The fine threads that are woven between the groom and the bride are strings that play the music of the Divine Presence at Mount Sinai.

(Rabbi Shlomo Wolbe, *Alei Shur* 1)

Further reading: For more on love of God, see p. 107.

Old Age

The first human was also the first to be condemned to death. Every individual ages and eventually reaches the end of his days. Over the years, one's strength and physical desires weaken, and he becomes more able to strengthen his mind and to connect to God. A person who, in his youth, has developed his intellect and has chosen an upright path will see with the years how his mind becomes more composed. In contrast, one who allowed his impulses and physical desires to rule over him will notice over the years that his strength leaves him and his life loses its savor.

We must value the rich life experience of the elderly, and make use of it. The elderly themselves can make time for Torah study and spiritual pursuits without having to be concerned with making a living.

The Distinction between Young and Old

When one is young his physical strength is dominant, but as he gets older, his physical strength leaves him, as do his desires. At this time he can rejoice in his intellectual achievements. One who invests in the intellect and rejoices in it will be able to yearn for God and desire to connect to Him in old age.

The philosophers clarified that during the period of youth, physiological forces are an obstacle to reaching almost all levels of virtue, and all the more so to acquiring the clear thinking that comes from perfection of the mind and that causes one to desire God, may He be exalted, as this is not possible when the bodily fluids are boiling. However, as physical strength weakens and the fire of one's desires fades, the intellect grows stronger and its light spreads, and its understanding is purified, and one rejoices in that which he has understood [and the desire for God increases].

(Rambam, *Guide of the Perplexed* III:51)

Further reading: For more on the Jewish attitude toward the elderly, see *A Concise Guide to Halakha*, p. 612.

If one chooses a good path in his youth and does not submit to physical desires, then as the years pass and his physical strength leaves him, his mind becomes serene and he rejoices over the fact that he chose the good. In contrast, if one chooses to follow worldly pleasures in his youth, and subdues the voice of the intellect, then as the years pass and his physical strength leaves him, his mind is unsettled and he cannot make peace with the choices of his youth.

The minds of older Torah scholars are settled:

"Ignorant people's minds grow unsettled as they age, but the minds of Torah elders become composed as they age" (Mishna *Kinnim* 3:6). This does not mean that as they become older their wisdom increases, as this may not be the case. Since the mind requires physical vessels, it is possible that when someone becomes very old, those vessels will become very weak, and the mind too will become weak... Rather it says: "Their minds become composed," and the explanation is that Torah elders, who in their youth set aside worldly appetites and chose the good path, become more and more content as they grow older, and their minds are at ease with regard to their choices.

Young people experience conflict between their reason and their physical desires:

This is because it is impossible that their immaturity does not cause them occasionally to submit to temptation in their youth, even though they have committed to renounce worldly appetites and excesses and they know they are not behaving rationally. Torn as they are between these opposing forces [reason and appetite] their minds cannot be entirely settled. However, once they begin aging and their appetites weaken, and they perceive that whatever they imagined concerning matters of this world is totally null and void, fleeting and insignificant, then reason is not in conflict [with that perception], and they are settled of mind because they see clearly that they chose the good and were committed to it, and all the pleasure they took in the world is meaningless, so they should not regret having given it up.

Ignorant people are unsettled in their old age.

However, the opposite occurs to ignorant people; in their youth they are tempted by their worldly desires, and their minds are susceptible at that time, and at ease, and they are not concerned about the fact [that their behavior] is irrational. As they age, and [pleasure in] the [physical] world slips away from them, and they from it, they perceive that all of their appetites and preferences in the days of their youth were nothingness and emptiness... because of this their minds are unsettled with regard to their former lifestyle.

(Rabbeinu Nisim Gerondi, *Derashot HaRan* 10)

What Should One Do in Old Age?

In a world where the main measure of a person's contribution is his productivity as a worker, a person who reaches old age often retires or is dismissed from his job. However, the old have a significant advantage over the young, as they are more stable and possess rich life experience. An employer who fires his older workers is harming himself.

In old age, one can study Torah while in a state of spiritual and physical tranquility, and can strengthen the spiritual aspect of his life.

The accepted practice of the elderly leaving their workplaces is mistaken:

From the concealed and dark aspects of the world a false understanding was generated, that since old age brings with it physical weakness, the elderly are therefore unable to work, create, or accomplish. Therefore, they are required to leave their jobs and give up their work. It is obvious that such an assumption inspires dejection and depression in the elderly: They are old, they are no longer capable of anything substantial, they are a burden on their families...

According to the Torah, in all matters of wisdom and intellect, the elderly should be the most involved:

According to the truth of the Torah, the exact opposite is the case: Aside from physical weakness, in old age one has attained the quality of "the multitude of years should expound wisdom" (Job 32:7), and: "the minds of Torah elders become composed as they age" (Mishna *Kinnim* 3:6). Even those who are not Torah scholars still have the advantage of intellect and wisdom, as a result of "the many experiences they have had" (*Kiddushin* 33a). Because of the rich life experience that elderly people have acquired over the years, young people need their advice. Since one's intellectual capacity, which is the most essential part of a person, does not deteriorate but on the contrary, "the multitude of years should expound wisdom," it is obvious that in matters of wisdom and intellect they should be extremely active....

As a result of the dismissal of the aged, businesses too are adversely affected:

From this it becomes clear, with regard to something that is accepted as part of the normal course of events, that when people reach old age they are partially or completely dismissed from the place where they made a living, that this is detrimental to the business and detrimental to them, even though the intentions of those who institute this policy may be good...

Old age is the time to study Torah with spiritual tranquility:

Since the elderly have reached old age with God's blessing, the intention of the Holy One, blessed be He, is that out of "weakness of body" will emerge "might of soul," that they should use their time...to study Torah with spiritual and physical calm, without confusion or concerns about the troubles of making a living.

(Rabbi Menaḥem Mendel Schneerson, *Siḥot*, 20 Av 5740)

Rabbi Yehuda Aryeh Leib Alter, the *Sefat Emet*, who was the third rebbe of the hasidic dynasty of Ger, passed away at the age of fifty-eight. When his sons were returning from their father's funeral, his eldest son, Rabbi Avraham Mordekhai (author of *Imrei Emet*), said to his brother, Rabbi Moshe Betzalel: "Thank God, our father merited a long life."

Astonished, his younger brother responded: "But our father did not even reach old age!"

Rabbi Avraham Mordekhai answered him: "It is true that our father did not live for many years, but all of his days were certainly long and full."

When one reaches old age...he should attach himself to Sages and to books of knowledge, and his eyes will be opened to these matters, and he must not waste this precious free time.

(Rabbi Eliezer Papo, *Peleh Yo'etz, Zikna*)

Righteous people become mightier in their old age; they gather strength and gain power for the service of God.

(Rabbeinu Yona, *Sha'arei Teshuva* 2:9)

"Train the lad in accordance with his way; even when he grows old, he will not turn from it" (Proverbs 22:6); even when he is an old man, he should constantly be educating himself.

(Rabbi Menaḥem Mendel of Kotzk)

Further reading: For more on studying Torah as required, see p. 269; *A Concise Guide to the Sages*, p. 454.

Death and Mourning

After the sin of the tree of knowledge, all human beings were condemned to die. At the moment of death, the soul separates from the body. Where does it go? One who has yearned to connect to God while in this world will be granted a way to ascend after his death.

The relatives of the deceased are obligated to mourn for him and to reflect on their sorrow, so that they improve their ways and repent. Nevertheless, the Sages instructed that one should not mourn too much, as it is important to remember that, even after a loss, we are the children of God, and He comforts us in our mourning. We must receive this comfort and not reject it. For the sake of the soul of the deceased, his children say Kaddish, elevating the soul from one level in the Garden of Eden to a higher one.

Death Was Decreed for All Humankind

The sin of Adam and Eve, i.e., eating from the tree of knowledge, caused death to be the fate of all. The separation of body from soul is a punishment for the sin of Adam and Eve, who separated the fruit from the tree of knowledge.

If Adam and Eve had not sinned, they would have lived forever like the ministering angels:

It is known that death was decreed for Adam, who was the root of the world and the source of all humankind, and no one can escape it. For he died for his sin, and if not for his sin he would have lived forever like the ministering angels...

The sin involved the separation of the fruit from the tree of knowledge, and the resulting punishment is the separation of the body from the soul:

It is known from nature that when a root is deficient or damaged, the branches also sustain partial damage. The death of man means the separation of the soul from the body, and the punishment matched the sin of separating the fruit from the tree. This is the meaning of the statement of the Sages: "He clipped the saplings" (*Tikunei Zohar* 69); Adam is described as doing so because he sinned by separating, in action and in thought.

 **Further reading:** For how we prepare for death, see *A Concise Guide to Halakha*, p. 77.

Because of the death decreed for Adam, even the perfectly righteous die:

Therefore, death is the way of the world for all, because they are the branches from that root, the descendants of Adam. It is unnecessary to state that this is the case concerning righteous people who sin, because even the perfectly righteous, who have never sinned, are included in the punishment of death, due to the decree against Adam, for we have encountered perfectly righteous individuals who never sinned, yet have died.

(Rabbeinu Baḥya ibn Ḥalawa, *Kad HaKemaḥ, Evel* 1)

Yearning for Above

After death, one stands in judgment before God for his actions during his lifetime. When the soul passes from the world, it does not know where it is being taken. But if the person had yearned for God in this world, he will be given the opportunity to ascend toward Him as a result.

At the time of his death a person does not know where he will come to:

When the time comes to be taken from this world, every individual approaches the heavenly King [to be judged]. This is as it is written: "The time for David to die approached" (I Kings 2:1); "The time for Israel to die approached" (Genesis 47:28). For when a person is in this world he does not notice or pay attention to where he stands; rather, every day he thinks it is as if he is walking on emptiness. For, when a soul departs this world it does not know along which path it is being led, for not all souls are admitted to the path leading upward to where light shines from the highest souls. For along [the path] one followed in this world, so he will continue after he leaves it.

One who yearns for God merits that his soul is drawn toward God even after his death:

Come and see: If a person is drawn toward the Holy One, blessed be He, and his desire in this world is for Him, then afterward, when he departs from it, he is drawn toward Him and he is granted a way to ascend, along the same path that he wished to be drawn every day in this world.

(*Zohar* 1:99a–b)

Further reading: For the story of the tree of knowledge, the source of death in the world, see *A Concise Guide to the Torah*, p. 8.

The Soul's Departure from This World

A soul's departure from this world does not happen in one moment. According to the mystical Torah, the soul undergoes seven journeys, some just before and others after death, in order to become fully detached from the world. The stages of this detaching are reflected in the *halakhot* of mourning, which end only after the soul's complete detachment from the body.

One month before death:

The life force, along with the soul, departs from the body in seven stages... (1) Thirty days before death the soul begins a partial departure... (2) In the last hours the [spiritual] image [that accompanies a person from the time of his birth] withdraws from him... (3) The life force is extinguished [i.e., the actual moment of death], and the spirit returns to God... and on that day the bereavement at his passing is most intense.

The seven days of mourning:

(4) Three days after death, the soul abandons the body... and during those first three days, when the soul has not entirely departed the body, the *halakhot* of mourning are at their peak... as it is said: "Three days for weeping" (*Moed Katan* 27b)... (5) After the seven days, there is a further departure, and this is why most of the *halakhot* of mourning apply for seven days... and this is as it is written in *Sha'ar HaMitzvot*:

Seven surrounding lights ... remain in the home, in the place where he died... during all seven days of mourning, the soul comes and goes, and it is hard for it to depart from there, and it is also hard for it to separate from its inner soul. Therefore it goes back and forth from the house to the grave and from the grave to the house. On each of the seven days of mourning, one of the seven surrounding lights attaches to the soul. When the seven days of mourning end, they have all separated from the house, and they come to rest on the grave.

From the end of the seven days of mourning, until one year after the death:

(6) After thirty days, the soul moves up an additional level... (7) The final stage is at the conclusion of twelve months. At that point, the soul departs from all matters of the material world, ascends to its heavenly source, and is not concerned with inconsequential material accomplishments... and since the soul has not totally departed from the body until twelve months have passed, there are mourning practices for one's father and mother for the entire twelve months.

(Rabbi Yeḥiel Mikhel Tukachinsky, *Gesher HaḤayyim* 2:26)

Why Is There a Commandment to Mourn?

It is natural for a person to feel sorrow when a relative passes away, but according to the Torah this natural sorrow is not sufficient, and one is required to mourn through *halakhot* and actions. This forces the person to contemplate his sorrow and consider what sin brought it about, so that he will be able to repent and live a better life.

One of the reasons for this mitzva [of mourning for a relative who has died] is something I have written many times with regard to the previous mitzvot: A person is influenced by his own actions. Since he is a physical being, he is not affected by anything abstract until he converts it from the potential to the actual. Therefore, when the punishment of the death of a relative, whom nature compels one to love, befalls him, the Torah requires him to act, which will drive him to keep his thoughts on the sorrow that has befallen him. Then he will contemplate in his soul how his sins caused this sorrow to come upon him…and this is the absolute belief of those of the precious Jewish faith. When one pays attention to this matter in the process of mourning, he will resolve to repent and will refine his deeds as much as he can.

(*Sefer HaḤinnukh* 264)

Do Not Mourn Excessively

Along with the obligation of mourning, the Sages taught us not to mourn too much. Even after the loss of a close relative, we are the children of the eternal God. Eternal life, which the deceased has attained, is better than anything in this world.

It is not fitting to exhibit excessive agony and grief over a deceased relative if a relative who is more distinguished and has more potential for good remains. Therefore [the Torah says] that you are the Lord's children (Deuteronomy 14:1). [For you,] whose Father exists forever, it is not fitting to fully agonize and mourn for any deceased person.… Additionally, one should not be overly aggrieved about the harm that came to the deceased at his death. "For you are a holy people" (Deuteronomy 14:2), destined for the World to Come, where [a moment of] contentment is better that all of life in this world.

(Sforno, Deuteronomy 14:1)

Further reading: For the *halakhot* of mourning, see *A Concise Guide to Halakha*, p. 105.

The soul of the deceased itself wants the remaining relatives to carry on with their lives in joy. When they fall into sadness and grief beyond that which is required, it saddens the soul of the deceased.

The will of the soul:

When a close relative passes away, in accordance with God's will, those who remain here can no longer see him with their eyes nor hear him with their ears. The soul, however, is in the World of Truth and can see and hear, and when it sees that its relatives are grieving excessively due to its physical absence, this matter causes it pain. Conversely, when it sees that after the mourning period established by the Torah, life returns to normal and is full of positive, productive activities, it can joyfully rest in peace in its resting place.

The evil inclination tries to drag people into unnecessary sadness and pain:

One should be wary of the evil inclination, which is very cunning…the evil inclination even encourages a person to give charity for the elevation of the soul of the deceased, and to study Torah and do mitzvot in memory of the soul, as long as each such act entails sadness and pain. But as mentioned above, this is the exact opposite of the objective, which is to bring joy and gratification to the soul of the deceased.

(Rabbi Menaḥem Mendel Schneerson,
Torat Menaḥem, Menaḥem Tziyyon, p. 546)

Kaddish

Children recite Kaddish after the death of a father or mother. Reciting Kaddish not only saves the soul of the deceased from being sent to Gehenna; it also allows one's parents to enter the Garden of Eden and elevates them from one level to the next.

I believe that I heard from my teacher of blessed memory [the Arizal] that it is good to recite this [the orphan's] Kaddish for the death of one's father or mother for the entire year, even on Shabbatot and festivals, since the reason [for the recitation of Kaddish] is not what many of the people think, that it functions only to save the soul of the deceased from being sentenced to Gehenna [and on Shabbat one is not punished with Gehenna]. Rather, there is an additional benefit, which is that it brings the soul into the Garden of Eden and elevates it from level to level.

(Rabbi Hayyim Vital, *Sha'ar HaKavanot, Derush HaKaddish*)

Further reading: For more on the recitation of Kaddish, see *A Concise Guide to Halakha*, p. 504.

There is a Torah commandment to mourn one's dead, and this is entirely a service of God.

(Rabbeinu Baḥya ibn Ḥalawa, *Kad HaKemaḥ, Evel*)

When a child says Kaddish for his father or mother, it is as though he has sent them his greetings. When he learns a chapter of Mishna for their sakes, it is as though he has sent them a letter. When he does mitzvot and performs good deeds for the good of their souls, it is as though he has sent them an entire parcel.

(Rabbi Aharon of Karlin)

Death is nothing; it is merely like walking from one room to another and opting for the more beautiful one.

(Rabbi Menaḥem Mendel of Kotzk)

The Torah commandment to mourn serves to emphasize the loss of the treasure of life, which allows one to continue to ascend without limit. For this tremendous purpose, the Holy One, blessed be He, brings [a person] into the world. The living person should take heed and occupy himself with the purpose of his birth.

(Rabbi Yeḥiel Mikhel Tukachinsky, *Gesher HaḤayyim* 3:1)

Further reading: For the *Yizkor* prayer, which is recited on festivals for the elevation of the souls of deceased relatives, see *A Concise Guide to Halakha*, p. 171.

Cycle of the Jewish Year

Shabbat

Shabbat, the seventh day of the week, has been a special day since Creation. It is a day of rest, of spiritual elevation, and of connection with the Creator.

Many reasons have been given for Shabbat and for the obligation to rest on it from certain types of labor. The sources below offer three: First, God's cessation from His creative activity on the seventh day is the foundation of remembering Shabbat. Second, the prohibition of labor serves to commemorate the exodus from Egypt. Finally, Shabbat alludes to the World to Come, wherein souls find rest.

What is one supposed to do on Shabbat? It is the principal day for study of both the Written Torah and the Oral Torah, and on Shabbat one gains the ability to return to his source and cleave to God. The *Zohar* mentions an additional soul which adorns a Jew on Shabbat, and which brings special joy.

Awareness of the Creation and Commemoration of the Exodus

The mitzva of Shabbat appears in the Ten Commandments. These appear twice in the Torah, once in the book of Exodus and once in the book of Deuteronomy. In each version a different reason is presented for the mitzva of Shabbat. Rambam discusses these two reasons and asserts that they reflect two aspects of Shabbat: First, it is a day when people rest from their labors, and this strengthens faith in the Creator, who created the world in six days and rested on the seventh day. Second, the mitzva to keep Shabbat was given to us because we were slaves in Egypt and were unable to rest when we wished to, and the cessation of labor reminds us that the Creator brought us out of Egypt.

Resting strengthens our awareness of Creation:

You know already from what I have said that opinions that are not confirmed, established, and made permanent in public by [the performance of] actions do not persist. Therefore, He commanded us to honor this day, in order to confirm thereby the principle of Creation which will spread in the world, when all people will rest on one day [each week]. When people ask: "Why is this is done?" The answer will be: "Because in six days the Lord made [the heavens and the earth...]" (Exodus 20:11).

The different reasons given for Shabbat in the two versions of the Ten Commandments express two different aspects of the day:

Two different reasons are given for this mitzva, because of two different objectives. The first version of the Ten Commandments gives the reason for honoring Shabbat as it says: "Because in six days the Lord made [the heavens and the earth, the sea and everything that is in them, and He rested on the seventh day; therefore, the Lord blessed the Sabbath day and sanctified it]" (Exodus 20:11). In the book of Deuteronomy it says: "You shall remember that you were a slave in the land of Egypt, [and the Lord your God took you out from there with a mighty hand and with an outstretched arm]; therefore, the Lord your God commanded you [to observe the Sabbath day]" (Deuteronomy 5:15).

The first reason relates to Shabbat as a day that strengthens belief in Creation. The second reason concerns the need to remember that we were slaves in Egypt and that God redeemed us:

This difference can easily be explained. In the former, the reason given is the sanctification of the day and its honor: "Therefore the Lord blessed the Sabbath day and He sanctified it" (Exodus 20:11), and the reason for this is "Because in six days...." But the fact that God gave us the laws of Shabbat and commanded us to keep it is the consequence of our having been slaves; for then we did not work by choice, nor at the time we wished to; and we could not rest.

Shabbat is meant to increase awareness of these two fundamental concepts:

Therefore, God commanded us to abstain from labor and to rest so that we should combine the two purposes: (1) That we believe the true principle, that the world was created ex nihilo, which clearly leads to the principle of the existence of God. (2) That we might remember how kind God was in freeing us from the burden of the Egyptians. Shabbat is therefore a double blessing: it gives us correct notions, and also promotes the well-being of our bodies.

(Rambam, *Guide of the Perplexed* II:31)

Further reading: For more on Shabbat, see *A Concise Guide to the Torah*, pp. 174, 192, 226; *A Concise Guide to the Sages*, p. 275; *A Concise Guide to Halakha*, p. 379. For more on the difference between the two renditions of the Ten Commandments, see *A Concise Guide to the Sages*, p. 277.

A Day That Alludes to the Future

Shabbat is not only a commemoration of the creation of the world in the past, but also intimates a future in which souls find rest in the World to Come. Refraining from certain physical activities on Shabbat is a reminder of where we came from, while the spiritual aspect of Shabbat is a reminder of where we are going.

Only in the spiritual realm is there true rest. The tranquility of Shabbat alludes to the soul's rest in the spiritual realm:

The mitzva of Shabbat does not only teach the aspect of the creation of the world, but Shabbat also alludes to the spiritual realm [i.e., life after death], where there is true rest and respite because that is where there will be true cessation from all labor and an end to material concerns. The purpose of labor is [the attainment of the spiritual realm] and there, there is no labor. For this reason, the Sages called it "the great Shabbat." They say about it: Whoever toiled before Shabbat will eat on Shabbat. Accordingly, workdays are an allusion to human activities in this world, which bring us toward the objective. The seventh day is an allusion to that objective.

Every Shabbat has two aspects:

Accordingly, we have two Shabbatot: One is the physical Shabbat, in remembrance of the Creation and the beginning of the world; and the other is the spiritual Shabbat, in remembrance of the permanence of the soul and the gratification it experiences after death.

(Abravanel, Exodus 31)

The Purpose of Abstaining from Labor on Shabbat

The point of Shabbat is the devotion of significant time to studying the Written Torah and the Oral Torah. On this day, each individual – whether man or woman, old or young – invests effort in developing his spiritual side and strengthening his connection to the Creator. Torah scholars derive pleasure from Shabbat because they are able to teach, and the entire nation learns from them and is uplifted.

Why was a day established on which we do not work? So that we will be free to study Torah:

The establishment of one day in the week on which we rest from all transitory, worldly matters is a powerful cause for many of the nation to be available to gather together, to congregate to hear from a teacher, and to call out the name of the Lord, [by studying] Bible, Mishna, and Talmud, each person according to his stature. The scholars will be content, because the people seek Torah from them. They will caution them about the mitzvot, and teach them the *halakhot* of each day and each week, as it has been found that this is the established custom of the entire Jewish people, wherever they live. With regard to this it says in the Jerusalem Talmud: "Shabbatot and festivals were only given to Israel so that they will study Torah on them" (Jerusalem Talmud, *Shabbat* 15:3). This is an aspect of the enhanced soul, as the Sages have said (*Beitza* 16a) that people have this [additional level of their souls] on Shabbat.

Abstention from labor is an opportunity for the entire nation to engage in Torah:

[Shabbat] contains a tremendous opportunity for the entire nation, including all its various factions, to study the divine texts, with their interpretations, and their insights. By this means, men, women, and children will hear and learn all of God's mitzvot and perform them. We have found [it said] that Shabbat is equivalent to all the mitzvot [combined], due to its benefit that [all may] engage in the Torah, Prophets, and Writings [on it], and this is a very suitable purpose.

(Rav Yitzḥak Arama, *Akedat Yitzḥak*, Exodus, Section 25 – *Vayak'hel*)

The Soul's Return to Its Source

God's ceasing to create on the seventh day reflects a stage where the spiritual forces that have descended to the world of action return and ascend to their heavenly source. Likewise, ceasing work on Shabbat enables us to transcend the activities of the six days of the week and return to ourselves, to the soul being connected to its source.

God's ceasing [His labor] on Shabbat is a metaphor based on human resting from labor.

The term "rest" that is said with regard to the Holy One, blessed be He: "Because on it He rested" (Genesis 2:3), is a metaphor based on a person who rests and ceases the work he has performed. While acting, his mind and thoughts were engaged in the action, and afterward, when he rests, his mind and thoughts return to their source. The deed itself is also contained in his mind, as an element of the action was [already] in his mind in that the action that he was performing was present in his mind [as an intention]. The discharged spiritual force, i.e., the cognitive and conceptual aspect of the action, ascends and returns to become a part of its source, i.e., [divine] cognition and conceptualization. So too, on Shabbat, the force that was extended for the six days of [divine] action via the ten sayings with which the world was created, ascends to the level of thought…

Shabbat resembles repentance, in that both involve the soul returning to its source:

Therefore, Shabbat is made up of the same letters as the word "you shall repent [*tashuv*]," as the concept of Shabbat and the concept of repentance are one: the return of matters to their source. For repentance is not simply [the rectification of] one's sins, but rather [the point of repentance] is to restore the soul that has descended very low and has become clothed with materiality to its source, to cleave to Him, may He be blessed.

(Rabbi Shneur Zalman of Liadi, *Likutei Torah*, Deuteronomy 66:3)

The Joy of Shabbat

It is customary in hasidic communities, to read a passage from the *Zohar* before the evening prayer service on Friday night. This passage describes the events that occur in the upper worlds on Shabbat. The evil forces that cling to the *Shekhina*, the Divine Presence, on weekdays depart, and the *Shekhina* can receive the heavenly light that shines from above. This light also shines on the people praying the evening service, resulting in their being adorned with an additional soul, bringing joy and good will.

When Shabbat begins, [the *Shekhina*, the kabbalistic *Sefira* of *Malkhut*, majesty,] is refined and separates from the "other side" [i.e., from the forces of evil], and all judgments are removed from her, and she remains in her singularity of holy light, adorned with a number of crowns for the holy King. All the proponents of anger and the accusers flee, and there is no other dominion in all of the worlds. Her face glows with a heavenly light, and she is adorned below by the holy nation, and all are adorned with new souls [i.e., renewed souls, upon which a sublime light shines]. Then the prayers begin and we bless her in joy, with shining faces, saying: "Bless the Lord, the blessed One."

(*Zohar* 2:135a)

On Shabbat there is great joy in the upper worlds, and from there a special joy pours forth to each and every Jew. Nevertheless, the ability to feel this sublime joy depends on the individual's degree of purity and refinement.

The joy and delight of Shabbat are first revealed in the upper worlds, and from there they are roused in every Jew:

For it is a day of joy, happiness, and great delight before the rock of Israel, blessed be He, and the light of the joy of Shabbat appears and illuminates the tremendous brilliance of His splendor and produces a glow in all of the holy worlds. There is nothing similar to this on any of the other days of the year, because the light that shines on it is illuminated by itself, without any stimulation from us. We, the Jewish people, who are called: "Children of the Omnipresent" (Mishna *Avot* 3:14), and "The allotment [*ḥevel*] of His inheritance" (Deuteronomy 32:9), are tied with this allotment [*ḥevel*, meaning allotment or portion, can also mean rope] with a cord [*tikva*] of scarlet thread, about which it is said: "There is hope [*tikva*] for your future"

(Jeremiah 31:16). The soul of each and every Jew has its source above, and from this source light comes down from above to his soul below, via that cord of hope. All this is known to those who know the mystical teachings. When the immense happiness, wondrous joy, and great delight are stirred up at the source of our souls to its full extent, then within each and every individual in Israel, His holy nation, boundless happiness and joy are necessarily awakened, the joy of the soul and the body, in every Jew, in accordance with his soul's stature and the source of his portion in the upper worlds.

The purer one is, the more joy of Shabbat he merits to receive. If a person is not purified then there is a barrier within him, between the source of his soul and the spark of the soul that is in him:

This depends on the extent of the refinement of one's body: The more purified one is, his body does not break the bond between the spark of the soul that is within him, and the source of his soul above, and the connecting cord brings immeasurable illumination from the source of the soul above, which receives the light of the joy of worlds on Shabbat, to the spark inside the person. But when one's body is not pure, it constitutes a division between the source of his soul above and the spark of his soul inside him, and it does not receive the illumination of the enduring spiritual joy of Shabbat.

A little of the joy of Shabbat shines even on one whose body is not pure, for two reasons: The light of Shabbat is especially exalted and powerful, and the light of Shabbat shines on the common source of the souls of Israel and therefore it shines on all the Jewish people:

Nevertheless, even with regard to the lowest of the low, it is certain that delight will be roused within him on Shabbat, because the light of Shabbat is immense and awesome beyond the light of the mitzvot, in its self-illumination. Furthermore, it is expressed in the full extent [of spiritual levels] where the source of the soul of all of Israel can be found, so [the light of Shabbat] will certainly be awakened in all of Israel.

Sadness and anger disappear on Shabbat due to the illumination of Shabbat, which fills all worlds with joy:

Through this you can understand the statement of the *Zohar*, which says: In the merit of that [addition to the] soul [on Shabbat], all sorrow and anger are forgotten by a person, and only joy and happiness are present both above and below. In other words, this is what takes place: All types of sorrow and strife are forgotten by a person and he is filled with joy and happiness from the enhanced soul and by that spirit.

(Rabbi Ḥayyim Tyrer, *Sidduro Shel Shabbat* 5:3:1)

Further reading: For more on the "rope" that ties people's souls to the Creator, see p. 320.

Shabbat: The Source of Blessing and Abundance from Above

Shabbat is the source of blessing and abundance for the entire week, both spiritually and materially. Candle lighting, *Kiddush* (the blessing recited over wine to sanctify the Shabbat day), and the loaves of *halla* symbolize basic human needs, on which Shabbat has an effect.

The days of the week are like the branches of the candelabrum in the Temple:

The body of the candelabrum, [on] which is the middle lamp, alludes to Shabbat. There are three lamps to the right and three to the left. Three allude to Wednesday, Thursday, and Friday, when we prepare for Shabbat; and three allude to Sunday, Monday, and Tuesday, as on those days some of the enhanced soul, spirit, and life force of Shabbat still remain...

Candle lighting, *Kiddush*, and *halla* hint to all human needs, which are blessed on Shabbat:

It is known that all sustenance that is allotted to us is a result of the sanctity of Shabbat. Therefore, at the beginning of Shabbat, when night falls, we sanctify Shabbat with grain, wine, and oil. There must be a table with bread on it, i.e., grain, and one must make *Kiddush* on the wine, and light the candles using oil. It is known that the general blessing of sustenance of humankind includes "your grain, your wine, and your oil" (Deuteronomy 7:13 inter alia).... Divine abundance of food comes to Israel as a result of the holiness of Shabbat, as the Sages said: "The blessing of the Lord, it will enrich" (Proverbs 10:22); this is Shabbat (*Bereshit Rabba* 11:1).

(Rabbi Yosef Ḥayyim, *Ben Ish Ḥai*, Year 2, *Pekudei*)

Further reading: For more on the smelling of spices at *Havdala*, an act that relates to the additional soul of Shabbat, see *A Concise Guide to Halakha*, p. 400.

Rabbi Nata of Avritch, one of the students of the Ba'al Shem Tov, used to refrain from sleeping on Shabbat. He would say: The Torah commanded: "The children of Israel shall keep [*veshamru*, literally guard] Shabbat" (Exodus 31:16); and would a guard sleep while standing at his post?

When word spread of Napoleon, it was said that the emperor slept very little, saying: "It would be a pity to waste a moment of my reign by sleeping." This statement reached Rabbi Nata, who saw it as justification of his custom: For on Shabbat, all of Israel are kings; and would a person who has been appointed king for one day waste the moments of his reign by sleeping?

Shabbat is greater than the World to Come, as Shabbat is the spring from which the World to Come was drawn.

(Rabbi Barukh of Medzhybizh)

On Shabbat, heavenly joy is revealed in actuality.

(Rabbi Shneur Zalman of Liadi)

Shabbat is like the World to Come, because on this day one allays every thirst in his soul and spends an entire day satisfying its desires and longings to connect to its blessed Creator, without any external hindrances.

(Rabbi Menaḥem Ekstein, *Tena'ei HaNefesh LeHasagat HaḤasidut*)

Further reading: For more on the World to Come, see p. 165.

Rosh Hodesh

The first mitzva that the children of Israel were commanded to perform was the sanctification of the new month. Each time the moon is concealed and then "reborn," a new month begins, and the act of determining the first day of each month symbolizes constant renewal. From the moon, the Jewish people learn how to renew themselves within a fixed reality. Each month involves a different type of renewal, and each year we have twelve different ways in which to renew ourselves. *Rosh Hodesh*, i.e. the day sanctified as the beginning of a new month, which is fixed according to the moon, bears special significance to women, who also have a monthly cycle of renewal.

Starting Over

God commanded the Jewish people to learn from the moon and renew themselves. In a world that proceeds as though everything is predetermined, we are instructed to sanctify the new month and to believe in constant renewal.

The pagan outlook espouses preserving the status quo, not renewal.

Paganism does not recognize anything new, not on earth, nor in people, nor in the gods and idols it sets above the world and humankind. Everything has iron necessity: Today evolves from yesterday, and tomorrow from today, necessarily. Just as paganism denies the concept of creation *ex nihilo*, i.e., unrestricted creation in accordance with the free will of the Creator, so too it rejects the notion of creation *ex nihilo* with regard to one's moral state, [i.e., the ability to bring about personal change,] and with regard to one's fate. Guilt and evil are forced to generate guilt and evil, and so forth. Accordingly, a person's heart lacks any connection to a free, unlimited God; according to it [the pagan worldview], there is no free God ruling in and over the world. Everything is swept down an unseeing, unchanging, and unavoidable course. All freedom is just an illusion; anything new is an extension of the old.

Further reading: For more on *Rosh Hodesh* and its prayers and customs, see *A Concise Guide to Halakha*, p. 237.

The mitzva to sanctify the new month was given specifically in Egypt, in order to negate its pagan worldview:

Therefore, it states [in the verse containing the commandment to sanctify the new month] "in the land of Egypt" (Exodus 12:1), i.e., in the land that consistently embraced paganism, in the land where pagan stagnation spread even to the social structure of the region, creating the restrictions of the class system. It was in Egypt, therefore, that God called the future leaders of His nation [Moses and Aaron], and showed them the crescent of the moon struggling to escape from the darkness into a new light, and said: This will be an example for you. Just as this one, which is restrained, [i.e., covered and hidden,] returns to its youth, so shall you take renewal for yourselves, in freedom. Whenever it appears, it will remind you of the renewal of your youth in freedom. When I renew you and when you renew yourselves, you, like this moon, will pass through the night sky of the nations, proclaiming everywhere the teaching of renewal; the teaching of God, who creates in freedom and brings us out into freedom; the teaching of man who receives from the hands of this God the freedom of morality and the freedom of destiny. This renewal is in fact directly derived from the meaning of the name *heh-vav-yod* [the Tetragrammaton], the God who brings about, through freedom, every moment of the future. Every Jew calls God by this name when he serves Him silently in the depths of his heart.

(Rabbi Samson Raphael Hirsch, Exodus 12:1)

Each month constitutes a unique path of renewal, and the Jewish people are commanded to find the opportunity for renewal every month:

These twelve days, the first day of each month, are twelve channels, or gates, for bringing renewal into the world of nature. The Jewish people brought this about, meriting to open up these pathways. With regard to this it is said [in the *Musaf* prayer on *Rosh Hodesh*]: "You have chosen Your people Israel from all nations, and have set for them rules for the New Moon."

(Rabbi Yehuda Aryeh Leib Alter, *Sefat Emet, Bo*)

The moon is renewed each time as it is once again illuminated by the sun. Likewise, the Jewish people are renewed because they again receive the light of God:

"This month [Nisan] is ... the beginning of months" (Exodus 12:2), because it is the beginning of all [the moon's] renewals. For each renewal occurs through receiving light that the sun emits in accordance with its orbit. As the sun emits light in that month, i.e., at that time of the year, with the changes of its course in the different periods of the year, so it is with the renewal of the moon, which receives from [the sun]. Likewise, the renewal of the Jewish people is through receiving the light of the Lord [YHVH],[1] who illuminates them with the emanation of His light, emanating conceptual light upon the lower world. This is the light of His *Shekhina,* which rests in the souls of the Jewish people, such that they are able to attain this light.

(Rabbi Tzadok HaKohen of Lublin, *Maḥshavot Ḥarutz* 7)

Rosh Hodesh: A Special Day for Women

It is customary for women to refrain from performing labor on *Rosh Hodesh* because they did not sin at the Golden Calf. The strong faith of women relates to their spiritual source, the *Sefira* of *Malkhut,* which is symbolized by the moon. The moon receives its light from the sun, and its light depends on the sun alone. Women perceive their relationship to the Creator in the same way.

Rosh Hodesh was given to women as a reward for having resisted participating in the sin of the Golden Calf:

It is necessary to understand: Why was the festival of *Rosh Hodesh* given specifically to women as a day on which they are prohibited from performing labor? Are not women exempt from positive, time-bound mitzvot [and therefore it is odd that they would have such a specifically time-bound custom]? There are many reasons for this... In *Pirkei deRabbi Eliezer* there is a reason for this: When the mixed multitude [gentiles who joined the children of Israel for the exodus from Egypt] caused Israel to go astray and make the Golden Calf, and said to them: "Remove the gold rings" (Exodus 32:2), the women did not contribute, and therefore they were given a reward, the holiday of *Rosh Hodesh.*

The spiritual explanation for the women's refusal to participate in the sin of the Golden Calf relates to their spiritual source:

The women did not accept that thinking [behind the sin of the Golden Calf], because women are of the feminine realm, whose source is from [the *Sefira* of] *Malkhut*... and *Malkhut* is the source of all things that have been created, and a revelation from it can be felt in a person's soul. The women felt this [revelation of divine providence], and did not accept that thinking, and did not remove their gold rings.

1. YHVH refers to the ineffable name of God expressed by the Tetragrammaton.

Rosh Hodesh symbolizes the connection between the moon and the sun, and at the same time, between the world and the divine light:

Because on *Rosh Hodesh* the moon receives reflected light from the sun, and its light essentially comes from the sun. The moon represents *Malkhut,* which is God's name *Elohim* [symbolizing God's revelation in the world], which receives all its power from the Tetragrammaton [symbolizing God's mastery of the world], and this relates to the unity of the Tetragrammaton and *Elohim.* Therefore women, whose source is from *Malkhut,* the name *Elohim,* and who did not put their faith in the Golden Calf, were rewarded with the cessation of labor on *Rosh Hodesh,* which is about the unity of the Tetragrammaton and *Elohim.*

(Rabbi Shmuel Schneersohn, *Torat Shmuel* 5640, vol. 1, *Noah*)

Rejoice with the Blessing of the Moon

By: Rabbi Yosef Ḥayyim

Rejoice, rejoice, with the blessing of the moon

The renewal of the moon, when my heart is joyous and we will pummel our foes by the light of the *Shekhina.*

He who acts in truth, His actions are truth, and it will be completed in the completion of its construction.

The lady shall be renewed with the raising of the crown, all the way to the crown [the *Sefira* of *Keter*] of glory [the *Sefira* of *Tiferet*] with the glory [*Tiferet*] of understanding [*Bina*].

O He who brings salvation, dissolve the oath, come and reveal Yourself in the heavenly city.

The renewal of souls will be in all the worlds, the Names will shine all around and at [every] corner.

Implore now before God: May He send the redeemer, gathering Israel whom He has acquired.

Lord, hear now this plea and send now reprieve, please save, please bring success.

Further reading: Concerning the blessing of the New Moon and how it is performed, see *A Concise Guide to Halakha*, p. 240.

The Months of the Year

Each of the twelve months of the year has its own character and spiritual significance. Each one of them is associated with one of the twelve combinations of the Tetragrammaton. The twelve months also correspond to the twelve tribes.

In addition to the festivals and special periods that take place in each month and that influence the entire month, each month has its own essence that is worth examining:

Tishrei

In the Written Torah the counting of the months begins from Nisan, making Tishrei the seventh [*shevi'i*] month. *Shevi'i* alludes to satiety [*sova*] and divine abundance [*shefa*]. This is a month replete with goodness: Rosh HaShana, Yom Kippur, *Sukkot*, and *Shemini Atzeret*. We perform many mitzvot in this month, from blowing the shofar to taking the *lulav*[2] and sitting in the *sukka*.[3] At the beginning of the month, all human beings stand in judgment before the Creator.

This month is holy, as it is the seventh, and is set aside for many mitzvot. It is what [the Sages] called "mighty in mitzvot" (*Rosh HaShana* 11a), derived from the verse: "In the month of Etanim [literally, the strong ones]" (I Kings 8:2). Just as the number seven is special compared to the other numbers, so is this month superior to the other months in [the quantity of] its mitzvot, as many mitzvot are performed in it: Rosh HaShana, shofar, Yom Kippur, *sukka, lulav*, willow branches,[4] and the libation of water.[5]

There is great inspiration [to be found] in this month [as represented by its] astrological sign [Libra]; the scales allude to the function of this day, [Rosh HaShana, on the first day of Tishrei,] when every person is weighed

2. The *lulav*, palm branch, is one of the four species of plants (a palm branch, a myrtle branch, a willow branch, and a citron fruit) that it is a mitzva to take up on *Sukkot*.
3. The *sukka* is a booth in which it is a mitzva to live during the seven days of *Sukkot*.
4. This is the custom of taking a willow branch on the seventh day of *Sukkot* (*Hoshana Rabba*). In the Temple, willow branches were placed around the altar.
5. Ordinary libations in the Temple were of wine. On the festival of *Sukkot*, there was an additional libation of water.

on the scales, so that each individual will be rewarded in accordance with his ways and in accordance with his actions.

(Rabbeinu Baḥya ibn Ḥalawa, *Kad HaKemaḥ*, *Rosh HaShana* 2)

Further reading: For more on the festivals of Tishrei, see p. 57; *A Concise Guide to the Sages*, p. 282; *A Concise Guide to Halakha*, p. 129.

Marheshvan

After the month rich in festivals comes Marheshvan. The unique meaning of this month is hidden in its name; Marheshvan is like *lehaḥashot*, to fall silent. This is the month of silence.

In [interpreting] the name of the month of Marheshvan, one should distinguish between the root of the word, *ḥet-shin-vav*, and the final *nun* [which is not essential to the word]. This root indicates the nature of the month – to be silent [*laḥashot*]. The month before it was entirely hustle-bustle, with many festivals and communal activities, and now the Jew enters the month of Marheshvan, a month of calm and quiet, during which more emphasis is placed on the individual. Now the individual, in the solitude of his private world, relives all the events and experiences that occurred in Tishrei.

(Rabbi Samson Raphael Hirsch, *BeMa'agalei Shana* 1, p. 172)

Kislev

According to *Sefer Yetzira*,[6] the month of Kislev inspires a tendency toward sleep, but the Jewish people overcome this tendency, and strengthen their desire for holiness in this month. Kislev is also connected to the tribe of Benjamin.

Kislev is linked to the kidneys and to desire:

The name of the month Kislev is derived from the term *kesel*, and the kidneys are called *kesalim*, and desire comes from the kidneys. [The term for kidneys, *kelayot*, derives from the root *kaf-lamed-heh*]... meaning longing and desire.

The astrological signs of the months cause particular tendencies, but the nation's patriarchs worked so that the Jewish people would be able to overcome these natural tendencies:

It can be explained according to the words of my honorable, holy father, our master, teacher, and rebbe [Rabbi Avraham Bornsztain, author of *Avnei*

6. *Sefer Yetzira* is an early mystical work that uses the letters of the Hebrew alphabet to propound its system.

Nezer], that the twelve tribes correspond to the twelve months of the year. Namely, the astrological signs cause people to be naturally drawn toward the quality that the astrological sign in question dictates, and the twelve tribes acted in righteousness so that Israel could overcome the astrological sign and not be drawn after that which is prescribed by the astrological sign, for there is no astrological sign [that affects] Israel.

The natural tendency in the month of Kislev is to sleep, but the tribe of Benjamin turned this into a desire for holiness:

The opposite of the attribute of desire is [the attribute of] one who performs actions lazily, and "sloth casts a deep sleep" (Proverbs 19:15); therefore the astrological sign of the month of Kislev calls for sleep, and relates to the stomach, but Benjamin, in his saintliness, changed it into his attribute, the attribute of desire, and it is called Kislev, which is an expression of desire.

(Rabbi Shmuel Bornsztain, *Shem MiShmuel, Rosh Hodesh Kislev* 5672)

Further reading: For more on the influence of astrological signs on the Jewish people, see *A Concise Guide to the Sages*, p. 423.

Tevet

In the month of Tevet we sink into the deep sleep of winter and there is great darkness in the world. What gives us the strength to overcome the darkness? The Hanukkah candles that we light at the beginning of the month.

Rosh Hodesh Tevet, which takes place during Hanukkah, receives the light of the candles upon all the days of the month, since everything depends upon *Rosh Hodesh*. The fact that we light [a total of] thirty-six candles [on Hanukkah] may allude to the notion that the candles bring light from the beginning of Hanukkah until the end of Tevet [a total of thirty-six days]. I heard from my teacher, my grandfather, of blessed memory, [Rabbi Yitzḥak Meir Alter of Ger, author of *Ḥiddushei HaRim*,] that the word Tevet comes from the term "preparation [*hatavat*] of the candles." It is possible to explain, as it is written in the [holy] books, that the days of Tevet are days of [God's] concealment, and therefore He provided the remedy ahead of time, because the candles provide illumination during these dark days as well, and ["God saw the] light that it was good" (Genesis 1:4).

(Rabbi Yehuda Aryeh Leib Alter, *Sefat Emet*, Hanukkah 5650)

Shevat

In the middle of winter, in the month of Shevat, the new year of the trees is celebrated. Sometimes the almond tree is already in blossom, but most of the trees are still far from beginning to blossom. So why don't we wait until spring? Because even when it seems, on the outside, that everything is frozen, internal renewal has already begun, and it is already possible to celebrate the approaching spring with joy.

Ancient Jewish tradition directs our attention to bare trees [by establishing the fifteenth of Shevat as the new year of the trees], while the snowy winter days are still at their height, and provides us with a sweet secret, whispering a lesson in our ears: Today, these trees are already celebrating the renewal of the coming spring. Inside the frozen, fragmented, gray, and cold external covering that enshrouds the naked trees, fresh, new life, in all its warmth, has already begun to well up. How penetrating and instructive is the moral lesson concealed in these tidings of spring that we hear from the winter trees covered in white snow.

(Rabbi Samson Raphael Hirsch, *BeMa'agalei Shana* 2, p. 108)

Adar

The month of Adar invites us to become stronger in our connection to God, and through the great joy of this month we are able to achieve greater holiness.

Adar [represents] strengthening, as it is written: "The Lord is mighty [*adir*] on high" (Psalms 93:4)...and the name of this month that is called Adar teaches that it is a time of becoming stronger, and of Israel's yearning for their Father in Heaven. [Coming closer to Him] is possible only through joy, as the Sages said: "When Adar begins, there is extra rejoicing" (*Ta'anit* 29a). Through this joy we increase holiness.

(Rabbi Shmuel Bornsztain, *Shem MiShmuel, Mishpatim* 5671)

Nisan

The world was created in the month of Tishrei, and accordingly Rosh HaShana is on the first of Tishrei. Nevertheless, at the time of the redemption from Egypt, in the month of Nisan, we were commanded to make Nisan the first month. Our calendar is special in that it is connected to the redemption and to the Torah, and not only to Creation and nature.

"This month is for you" (Exodus 12:2): Although it is not in itself fitting that it should be "the beginning of months" [since the world was created in Tishrei], it is fitting for you that it comes first, since you were redeemed in it, and the Torah began for you in it. It is fitting that all of our timekeeping be rooted in the Torah and not the natural order, because we do not operate in accordance with nature, but rather entirely according to reward and punishment.

(Rabbeinu Nisim Gerondi, *Derashot HaRan* 3)

Iyar

Iyar is a month of preparation for the receiving of the Torah. On each day of the month we count the *omer*[7] and move forward, day by day improving our character traits and spiritual qualities. The improvement of character traits is the healing for the soul, and therefore this is an especially good time for repentance and healing.

It is written in the book *Ohev Yisrael* that this month is [particularly] suitable for repentance. There is an allusion to this fact in that the world sees it as a time of healing, and the main thing is the healing of the soul... [The prayer said after the counting of the *omer* includes the petition] "to purify us from our external layers and from our impurities."

(Rabbi Tzadok HaKohen of Lublin, *Peri Tzaddik, Vayikra, Rosh Hodesh Iyar* 4)

Sivan

The astrological sign for Sivan is Gemini, the twins. This alludes to the complexity necessary for learning the Torah, which was given in this month. The Torah comprises the Written Torah and the Oral Torah, and it was given to us in the third month, a time that reflects its complexity. This complexity ultimately leads to recognition of the unity [of the Torah].

Because Jacob [the third patriarch] is [designated by the sign Gemini, i.e., the] twins,[8] the Torah was given to his children in the month [whose sign is] twins, and the Torah is the mystical concept of twins, namely, the Written Torah and the Oral Torah. It was given in the third month, to the nation of three [sections: priests, Levites, and Israelites], with the qualities of the three [patriarchs]. It is a threefold Torah: Torah, Prophets, and Writings. All this is one [i.e., the mystical concepts of twins, and of these groups of three, give rise to a unified view of everything].

(*Zohar* 2:78b)

7. The mitzva to count the days between Passover and *Shavuot*.
8. Jacob represents the merging of the aspects of Isaac and Abraham. For this reason, he represents the ability to comprehend things from multiple points of view, which is mystically represented by twins.

Tamuz

Tamuz and Av are months in which we mourn the beginning of the exile and the destruction of the Temple, and we pray for the redemption and for the building of the Third Temple. The spiritual roots of exile came from not looking upon others with benevolence, nor being able to hear good about them. Within this understanding lies the key to redemption: The redemption of our senses of sight and hearing.

According to *Sefer Yetzira*, a person's sense of sight corresponds to the month of Tamuz and a person's sense of hearing corresponds to the month of Av.... The spies went to scout the land on the twenty-ninth of Sivan, so they necessarily went in Tamuz, namely, the month of sight: "They saw the land, and they disheartened the children of Israel" (Numbers 32:9), and the sense of sight was damaged. Then, "they returned from scouting the land at the conclusion of forty days" (Numbers 13:25), in the month of Av, the month of hearing, and they spoke slander against the land, and "the entire congregation raised and sounded their voice and...wept" (Numbers 14:1), because they had listened to the [spies'] words and the sense of hearing was damaged.... Therefore, we pray [in the *Tahanun* prayer]: "Incline Your ear, My God, and hear; open Your eyes and see" (Daniel 9:18), so that sight and hearing will be corrected.

(Rabbi Tzvi Elimelekh Shapira, *Benei Yisaskhar, Tamuz–Av* 1:3)

Av

At the beginning of the month of Av, the mourning over the destruction of the Temple intensifies, and the Sages said that one should reduce joy from *Rosh Hodesh* onward. Nevertheless, joy occupies a central place in hasidic thought, and it is explained that it is pain and worry that need to be decreased, by rejoicing.

"When Av begins, one reduces joy" (Mishna *Ta'anit* 4:6); the [hasidic] interpretation is: We reduce sadness and worry with joy, meaning: By rejoicing. Through the joy that a person has, he lessens the exile of the *Shekhina*.

(Rabbi Kalonymus Kalman Epstein, *Ma'or VaShemesh, Vayeshev*)

Elul

Before we crown God as King on Rosh HaShana, there is a month in which He approaches us, and we approach Him. In the month of Elul, God receives everyone with joy and allows everyone to appear before Him.

Elul is the time of the revelation of the thirteen attributes of mercy. To understand why these are regular weekdays and not holidays...it may be understood with an allegory of a king. Before he arrives in a city, the people of the city go out toward him and greet him in the field. Anyone who wishes is permitted to approach, and he receives everyone warmly and with a smile. When he enters the city, they follow him. Afterward, when he enters into his royal court, no one may enter unless granted permission to do so, and even this pertains only to high-ranking people and distinguished individuals. This is the idea by way of analogy: In the month of Elul we go out to greet the shining face of God in the field [not on a holiday when He is in His royal court].

(Rabbi Shneur Zalman of Liadi, *Likutei Torah, Re'eh* 32:2)

Further reading: For special customs of the month of Elul, see *A Concise Guide to Halakha*, p. 373.

Sweetness of Months[9]

By: Rabbi Avraham Yitzḥak HaKohen Kook

[Tishrei:] Repentance and good actions,
Shatter and refute the statements of those who find liable,
Refined and cleaned from filthy sins,
They will confess their sins, past deeds are forgotten.

[Marheshvan:] Heat has passed from the lands,
The joy of nature has ceased now,
In our land for rain and dew
We pray and beseech fervidly.

[Kislev:] The enemy's chains are broken; they overcame him,
His oppression they removed, his yoke they broke,
The priests of God fought like lions,
And in God's Temple, they set up the lamps.

[Tevet:] The recording elders hid the pearls
In the Greek translation they refrained from revealing,
The Torah of God they concealed, showing just the exterior.

[Shevat:] Rejoice, trees of the forest, Shout out creation!
At the consecration of the festival of the new year for trees,

9. In the original Hebrew, the first letter of each line spells out the name of the month in each verse.

Refreshed nature returns to life.

[Adar:] A sign and wonder are the days of Purim for us,
The words of the megilla [the book of Esther] are preserved forever,
God's mercy covers us like eagles' wings.

[Nisan:] He showed wonders to His nation,
His hand crushed the enemy; they knew His wrath;
Mighty horses he sent down to the deep;
The waters stood; these passed through and those drowned there.

[Iyar:] Merriment has ceased; in the days of the *omer* it stopped;
Painful is the tragedy of Rabbi Akiva's students, descended to the grave.
The sadness passes on the eighteenth, with the *hilula* [celebration] of Rabbi Shimon,
First among masters of secrets, the pillar of fire and cloud.

[Sivan:] The book of books was given with sound and lightning,
Yeshurun ascended to become a kingdom of priests, to the heights of heaven.
The eternal covenant will never be abandoned.
The covenant made with Israel, who are armed with His Torah.

[Tamuz:] A graven image was erected in the Temple;
The enemy camp spread around the city;
In his criminal rage, he avenged with fury;
The daily sacrifice he cancelled, destroyed the beloved.

[Av:] National mourning wraps every Jew in sadness;
Weeping and long lament for two thousand years; it is endless.

[Elul:] Last of the months, end of the year,
The heart of the Jew is shaken; he will find time despite his troubles;
In his soul, the voice of God calls out a holy roar:
Repent! Act righteously and come into the gates of Torah.

Holidays

The holidays listed in the Torah are also called "holy convocations" (Leviticus 23:2 inter alia) and on these days labor is prohibited. They are: Rosh HaShana, Yom Kippur, the first and last day of *Sukkot*, the first and last day of Passover, and *Shavuot*. In the diaspora, a day is added to each of these: the first two and last two days of Passover and *Sukkot* are holidays and *Shavuot* is extended an additional day.

While each festival has a unique meaning and its own practices, the elements that these days of holy convocation share are also of great significance to Jewish life.

Why Do We Refrain from Labor on Festivals?

Each festival was established for a different reason, but there is a common aspect to all of the holidays: It is prohibited to perform labor on these days. Why? So that families have time to be together, and so that rabbis are able to speak to the entire community. The festivals have a purpose, and the cessation of work prevents us from becoming distracted from this purpose.

Not working allows people to pay attention to the essence of the day:

The reasons for this mitzva [of refraining from labor on holidays] include: For Israel to remember the great miracles that God did for them and their patriarchs, and for them to speak of them, and make them known to their children and to their children's children. Resting from the affairs of the world will free them to engage in this. If work, even light work, were permitted, each and every person would turn to his affairs, and the honor of the festival would be forgotten from both children and adults.

Free time is dedicated to Torah study:

Furthermore, there are many advantages to cessation of labor, as the entire nation gathers in the synagogues and study halls to hear the words of the Torah, and the leaders of the nation guide and instruct them, as the Sages said: "Moses instituted for the Jewish people that they should expound the *halakhot* of Passover on Passover, and the *halakhot* of *Shavuot* on *Shavuot*" (*Megilla* 32a).

(*Sefer HaḤinnukh* 298)

Further reading: For more on the cessation of labor as an opportunity to gather for communal learning, see p. 35; *A Concise Guide to the Sages*, p. 125.

The holidays are not only opportunities for families and communities to gather together; they are holy days, when everyone assembles to pray and to praise God. Nevertheless, we do not stay in the synagogue the whole holiday; we must rejoice in our homes as well, with good meals and with concern for those who do not have enough to eat.

The reason that [the holidays are called] "holy convocations," is because on this day everyone convokes to sanctify it. For it is a mitzva given to Israel to gather in the House of God on the day of the festival, to sanctify the day in public, with prayer and praise of God, in clean garments, and to make it a day of feasting. As it says in the Writings: "Go, eat rich foods and drink sweet beverages, and send gifts to whomever does not have anything prepared, as this day is holy to our Lord. Do not be saddened, as joy in the Lord is your strength" (Nehemiah 8:10).

(Ramban, Leviticus 23:2)

The Holiness of the Festivals

When we determine the times of the festivals, we summon the holiness from above to shine upon us, and holiness pours forth upon the Jewish people.

We shall address this matter [of why the festivals are called "holy convocations"] by noticing that God commanded the human court to determine [the specific date of] the festivals, saying: "You shall proclaim them [*tikre'u otam*]" (Leviticus 23:2 inter alia); and [the spelling of *otam* is deficient;] it is written [as if it said] "You yourselves shall proclaim [*tikre'u atem*]" (*Rosh HaShana* 24a). By determining that a certain day is a festival, the court of the devoted of Israel imparts holiness to that day. As a result, [of the human court's action,] the holiness above which is the root of each festival awakens and that holiness also establishes the day as a festival and pours out from above the abundance of holiness that is specific to that festival. Therefore, it is called "a holy convocation," because on it, holiness from above is summoned, and the divine abundance of holiness descends to Israel below, and the day becomes holy.

(Alsheikh, *Torat Moshe*, Leviticus 23)

Further reading: For the specific *halakhot* of each of the festivals see *A Concise Guide to Halakha*, p. 464.

Happening Here and Now

A festival not only commemorates the past. Every time the Jewish people keep a festival, they merit to receive new light pouring forth toward them from the heavens.

Celebrating the festivals restores the revelation of the original light:

When the holy Rabbi Moshe Zacuto [1625–1697], may his memory be blessed, discussed [the holiness of the festivals] in his book *Tikkun Shovavim*, he wrote that this is a mystical [meaning] of "these days are remembered and observed" (Esther 9:28): That when they are remembered below [in this world], they are carried out above... and it is possible that this can be found in the wording [of the blessing] established by the Sages: "Who performed miracles for our ancestors in those days, at this time," meaning, "in those days" God did great things, pouring forth abundance, salvation, and mercy, and a miracle occurred for them; likewise, "at this time," the divine abundance of mercy is renewed.

Accordingly, it is possible to understand why the festivals are celebrated even in places where the miracles themselves did not occur:

The Jews in Spain and Africa were not under the rule of Ahashverosh, so why are all Jews today obligated to observe Purim? I, with all humility, have arrived at the resolution of this issue via reasoning or by tradition, and it is in accordance with the way of truth [the Kabbala]: Since every year a great radiance shines brightly on Purim, to the same degree as was seen in the days of Mordekhai and Esther, all of Israel must keep these days of Purim at the appropriate time.

(Rabbi Ḥayyim Yosef David Azulai, *Lev David* 29)

What Do the Festivals Reveal to Us?

Every festival reveals the will of God and reinforces the awareness that the world does not operate according to nature, but according to His will.

The revelation of [God's] will is through the festivals. Because each festival proclaims and reveals the will, the fact that everything behaves according to His will alone. This is the aspect of "holy convocation," [or holy proclamation,] as the festival is holy, and it proclaims the will [of God], since on every festival God performed awesome signs for us, which are the very opposite of nature, and through this, the will was revealed, that everything is in accordance with His will, and there is no natural necessity at all. On Passover, it was the exodus, that He took us out of Egypt with awesome signs. On *Shavuot*, it was the giving of the Torah, that He gave us the Torah with awesome signs. On *Sukkot*, it was the presence of the surrounding clouds of glory.

Therefore, each and every festival proclaims the will, in the sense of a "holy convocation," as mentioned above.

(Rabbi Naḥman of Breslov, *Likutei Moharan Tinyana* 4:6)

"A person on a festival must [dedicate himself to] either eating and drinking or to sitting and studying" (*Pesaḥim* 68b), because through eating and drinking in the physical realm, the soul is able to cling to the spiritual.

(Rabbi Yaakov Yosef of Polnoye, *Ben Porat Yosef, Noah*)

Therefore, the festivals were called good days [*yamim tovim*], because through them, heavenly good [*tov*] was revealed.

(Rabbi Zev Wolf of Zhitomir, *Or HaMe'ir, Bo*)

Further reading: For more on miracles and their meaning, see p. 213.

Rosh HaShana

The first day of the Jewish year is called Rosh HaShana. In the Torah, this day is referred to as the Day of Remembrance and as the Day of the Sounding of the Shofar, and in the Oral Torah it is called Rosh HaShana and the Day of Judgment. Just as the human body has a head [*rosh*], the location of the brain, from which the operations of the entire body are controlled, so too, the year has a head that affects the entire year. On this day, the Creator judges all the deeds of human beings and determines what divine abundance will descend to the world in the coming year.

It is a great kindness to humankind that the Creator does not judge a person only at the end of his life, but rather on each Rosh HaShana. When our Father in Heaven judges His children, He dispenses the judgment in a way that conforms to His will. On this day, we crown God as the king and fulfill the mitzva of sounding the shofar, which is full of mystical significance.

A Day of Judgment and of Kindness

The Day of Judgment is not only after death or at the end of the world; rather, all people stand in judgment before God each year on Rosh HaShana, and there is a great kindness in this.

Why does one need to stand in judgment before the Creator every year?

The reasons for the mitzva of this festival include: That it was one of the kindnesses of God to His creatures to remember them and examine their deeds on one day each year, so that their sins will not proliferate, and the possibility of atonement will remain. He is "abounding in kindness" (Exodus 34:6), inclined toward kindness, and since [the sins] are few, He tolerates them [and does not punish]. If perhaps there are among them sins that [defile the sinner] and require cleansing [i.e., punishment], He punishes them little by little, and this is like what the Sages said: "His beloved, He punishes him little by little" (*Avoda Zara* 4a). If He did not reckon with them for a long period, [their sins] would proliferate so much that the world would almost be deserving of destruction, God forbid.

That being so, is Rosh HaShana a day of celebration or a day of fear and trembling?

Consequently, this important day [ensures the continuing] existence of the world, and therefore it is fitting to make it a festival, and it is fitting for it to be counted among the special periods of the year. Nevertheless, as it is the day of the judgment of all living beings, it is appropriate to stand in fear and awe on it, to a greater extent than on any of the other festivals of the year. This is the idea of "a remembrance by means of an alarm blast [*teru'a*]" (Leviticus 23:24), mentioned with regard to [Rosh HaShana], as the *teru'a* is a fragmented sound, indicating that each individual should shatter the force of his evil inclination, and should regret his evil deeds.

(*Sefer HaḤinnukh* 311)

Further reading: For more on Rosh HaShana, see *A Concise Guide to the Torah*, p. 317; *A Concise Guide to the Sages*, p. 282; *A Concise Guide to Halakha*, p. 129.

God watches over all the deeds of mankind, and when the Day of Judgment comes, the accusers present our evil deeds, but God directs the ruling in accordance with His will.

On Rosh HaShana, the angels stand before the Creator, and among them is the accusing angel:

Rabbi Elazar began [his homily]: "It was one day, and the children of the great came to stand before the Lord, and the accuser too came among them" (Job 1:6). "It was one day": This is Rosh HaShana, when the Holy One, blessed be He, stands in judgment over the world. Similarly: "There was one day that he came there" (II Kings 4:11). That day was the festival of Rosh HaShana.

God rules in favor of Israel:

"The children of the great came"; these are the great angels appointed and sent into the world to observe the actions of human beings. "To stand before the Lord"; as it is stated: "All the host of the heavens attending Him on His right and on His left" (I Kings 22:19). "The accuser too came among them…" "Too": To include him over them, as they all come to serve as accusers of Israel, and this one is added to them because he is the greatest denouncer of them all, the greatest accuser. When the Holy One, blessed be He, sees that they are all coming to accuse, immediately, "the Lord said to the accuser: From where have you come?" (Job 1:6). Did not the Holy One, blessed be He, know where he had come from? Rather, it is to direct the [accuser's] action by His will.

(*Zohar* 2:32b)

Further reading: The combination of joy and of trembling due to the fear of judgment is also expressed in the festival meals; see *A Concise Guide to Halakha*, p. 141.

Repentance on Rosh HaShana

The mitzva of Rosh HaShana is the sounding of the shofar. What is the connection between the shofar and the Day of Judgment? The shofar spurs us to leave our evil ways and think about how to repent and do more good deeds.

The sounding of the shofar is a wake-up call to arouse us:

Even though the sounding of the shofar on Rosh HaShana is a [divinely legislated] Torah edict [for which there is no explicit reason], there is an allusion associated with it, as though it is saying: Awaken, sleepers, from your sleep; and slumberers, arise from your slumber, examine your actions and repent, and remember your Creator. Those [of you] who forget the truth due to the futilities of the time, and err all year long with emptiness, which provides neither benefit nor salvation: Look into your souls and improve your ways and your actions, and each one of you should abandon his evil path and his thoughts that are no good.

One is obligated to view himself as though he is being judged at every moment, and as though the two sides of the scale are equally balanced. An act in one direction or the other determines how the scale will tilt:

Therefore, every person needs to view himself all year long, as though he is half innocent and half guilty, and likewise, the entire world is half innocent and half guilty. If he has commited one sin, he has tilted the scale for himself and for the whole world in the direction of guilt, and has caused its destruction. If he has fulfilled one mitzva, he has tilted the scale for himself and for the whole world in the direction of innocence and has brought about salvation for himself and for them, as it is stated: "The righteous is the foundation of the world" (Proverbs 10:25); he who has acted righteously tilted the whole world to [a ruling of] innocence, and saved it. Because of this matter, the entire house of Israel customarily increases charity and good deeds and occupies itself with the performance of mitzvot from Rosh HaShana until Yom Kippur, more so than during the rest of the year.

(Rambam, *Mishneh Torah, Hilkhot Teshuva* 3:4)

Further reading: For the *halakhot* of how and when to blow the shofar, see *A Concise Guide to Halakha*, p. 147.

The Sound of the Shofar

The sounding of the shofar, which is the central ritual of Rosh HaShana, reminds us of a variety of matters related to the festival, to the Jewish people, and to their relationship with the Creator.

Ten reasons for the sounding of the shofar:

Rav Se'adya [Gaon] wrote that the Creator's commandment for us to sound the shofar on Rosh HaShana has ten reasons:

Crowning the Creator:

The first reason: Because this day was the beginning of Creation, when the Holy One, blessed be He, created the world and became its king. So it is with kings at the beginning of their reigns; trumpets and horns are sounded before them to announce in every place the beginning of their reign. Likewise, we crown the Creator as king over us on this day. This is what David said: "With trumpets and the sound of the shofar make loud sound before the King, the Lord" (Psalms 98:6).

A warning and a reminder to repent:

The second reason: Rosh HaShana is the first day of the ten days of repentance [between Rosh HaShana and Yom Kippur], and the shofar is sounded on it to proclaim this to us, like one giving warning, saying: Anyone who wants to return should return. If he does not, he should not complain of injustice toward himself [by claiming that he did not know that repentance was required]. This is what kings do; they initially warn the world of their decrees, and anyone who transgresses after the warning, his claim is not accepted.

Mount Sinai and receiving the Torah:

The third reason: To remind us of Mount Sinai, about which it was stated: "The blast of a shofar, extremely powerful" (Exodus 19:16). We accept upon ourselves that which our forefathers accepted upon themselves: "We will perform and we will heed" (Exodus 24:7).

The exhortations of the prophets:

The fourth reason: To remind us of the exhortations of the prophets [to return to God], which were compared to the sounding of the shofar (Ezekiel 33:4).

The destruction of the Temple and beseeching God to rebuild it:

The fifth reason: To remind us of the destruction of the Temple and the sounds of war made by the enemies, as it is stated: "As the sound of a shofar, you heard, my soul, the sound of an alarm of war" (Jeremiah 4:19). When we hear the sound of the shofar, we appeal to God to rebuild the Temple.

The binding of Isaac and self-sacrifice:

The sixth reason: To remind us of the binding of Isaac,[10] who was willing to give his life for Heaven. Likewise, we [are willing to] give our lives to sanctify God's name, and may our remembrance ascend before Him for good [on Rosh HaShana].

Fear and trembling:

The seventh reason: At hearing the sound of the shofar, we will be afraid, tremble, and break down before the Creator. For this is the nature of the shofar; it causes trembling and shaking, as it is stated: "Will the shofar be sounded in a city, and the people not tremble?" (Amos 3:6).

The great Day of Judgment in the future:

The eighth reason: To recall the great Day of Judgment [at the End of Days] and to fear it. As it is stated: "The great day of the Lord is near; it is near and hastens greatly... A day of trumpeting [*shofar*] and alarm" (Zephaniah 1:14–16).

Ingathering of the exiles – the return to Zion:

The ninth reason: To remind us of the ingathering of the exiles of Israel and yearn for it. As it is said: "It will be on that day that a great shofar will be sounded, and the lost in the land of Assyria [and the outcasts in the land of Egypt] will come..." (Isaiah 27:13).

Resurrection of the dead:

The tenth reason: To remind us of the resurrection of the dead and to evoke belief in it. As it is stated with regard to it: "All inhabitants of the world and dwellers of the earth: When a banner is raised on the mountains you will see, and with the sounding of the shofar you will hear" (Isaiah 18:3).

(Rav David Abudarham, *Seder Tefillot Rosh HaShana*)

10. According to a tradition of the Sages, the binding of Isaac occurred on Rosh HaShana, and the ram's horn used to make the shofar recalls the ram that was sacrificed in place of Isaac.

Further reading: Some of the allusions described here with regard to the shofar derive from statements of the Sages; see *A Concise Guide to the Sages*, p. 284.

The sound of the shofar is like a cry without words. It is the cry of the soul which has been distanced from the Creator. This can be compared to the son of a king who was sent far away from his father for so long that he forgot the language spoken in the palace. In order to make himself known to the king he simply cries out, and this is how the king recognizes him.

The sound of the shofar is a pure cry:

The sound of the shofar is a simple sound, a simple cry from within the depths of one's heart at his separation from the one God. It is [sounded] with the horn of an animal, in accordance with: "Lord, You save man and beast" (Psalms 36:7).

The analogy of a king whose only son went far away from him:

A parable for this was related in the name of the Ba'al Shem Tov, of a king who had an only son who was especially learned, and who was the veritable apple of his eye. The father and his son concluded that he should travel to other lands to learn wisdom and to know the practices of [other] people. His father the king then gave him officials and servants and great wealth so that he could tour countries and the islands of the sea, so that the son would reach a higher level than where he was while with his father in his house…

In any case, he went to a land so distant that even his father was not known there at all, and when he said that he was the son of King So-and-So, aside from the fact that they did not believe him, his father's name was not known at all. When he saw that all his attempts to recover and make his living had failed, he decided, in his distress, to return to his father's land. However, since such a long time had passed, he had even forgotten the language of his country. When he came to his country, what could he do since he had forgotten the language? He began to signal them [by means of gestures] that he was the son of their king, and he became a laughingstock; could it be that the son of such a mighty king would walk around so ragged and worn out? They struck him on his head and he became full of sores and wounds.

Ultimately, he arrived at the king's court and began to signal to them that he was the son of the king, and they paid him no attention whatsoever, until he began to cry out in a loud voice so that the king would recognize his voice. When the king heard the sound, he said: "Is this not the voice of my son crying out in his distress?" Love was awakened within him and he hugged him and kissed him…

Likewise, Jewish souls are God's children who have become distanced from Him:

The above parable should be understood this way: Jewish souls are called the children of the Omnipresent... and He sent the soul down into the body. This is like the parable of the son of the king who went far away in order to become learned. Through the mitzvot and good deeds, souls ascend to a higher level than that which they had been on previously. Indeed, due to the passion of the body and the desire for money, and the other desires of human beings, and through being entrenched [in these desires], one moves very far away, to a place where no one knows the name of his Father, [no one recognizes God]...until he begins to return, and cries out with a simple cry so that his Father will know it is him by recognizing the voice.

The sound of the shofar is a spiritual cry, and forgiveness and absolution are God's loving response to us:

This is the sound of the blowing of the shofar, which is, in a sense, a spiritual cry from the depths of the heart concerning one's regret with regard to the past and his acceptance upon himself to listen to the voice of his Father in the future. As a result of this cry, the King of kings, the Holy One, blessed be He, awakens and shows His love for His only son, and forgives him for what happened in the past.

(Ba'al Shem Tov, *Keter Shem Tov, Hosafot* 194)

Further reading: For the story of a simple cry that came from the depths of the heart and split open the gates of Heaven, see p. 70.

The Crowning of God

On Rosh HaShana, God's desire to rule over the world is renewed. On this day, one is required to accept God's kingship upon himself.

Rosh HaShana contains within it everything that will occur over the course of the year:

All the months are called "the months of the year" (Exodus 12:2), whereas Tishrei is called, simply, "month" (Psalms 81:4). It is a general renewal of all worlds and their coming into being from nothingness, because Rosh HaShana takes place in it, and [Rosh HaShana] represents [in kabbalistic symbolism] the head and the brain of the year... just as a soul has [the aspect of] head and brain, from which is manifest the general life force, from which spreads the particular life force of each organ in accordance with its own nature and attributes, so too...on Rosh HaShana there is a manifestation of the general life force, and from it, the distinct spiritual force of each month is drawn.

The judgment on Rosh HaShana concerns accepting God's kingship:

The principal time in which [God's] will [to rule over the world] is manifest is on Rosh HaShana, when there is a renewal of the general life force for the coming year. The manifestation of the general life force of the previous year is understood to depart at the beginning of Rosh HaShana evening. Therefore, Rosh HaShana is the day of judgment, on which people are judged for their actions during the past year. For the possibility of a renewal of the general life force for this year [is in question because] there are a number of [angels making] accusations against humankind with regard to whether they deserve His heavenly will to be manifest in the revelation of His kingship. [These are] due to [occasions where] they cast off the yoke [of God's kingship]. Some do not constantly accept the yoke of the kingdom of Heaven willingly and with love, but do so only occasionally, when they recall the King of kings, the Holy One, blessed be He. On the contrary, such a person is preoccupied with his own thoughts, each according to what is in his mind. In particular, there are those who are neither careful to abandon evil nor to do good, each person on his level. For the manifestation of the will of Heaven to reveal His kingship [and renew life in this world] is impossible when below, God forbid, there is casting off of the yoke of the kingdom of Heaven, when people do not willingly accept upon themselves the yoke of His kingdom.

(Rabbi Shneur Zalman of Liadi, *Likutei Torah*, Rosh HaShana 53:4)

The Ba'al Shem Tov once instructed one of his students, Rabbi Zev Kitzes, to study the mystical intentions associated with the service of sounding the shofar, since he would be the one to sound the shofar for him [the Ba'al Shem Tov] on Rosh HaShana. Rabbi Zev studied the mystical intentions and wrote them on a special piece of paper and put the paper in his pocket so that he would be able to look at it during the sounding of the shofar. This did not please the Ba'al Shem Tov, and the paper was lost. When Rabbi Zev was about to sound the shofar, he began searching for the paper with the mystical intentions on it, and since he could not find it, he did not know which intentions to have. This greatly distressed Rabbi

Zev and he wept bitterly with a broken heart while he was forced to sound the shofar without any intentions.

After the prayer service, the Ba'al Shem Tov said to him: In the king's palace there are many rooms and halls, and there is a different, unique key for each door, but there is one instrument with which it is possible to open every lock, and that is the ax. The mystical intentions are the keys to the heavenly gates, and for each gate there is a different intention, but a broken heart can unlock each and every gate and hall.

After the shofar is sounded, a new, higher light descends; a light so heavenly that has never shone before.

(Rabbi Shneur Zalman of Liadi, *Tanya, Igeret HaKodesh* 14)

Further reading: For the Ba'al Shem Tov statements on a broken heart as the key to every gate, see p. 308.

Yom Kippur

One day a year, everything stops. Though it can occur on a weekday, it is called the "Sabbath of Sabbaths." We do not eat or drink on it; we only pray, confess, and make a personal account of our lives. The day opens with the *Kol Nidrei* prayer and closes with the *Ne'ila* prayer, and on this day God forgives all of our sins. This day is Yom Kippur.

On Yom Kippur, God examines our hearts, receives us as His children and His servants, and forgives all sins. On this day, we renounce the needs of the body and behave like the angels. It is a day when people forgive one another, and all become purer. We correct everything that requires correction and embark on a new path.

A Day of Freedom

On Yom Kippur, God examines the extent of his children's progress over the course of the year. When we come properly prepared, the community of Israel – the source of all Jewish souls – merits to unite with the holy King, and we are all judged to live in freedom and joy.

The community of Israel is compared to a queen who is appointed over the education of the king's children:

The holy King left His palace and His household under the control of the queen [namely, the community of Israel, understood as a spiritual entity]. He left His children with her, so that she would lead them…if they are deserving, the queen enters in joy and honor to the King. If they are not deserving, both she and they return to exile.

Prayers and fasting on Yom Kippur make forgiveness possible:

Therefore, there is one day in the year on which [God] examines them [the Jewish people]. When this day arrives, the mother above, in whose hands all freedom is found, [as true freedom is freedom from sin,] appears before Him, to look upon Israel. Israel are diligently engaging in various services, prayers, and afflictions, all to their merit. Then they are free, as freedom comes from that place, and all freedom is in the hands of the queen. The King's children, her children, over whom she was appointed, are all found to have merit; all are without sin, without wrongdoing. Then she unites with the King, in light and joy, completely and willingly, as she has raised the children of the heavenly King in the proper manner. And when they are not found to be deserving on this day, woe to them! Woe to their emissaries!

Alas, the queen has grown distant from the King. The mother above withdraws, and freedom does not descend from her to the worlds.

The joy of the Jewish people on Yom Kippur:

Happy are Israel, as the Holy One, blessed be He, taught them His ways so that they would be saved from judgment, and be found righteous before Him. This is as it is written: "For on this day He shall atone for you, to purify you" (Leviticus 16:30).

(*Zohar* 3:102b)

Further reading: For more on Yom Kippur, see *A Concise Guide to the Torah*, pp. 293, 318; *A Concise Guide to the Sages*, p. 285; *A Concise Guide to Halakha*, p. 167.

Atonement for Sins on Yom Kippur

Following the crowning of God as king on Rosh HaShana, His kingship is expressed on Yom Kippur by His absolving our sins. God is the King of the Universe, and accordingly, He removes us from our slavery to the evil inclination, and brings us into His domain.

Entering the domain of the King of the Universe:

An aspect of Yom Kippur is...that the world is the King's, God's, just like a servant belongs to his master. Consequently, the Holy One, blessed be He, absolves their sins, because they [the Jewish people, or perhaps mankind] are His...and from the fact that He is the King of the Universe, and everything in it is His, under His domain and no one else's. So on Yom Kippur they emerge from the domain of that king, the evil inclination, with whom they became entangled during the year, and they enter the domain of the Holy One, blessed be He, because they are called by the name of the King, the Lord of hosts.... The sinner is sold into the hand of the evil inclination through his sins, until he is able to come under the domain of another; and on Yom Kippur, he emerges [from the domain of the evil inclination].

(Maharal, *Gevurot Hashem* 46)

Further reading: With regard to the *Kaparot* ceremony that takes place before Yom Kippur, see *A Concise Guide to Halakha*, p. 158.

Why Do We Fast on Yom Kippur?

Fasting is a cleansing process. By relinquishing the needs of the body and our animalistic nature, we cleanse ourselves of undesirable thoughts and deeds. Engaging in lofty matters enables us to repent completely.

Cleansing the soul of all confusion:

The solemn fast day: On this day, one becomes purified from every sin he has committed in the past and completes anything not achieved on Shabbatot and *Rosh Hodesh* [which are also days of purification]. On this day, the individual is purified of all confusions of the mind, the forces of anger and desire, and will wholly repent from holding on to them in thought or deed. If it is impossible for him to remove them from his mind, because his habitual thinking that he has retained since his youth overcomes him, as a result of songs he has heard or from stories and the like, then it is sufficient that he become purified in his actions, and that he seek to atone for his thoughts and accept upon himself not to bring them to his lips, as it is said: "I pondered, and nothing passed my lips" (Psalms 17:3), and all the more so, not to express them through any action.

What is the benefit of fasting?

The fast on this day makes the pious one almost like the angels, as the day passes by in humility and in submission, while standing and bowing, praising and giving thanks. All of one's physical powers abstain from the natural needs [of the body] and are occupied only with fulfilling mitzvot, as if he did not have an animalistic nature at all.

(Rav Yehuda HaLevi, *Kuzari* 3:5)

On one day a year, we come closer to God and to holiness. In order to receive the special light of this day, all fast on Yom Kippur, emulating the angels to some degree.

The purpose of Yom Kippur:

The idea of Yom Kippur is that the Master, blessed be He, prepared one day for Israel when repentance is readily accepted and sins are easily wiped away. That is to say, it is to repair all the damage that has been done and to remove all the darkness that has taken over as a result, and to bring those who repent back to the level of holiness and closeness to God, from which they were distanced as a result of their sins.

The way to receive the special light of Yom Kippur is through fasting:

On this day there is a light shining, by whose power this entire matter [of coming close to God, and of the atonement for sins] is achieved. In order to receive this light, Israel must observe that which they were commanded concerning this day, and in particular with regard to afflicting [the body], through which they become thoroughly disconnected from physicality, and ascend a little toward resembling the angels.

(Rabbi Moshe Ḥayyim Luzzatto, *Derekh Hashem* 4:8:5)

The Day That Illuminates All Other Days

On Yom Kippur an especially sublime light emanates from the upper worlds, and even the Accuser is unable to make accusations. Yom Kippur influences the entire year, and therefore one should greatly rejoice as it approaches.

A day like no other:

Because Yom Kippur is like the World to Come, and it is a day that is more special than all other days of the year, as they said ... with regard to the verse: "'Of the days that were created, one is His' (Psalms 139:16), this is Yom Kippur," on which there is illumination from the upper world. Even the Accuser is not permitted to make accusations.

Yom Kippur influences the entire year:

Therefore, this day illuminates all the other days ... and likewise, this day elevates all the other days ... meaning that this day elevates all the other days to a level that is above nature, like it is explained in another place, that existence is dependent on the ability to nullify [the self and to cleave] to the transcendent source [of all things]. Therefore, one should rejoice when this holy day approaches ... and illumination is channeled through this joy from Yom Kippur to all the other days.

(Rabbi Yehuda Aryeh Leib Alter, *Sefat Emet*, Yom Kippur 5652)

Further reading: For more on resembling the angels on Yom Kippur, see *A Concise Guide to the Sages*, p. 231; *A Concise Guide to Halakha*, p. 169.

The Significance of Confession

Even when we regret our improper behavior and resolve to change our ways, it is sometimes very hard for us to take the necessary steps. Confession, which is a central element of the Yom Kippur prayers, makes this possible. When we openly admit that we have erred, we are able to stand before God and to embark on a new path.

The problem: The disparity between how one feels on the inside and what he expresses on the outside:

At times one knows beyond any doubt that he has sinned and strayed from his life's purpose, because he has betrayed all his values. He knows why, but he is not prepared to say it openly or to hear it from others [like in the talmudic expression]: "Anyone who says ... will be stabbed" (*Ketubot* 104a). In his bed at night he thinks of it, and his soul cries in secret, but in the light of day, in the eyes of others, he is happy and content. In order to cover up the truth that is eating away at his soul, he continues to sin, increases his pace, and keeps charging toward the precipice.

The solution: To explicitly state the difficult reality:

Confession compels a person to recognize, through tremendous suffering, the simple facts, and to articulate the truth as it is clearly. This involves a kind of sacrifice, a kind of breaking of one's will, and a painful action that is contrary to nature. It involves not only regret, but also shame. "You have taught us, Lord our God, to confess before You all our iniquities" (*Ne'ila* prayer), to look the truth straight in the eye, face-to-face, to really look; to break down our defense mechanisms; to shatter the artificial barriers; to go against human nature, which tells us to conceal ourselves; to tear up our masks; to determine with our lips that which our hearts had previously determined. All this is so that: "We may end the oppression that is performed by our hands," and subsequently: "That you may receive us back in perfect repentance before You, like burnt offerings and their sweet savor." Just as an offering is burned on the altar, so too, through the act of confession, we burn our well-guarded serenity, our meticulously maintained pride, our artificial existence. Then, and only then: "Before the Lord you shall be purified" (Leviticus 16:30).

(Rabbi Yosef Dov Soloveitchik, *Al HaTeshuva*, pp. 61ff)

Further reading: For more on the confession that we say on Yom Kippur, see *A Concise Guide to the Sages*, p. 287; *A Concise Guide to Halakha*, p. 170.

One year, on Yom Kippur, the Ba'al Shem Tov saw that there was a severe decree against a particular Jewish town. He endeavored with all his might to reverse the decree through his prayers, but to no avail. When they came to the *Ne'ila* prayer and the decree was still in force, the Ba'al Shem Tov was very grave, and he sobbed with great intensity, as did all his holy followers and all the others praying in his study hall.

There was a Jewish youth, an uneducated shepherd, who had come to the synagogue for the Yom Kippur services. While everyone had been praying, he merely stood and stared into space. But during *Ne'ila,* when everyone began wailing from the depths of their hearts in prayer to the

Master of the Universe, his heart stirred, and a strong desire to pray was ignited in his soul. For a long time he had marveled at the call of the rooster, and now, before he knew it, a resounding cry suddenly emerged from his lips: "Cock-a-doodle-doo! Master of the Universe, have mercy!"

There was a commotion in the study hall, and some of the worshippers wanted to throw the ignorant villager out, but suddenly a joyful tune was heard from the Ba'al Shem Tov, and he quickly finished the prayers, his holy face shining with exultation.

When the holy day came to an end, the Ba'al Shem Tov told his followers that an accusation had been voiced against the residents of the town, who lived among gentiles and distanced themselves from the Holy One, blessed be He. But when the pure cry of the villager, whose soul had spilled over in prayer to the Master of the Universe, was heard, this cry caused delight in the highest heights and nullified all the decrees.

I desire to live, because in the World to Come there are no Days of Awe, and what would the soul of a Jew do without Yom Kippur? What is the point of living without repentance?

(Rabbi Shmelke of Nikolsburg)

In the *Ne'ila* prayer, the *yehida* aspect of the soul, which is unified with God, is revealed, and at that time there is place for nothing but God and the Jewish people.

(The Lubavitcher Rebbe)

If Yom Kippur were given to us only once every seventy years, and we knew that the day on which all our sins are forgiven was approaching, how great would our joy be! Now, since Yom Kippur comes every year, our joy should be more than seven times greater!

(Rabbi Yisrael Salanter)

Further reading: For more on the holiness of simple Jews, see p. 226.

Sukkot

The Days of Awe are followed by the joy of *Sukkot*. Holding the four species (palm branch [*lulav*], citron [*etrog*], myrtle [*hadas*], and willow [*arava*]);[11] dwelling in the *sukka*, a temporary structure, for the entire week; and the *Simhat Beit HaSho'eva* (festive gatherings in memory of the water libation ceremony that took place in the Temple on *Sukkot*), make the festival colorful and joyous. In fact, the Torah commands us to be particularly happy during *Sukkot*.[12]

In the Torah, *Sukkot* is called the Festival of the Harvest, because at that time we finish bringing the produce inside before winter. On this festival, we also collect all the spiritual fruits of Torah and mitzvot from the preceding year. We hold the four species, which symbolize the beauty of the Land of Israel, as well as control over a person's physical forces. The totality of the four species also hints at unity, which is the prerequisite for the resting of the Divine Presence. When we sit in the *sukka*, it is as if we are returning to the Garden of Eden.

 **Further reading:** For more on the festival of *Sukkot*, see *A Concise Guide to the Torah*, pp. 318, 472; *A Concise Guide to the Sages*, p. 290; *A Concise Guide to Halakha*, pp. 176ff.

The Harvest Festival

Just as one gathers the produce from the field and brings it into the storehouses, so too, he gathers the spiritual fruits of the mitzvot that he has fulfilled during the year, and brings them into the heavenly storehouse. Before placing produce in one's storehouses, he must clean it of all refuse, and likewise, before bringing Torah and mitzvot into the heavenly storehouse, we have the Days of Awe, during which we cleanse ourselves of all spiritual waste.

The analogy of bringing the produce into the storehouses on *Sukkot*:

The festival of *Sukkot* is also called: "The Harvest Festival" (Exodus 34:22). It is known that all physical matters are analogous to spiritual matters. Therefore, it is evident that just as in the physical realm this is the time for

11. See Leviticus 23:40, "You shall take for you on the first day the fruit of a pleasant tree [*etrog*], branches of date-palms [*lulav*], and a bough of a leafy tree [*hadas*], and willows of the brook [*arava*], and you shall rejoice before the Lord your God seven days."
12. See Deuteronomy 16:15, "Seven days you shall celebrate to the Lord your God in the place that the Lord shall choose, as the Lord your God will bless you in your entire crop, and in all your endeavors, and *you shall be completely joyous*."

gathering all the produce of the field, so too, in the spiritual realm, all Torah, mitzvot, and good deeds that a person has accumulated over the course of the year are gathered on *Sukkot*.

To be able to store one's spiritual harvest, one must cleanse it:

And just as in the physical realm, we first remove any waste from the produce, and only afterward put it in the storehouse... so too in the spiritual realm, with regard to all Torah, mitzvot, and good deeds: If they contained any unworthy thoughts or any outside considerations that were not for the sake of Heaven, these are like chaff in the produce, and we do not put such mitzvot in the heavenly storehouse.

On the Days of Awe, all spiritual waste is purged:

But on Rosh HaShana and Yom Kippur: "Wholly wicked people are immediately written and sealed for death" (*Rosh HaShana* 16b). My holy father, our master, teacher, and rabbi [Rabbi Avraham Bornsztain of Sochatchov], of blessed memory, said that just as wholly wicked people are included in this principle, so is every aspect of every person and every mitzva. The evil part of every individual is purged and the waste from every mitzva is expelled. It is therefore obvious that after Rosh HaShana and Yom Kippur, when all Torah, mitzvot, and good deeds are cleansed of waste, it is the most auspicious time to put them in the heavenly storehouse.

(Rabbi Shmuel Bornsztain, *Shem MiShmuel, Sukkot* 5672)

The Four Species – the Beauty and Goodness of the Land of Israel

On *Sukkot* we joyfully wave and shake the four species: a palm branch [*lulav*], a citron [*etrog*], three myrtle branches [*hadas*], and two willow branches [*arava*]. The four species comprise three different types of branches and one fruit. They are some of the most beautiful plants of the Land of Israel and represent the Israelites' emergence from the wilderness and entrance into the Land of Israel.

Why do we wave the four species on *Sukkot*?

It seems to me that the four species of the mitzva of *lulav*[13] represent joy and delight at having emerged from the wilderness, which is: "Not a place of seed, or figs, or vines, or pomegranates, and there is no water to drink" (Numbers 20:5), and their having arrived at a place of fruit trees and rivers.

13. In addition to being one of the four species, *lulav*, as the largest and most conspicuous of them, is used as a general term for all four species.

Therefore, one holds, as a reminder of this, the most beautiful fruit of all, the citron; the one with the best fragrance, the myrtle; the one with the most beautiful leaves, the palm branch; and the most beautiful plant, that is, the willow of the brook.

The unique characteristics of the four species:

These four species possess three advantageous qualities: First, they are very common in the Land of Israel during the season of *Sukkot*, and are accessible to everyone. Secondly, they are beautiful and fresh, and some of them – the citron and the myrtle – have a pleasant fragrance, while the palm branch and willow have neither a bad odor nor a fragrance. Thirdly, they remain fresh for seven days, which is not the case with regard to peaches, pomegranates, quinces, pears, or the like.

(Rambam, *Guide of the Perplexed* III:43)

Further reading: Read about how to choose the four species in *A Concise Guide to Halakha*, p. 180.

The Four Species: Four Major Organs

The four species resemble some of the most important organs in the human body. They hint that one must use all these body parts to serve the Creator.

These four species possess an additional attribute, which is that they resemble human organs of great significance. The citron resembles the heart, which is the locus of understanding, symbolizing that one must serve his Creator with his understanding. The palm branch resembles the spine, which is a person's main support, symbolizing that one should set his entire body upright to serve God. The myrtle [leaf] resembles the eye, symbolizing that one must not stray after his eyes "on the day of his joy."[14] The willow leaves resemble the lips, with which one completes all his acts of speech, hinting that one should exercise restraint over his mouth and control his speech, and should fear God, even at a time of rejoicing.

(*Sefer HaḤinnukh* 324)

Further reading: For more on the symbolism of the four species, see *A Concise Guide to the Sages*, p. 291.

14. This phrase alludes to a time of levity. See Song of Songs 3:11.

The Four Species: Symbol of Unity

Divine flow is given only where there is unity. Each of the four species exhibits unity in a distinctive way. The leaves of the palm branch are attached to its spine, making it look as though it is one branch. Myrtle leaves overlap with each other. Willows grow close together, as though they are friends, while the citron grows through all four seasons of the year.

Divine flow from above comes only to a place where there is unity:

Elicitation of the infinite light occurs only in a place of oneness, that is, in a place where there is unification, and not in a place of division.... With regard to these four species, each one of them possesses the element of oneness and integration.

Unity expressed through the palm branch:

With regard to the palm branch, all its leaves are integrated, and they combine and ascend together as one with the spine, and they are all attached and unified with each other as though they are one entity.

Unity expressed through the myrtle:

The myrtle, too: Its leaves grow in triads, that is, three leaves emerging from one point. As is known, this is an aspect of oneness and integration. The myrtle is also called "a bough of a leafy tree" (Leviticus 23:40), because the foliage covers the tree [that is, the wooden stem of the branches], which demonstrates unification, as one leaf covers the next, such that it looks like one surface.

Unity expressed through the willow:

The "willows of the brook" (Leviticus 23:40) are called "*ahvana*" in the Talmud (*Shabbat* 20a), because they grow in fellowship [*ahva*], that is, they grow in such a way that they are joined together like beloved friends.

Unity expressed through the citron:

The citron is called "the fruit of a pleasant [*hadar*] tree" (Leviticus 23:40), because it "dwells [*dar*] in its tree from year to year" (*Sukka* 31b) [i.e., the citron can stay on the tree throughout the entire year without falling off or rotting]. This is because it, too, contains an element of oneness and integration. For all fruits do not survive from year to year, due to the changes in the seasons. The cold or the heat of summer or winter affect them, and they are unable to endure two opposites, like cold and afterward hot, and they therefore spoil and rot. But the fruit of the citron tree is not affected by these changes; that is, it is able to endure all the changes of the seasons, of cold and heat, because it possesses an element of oneness and integration. Therefore, it can endure the combination of different kinds of opposites [and in this way, it unites within it the effects of the four seasons].

(Rabbi Shneur Zalman of Liadi, *Sefer HaMa'amarim* 5568, p. 447)

Further reading: For more on the unity of the Jewish people, see p. 113.

Dwelling in the *Sukka*: A Taste of the Garden of Eden

When Adam, the first man, was created, God placed him in the Garden of Eden; but when he sinned, he was expelled from it. Each year, we are able to feel glimmers of the Garden of Eden when we dwell in the *sukka* sheltered by God, and are able to rejoice on *Sukkot*.

Sukkot is called "our time of rejoicing," in the festival prayers, because God granted us the merit of dwelling in His shadow [that is, His shelter, the *sukka*]. This is somewhat like the Garden of Eden, as it is written: "He placed there the man" (Genesis 2:8). The main idea of Creation was that man's dwelling place would be there [that is, in the Garden of Eden], and that was where joy was found, as it is written in the wedding blessings: "As You gave joy to Your creations in the Garden of Eden," but it is also written: "He banished the man" (Genesis 3:24). Nevertheless, there are times when a little of the illumination from the Garden of Eden glimmers; God brings us into this dwelling [that is, the *sukka*] that bears the name of Heaven [as it has the status of an article used in the performance of a mitzva]...therefore, this dwelling brings joy.

(Rabbi Yehuda Aryeh Leib Alter, *Sefat Emet, Sukkot* 5643)

Sukka and *Lulav*

By: Rabbi Moshe ben Yaakov Adhan

Sukka and *lulav* for the chosen nation; together they sing and express appreciation.
God delivered us from the land of Egypt, and made heard to us His sacred words.
He surrounded us with clouds of glory,
on all four sides, above and below.
He told us of His pleasant ways,
and appeared to us in His light and splendor.
Knowledge is expressed from day to day;

knowledge is uttered night by night.
Israel will rejoice in the shade of His *sukka*,
taking shelter under His wing.
His ineffable name as written and read,
carries the value of *sukka*.[15]
How great are the secrets of the four species,
their lessons are so precious to me.
Praised is the purehearted, who focuses his gaze
on the secrets of this mitzva, so elevated.
Within the *lulav* lies the name that has four;[16]
the addition of the letter *heh* adds to the count.
The spine of the *lulav* is surrounded,
encircled by its species.
The myrtle hints to our patriarchs three;
Moses and Aaron – branches of the willow tree;
Joseph the *lulav* desired by all;
David – the citron – like a bride at her wedding.
Provide a deed of release to Your children,
a gift to the nation that is Yours,
who await and hope for Your salvation.
May Your name be sanctified in our words, sela.

Rabbi Mikhel of Zloczow owned a pair of very valuable *tefillin* that he had inherited from his saintly father. More than once, people had offered him large sums of money for them. Rabbi Mikhel was desperately poor and lived in dire need, and his wife had tried to convince him to sell the *tefillin* so that they would be able to provide for their household, but he refused to hear of it.

One year, the festival of *Sukkot* was approaching, and there was no citron to be found in Zloczow. Just as the festival was about to start, a Jewish man entered the town with a most beautiful citron. He was asking a high price for it. Rabbi Mikhel immediately went and sold his *tefillin*, and bought the citron.

15. This is a reference to *gematriya*, the system whereby each Hebrew letter has a numerical equivalent, leading to connections between words.
16. This is a reference to the four-letter name of God.

When he brought it home, his wife realized that it was worth a fortune, and she began to question her husband about where he had obtained the money to buy it. He had no choice but to tell her the truth, that he had sold the *tefillin*. When she heard this, his wife was furious, and in her anger she picked up the citron and broke off the wood-like protuberance at its end, disqualifying it for use for the mitzva.

When the saintly man saw this, he lifted up his eyes and said: "Master of the Universe, I have no *tefillin*; I have no citron. Should I become angry too, and lose my World to Come? No; I will not become angry."

This is why God gave us the mitzva of *sukka*; it protects [us] from the might of the nations. It alludes to this by protecting us from the sun, which signifies the might of the nations.... That is why this festival is called *Sukkot*.

(Rabbi Shmuel Bornsztain, *Shem MiShmuel, Sukkot* 5677)

On *Sukkot* the strength and love of the generation of the wilderness[17] is awakened... this is the *sukka*, which recalls the clouds of glory in which God protected the Israelites in the wilderness. "And his banner upon me is love" (Song of Songs 2:4); the *lulav* is the banner.

(Rabbi Yehuda Aryeh Leib Alter, *Sefat Emet, Sukkot* 5662)

The greatest joy on this festival comes from the illumination of the soul that the Jewish people merit after they were purified on Yom Kippur... and wherever there is a revelation of the soul's illumination, there is joy.

(Rabbi Yehuda Aryeh Leib Alter, *Sefat Emet, Sukkot* 5662)

Further reading: For more on the special joy of *Sukkot*, see *A Concise Guide to the Sages*, p. 292.

17. Those who were redeemed from Egypt and traveled in the wilderness for forty years.

Hanukkah

In the depth of winter, when the nights are especially long, we light the eight Hanukkah candles and remind ourselves that a little light overcomes much darkness, just like in the war of the Hasmoneans against the Greeks, where the few triumphed over the many. The days of Hanukkah are considered regular weekdays, yet they are days of great illumination. Dreidels and fried doughnuts and potato pancakes are customs that were added to the main mitzva of this festival, which is the lighting of the candles.

Lighting candles inspires us; it reminds us that we can "catch fire". Hanukkah is the commemoration of the devotion and self-sacrifice of the Hasmoneans, which allow us to draw on the light of the infinite and strengthen our commitment to Torah and mitzvot. We understand that our struggle against the Greeks is not a war fought on the battlefield but one that takes place in our minds and souls, over the meaning of life, morality, and holiness.

Further reading: For more on Hanukkah, see *A Concise Guide to the Sages*, p. 295; *A Concise Guide to Halakha*, p. 244.

Passion and Renewal

Hanukkah is a time of igniting a fire, both in the candles and in ourselves, in our fervor for God's commandments. Contemplating the miracles of Hanukkah teaches us that the world does not merely conform to natural laws; everything is constantly being created anew by the Creator. Hanukkah is a time of renewal and of recognizing the power of God, who in His goodness continually renews the work of Creation day after day.

Passion for doing mitzvot:

"Blessed are You, Lord, our God, King of the universe, who has sanctified us with His commandments and commanded us to light the Hanukkah lights." It is known that a person's main duty in prayer, Torah, and mitzvot is to impassion his soul and heart for [serving] God, with wondrous love and desire, by contemplating God's greatness through delving deep into wisdom. Accordingly, one's soul will be passionate about God, amid pleasantness, sweetness, and affection. It is known with regard to the joy of mitzvot that the most important thing is to do each and every mitzva with great love and desire and with immense enthusiasm (see *Zohar* 3:8a). This is the interpretation of the blessing: "Blessed are You, Lord…to light," that is, we bless and praise God, who chose us as His people of distinction to perform His commandments while ablaze, with great passion, like a flame that ignites by itself [and does not need to be lit from an external source].

The miracle of Hanukkah is a concealed miracle:

Know that the miracles that the Creator, blessed be He, performs for us can be broken down into three types. There are concealed miracles and there are revealed miracles. The revealed miracles are like those that were performed for our patriarchs in Egypt... and the splitting of the Red Sea, which were changes to the natural order, and everyone saw these miracles plainly. There are also concealed miracles, like the miracle in the days of Mordekhai and Esther, where events appeared to follow a natural course... and the miracle mentioned in the *Al HaNisim* prayer said on Hanukkah, namely, that God delivered "the many into the hands of the few, the impure into the hands of the pure." This too was a concealed miracle, as it was by means of a war. And the act of Judith [who killed the Greek general] was also to some degree in accordance with nature. Of course, it was really a miracle, and not the natural course of events, but it was a concealed, and not a revealed, miracle.

Further reading: For more on concealed and revealed miracles, see p. 215.

The natural order of the world is also directed in accordance with God's will:

If a person, God forbid, does not believe in concealed miracles, then he thinks that this is the natural order of things, that is, that the sun shines during the day and the moon shines at night, and at night one sleeps and in the day he is awake, and one who expands his trade becomes richer, and one who travels far makes a profit, and when one is sick he should take medicine. He believes that this is the natural order. Yet when one sees concealed miracles, for example, when God, the Creator, blessed be He, delivered the strong into the hands of the weak, or the downfall of Haman, and all the more so with regard to revealed miracles, then a person sees that the world does not behave in accordance with habituation. Rather, God is the One who sets captives free and who raises those who are bowed down; He is the One who rolls away the light before the darkness [every evening]; He is the One who forms light and darkness; and God is the One who heals the sick.

The Holy One, blessed be He, renews the existence of the world every day:

The Creator, may His name be blessed, is the King of the Universe, and as King, He renews His world in accordance with His will, and there is no natural order that dictates the way the world always behaves. Rather, even with regard to the natural order, the Creator, may His name be blessed, who is the King of the Universe, renews it. By His will He renews the natural order, and by His will He negates the natural order. He does not say that that which was yesterday is what will be; rather, every single day [and every single moment], the Holy One, blessed be He, creates all His creations anew.

Why is this festival called Hanukkah, and what is the significance of the blessing: "To light the Hanukkah lights"?

The term Hanukkah comes from "dedication [*hanukat*] of the Temple," an expression of newness. We acknowledge the concealed miracles and the fact that God constantly renews even the established natural order of the world, that is, that the world does not automatically behave in accordance with natural laws, God forbid. And this is [the spiritual meaning of the blessing] "to light the Hanukkah lights," that is, this idea that God renews the world at each and every moment should always be emitting its light in our thoughts and should purify our hearts to serve Him, since we [learn from this concept that we are entirely] in His hands.

(Rabbi Levi Yitzḥak of Berditchev, *Kedushat Levi*, Hanukkah)

The Jug of Oil in Each of Us

The small jug of ritually pure oil that was found in the Temple, when all other oil there had been desecrated by the Greeks, symbolizes the drop of goodness and light that exists in every Jew and in every situation. The mitzvot, and in particular the Hanukkah lights, help people to find this concealed element.

This jug is an allusion to the fact that there always remains in every Jew an element that the Holy One, blessed be He, protects, where there is no admittance to outsiders [alien influence]...yet this element must be searched for. If one believes that there is a concealed element [of purity] in everything, and searches with all his might, he will find it.... This is the essence of the Hanukkah candles; they shine so that we are able to find the concealed element. Just as in the exile there is a concealed element that does not become defiled...so too, within every Jew there is such an element, a divine soul from above. The mitzvot are candles with which we are able to find this element.

(Rabbi Yehuda Aryeh Leib Alter, *Sefat Emet*, Hanukkah 5633)

Lighting the Darkness

One lights the Hanukkah candles at the entrance of his home, facing the public domain, after night has fallen. In this way, the Jewish people illuminate the darkness outside. A tremendous light emanates from these candles, a light of devotion. It draws its power from the heavenly light, which is above the bounds of nature.

The purpose of the Hanukkah candles is to illuminate the darkness. As a result of the war against the Greeks, who tried "to make them forget Your Torah and to force them to transgress the statutes of Your will" [from the *Al HaNisim* prayer said on Hanukkah], and especially due to the fact that they entered the Sanctuary and desecrated all the oil that was there, there was a strengthening of the force of darkness that opposes holiness. Therefore, when the Hasmoneans prevailed and defeated the Greeks, they instituted the [lighting of] Hanukkah candles in order to illuminate the darkness. And this is why the time for their lighting is after sunset, as the idea of the Hanukkah candles is to illuminate the darkness. They are positioned outside (facing the public domain), to the left of the entrance, in order to illuminate the darkness of the public domain as well, the mountains of separation,[18] which draw [vitality] from the left side.

(Rabbi Menaḥem Mendel Schneerson,
Torat Menaḥem, Sefer HaMa'amarim Melukat, vol. 2, p. 131)

The Spiritual War against the Greeks

The Greeks were lovers of wisdom and knowledge. Their objection was not to the elements of Torah and mitzvot that are understood by the human mind, but to the notions of "God's Torah" and "God's mitzvot," i.e., that there is an element of the Torah and mitzvot beyond what is understood by the rational mind.

The objection of the Greeks was to our connection to the divine:

Even the Greeks acknowledged that one needs to study and fulfill Torah and mitzvot, as the Greeks are lovers of wisdom and possess understanding, and as a result they, too, say that Torah and mitzvot are good and that it is impossible to endure without them. But which Torah and mitzvot are good, according to the Greeks? The Torah that derives from human reason, and the mitzvot that constitute uprightness of character and ethical behavior in accordance with human understanding. But the Greeks would wage war against the Torah associated with the Tetragrammaton and the mitzvot

18. This is a kabbalistic expression that refers to a place where there is no revelation of the unity of the Creator or of the divine.

associated with the Tetragrammaton [which emphasize one's relationship with and connection to God].

The purpose of studying Torah and doing mitzvot is service of the Creator:

In truth, the real purpose of Torah study is not only to attain knowledge of the *halakha* or to grasp the subject [being studied]. Rather, the most essential aspect of this activity is that one's heart and mind must be bound in service to Torah and to the One who gives the Torah.... Likewise, with regard to the mitzvot, the most essential aspect is the acceptance of the yoke of Heaven, and the fear of Heaven involved in the fulfillment of mitzvot.

(Rabbi Yosef Yitzḥak Schneersohn, *Sefer HaMa'amarim* 5692–93, p. 185)

The Difference between Greek Culture and Jewish Culture

Judaism is full of the spirit of life, but it does not view life only in terms of external beauty; rather, it sees the religious, moral aspect of nature as well. The Jewish faith is not an encumbrance on one's ability to live his life, but its spirit influences every creative act.

The distinction between Greece and Israel:

The difference between Greece and Israel has already been explained: The Greeks are the nation of beauty, and the Jews are the nation of the spirit. This expression has become somewhat distorted as a result of having been rehashed so many times. It would be more precise to say that the Greeks viewed the world from the perspective of beauty. The sights of nature and the evaluation of those experiences were processed from the point of view of aesthetics. The multiplicity of color and hue that is found in the experience of nature excited aesthetic pleasure in the Greek viewer. By contrast, the Jewish prophet experiences nature also from a religious, moral perspective.

How the Greek poets sang of the beauty of the forest, and how the poets of Israel did so:

The Greek poets sang of the forest. Its blossoming trees lined up in their unique way roused their lyrical senses. This is revealed in numerous representations of the beauty absorbed by their eyes and souls from this magnificent sight. The religious poet was also moved by the forest, and his lyrical sense, too, was inspired to form images, but these images are entirely different: "All the trees of the forest will then cry out for joy before the Lord when He comes" (Psalms 96:12–13). This is not merely a poetic phrase, but reflects the sensory vision of Jewish religiosity, which perceives trees as praying softly.

The Jewish approach to the spirit of vitality:

Jewish religiosity is not a reaction against the spirit of vitality; rather, it is itself the surging experience of life. It does not come in order to suppress creativity; rather, it is a bursting forth of creative abundance. Therefore, we see that the Jewish faith does not view life with anger, nor does it consider it to be its competitor.

Judaism influences everything that the human spirit contemplates:

The Jewish faith was never considered by its followers as a stumbling block to a vital life. The spirit of life and the spirit of religion were not hostile competitors; rather, they merged and blended together. Religion did not constrict itself or life; rather, it expanded to all areas of life and impressed its seal on them. It did not constrict itself to the four cubits of religious worship [that is, to that which pertains directly to Torah and mitzvot]; rather, it enfolded all human activity and thought within itself, and its spirit cultivated and influenced all creativity, whether in nature or art, science or politics, everything that the human spirit pondered.

(Rabbi Yeḥiel Yaakov Weinberg, *Lifrakim*, vol. 1, pp. 180ff)

Further reading: See p. 290 for another example of religious significance that is found in a seemingly secular matter.

It was Hanukkah in the Bergen-Belsen concentration camp. A large group of Jews gathered together, and the Bluzhever Rebbe lit the Hanukkah candles. After he had recited the blessings and lit the candles, one of the inmates approached him and asked:

"Rebbe, I thought that in terrible circumstances such as these it is better not to light Hanukkah candles. But if you do insist on lighting the candles and making the blessings, how could you say the *Sheheḥeyanu* blessing? Why would one say the blessing, 'Who has given us life, sustained us, and brought us to this time,' when thousands of Jews are suffering and being murdered in unspeakable ways?"

The Rebbe answered him: "I also considered this, and in the end, I found the answer. In such terrible circumstances, when so large a group of prisoners come together with true self-sacrifice to see and hear the lighting of the Hanukkah candles, we must recite *Sheheḥeyanu* over the fact that there are still Jews such as these!"

Self-sacrifice for God and His Torah is not the pinnacle of strength that it is possible to have for the sake of Torah. Instead of dying for Torah, it is better to live for it, and to fight courageously for its triumph.

(Rabbi Samson Raphael Hirsch)

The primary illumination of Hanukkah for everyone who is able to do so is to extend the holiness toward those who are still standing outside and who cannot perceive that holiness, and to illuminate the world so that all will recognize and know that God alone is the Ruler over all the earth.

(Rabbi Yisrael of Kozhnitz, *Avodat Yisrael*)

Purim

Jewish tradition attaches great importance to Purim, and already in the book of Esther it says: "These days of Purim will not pass from among the Jews" (Esther 9:28). There are special mitzvot that are observed on Purim: the reading of the megilla, *mishlo'ah manot* (gifts of food sent to friends), gifts to the poor, and feasting and rejoicing. It is also customary to dress up in costumes and to reveal hidden aspects of our personalities.

What can we learn from the book of Esther? It is a story that appears to unfold within the bounds of nature, yet reflecting on it reveals an extraordinary level of divine providence. Additionally, we observe that what brought about the decree against the Jews was divisiveness among the Jewish people, while unity brought about its cancellation. This unity is reflected in the mitzvot of *mishlo'ah manot* and gifts to the poor. The mitzva of rejoicing and feasting is an extension of the joy that was felt at the cancellation of the decree. There is also a special mitzva to drink wine, as through drinking and attenuation of our awareness we have the capacity to reach the supernal root of the soul.

Further reading: For more on Purim, see *A Concise Guide to the Sages*, p. 298; *A Concise Guide to Halakha*, p. 262.

Concealed Providence

The miracle of Purim was not outside of the bounds of nature, but reflection on the progression and combination of events reveals God's providence and His direction of it all. From this, we can learn that God is watching over every individual and directing everything that happens to him.

The events of the megilla are concealed providence:

When we read the book of Esther we do not find anything that is outside the normal bounds of nature, because all the events that occur in it are ostensibly common and natural. Esther was taken to the king's palace because of her beauty, she was pleasing to him, and he placed the royal crown on her head. Likewise, in the incident with Bigtan and Teresh, Mordekhai heard that they were planning to attack King Ahashverosh. He told Esther, and she told the king; this is also a plausible event. Every event developed as a result of natural and reasonable circumstances, yet one [must] reflect on this matter and consider the way in which all the circumstances combined: Vashti defied the king; the king regretted his act; Esther, who was raised in the house of Mordekhai, was pleasing to the king, and he crowned her in place of Vashti;

and then Mordekhai overheard Bigtan and Teresh. The king's sleep was disturbed on the very same night that Haman had been advised by his family and friends to build the gallows for Mordekhai. As a result of these developments and the combination of all these circumstances, we find that Haman prepared his own hanging, and the Jewish people were saved. Anyone who reflects on this will see plainly that God's hand made all of it happen and was the [real] cause of all these [seemingly natural] circumstances.

Everyone is attended by divine providence:

In this manner each individual will see for himself the divine providence in his life, at every step he takes. In particular, the pious Jew, when he reflects on everything that happens in his life, sees the hand of God bringing it all about, despite the fact that everything develops from natural circumstances.

(Rabbi Yosef Yehuda Leib Bloch, *Shiurei Da'at*, vol. 1, p. 83)

Further reading: For more on divine providence, which accompanies every individual on every step of the way, see p. 91.

The Key to Victory: Unity

What should we do in order to save ourselves from harsh decrees? We must unite. Exile leads us to assimilate among the nations, but the nations' hatred of us makes us come together as one, and this unity brings about redemption.

The verse states: "One nation that is scattered and dispersed among the peoples" (Esther 3:8). Indeed, as a result of exile and of being assimilated among the nations, the Jewish people are unable to unite properly.... But in truth, every act of Heaven is certainly for the good, for as a result of the fact that [the Jews] attended the feast of Ahashverosh [which, according to the Sages, was the spiritual reason for the decree of annihilation], and associated with wicked people, they were unable to unite [with one another].

Unity brings salvation:

But afterward, the hatred that made the nations decide to destroy them was itself the cause of salvation, as they became [our] enemies and the Jewish people united [out of fear, due to the decree], as it is written: "Assemble all the Jews" (Esther 4:16), and it is written that they "assembled and defended themselves" (Esther 9:16). Therefore, the basic mitzva of megilla is [that it should be read] in the presence of ten [that is, a *minyan*, the minimum quorum for public prayer]: "Each and every family" (Esther 9:28), indicating that the primary salvation occurred because the Jewish people gathered together to become united.

(Rabbi Yehuda Aryeh Leib Alter, *Sefat Emet*, Purim 5653)

The mitzvot of Purim of *mishlo'ah manot* and gifts to the poor reveal the importance of unity among the Jewish people:

This is found throughout the megilla. When the Jews were endeavoring to emerge victorious, it is written: "Go, assemble all the Jews" (Esther 4:16), and: "The Jews assembled" (Esther 9:2), and all this is because when Israel is one nation, then God, who is One, is with them, and this is how they defeat Haman and his progeny, who signify the opposite of God's oneness. Therefore, specifically on Purim, this is the mitzva: "Sending portions one to another, and gifts to the poor" (Esther 9:22), because the basis of these mitzvot is the fact that Israel is one nation, to a greater extent than are all the other nations.

(Maharal, *Or Ḥadash*, Esther 9:22)

Feasting and Rejoicing on Purim

Every year, history repeats itself. After the miracle of Purim occurred, the Jews celebrated, making these days into a time of feasting and rejoicing. When we commemorate this today and observe the mitzvot of Purim, the light of these miracles shines on us too, and we receive the divine outpouring of holiness.

The Jewish people create the holiness of Purim:

"These days are remembered and observed" (Esther 9:28); the interpretation of this is that through remembering, and through the reading of the megilla [and the observance of the other mitzvot of Purim each year], the [spiritual] force of the miracle is revived. This is the meaning of the verse: "To *make* them days of banquet and joy" (Esther 9:22), as through the mitzvot of Purim, these days are *made* into days of feasting. [Consequently,] during these days, a divine outpouring of holiness and the light of miracles are revealed.

Further reading: For more on the idea that remembering can bring about a renewal of past events, see p. 54.

Joy for the sake of Heaven brings about the light of Purim:

Indeed, that generation put this into effect, as it is written: "And it was *made* a day of banqueting and joy. Therefore, the Jewish villagers, who live in open towns, *make* the fourteenth day of the month of Adar [a day of] joy and feasting and a festive day" (Esther 9:18–19). Because they made it into a day of feasting, and their joy was for the sake of Heaven, and they rejoiced at having sanctified His blessed name, [the essence of Purim was established as being joyous] and "[Every] mitzva that they accepted [upon themselves] with joy…they still perform with joy" (*Shabbat* 130a). Likewise, today, the more we receive these days with joy and for the sake of serving the Creator, the more the days are illuminated [with a heavenly light].

(Rabbi Yehuda Aryeh Leib Alter, *Sefat Emet*, Purim 5660)

The joy of Purim is the joy of performing a mitzva, and it does not allow for any degree of licentious or unruly behavior:

Even with regard to those individuals who become drunk [at the Purim meal], their intentions should be for the sake of Heaven, in order to remember the miracle, which came about through a wine fest. They should not behave like those people who become drunk in order to fill their throats [to satisfy their desire to get drunk]…and [the notion that] anyone who behaves in a crazed fashion is worthy of praise [is baseless], for all this is certainly wicked and a serious sin.

(Rabbi Moshe Met, *Mateh Moshe, Inyan Purim* 1012)

The Revelation of the Soul's Heavenly Source

On Purim, the heavenly source of the soul is revealed, just as it is on Yom Kippur. On Purim, however, it is not revealed by means of fasting, but through feasting and rejoicing.

Purim is similar to Yom Kippur:

Purim and Yom Kippur are of the same essence.[19] Purim is called by this name because of the lot, due to the pretensions of Haman, who "had cast a *pur*, which is the lot" (Esther 3:7), as he wanted to imitate the lot of Yom Kippur.[20] And just as Yom Kippur contains supernal repentance: "Before the Lord you shall be purified" (Leviticus 16:30), so too, on Purim, the Jews merited supernal repentance through fasting and crying out, and being ready to give up their lives to sanctify God's name. For Haman did not

19. This is reflected in the rabbinic homily based on the alternative name of Yom Kippur, *Yom Kippurim*: *Yom Kippurim* is a *yom kePurim*, meaning, a day like Purim.

20. The lot that Haman cast corresponds to the lot cast by the High Priest in the Temple on Yom Kippur over the two goats, one of which was offered as a sacrifice and one of which was taken to be sent over a cliff (see Leviticus 16:8).

want anything other than to eradicate the Jews [those who live and believe according to the tenets of Judaism], and if they had, God forbid, denied their faith he would not have acted against them in any way. Accordingly, our Sages said (*Shabbat* 88a) that in the time of Ahashverosh they accepted the Torah willingly. As a result, their souls were raised up to the lofty source from which they were carved, through the aspects of "initial thought," and "repentance preceded the world." [Terms referring to the ability of repentance to elevate the soul to the most lofty source of existence. See Rashi, Genesis 1:1; *Midrash Tehillim* 90.]

The difference between Yom Kippur and Purim:

The revelation of this aspect of the soul on Yom Kippur [requires] not eating or drinking. But on Purim, which occurred during the exile, it is [revealed] specifically through the drinking of wine. Wine intoxicates, that is, it eliminates [normative and mundane] awareness and comprehension [thereby elevating the individual to a higher level].

(Rabbi Shneur Zalman of Liadi, *Torah Or*, Esther 95:4)

Costumes

What is the origin of the custom of dressing up in costumes on Purim? Firstly, when the Jews went into exile they were compelled to put on an act, bowing down to the statue of Nebuchadnezzar. On a deeper level, costumes recall the spiritual garments that Mordekhai and Esther merited to receive.

The straightforward explanation of why we dress up:

The customs of Israel are as binding as the Torah. They were accustomed to transform themselves with unusual attire at the time of the festive meal and the rejoicing on Purim, and this is no meaningless behavior. And I have pondered the teaching of our eminent teacher, Rabbi Moshe Hagiz [Jerusalem, 1672–1750], that it is because of what our Sages said: "They did so [that is, bowed down to the idol in the days of Nebuchadnezzar] only for appearance. So too, the Holy One, blessed be He, acted with them only for appearance [as there was a decree issued against them, but it was not carried out]" (*Megilla* 12a). Therefore, we likewise transform ourselves, with unusual attire, at the time of rejoicing, making our appearances unrecognizable. This is a precious explanation of the straightforward meaning of the custom.

An additional explanation for the custom of dressing up:

But I will tell you that which is in my heart…the customs of Israel are as binding as the Torah. They were accustomed to dress in unusual attire at the time of rejoicing to remember the miracle and the wonder that God performed for Mordekhai and Esther, that they were dressed in precious, spiritual garments, those which saintly people wear in the Garden of Eden.[21]

(Rabbi Tzvi Elimelekh Shapira, *Benei Yisaskhar, Ma'amarei Ḥodesh Adar* 9)

Further reading: For more on the Jewish people's insincerity when bowing down to the idol, see *A Concise Guide to the Sages*, p. 299.

The Gerer Rebbe, writer of *Ḥidushei HaRim*, once said, at a Purim banquet: "When we begin reading the book of Esther, we are astonished by the fact that it is filled with stories about a Persian king: It tells of the feast he arranged to mark the third year of his reign; it describes Queen Vashti, who did not want to come before him; it outlines the arrangements involved in selecting a new queen. And all the while, we are wondering: What does this have to do with us?

"Only at a much later stage in the megilla do we suddenly understand that all the earlier incidents were part of a chain of events that resulted in the miracle of Purim."

When the saintly man had finished speaking he was silent for a moment, deep in thought. Then, he stood up and said: "The messiah will arrive in the same way. Various unusual events will occur, and then, all at once, everyone will understand that they were all connected to the redemption."

It is better for a person to increase his gifts to the poor than to enlarge his banquet or the portions sent to his friends, as there is no greater or more glorious joy than that of bringing joy to the hearts of poor people, orphans, widows, and converts.

(Rambam, *Mishneh Torah, Hilkhot Megilla VeḤanukah* 2)

21. The *Zohar* states that the "royal garments" (Esther 8:15) that Mordekhai and Esther wore were the spiritual garments that are worn by the righteous in the Garden of Eden, and when they wore them they looked like angels.

The Purim miracle led Israel to experience gratitude, and as a result, they merited connection to God.

(Rabbi Eliyahu Eliezer Dessler, *Mikhtav MeEliyahu,* vol. 2, p. 134)

Through the Purim feast, we will be filled with God's blessing... and it is a glimpse of the feast in the World to Come.

(Rabbi Tzadok HaKohen of Lublin, *Likutei Ma'amarim* 141)

Further reading: For more on how to fulfill the mitzvot of *mishlo'ah manot* and gifts to the poor, see *A Concise Guide to Halakha*, p. 265.

Passover

Egypt was the crucible in which the Jewish nation was formed. For many years, we were enslaved under harsh conditions, and then God brought us out to eternal freedom, performing miracles and wonders that demonstrated to the entire world that He is the sole ruler. Each day we remember the exodus from Egypt when reciting *Shema*. Likewise, each Shabbat we cease our labor in memory of the exodus. While there are a great number of mitzvot that commemorate the miracles that occurred at that time, the Passover *seder* is entirely focused on the exodus. The whole family gathers together, and the tradition is passed from one generation to the next.

On *seder* night, when we tell the story of the exodus from Egypt [*Mitzrayim*], it is proper to consider the straits [*metzarim*] from which we must emerge, in every generation. We eat matza on this night, which strengthens our faith. We also refrain from eating *hametz* for the entire seven days of Passover (eight outside the Land of Israel); we are wary of pride and the evil inclination symbolized by *hametz*, and we return to eating matza, the simple food of faith.

 **Further reading:** For more on Passover and the exodus, see *A Concise Guide to the Torah*, pp. 135ff, 161, 315, 471; *A Concise Guide to the Sages*, pp. 84, 306; *A Concise Guide to Halakha*, pp. 274ff.

The Meaning of the Miracles

Although the exodus took place thousands of years ago, it has significance for each one of us to this day. At the time of the exodus, we received our "spiritual eyes," namely, the ability to perceive that the world does not consist only of what we sense in the physical plane.

In truth, the main purpose of the exodus from Egypt was for us to have faith in the existence of miracles. Chiefly, this means recognizing the spiritual side of creation, and knowing that creation is not merely that which one sees with his eyes, nor that which he feels with his bodily senses. The physical matter that we see constitutes only the outer garment of true creation. What is true creation? It is the spiritual force behind the physical world.

(Rabbi Yeruḥam Levovitz, *Da'at Torah*, Exodus, p. 95)

The miracles of the exodus made it apparent that the Jewish people have a unique role in the world, and that the entire world was created for them. The miracles served a dual purpose; they provided both proof that God is the Creator of the world, and proof that the world was created for the Jewish people.

God altered nature for the children of Israel at the exodus from Egypt [for example, with the ten plagues and the splitting of the sea]. This was proof with regard to the Creator, that is, that He is the Creator and He acts in accordance with His will [and can even alter the course of nature if that is His will]. In addition, it was proof with regard to the children of Israel that the entire world was created for them; this is why God altered nature for them. Indeed, God could have redeemed us in accordance with the laws of nature, but the whole purpose of the exile in Egypt and the redemption from there was to make it clear that God would alter His world for the Jewish people.

(Rabbi Yehuda Aryeh Leib Alter, *Sefat Emet, Bo* 5649)

The Exodus Today

Why do we celebrate becoming free at the exodus, given that we have since been subjugated again? At the exodus, the Jewish people acquired their essential identity as free people. This is therefore a dramatic event for all generations.

When the Israelites left Egypt they received essential goodness until they were inherently fit to be free. This is the essential nature of Israel, that they are fit to be free people in their very essence. That which is incidental can never negate that which is essential. The Jewish people retain this quality of being free people in their essential nature, despite occasional subjugation.

(Maharal, *Gevurot HaShem* 61)

Matza: Bread of Faith and Healing

On Passover we eat matza, and this contains the secret of strengthened faith. Once a person's faith has been strengthened by eating matza, he is able to eat anything without it doing him any harm. For one week (or eight days outside the Land of Israel), we refrain from eating *hametz*, and it is a period of spiritual cleansing and healing for the soul.

Eating matza reminds us of the secret of faith in God:

It is a mitzva to eat matza on Passover because it is a reminder, for all future generations, of the secret of faith. The Sages explained this: At the time of the exodus, the Jewish people also relinquished other errors [that is, idol worship] and obtained the secret of faith, and the Sages have explained this secret in numerous places.

If *hametz* is seen in such a negative light, why, in the Temple, do the priests bring the offering of the two loaves, which are *hametz*, on the festival of *Shavuot*? This is likened to the case of a prince who was very sick and required medicine.

We must consider the fact that on Passover, the Jewish people relinquished the bread that is called *hametz*... and now [on *Shavuot*], when they have merited to receive a much loftier bread [that is, the Torah, which is bread for the soul], is it not proper that all *hametz* be nullified and out of sight like on Passover? Why do we have this offering of *hametz*? This is comparable to a king who had one son who became sick. One day, the son desired to eat. It was said: The king's son must eat a specific medicinal food, and until he has done so, there are to be no other foods found in the palace. This was carried out. Once his son had swallowed the remedy, the king said: From now on, he may eat whatever he desires, for it cannot harm him.

The king's son represents the Jewish people, who were in need of healing when they left Egypt.

When the Jewish people left Egypt, they did not know the basis of the secret of faith. The Holy One, blessed be He, said: Israel must taste this remedy, and until they do so, they must not have another food. Once they had eaten the matza, which was the means to ascend and to understand the secret of faith, the Holy One, blessed be He, said: From this point forward, they may eat *hametz*, as it cannot harm them.

(*Zohar* 2:41a, 183b)

Hametz: Symbol of Pride and of the Evil Inclination

Hametz is an allusion to the evil inclination. Concealed within the commandment to search for *hametz* everywhere, burn it, and nullify it, lies the answer to the question of how one should combat the evil inclination.

It is known with regard to this prohibition, that *hametz* contains an allusion to the evil inclination. One's good inclination must overpower his evil inclination.... This alludes to the notion that just as we are commanded by Torah law to nullify the *hametz* in our hearts,[22] so too, we are obligated to nullify the evil inclination in our hearts so that it does not rule over us. And just as the tradition comes[23] [that is, rabbinic law dictates] to burn the

22. The Torah commandment is: "You shall eliminate leaven" (Exodus 12:15), and this is interpreted to mean that one must mentally nullify all *hametz*, in order to relinquish ownership of it.
23. The Sages ruled that it is not enough merely to mentally nullify *hametz*; we must also physically destroy it.

hametz and to search our houses for it in every hole and crack, so too, are we obligated to search deep inside ourselves for evil thoughts.

(Rabbeinu Baḥya ibn Ḥalawa, *Kad HaKemaḥ*, *Pesaḥ* 1)

Further reading: For more on *hametz*, what it is, and how to destroy it, see *A Concise Guide to Halakha*, pp. 274, 286.

Hametz is different from matza in that it rises. As a result, *hametz* symbolizes pride, whereas matza symbolizes humility and self-abnegation.

Matza reflects the real nature of things, without any inflation of the truth:

As it contains no leaven, matza does not rise, expand, or become thicker or heavier after baking. Rather, it remains the same after baking as it was at the outset, without any expansion. It comprises just the essential elements of flour and water, kneaded together.

By contrast, *hametz* signifies an inflated image of one's true essence:

This is not the case with regard to leaven; it expands within the dough, making it rise considerably. The dough appears large and substantial, having expanded and thickened on all sides, and is much larger than it was previously. And it expands in a way that signifies haughtiness, as its height increases gradually [and increased height indicates haughtiness].

The puffed-up *hametz* symbolizes pride, whereas matza symbolizes self-nullification and humility:

The Jewish people were commanded to eat matza ... so that they would possess the attribute of complete self-nullification.

(Rabbi Shneur Zalman of Liadi, *Siddur Im Derekh Etz Ḥayim*, p. 284)

Further reading: For more on humility and pride, see *A Concise Guide to the Sages*, p. 432.

The Fifth Son

The haggada describes four sons, who represent the range of different types of Jewish people. There is the wise son, the wicked son, the simple son, and the son who does not know how to ask. There is a commandment to tell each one of them, in the way that is right for him, the story of the exodus. But these four sons are all sitting at the *seder* table, taking part in the Passover experience. Nowadays, a fifth type of Jew has emerged, who does not even come to the *seder* table. It is our duty to find Jews such as these and bring them closer to Judaism.

The common denominator of the four sons:

Notwithstanding the differences between the four sons and their being opposites of one another, they do have something in common: Even the wicked son is present at the *seder*.[24] He encounters and lives with those who live the life of Torah and observance of mitzvot, and it interests him.

Nowadays there is a fifth son:

But sadly, there is another type of son, particularly in our time, when darkness abounds: The son who cannot be found at the *seder* at all. He does not ask questions because he has no sense of connection to Torah and mitzvot or to the authentically Jewish *halakhot* and customs. He does not know about the existence of "this service":[25] the Passover *seder*, the exodus, and the receiving of the Torah.

What should our reaction be to this absent son?

One must devote a great deal of time to these children before Passover, before the *seder* night. One must do so with self-sacrifice and out of love for one's fellow Jews. For it is forbidden to abandon even a single Jewish child, and one must employ all available resources in order to rescue such a child from his current state and return him to the Jewish *seder* table.... It is forbidden for a Jew to despair. It is forbidden to give up on another Jew. With the correct approach, that is, if one comes from a place of love for one's fellow Jews, people like this will be brought inside and will sit among the four sons. And eventually, they will even be brought to a point where they are considered "wise sons."

(Rabbi Menaḥem Mendel Schneerson, *Mikhtav Klali*, 11 Nisan 5717)

Further reading: For more on the four sons, see *A Concise Guide to the Sages*, p. 307.

Every year on the first night of Passover, before returning home to lead the *seder*, Rabbi Tzvi Elimelekh of Dinov would walk through the streets of his town to hear how the townspeople observed the *seder*. The words and songs of the haggada would emerge from every house.

One year, as he passed by one of the houses, he heard a Jew reciting the passage concerning the four sons. Each time the Jew said the word

---

24. In particular, he is present for everything related to the Passover *seder*. But this can also refer to the entire order [*seder*] of Torah and mitzvot.
25. As the *seder* is described to the wicked son.

"one" (as in: "One is wise, one is wicked..."), he cried out loudly and with intention, like in the recitation of *Shema* when we say: "Hear O Israel... the Lord is One."

Standing outside, the saintly man said in wonder: This Jew has formed a prayer out of all four sons, including the wicked son, as holy as the *Shema*.

Each Passover, the forces of holiness are purified of their outer shells and adjoined to the Jewish people... because there is not only one exodus, rather, God brings them out every year.

(Rabbi Ḥayyim ben Atar, *Or HaḤayyim*, Numbers 23:22)

The Jewish people's exodus from Egypt will forever remain the spring of the world.

(Rabbi Avraham Yitzḥak HaKohen Kook, *Meged Yeraḥim*, Nisan)

Further reading: For more on constantly remembering and experiencing the exodus, see *A Concise Guide to the Sages*, p. 307.

Shavuot

We count the seven weeks of the *omer* beginning at Passover. At the conclusion of the seven weeks, on the fiftieth day, we celebrate the festival of *Shavuot*. According to the Sages, this was the day of the revelation at Mount Sinai, when the Jewish people received the Torah, although in the Written Torah no explicit date is mentioned with regard to this event.

What do we do on *Shavuot*? Why does the Torah have so many names for this festival? And why is it not stated explicitly that it is the day on which the Torah was given?

Every year, we engage in preparations to receive the Torah, recognizing our obligation to demonstrate that we truly want it. The giving of the Torah was not a one-time event. Each day, and each year, we relive that wonderful experience of connecting to the Giver of the Torah.

What Do We Do on *Shavuot*?

Shavuot night is a time of preparation for receiving the Torah. The giving of the Torah is not just an event that took place thousands of years ago; rather, each year on this day, we receive the Torah anew, and are like a bride entering the wedding canopy with her husband, that is, with God.

On *Shavuot* night, the Jewish people spend their time studying the Torah, which is likened to the jewel worn by a bride:

Rabbi Shimon would sit and engage in Torah study on the night when the bride joins her husband [that is, on *Shavuot*]. As the Sages taught: On the night before a bride is to come under the wedding canopy with her husband, all those friends [that is, Torah scholars] who are close to the bride [that is, the community of Israel] must remain with her all night and rejoice with her during her preparations. They engage in the Torah, Prophets, and Writings, in interpretations of the verses, and in the concealed wisdom, because these are her enhancements and jewels. She enters and stands at the head of her attendants and is adorned by them. She rejoices with them all that night, and the next day she enters the wedding canopy accompanied by them. They are known as the wedding party. When she enters the wedding canopy, the Holy One, blessed be He, asks about them and blesses them, and crowns them with the crown of the bride. Fortunate is their lot.

Those who study Torah on this night receive protection:

Sit, honored ones, sit, and we will renew the preparation of the bride on this night. As everyone who joins her on this night will be protected, both above and below, for the entire year, and will end his year in peace. With regard to such people it is written (Psalms 34:8–9): "The angel of the Lord encamps around those who fear Him, and rescues them. Consider and see that the Lord is good."

(*Zohar* 1:8a)

Further reading: For more on learning Torah throughout *Shavuot* night, see *A Concise Guide to Halakha*, p. 349.

Beyond feeling joy and gratitude at having received the Torah, we must strive to make it a meaningful part of our lives. *Shavuot* is the day of judgment with regard to the extent of our connection to Torah:

One is obligated to greatly rejoice on this festival because it is the day on which we merited to receive the crown of Torah.... Nevertheless, it is written: "Rejoice with trembling" (Psalms 2:11); this joy is a spiritual joy of thanks and praise to God for giving us the Torah. One's heart is roused and he resolves to become sanctified, to rectify his ways, and to be crowned with the crown of Torah, in order to fulfill: "And you shall ponder it day and night" (Joshua 1:8). For this holy day is the day of judgment.

(Rabbi Yeshaya HaLevi Horowitz, *Shenei Luḥot HaBerit, Masekhet Shavuot, Ner Mitzva*)

Names of the Festival: *Shavuot*

Why is this festival named after the seven weeks that were counted starting from Passover, which culminate on this day? These weeks build up the bond of love between us and God. We renounce all else for the sake of our love for Him.

The counting of these weeks is similar to the counting of the seven days [free of menstrual blood] before a wedding:

The counting of weeks is to teach us that at the giving of the Torah we became joined to God like a bride entering the wedding canopy.... Now she will direct her love to him alone, and therefore she counts seven days especially for this bridegroom.... In the same way, aside from our obligation to observe the mitzvot, we became obligated to direct our love to Him alone.

The seven weeks symbolize the period of preparation and the bestowal of our love upon God. This is why the festival is called *Shavuot*:

Since it is not an easy matter for a person to direct his love to God like a woman does toward her husband, God commanded us to count seven weeks [*shavuot*]. This is why the festival is called *Shavuot*, that is, the Festival of Weeks, and not the Festival of Days [even though the days are also counted during the *omer*]. It is to enable us to understand that we must direct our love to God and restrain ourselves [*ne'etzar*] before Him [to disconnect from all mundane matters in order to concentrate on God]. This is why this festival is called *Atzeret* by the Sages; this is the purpose of *Shavuot*.

(Netziv, *Ha'amek Davar*, Numbers 28:26)

Further reading: For more on *Shavuot*, see *A Concise Guide to the Torah*, pp. 192, 317, 472; *A Concise Guide to the Sages*, p. 309; *A Concise Guide to Halakha*, p. 340.

Names of the Festival: *Atzeret*

The Sages called the festival of *Shavuot*: *Atzeret* [literally: restraint or cessation], because there are no specific mitzvot associated with the festival through which our connection to God is expressed. Therefore, it is a unique day, as the illumination that comes from above is not limited to specific types of connections.

There are two types of divine light: that which comes as a result of observing the mitzvot, and that which is tied to a particular time:

Why is *Shavuot* called *Atzeret* [in the Mishna], and likewise, why is the festival on the eighth day of *Sukkot* called *Atzeret* [see Leviticus 23:36]? There are two lights that the Creator shines upon the Jewish people. He shines the first one upon them because they fulfill His mitzvot. The other is not connected to the observance of mitzvot; rather, it comes as a result of the abundance of holiness at specific times. Now we will explain the difference between them: The light that comes as a result of the observance of mitzvot is limited and finite, as the mitzvot themselves are finite [that is, they each have a defined time, place, and procedure]. But the light that comes as a result of abundant holiness has had no limits set upon it.

When the divine light is revealed through a certain mitzva, the illumination corresponds to the mitzva and is therefore limited. But illumination that is not linked to a particular mitzva is unlimited:

On *Sukkot* and Passover the light shines due to the mitzvot that are fulfilled on these days, for example, the mitzvot of *sukka* and *lulav* on *Sukkot* and the mitzva of matza on Passover, in addition to the other mitzvot associated with these days. But on *Shavuot* and *Shemini Atzeret,* there are no unique mitzvot, and the light on these days has had no limits set upon it.

On these days of unlimited illumination, we must direct the light in accordance with our needs. The term *Atzeret* refers to the restraint and limitation of the light in furtherance of a certain purpose.

We must limit the light until the upper and lower worlds receive it, for if the light is unlimited, the lower worlds cannot hold it. Each individual must limit the light to the matter that he is in need of, for example, wisdom, children, life [health], or livelihood. For this reason these two festivals, that is, *Shavuot* and the eighth day of *Sukkot,* are called *Atzeret.* The word *Atzeret* hints to restraint and limitation, from the term: "And [the plague] was stopped [*vate'atzar*]" (Numbers 17:13). We must restrain and limit the light.

(Rabbi Levi Yitzḥak of Berditchev, *Kedushat Levi,* Numbers, *Shavuot*)

Why Is It Not Written in the Torah That *Shavuot* Is the Festival of the Giving of the Torah?

Is the day on which we received the Torah a joyous one? The gentiles did not want to receive it. In a certain sense it is the day we accepted upon ourselves obligations. Of course, we have accepted the Torah, and we rejoice over having received it. But since it is a day that also contains the necessity of servitude to God, the date is not explicitly mentioned in the verses that deal with the festivals.

God gave the times for the festivals, which are the joy of Israel, as they merited receiving goodness. For example, the verse states with regard to Passover that Israel left the house of bondage, and with regard to *Sukkot* that "I had the children of Israel dwell in booths" (Leviticus 23:43).... But on *Shavuot,* God gave us the Torah, which is a burden on Israel. Indeed, the nations of the world did not want to receive it. Even though we say: "The time of the giving of our Torah" (*Shavuot* prayer), that is, we ourselves accepted the Torah, saying: "We will perform and we will heed" (Exodus 24:7), nevertheless, God, who gave us the Torah, held the mountain over the children of Israel to force them to accept the Torah,[26] because it is a burden upon them.

26. A Talmudic midrash relates that God held Mount Sinai over the heads of the children of Israel like a barrel, and said to them that they must accept the Torah or this will be their burial place (*Shabbat* 88a).

How could the time of the giving of the Torah be written in the Torah when God gave it with a decree against man?

(Maharal, *Tiferet Yisrael* 27)

A fixed date limits the event that is said to have taken place on that date. One should accept the Torah every day and become renewed by it. Therefore, the Torah does not specify a date on which the Torah was given.

God did not want to limit the giving of the Torah to a specific day because on every day of the year one should feel as though he has received the Torah from Mount Sinai that very day.... If so, the Torah is given every day to those who study it; therefore, it is not fitting to specify the day on which it was given. With regard to this, our Sages said (see Rashi, Deuteronomy 26:16) that the words of Torah should be for you as if they were brand new.

(Rabbi Shlomo Efrayim Luntschitz, *Keli Yakar*, Leviticus 23:17)

The Day We Stood at Sinai

By: Rabbi Yitzḥak ibn Ghiyyat

When the day we stood at Sinai comes to mind, I am overcome with shudders of trembling.
The north and east feel fear, the western sea crawls;
All fear You, Your glory, when it was revealed.
Mighty Lord is Your name, my king, when You began by stating "I am,"
All creatures fell silent, they could not say a word.
When they heard Your voice, they bowed cowered,
trembled and stirred, those above and below.
Living God, who can evaluate Your greatness?
You have no beginning, no end.
When my heart will see this, then deep inside of me
Fear will enter, trembling and panic.
He limits my plans, He investigates my thoughts;
my spirit and soul will acknowledge You, sela!

The sharpness and wit of the Gerer Rebbe, Rabbi Yitzḥak Meir Alter, author of *Ḥidushei HaRim*, was already evident when he was a child. The scholars of the city loved to discuss matters of Torah with him and enjoyed his insights. Once, one of the scholars asked him: In the passage that addresses the giving of the Torah, the verse states: "All the people were seeing the voices" (Exodus 20:15). Why did they need to see the voices? Even if they had only heard the words of God, wouldn't these words have penetrated their hearts?

The boy answered immediately: If the Jewish people had not seen the voices, there would have been room to shrewdly claim that it does not say: "You shall not [*lo*] steal" (Exodus 20:13), but rather: "You shall steal for him [*lo*]," which in Hebrew sounds the same but is spelled differently. In other words, one could have asserted that it is permitted to steal for the sake of Heaven. Therefore, they saw the voices; everyone saw that it says: "You shall not steal," so there is no room for any excuses or rationalizations.

Each year on *Atzeret*, it is like the day that we stood before Mount Sinai; we receive the Torah anew.

(Rabbi David Frankel, *Korban HaEda, Rosh HaShana* 4)

Every year on this festival, each Jew receives everything that he is going to understand and reveal in Torah in the future.

(Rabbi Yehuda Aryeh Leib Alter, *Sefat Emet*, 5635)

We must take the central purpose of *Shavuot* to heart and remember that it is the day on which we became the servants of God. We must wholeheartedly reaccept the yoke of Heaven upon ourselves and observe all the statutes of the Torah.

(Rabbi Yaakov Tzvi Mecklenburg, *HaKetav VehaKabbala*, Deuteronomy 16:10)

Further reading: For more on the revelation at Mount Sinai, see *A Concise Guide to the Sages*, pp. 103ff.

Torah Concepts

Love of God

Each day, religious Jews recite the verse "You shall love the Lord your God" (Deuteronomy 6:5). What does it mean to love God? How can we experience this feeling? How does love of God affect one's life?

To love God is to crave a connection with the Creator. Love of God comes through contemplation of all that He has created and appreciation of God's greatness. Natural love of God lies concealed within every Jew. It does not need to be generated, but only to emerge from where it is hidden. One who loves God is happy, not confused, and this love can be gauged by how one prioritizes God over all else.

What Is Love of God?

Love of God is yearning for Him. One's soul is a spiritual rather than material entity. Therefore, it yearns for that from which it benefits and which brings it strength. Love of God encompasses all areas of life. One who loves God will continue to serve Him and trust in Him even when it is difficult.

Love of God is the soul being drawn toward God:

But what is the love of God? It is the yearning of the soul, its inclination toward the Creator so that it can connect to His supernal light.

The soul is connected to God and is distinct from the body:

That is, the soul is an immaterial, spiritual entity. It is inclined toward that which is similar to it, i.e., spiritual beings, and naturally distances itself from that which is opposite to it, i.e., physical entities. The Creator tied the soul to this coarse, unclean body that is full of darkness, because He wanted to test the soul in its control of the body. Accordingly, He roused it to have compassion on the body and to bring benefit to it for the good of the partnership and connection that was generated between them from the outset.

The soul is drawn toward that which gives it light and strength:

When the soul senses something that is of use to the body and advantageous to its constitution, it will be inclined toward it and desire it, seeking rest from the afflictions and ailments of the body. This is like a person who desires an expert doctor when he is sick, so that he has someone to attend to him and think about him. When the soul senses something that adds light and strength to its essence, it thinks of that thing, clings to the idea of it, and considers and desires it. This is pure love.

The actions of one who loves:

Then the soul will drink from the cup of love of God, and will enjoy the bliss of being alone with God, devoting itself wholeheartedly to Him, loving Him, putting its trust in Him, and yearning for Him. It will have no other occupation than His service, and no ideas or thoughts other than of Him. It will not move any of the limbs of its body except to perform actions which will gain His favor. It will not unbind its tongue except to refer to Him, praise Him, thank Him, and laud Him out of love for Him and out of longing to do His will. If He bestows a benefit on the soul, it will thank Him. If He brings suffering on it, it will patiently bear it, and will only increase its love for Him and trust in Him.

(Rabbeinu Baḥya ibn Pekuda, *Ḥovot HaLevavot* 10:1)

Further reading: For more on the human soul, see p. 218.

Love makes a person do things without receiving any reward, acting in accordance with the truth purely because it is the truth. When a person loves God, he performs the mitzvot out of love for Him. Great love accompanies one always, and one who loves God thinks only of Him.

Serving God out of love means acting in accordance with the truth purely because it is the truth:

One who serves out of love engages in Torah and mitzvot and walks in the paths of wisdom, not because of anything in the world, nor because of fear of misfortune, nor in order to acquire benefit; rather, he acts in accordance with the truth because it is the truth, and in the end, benefit will come as a result.

The level of one who serves God out of love:

This level is a very high level, and not every wise person attains it. It is the level of our patriarch Abraham, whom the Holy One, blessed be He, referred to as the one who loves Him (Isaiah 41:8), because he served God only out of love. This is the level with regard to which the Holy One, blessed be He, commanded us through Moses, "You shall love the Lord your God" (Deuteronomy 6:5). When one loves God with proper love, he will immediately perform all the mitzvot out of love.

What is proper love?

What is proper love? One must love God with great, exceedingly strong love, such that his soul is tied up with love of God. He should think of it always, like one who is lovesick, whose mind is never free from his love for a certain woman, and who is always preoccupied with her, whether he is sitting, standing, or eating and drinking. Love of God, in the hearts of those who love Him, is even greater. They think of it always, as He commanded us to, "with all your heart, and with all your soul" (Deuteronomy 6:5). This is what Solomon referred to by way of an analogy: "For I am lovesick" (Song of Songs 2:5), and all of Song of Songs [which describes the love between a man and a woman] is an allegory for this matter.

(Rambam, *Mishneh Torah, Hilkhot Teshuva* 10:2–3)

The Path to Love

The way to loving God is through reflecting on His actions and His creation. When we recognize the wondrous wisdom underlying them, we will yearn to know Him, and will love Him.

What is the way to loving Him?...When a person contemplates His great and wonderful actions and creations, and recognizes in them His wisdom, which is inestimable and infinite, he will immediately love, praise, and glorify, and will be exceedingly desirous of knowing the great name.

(Rambam, *Mishneh Torah, Hilkhot Yesodei HaTorah* 2:1)

Love of God is present in the heart of every Jew; we inherited it from our patriarchs. First we recognize that God is the source of life. We then recognize that God is our Father, and we contemplate this constantly. Even if initially this seems like a product of our imagination, it is the truth, and practicing such thinking makes the love come naturally.

A person loves God as he loves his life:

Love of God belongs equally to every Jewish soul and is an inheritance from our patriarchs. This is what the *Zohar* wrote concerning the verse "With my essence, I desired You at night" (Isaiah 26:9), that I desire and crave You like one who yearns for his own life. When he is weak and afflicted, he longs to return to himself. Likewise, when he goes to sleep, he longs for his essence to return to him when he awakens from his slumber. So too, I desire and crave the light of the infinite One, blessed be He, namely, true life, and to draw it within me through engaging in Torah when I wake up from my night's sleep. For the Torah and the Holy One, blessed be He, are one and the same [so clinging to Torah is the same as clinging to God].

A person loves God as he loves his father:

An even greater love than this, which is concealed also in every Jewish person as an inheritance from our patriarchs, is...to become accustomed, in one's speech, heart, and mind, to that fact that the infinite One, blessed be He, is our true Father and the source of our life, and to arouse toward Him the love a son has for his father. When one practices this [way of thinking] constantly, his habit will become his nature.

This is absolute truth:

Even if it seems to him as though this is imaginary, he must not be concerned, because it is absolutely true as an intrinsic aspect in the sense of concealed love. The advantage of its being revealed is that it brings about action: Studying Torah and observing mitzvot in order to bring pleasure to God, like a son serving his father.

(Rabbi Shneur Zalman of Liadi, *Tanya, Likutei Amarim* 44)

Further reading: For more on love of God, see *A Concise Guide to the Sages*, p. 232.

How is it possible to command people to love God? Can an emotion be commanded? The emotion in this case does not need to be generated; all one needs to do is to reveal the concealed love that already exists within us.

We need to understand how the language of command could apply to love. It is because by nature there is concealed love within every Jew. The commandment "You shall love" (Deuteronomy 6:5) does not concern love itself, as love itself is present, by nature, in every Jew. Rather, the commandment is to bring the light of this love out of concealment, so that it is revealed.

(Rabbi Shmuel Schneersohn, *Sefer HaMa'amarim* 5626, p. 225)

Further reading: For more on the relationship between a father and his children, and its resemblance to the relationship between God and the Jewish people, see pp. 28, 222.

The Nature of Love

When a person longs to achieve something that is difficult to achieve, it is usually distressing and confusing. Nevertheless, although God is unattainable, one's love for Him does not confuse the soul, but brings it joy. The highest form of love is when the individual considers only what is good and beneficial to his beloved, without thinking of his own interests.

Loving God brings joy to the individual:

Love of God brings delight and joy to the soul. When it is impossible or very difficult to grasp the object of one's love, the soul is usually troubled and confused, thinking of ways to attain the object of his love. Because of this, those who desire are always sad and troubled until they attain the object of their desire. However, love of God, although He is impossible to grasp, neither troubles nor confuses the soul; rather, the soul will rejoice, delight, and derive great pleasure from the small measure that he grasps.

Absolute love contains no selfish element; it is purely for the sake of the beloved:

Love that is for the benefit of the lover is like the love that a person has for animals, which results from the great benefit one derives from them. Love due to the protection from harm one receives is comparable to the love that a person has for dogs, which results from their protecting him from harm. Absolute love is when one loves another for the sake of the beloved alone, and has no purpose other than to fulfill the will of the beloved, whom he loves for no other reason... And since this is the highest kind of love, and is found only among those who possess wisdom and understanding [i.e., humans], one is to be praised or criticized on account of it [concerning the extent of one's selfless love for God].

(Rav Yosef Albo, *Sefer HaIkkarim* 3:36)

The perfectly pious person is one who loves God. This love can be assessed in ten different ways:

One's love may be assessed in ten ways with respect to the nature of the love: (1) One loves God's Torah. (2) One gains more pleasure from serving God than from any other kind of pleasure. (3) One abhors those who abhor the Creator and loves those who love Him. (4) One's love for the good in this world is like nothing to him when compared with serving the Creator. (5) Any exertion, loss, or suffering involved in loving God seems sweet to him. (6) One does not place any of his own concerns before those of God. (7) One tells others of his love for God and glories in it. (8) One does not listen to those who incite or tempt him from the service of God. (9) No matter what happens to him, good or bad, one does not abandon the service of God. (10) One does not serve [God] in order to receive a reward, because this would mean that his service is contingent on something. When these ten attributes are integrated within a person, he is considered one who loves God, and he is entirely pious.

(*Sefer HaYashar*, 2)

A great rabbi once said to the saintly Rabbi Avraham of Stretin: I have heard tell that the honored rabbi gives out spiritual remedies [*segulot*], and that his *segulot* are effective. I beg him for a *segula* that will help me to fear Heaven.

The saintly one answered him: I have no *segula* for fear of Heaven, but I do have one for love of Heaven.

The rabbi said: But love of Heaven is an even higher level than fear of Heaven. Would the honored rabbi give me this *segula*?

Rabbi Avraham replied: A great *segula* for love of Heaven is love of Israel. One who loves the Jewish people can easily come to love of Heaven.

Love of God is the ultimate objective of all our attributes and the culmination of all the levels of those who serve God. It is as though all character traits are on a ladder that leads to the level of love... there is nothing above it.

(*Orḥot Tzaddikim, Sha'ar HaAhava*)

When, due to his understanding, the believer's heart is emptied of his love of this world and consciously and rationally freed from his desires, then love of the Creator will come to rest in his heart and will be ingrained in his soul.

(Rabbeinu Baḥya ibn Pekuda, *Ḥovot HaLevavot* 10, Introduction)

One must do everything in his power to direct his thoughts at all times, so that there is not even one moment, day or night, when he does not remember his wholehearted love for God.

(*Sefer HaḤinnukh* 418)

The purpose of the mitzvot is to come to love of God.

(Rabbi Yehuda Aryeh Leib Alter, *Sefat Emet, Ekev* 5658)

"You shall love" (Deuteronomy 6:5); search for closeness to God by giving of your entire self. Closeness to God must be everything to you, and not just a means of attaining your desires.

(Rabbi Samson Raphael Hirsch)

Loving One's Fellow Jews

The Talmud tells of a convert who approached Hillel the Elder and asked him to teach him the entire Torah while he stood on one foot. Hillel replied, "That which is hateful to you do not do to another" (*Shabbat* 31a). This is the most fundamental principle in the Torah: "You shall love your fellow as yourself" (Leviticus 19:18).

The commandment to love others stems from the awareness that we all derive from God, who is One, and therefore we too are essentially one. But is it possible to love others in the same way that we love ourselves? Ostensibly, the realistic goal is to reach a point where we wish upon others only good, and are not jealous of their successes. But in truth, it is even possible to reach a level where we do not see other people as "others," but genuinely relate to them as we relate to ourselves. The way to reach this level is through reflecting on the divine element present in each individual. From this perspective, there is no separation between oneself and another.

The Oneness of the Nation as an Expression of the Oneness of God

God is absolute unity, and we, His people, are also required to express this oneness, through behavior that demonstrates that we are one nation.

"You shall love your fellow as yourself" (Leviticus 19:18), for this is "a fundamental principle in the Torah" (*Sifra, Kedoshim* 4:12). This teaches us that it is not fitting for there to be division between one person and another; rather, we must judge each person favorably, as we would judge ourselves. This is [why the aforementioned verse ends with the phrase] "I am the Lord" (Leviticus 19:18); just as I, the Lord, am one, so too is it proper that you will be one, undivided nation.

(Rav Avraham Saba, *Tzeror HaMor*, Leviticus 7)

Further reading: For more on loving one's fellow Jews, see *A Concise Guide to the Sages*, p. 373.

The Meaning of Loving Others "as Yourself"

The commandment "You shall love your fellow as yourself," requires us to be as concerned about others as we are concerned for ourselves, and even to wish more for others than we have ourselves.

The commandment to love someone "as yourself," contains an element of hyperbole, and its meaning is that we must desire good for others:

The explanation of "You shall love your fellow as yourself," is that it is an exaggeration, as one could not undertake to love another as much as he loves himself; and furthermore, Rabbi Akiva taught, "Your life takes precedence over the life of the other" (*Bava Metzia* 62a). Rather, the mitzva, from the Torah, is to love one's fellow in every matter, just as he loves himself, [wishing] everything good for himself.

The commandment to love one's fellow is a commandment against being envious of others:

It is possible that it [literally] says not "You shall love your fellow as yourself," but rather "You shall love *to* your fellow..." in order to equate them, meaning that the two loves [one's love for others and his love for himself] should be equal in a person's mind. Because sometimes, one's love for another person extends only to certain areas, e.g., he wants the best for the other person with regard to wealth but not with regard to wisdom. But if he loves his fellow in all matters, he will want the beloved to have wealth, possessions, honor, knowledge, and wisdom, and he will not just equate himself to him, but will want him to have more than he himself has, in all spheres. The verse commands us not to carry this abhorrent attribute, envy, in our hearts; rather, we must love another, wishing all good things upon him, as a person does himself, and not set limitations upon this love.

(Ramban, Leviticus 19:18)

An absolute connection between two individuals is expressed through making a covenant. This means that they are not separate from one another. They assist each other in every matter, to the point where they do not feel like distinct entities. The Torah commands us to love one's fellow in the same manner: One should feel as though he is not distinct from us; rather, he is an inseparable part of us.

Two people who make a covenant are as one body while they are alive, and only death can part them. Therefore, if a person feels that some harm or sorrow has come to someone with whom he has made a covenant, he will exert himself in order to save him, just as he would endanger himself. Likewise, he will not hide from this person any knowledge or sense that others are planning on harming him, or that others have thought badly of him. So too, he will reveal his secrets and hidden thoughts to him just as he reveals them to himself, because this person is not distinct from himself, and it is fitting that he love him as he loves himself. This is as the Torah states, "You shall love your fellow as yourself" (Leviticus 19:18), i.e., just as your love for yourself involves no other, so too, with regard to your love for your fellow, you should not think of him as being distinct from you, as the definition of absolute love is that the lover and the beloved become one. This is why the numerical value of the word love [*ahava*, which is thirteen], is the same as that of the word one [*eḥad*]; for the beloved is not separate from the lover at all.

(Rav Yosef Albo, *Sefer HaIkkarim* 4:45)

Further reading: For a discussion of whether one's life takes precedence over the life of another person, see *A Concise Guide to the Sages*, p. 162.

How to Perform This Mitzva

When we are focused on the body and its needs, it is impossible to love others without personal interest, because each individual has his own separate body. But if our principal focus is upon the divine soul, i.e., the divine spark within each of us, it is possible to truly love another, because souls are all connected to one another at their source.

We can come to love others by recognizing the centrality of the divine soul in each individual:

By realizing the things mentioned above, when one's body is despicable and abhorrent to him, and his joy is only the joy of the soul, this is the direct and simple way to fulfill the mitzva of "You shall love your fellow as yourself," with regard to every Jewish soul, great and small.

Bodies are distinct and different from one another, but souls are all connected:

Because his body is abhorrent and disgusting to him, whereas with regard to the soul and spirit, who can know the level of their greatness, as their root and source come from the living God. Additionally, all souls complement one another and have one Father, and therefore the Jewish people are called "brothers," as the source of their souls is from the one God, and only their bodies are separate. Therefore, those who consider their bodies to be the most important thing, and their souls to be secondary, cannot have true love and brotherhood between them; rather, their love is dependent on something [i.e., self-interest].

(Rabbi Shneur Zalman of Liadi, *Tanya, Likutei Amarim* 32)

Further reading: For more on the source of the soul, see p. 223.

We are all well aware of our own faults, but we are not distressed by them, because we love ourselves. Nevertheless, when another person points out our faults, we become angry, as he has emphasized our shortcomings and made them into an issue. The mitzva of "you shall love your fellow as yourself" instructs us to relate to the shortcomings of others as we do to our own, i.e., our love for another individual must not be diminished as a result of his shortcomings.

Due to self-love, we do not consider our shortcomings as serious:

Just as "a person does not find fault in himself" (*Shabbat* 119a) does not mean that he does not know his faults (on the contrary, he is able to perceive the extent of his deficiencies better than anyone else, as another person sees him with his eyes alone, whereas he can see into his own heart); rather, the meaning is that he does not consider his faults significant enough to become provoked by them. It is as though he does not see them. The tremendous love that he has for himself covers up all the sins he is aware of.

Why we become angry when another person exposes our shortcomings:

When another person perceives and understands one of his faults, he becomes exceedingly angry, even though he knows that it is the truth. The primary anger is not over the deficiency itself, as if his fellow has imagined something false, since he knows that it is in fact true. It is because his associate's knowledge of his deficiency makes it substantial and activating. This was not the case when [only] he knew of it, as love covered it up. He is angry at his associate for exposing his fault and bringing it out of concealment. It had been covered up by love such that it was completely invisible, and now, with regard to his fellow, it is visible, as something of substance.

As a result of our love of others, we should not make an issue of their shortcomings:

This is the explanation of (*Shabbat* 31a): "That which is hateful to you," i.e., the exposure [of your faults], "do not do to another." Do not see his faults and sins... as something of substance. Rather, your love for him should be so great that it covers up his sins. Do not react as a result of your knowledge of these sins. This is like when one has great passion for another person and is powerfully drawn to that person from the very essence of his soul. He does not acknowledge anything wicked that the person does to him that obstructs his love; such actions are like nothing to him when compared with the strength of his love.

(Tzemaḥ Tzedek, *Derekh Mitzvotekha* 28a)

The Outcomes of Loving Others

The love and connection between us make it possible for us to stand together before God. Therefore, before praying, one needs to accept upon himself love for every Jew, so that his prayer can ascend to God.

Before one says his prayers in the synagogue... he must accept upon himself the mitzva of "You shall love your fellow as yourself," and he must have the intention of loving every Jew as he loves himself. For this is how his prayer will ascend: Together with all the prayers of Israel, and in this way it will be able to rise up and produce a good outcome.

(Rabbi Yitzḥak Luria (Arizal), *Sha'ar HaKavanot, Derushei Birkot HaShaḥar*)

Loving Others Results in Perfection of the Self, and Redemption

Love and mutual responsibility make it possible for each individual to observe all the mitzvot, as one person can perform a mitzva for others. The mitzva to love the Jewish people contains within it a special power that brings the redemption.

Observing all the mitzvot is impossible unless we augment one another:

Every Jew is obligated to fulfill 248 positive mitzvot,[1] but it is impossible for each individual to do this. However, by means of the love that exists among the Jewish people, each individual's 248 can be completed through the actions of his fellow. Therefore, the number 248 [*resh-mem-ḥet*] contains the same letters as the word *raḥem*, which is the translation of the word love into Aramaic. This alludes to the fact that the 248 mitzvot are completed for each individual through *raḥem*, through the love that exists between us.

Loving one's fellow Jews hastens the redemption:

It is also known that when the attribute of love is fully manifest in the Jewish people, the redemption will come. Therefore, the verse states, "I will set redemption between My people and your people; tomorrow [*lemaḥar*]" (Exodus 8:19). [The word *lemaḥar* contains] the letters of *leramaḥ*, for 248, as well as the letters of *leraḥem*, for love. This means that in the merit of the 248 positive mitzvot that will be received at Sinai, and in the merit of the love that [the Jewish people] have for one another, "this sign [of redemption] will come to be" (Exodus 8:19).

(Rabbi Yosef Ḥayyim, *Ben Ish Ḥai*, Year 1, *Va'era*)

1. According to tradition, there are 613 mitzvot, in the Torah: 365 prohibitions and 248 positive obligations.

Torah Concepts

Further reading: For more on unity as a means of bringing redemption, see above, p. 87.

When he was five years old, the Ba'al Shem Tov lost his father, the saintly Rabbi Eliezer. In the last moments of his life, when he lay on his sickbed, the father turned to his only son and gave him his final instructions: "My son! Do not fear anyone or anything in this world except the Holy One, blessed be He. Love every Jew with all your heart and soul, no matter who or what he is." With this short will, the father provided his son with everything he needed for his journey through life.

The sigh that a Jew sighs over the pain of another Jew destroys the iron barriers of the accusing angels. The joy and the blessing of a Jew who rejoices in the joy of another Jew and blesses him are received by God like the prayer of Rabbi Yishmael the High Priest in the Holy of Holies.

(Ba'al Shem Tov)

A soul may descend into this world and live for seventy or eighty years solely in order to provide another Jew with a material, or especially a spiritual, benefit.

(Ba'al Shem Tov)

If only I could love the most saintly Jew as much as God loves the most wicked Jew.

(Rabbi Shlomo of Karlin)

Instill in our hearts that each one of us see the virtues of others, and not their shortcomings, and may each one of us speak to others in the honest and appropriate manner before You, and may no hatred arise in us against others, God forbid.

(Prayer of Rabbi Elimelekh of Lizhensk)

Further reading: For more on the soul's descent into this world, see p. 226.

Food

Eating is essential for the survival of the body, but our desire to eat can easily become a great appetite and cause harm to the body as well as to the soul. Are we to contend with this through fasting and self-denial? Judaism does not endorse fasting, except on certain days, but it does set restrictions on what is permitted and prohibited with regard to eating.

The objective is to eat for the sake of Heaven, in order to strengthen our bodies, and not merely to relieve a craving for food. There is an even higher level when it comes to the act of eating: partaking of food in order to raise up the divine sparks hidden inside it. To do this, one must make a blessing on the food and intend to connect to its spiritual essence.

Initially, it was forbidden for people to eat meat. Some believe that in the future, once the world has been entirely rectified, there will no longer be a need to eat meat.

Strengthening of Body and Soul

One must care for both his body and his soul, but he need give only that which is necessary to the body, whereas he must provide amply for the needs of the soul. One who cares only for the body weakens the soul.

One must be aware of the needs of both his soul and his body:

Your soul and body require care and consideration. The nourishing and proper care of the soul occur by making it accustomed to accepting admonishment and wisdom, guiding it wisely, teaching it good character traits, and preventing it from [acting upon] its animalistic desires. But for nourishing and proper care of your body, you must regularly provide it with good-quality, pleasant food and drink that suit its nature, bathe in tepid water, and constantly take notice of what is good for it and what its needs are.

We need to make sure that our bodies are able to survive, but with regard to the soul, we must give it even more than it requires:

If your thoughts are on care of your body and you give it all your attention, you will overlook the care of the soul. Likewise, if your thoughts are turned to enlivening your soul, your attention to it will cause you to overlook many matters of your body. If you are devout, you will give priority to your eternal soul over your mortal body, regarding and paying attention to it. But do not disregard matters that are essential to your body. Do not overburden it and weaken it, as this will cause weakness in both body and soul. Rather, give your body the sustenance that it needs to function, and give your soul more wisdom and admonishment than is within its power [i.e., than it requires].

(Rabbeinu Baḥya ibn Pekuda, *Ḥovot HaLevavot* 8:3)

Further reading: For more on caring for the soul, and the connection between the body and the soul, see pp. 222ff.

Eating for the Sake of Heaven

The Torah does not command us to be ascetic or to fast, as fasting is like taking medicine for an illness, whereas eating for the sake of Heaven is the healthy and proper way to live:

Part of the perfection of the Torah is that it commands us to fast on only one day of the year, revealing the underlying intention of the mitzvot, which is that one should walk the middle path [and not behave in an extreme fashion]. This is unlike the teachings of other nations, who have tried to imitate our Torah. When one eats for the sake of Heaven, it is better than fasting, because fasting merely heals the disease of excessive desire, but eating for the sake of Heaven[2] is considered an act of righteousness.

(Rav Yaakov Anatoli, *Malmad HaTalmidim, Nitzavim*)

At every moment, and with every act, one must serve God. This applies even while eating, which is when one is apt to forget Him. One must be particular to eat only the amount necessary to sustain his body, and must not eat in order to fulfill his desires.

Even while eating, one must cling to God:

Even while eating, when you are close to forgetting Him and separating your mind from the knowledge of Him, "Be cognizant of Him" (Proverbs 3:6), cling to Him. If you do this, then [as the verse concludes], "He will smooth your paths" (Proverbs 3:6); God will smooth the way for you on the path of life. This is referring to the triumph of the soul [when it receives its portion] in the World to Come.

One must eat only in order to sustain the body, and not out of desire:

Therefore, it is fitting for a person to eat only for the subsistence of the body. It is forbidden for him to be drawn to any indulgence unless it replenishes his body and opens his mind, so that his body is healthy and strong, subject to his will and the will of his Creator.... One who has this intention is

2. With the intention to use the energy that he gains from the food to serve God and perform good deeds.

considered "an angel of the Lord of hosts" (Malachi 2:7). But one who does not have this as his objective "is like the beasts that perish" (Psalms 49:13).

(Rabbeinu Baḥya, *Shulḥan Shel Arba* 2)

Further reading: For the *halakhot* of mealtimes, see *A Concise Guide to Halakha*, p. 513.

The spiritual force of permitted foods comes from the husk of Venus,[3] which contains both good and evil. When one makes use of food in the correct way, he reveals the good in it and elevates it to a level of holiness.

The spiritual force of kosher foods comes from the husk of Venus.

The souls of pure animals, birds, and fish that are permitted for consumption, and the existence of every inanimate object and every plant that may be eaten… are dependent on the second level of the husks and the "other side,"[4] which is the fourth husk, called the husk of Venus… which is in between the three completely impure husks and the aspect of holiness. Therefore, it is sometimes included among the three impure husks.… And it is sometimes included in the aspect of holiness [when used properly by people].

Eating as part of one's service to God elevates the food to the level of an offering:

For example: If one eats rich beef and drinks spiced wine to expand his understanding of God and his Torah in the manner that Rava described: "Wine and good scents [make me wise]" (*Yoma* 76b), or in order to fulfill the mitzva of enjoying Shabbat and festivals, then the spiritual force of the meat and wine, which came from the husk of Venus, has been refined, and ascends to God like an offering.

(Rabbi Shneur Zalman of Liadi, *Tanya, Likutei Amarim* 7)

Food's Spiritual Force

Everything was created by the word of God. Divine words are what grant food the vitality to nourish us. One who makes a blessing on his food evokes the spiritual force within it. But if a person eats without making a blessing, even though he is nourished by the spiritual force within that food, he does not gain from it in the same way as one who makes a blessing.

3. In kabbalistic thought there are gradations or levels of reality surrounding the pure divine reality. These husks (*kelipot*) are often associated with particular planets and astrological signs. The husk of Venus (*kelipat noga*), which could alternatively be translated as the husk that shines, contains elements that can be redeemed by human action.
4. The "other side" represents the forces of evil and has a complex structure. The husks are part of the "other side."

The divine words that are within our food replenish us:

"Man does not live by bread alone; rather, it is by everything that issues from the mouth of the Lord that man lives" (Deuteronomy 8:3); this refers to the statements that issued from God's mouth during Creation to extract each thing from the earth. Those [divine] words enter the food and nourish and give life to the person.

Making a blessing over food evokes the spiritual force that is within it:

Therefore, one must make blessings over food, because through the blessing, the spiritual force is evoked.... When one eats without a blessing, the spiritual force within it is not evoked. Eating...without a blessing does nourish part of the person's soul, but the good that is brought upon the soul when there is no blessing is not the same as the good that results when a blessing is recited.

(Rabbi Yitzḥak Luria (Arizal), *Likutei Torah, Ekev*)

The entire world was created via the power of the Torah, and therefore the spiritual force of everything lies within the Torah. One who reflects on a food's spiritual force can be satiated by it, but one who sees only the physical aspect of the food cannot reach this state.

The central component of bread and other foods is the spiritual force within them, as it is stated, "There is no bread but Torah" (*Midrash Tehillim* 41:7). Everything was created through the power of the Torah, and the spiritual force of everything is found in the letters of the Torah. But one's satiation [as a result of eating] depends on his outlook.... If he sees and believes that the spiritual force comes from the Torah and from the Holy One, blessed be He, then his soul receives the spiritual force [that is within the food], as the verse states (Proverbs 20:13), "Open your eyes; you will be sated with food."

(Rabbi Yehuda Aryeh Leib Alter, *Sefat Emet, Beshalaḥ* 5654)

Eating Meat

Killing animals and eating them are both acts that produce traits of wickedness in the soul. God commanded the first man to eat only plants, and no meat. Even when meat was later permitted, only certain types of meat were allowed to the Jewish people, and even this was out of necessity alone.

Eating meat desensitizes the soul:

Apart from the fact that killing animals involves cruelty and rage, teaching people the evil trait of spilling blood for no reason, eating the meat of some animals also causes coarseness, murkiness, and insensitivity in the soul. As the verse explains at the end of the passage that prohibits some animals to the Jewish people, "And you shall not be rendered impure by them, and become impure [*venitmetem*] through them" (Leviticus 11:43). The letter *alef* is missing [from the word *venitmetem*, rendering it similar to the word *atimut*, insensitivity], to teach that eating non-kosher animals causes coarseness and insensitivity.

The first man ate only plants:

As a result, even though the meat of some animals is edible for human beings, God preferred to withdraw the small amount of good that comes from eating meat in order to avoid the evil and great harm that could arise from doing so, and He therefore prohibited the consumption of meat. He compensated for the foods that he removed, by designating, especially for humankind, edible food from plants, such as wheat, barley, and everything that contains seeds that may be planted, including the fruit of the trees. To the rest of the animals, He gave "all green vegetation" (Genesis 1:30), rather than seeds that can be planted, and this [fact, that humans eat food that they grow from seeds while animals eat merely "green vegetation"] indicates the superiority of humans over other animals.

The consumption of certain animals was allowed out of necessity:

When the Torah was given to the Jewish people… it prohibited eating those animals that cause coarseness and murkiness in the soul. Even with regard to those which were permitted, the Torah spoke only in response to the evil inclination [to eat meat].

(Rav Yosef Albo, *Sefer HaIkkarim* 3:15)

One must have compassion for all creatures and not treat them with contempt or allow them to be wasted. Uprooting a plant or killing an animal is permitted only in order to elevate the object from the level of vegetable or animal, namely, to make it part of a human being.

One must have compassion for every creature as much as is possible:

One's mercy must be upon all creatures; he must not treat them with contempt, nor destroy them [needlessly]. For divine wisdom is extended to all of creation: mineral, vegetable, animal, or rational [human beings]. For this reason, we are forbidden to treat food with contempt. Just as the divine wisdom is not contemptuous of anything that exists, and is the source of everything, as it is written, "In wisdom, You made them all" (Psalms 104:24), so too, it is appropriate that a person's mercy be applied to all of God's works.... As a result, one should not treat any of the creations, all of which were created in wisdom, with contempt. One should not uproot any growing thing unless it is necessary, and one should not kill any animal unless it is necessary, and he should ensure that [any creature he does kill] receives a good [quick] death, with a knife that has been checked, in order to be as merciful as he can.

One may use means that appear cruel only in order to elevate things:

This is the principle: One must have compassion for all creatures, and must not cause them any harm; this stems from wisdom. The exception is in the case of an act that elevates something from one level to the next, such as from vegetable to animal [when an animal eats a plant], or from animal to speaker [when a human eats the meat of an animal]. In these cases, it is permitted to uproot the vegetable or to kill the animal. A person causes the object's loss in order to bring about its gain.

(Rabbi Moshe Cordovero, *Tomer Devora* 3)

The Torah allows the consumption of meat, but states that it is permitted only because we have not yet reached a high level of morality. In the future, we will achieve a purer morality and will append to the Torah's commandments the moral imperative to refrain from eating meat.

We eat meat because of our low moral level:

When the Torah permitted the consumption of meat after the consecration of [Israel through] the mitzvot at the giving of the Torah, it presented an extended description: "And you say: I will eat meat, because your heart will desire to eat meat; with all your heart's desire you may eat meat" (Deuteronomy 12:20). There is a subtle rebuke and the indication of a limit. In other words, [the Torah permits eating meat] as long as your inner morality does not cause you to be revolted by the consumption of the flesh of animals as you are already revolted by human flesh. The Torah did not need to give an explicit prohibition against [eating human flesh], as one does not need to be warned against that which he already knows intrinsically. [Intrinsic moral prohibitions of this sort] are equivalent to explicit ones. When the time comes for human morality to abhor the flesh of animals because of the moral repulsion it involves, then you will not desire meat, and you will not eat it.

When humanity reaches a perfect state, our relationship to animals will change:

When humanity reaches the objective of its bliss and complete freedom, when it reaches the height of perfection of the pure knowledge of God, and the holiness of a life that is full in its character... humanity will realize, with regard to its fellow creatures, the animals, what is fitting from the perspective of pure morality. There will no longer be a need for concessions of exigency, for the compromise between the attribute of compassion and the attribute of justice with respect to the individual,[5] or concessions where the Torah spoke [i.e., permitted something] only because of the evil inclination. Instead, he will walk on the path of absolute good.

(Rabbi Avraham Yitzḥak HaKohen Kook, *Ḥazon HaTzimḥonut VehaShalom*)

Further reading: For more on the proper treatment of animals, see *A Concise Guide to the Sages*, p. 435; *A Concise Guide to Halakha*, p. 613.

5. That is to say, a person will be able to be fully just without moderating justice with compassion. In this case the permission to consume meat is a concession out of compassion for humanity that craves it.

Faith

The basis of Jewish life is faith in God, who gave us the Torah and the mitzvot. One should not be satisfied with merely an emotional inclination to faith. Rather, one must strive to know that there is a God. In order to strengthen one's faith one can reflect on the miraculous aspects of the well-ordered universe or the wonders of the human soul. The word "faith" [*emuna*] is related to the term *imun*, meaning training. One is required to train himself to perceive the world's inner meaning, and not just its external appearance.

The Commandment to Believe

Before performing mitzvot, one needs to know that there is a supreme Ruler, the Master of the Universe, who created all the dimensions of reality.

The first mitzva is to know that there is a supreme Ruler:

"And you will know that I am the Lord your God" (Exodus 6:7). This mitzva is the first of all the mitzvot; it comes before all the mitzvot: To know the Holy One, blessed be He, in general. What does in general mean? Knowing that there is a supreme Ruler who is the Master of the Universe and who created all the worlds, the heavens, the earth, and all their hosts. This is what in general means. And ultimately: In specific ways. One must know Him in specific ways.

Before the exodus, God was known in a general way, and in the end, He was known in a specific way:

When the children of Israel departed from Egypt, they did not know the Holy One, blessed be He. When Moses came to them, he taught them this first mitzva, as it is written, "And you will know that I am the Lord your God, who takes you out from under the burdens of Egypt" (Exodus 6:7). Were it not for this mitzva, Israel would not have believed in all the miracles and acts of might that God performed for them in Egypt. Once they knew this commandment in a general way [that is, they knew about the existence of the Creator], miracles and acts of might were performed for them. Forty years later, when they strove to keep all the mitzvot that Moses had taught them, both those [mitzvot] that are performed in the Land of Israel and those that are performed outside the land, he then taught them specifically that which is written: "You shall know this day, and restore to your heart"

(Deuteronomy 4:39). Namely, it is only on this day [after receiving all the mitzvot, that you know] in detail that which was not optional beforehand: "That the Lord, He is the God." This is specific [knowledge of God] There are numerous mysterious subtleties associated with this. This mitzva and the one given at the beginning are one, that one in general and this one specifically.

(*Ra'aya Meheimena* 2:25a)

Further reading: For more on faith in God, see *A Concise Guide to the Sages*, p. 381.

Is It Possible to Know God?

The fact of God's existence is known, but it is not in our power to grasp His essence. The cognitive achievement is to fully comprehend our inability to know God.

As the wise person said when he was asked whether he knew God's essence, "If I knew Him, I would be Him." No one can grasp God's essence except for God Himself, although His existence is revealed by His works in a complete manner. Praiseworthy is the One who, in His perfection, has surpassed us, and whose mighty appearance is concealed from us, just as perception of sunlight and its pleasantness is concealed from those who have weak eyesight. Their inability [to see it] does not indicate its nonexistence. All that we can comprehend of God is that it is impossible to comprehend Him. As the wise person said, "The entirety of what we know of You is that we cannot know You."

(Rav Yosef Albo, *Sefer HaIkkarim* 2:30)

The commandment to have faith means gaining as much of an understanding of the Creator as possible, and to have faith with regard to everything that cannot be understood.

Therefore, King David states, "Know the God of your father" (I Chronicles 28:9). "Know" means that you must strive to grasp every aspect of His godliness that can be grasped in terms of knowledge, and consider these matters in depth. This is the knowledge of His existence and the fact that He is the source of life.... With regard to that which is impossible to grasp with knowledge [rational understanding], have it rest upon faith. Trust in Him with complete faith once you know of His existence and the fact that He is the source of life. Faith is a genuine experience like visual perception. Thus, that which is impossible to grasp [intellectually] is experienced as faith.

(Tzemaḥ Tzedek, *Derekh Mitzvotekha* 46a)

The Pillars of Faith

The foundations of the Torah rest on three pillars: the existence of God, reward and punishment, and the fact that the Torah is from Heaven.

In my opinion, the correct way to count the principles that compose the foundation of the divine Torah is this: There are a total of three general principles that are necessary for the true religion, and they are: the existence of God, providence with regard to reward and punishment, and Torah from Heaven.

(Rav Yosef Albo, *Sefer HaIkkarim* 1:4)

The Torah rests on six foundations: God knows what happens to His creations, watches over them, is omnipotent, and grants prophecy to the prophets, free will to human beings, and purpose to the world.

There are foundations and pillars that support the house of God, and whose reality make possible the truth of the Torah to be ordered by Him, may He be blessed. If one of them were missing, the [truth of] the entire Torah would collapse, God forbid. When we investigated, we found that these are six: (1) God's knowledge of reality, (2) His providence over it, (3) His power, (4) prophecy [which He gives to human beings], (5) free will, and (6) the purpose [of the Torah and the world, which is realized through humankind].

(Rav Ḥasdai Crescas, *Or Hashem* 2:1)

There are thirteen principles of Judaism, which constitute the specifics derived from three foundations: faith in God, His connection to human beings, and reward and punishment.

The foundations of faith in God:

There are thirteen principles, or foundations, of our religion: (1) The existence of the Creator, namely, a Being who is perfect in all ways. He is the cause of the existence of all creatures; their reality is dependent upon Him and derives from Him.... (2) The oneness of God, meaning that He, who is the cause of everything, is one.... (3) His incorporeity: He is not a material body, nor a physical force. Features of physicality, like movement and being at rest, do not apply to Him, either in essence or incidentally.... (4) Eternity: He is eternal[6] and nothing besides him is eternal as He is. Know that

6. Eternal, in this context, means always existent or, more precisely, that God is outside of time and cannot be described in temporal terms.

the great foundation in the Torah of Moses, our teacher, is that the world is created. God created it *ex nihilo* .... (5) God is the One whom it is fitting to serve and extol, to proclaim His greatness and perform His mitzvot. And one should not do these for anything whose existence is inferior to His.

The foundations of God's connection with humankind:

(6) Prophecy: One should know that in humankind there are those with a nature composed of exceptionally pure and elevated character traits and great perfections, whose souls are prepared.... These are the prophets, and this is prophecy, and that is what it concerns.... (7) The prophecy of Moses our teacher: We must believe that he was the father of all the prophets who came before him, as well as those who arose after him. All were on a level inferior to his.... (8) The Torah is from Heaven: We must believe that the entire Torah that we have today is the one given through Moses, the entirety of which came from the mouth of the Almighty.... (9) Abrogation: The Torah of Moses will not be revised or replaced, and no other Torah will ever come from the Creator. One must not add to it nor subtract from it. This refers to both the Written Torah and the Oral Torah.

The foundations of reward and punishment:

(10) God knows the deeds of human beings and does not ignore them.... (11) God rewards a person who fulfills the mitzvot of the Torah, and He punishes whoever violates the Torah's prohibitions. The greatest reward is the World to Come, and the harshest punishment is excision from the World to Come.... (12) The messianic era: Believing and trusting that the anointed one[7] will come, and do not think that he will be late: "If it [the end of days] tarries, wait for it" (Habakkuk 2:3). (13) The revival of the dead.

(Rambam, *Commentary on the Mishna, Sanhedrin* 10:1)

Further reading: For more on prophecy, see p. 203; for more on the Torah being from Heaven, see p. 269; for more on divine providence, see p. 173; for more on reward and punishment, see p. 256; for more on the messianic era, see p. 145; for more on the revival of the dead, see p. 295.

7. The anointed one is the messiah. Messiah is a form of the Hebrew *mashiaḥ*, which means "anointed one."

How Do We Acquire Faith?

When something is set up in an orderly fashion, it is obvious to us that someone arranged it so. If one finds a piece of paper with words written on it, it is obvious that someone wrote those words, and that the ink did not spill of its own accord and form the shapes of the letters.

Our world is arranged in an orderly fashion:

When we look at this world, we find it to be assembled and constructed. Not one of its parts lacks connection or arrangement. For we perceive it both through our senses and intellectually, as a completed house in which every necessity has been coordinated. The sky is like the ceiling; the land is spread out like a bed; the stars are arranged as lamps; and all the objects are gathered in it like hidden treasures, each one for its particular need. The human being is like the master of the house, who makes use of everything in it. The different types of plants are there for his use, and the different types of animals for his enjoyment.

Anything arranged in an orderly fashion could not have been created unassisted:

How could one say about the world that it came into being without the intention and wisdom of One who has power? We know that anything that occurs unintentionally contains no sign of wisdom or competence. If one suddenly spills ink on a blank page, it is impossible that orderly writing and legible lines, as though written with a pen, would result. If an individual brought before us orderly writing that could not have been formed without the help of a pen, and says that the ink spilled on the paper and the writing formed of its own accord, we would hurry to charge him with speaking falsely, as this could not have been produced without intention. Since it is impossible, according to our understanding, that this could occur with regard to written symbols, how can we say, with regard to something whose workmanship is more delicate and whose artistry is infinitely more remote [from our comprehension] and infinitely deep in our perception, that it could occur unintentionally and without the wisdom and power of One who is wise and powerful?

(Rabbeinu Baḥya ibn Pekuda, *Ḥovot HaLevavot* 1:6)

Faith means constant training. It is not acquired through a single experience of insight, but through repeatedly looking at the world and reflecting on its spiritual significance.

The most important thing is habit: Fixing in his heart and mind that everything he sees, the sky and the earth and its contents, is an outer garment of the King, the Holy One, blessed be He. In this way, one will always recall the spiritual essence and vitality of everything. This is referred to in the word for faith [*emuna*], which is a term of habitual activity, like a craftsman [*uman*] who trains [*me'amen*] his hands.

(Rabbi Shneur Zalman of Liadi, *Tanya, Likutei Amarim* 42)

By considering the human self we can gain an understanding of the extent of God's power, just as a person who looks at a map understands what the terrain looks like.

The wise person said: Whoever knows his own self knows his God. The verse "for He made man in the image of God" (Genesis 9:6), teaches that one who looks at this image understands the divine, i.e., one who looks at himself will gain from its image [i.e., from his perception of himself] an understanding of God. Although "to what likeness would you compare Him" (Isaiah 40:18), nevertheless, from the unlimited powers of his soul, which are more exalted than the physical processes, one may understand something of the exalted nature of God's power. This is the meaning of the verse "And from my flesh I will view God" (Job 19:26): That from one's own image, which is the image of God, one may perceive divinity. It is like one who looks at a map and understands the terrain. Even though there is no real resemblance whatsoever [between the actual terrain and the map], he will understand what he needs to understand.

(Rabbi Simha Zissel Ziv, *Ḥokhma UMusar*, p. 197)

Further reading: For more on learning to know the Creator by contemplating the self, see p. 221.

Simple Faith

Jews have simple faith because the heavenly part of the soul sees the divine. The source of faith is the connection of the soul's root to the divine.

There are two reasons why Jews believe in God with simple faith and do not require proof in this matter. [The first is] because "their *mazal* sees" (*Sanhedrin* 94a): The higher soul sees the divine (with perception that is beyond the intellect), and this inspires faith in God within the soul that inhabits the body. A further explanation is that the root of faith lies at the essence of the soul (which is higher than the level of "their *mazal* sees"). This essence of the soul is inherently tied to the divine [in that it itself is divine], in a manner that is independent of causation and does not depend on perception [of any sort,] even perceptions that are beyond the intellect.

(The Lubavitcher Rebbe, *Torat Menaḥem, Sefer HaMa'amarim Melukat* 3, p. 34)

The Land of Israel

The Sages' midrashic interpretation of the first verse in the Torah, "In the beginning, God created the heavens and the earth" (Genesis 1:1), understands "earth" as referring to the Land of Israel. This land is God's portion; He Himself watches over it, and those who dwell in it must be strict about maintaining a high spiritual level. In the Land of Israel, the Jewish people are able to connect to God, and therefore it is the site of prophecy.

The land's holiness is bestowed upon all who dwell there, and even upon those who are buried there, but the degree of its impact depends on the spiritual level of the individual. This holiness stems from God, who watches over the Jewish people who live in the land, as it says, "Always the eyes of the Lord your God are upon it" (Deuteronomy 11:12). Therefore, before the Jewish people entered the land, it was "a land that devours its inhabitants" (Numbers 13:32), and "spews them out" (Leviticus 18:25). Only when the Jewish people are in the land does it become "exceedingly good" (Numbers 14:7).

The Virtues of the Land of Israel

In contrast to all other lands, over which heavenly beings are appointed, God Himself watches over the Land of Israel, and therefore the land spews out those who defile it with idol worship or forbidden sexual relations. Because of the Jewish people's closeness to God, He punishes them severely when they sin.

The Land of Israel is the portion of God, and He Himself watches over it:

For God set the authority over the lower world into [the hands of] higher creatures, and appointed, over every nation in its land, a star and an astrological sign, as it states, "which the Lord your God distributed to all the peoples" (Deuteronomy 4:19). And above the astrological signs are the heavenly angels, [who serve] as officers, and God is supreme [Master of] the entire world. However, the Land of Israel is the center of the world, and is the portion of God. It is assigned to Him and not to the angels. He bequeathed it to His nation, which unifies His name.... Because they are set aside for Him, He gave them the land that is the portion of God, which spews out all who defile it with idol worship and forbidden sexual relations. Outside the land, although everything is God's, there is no perfect purity, because of the servants [the angels] who rule there. The nations go astray and serve their ministers.

The heavenly Temple is directly opposite the earthly Temple:

It is not permitted to explicate further with regard to the land [as it is a mystery to be revealed only to a few], but if you merit to understand the first land mentioned in the verse "In the beginning, [God created the heavens and the land]" (Genesis 1:1), and the one mentioned in *Parashat Behukotai* ["And the land, I will remember" (Leviticus 26:42)], you will know a sublime mystery, and will understand that which is stated, "The heavenly Temple is directly opposite the lower one" (*Tanḥuma, Vayak'hel* 7).[8]

The closeness to God in the Land of Israel requires higher standards of conduct.

We find that Israel's closeness to the Holy One, blessed be He, is what causes them to be distanced [when they sin]. [This applies] all the more so to those who merit to sit before the Holy One, blessed be He, in His land, as they are like those who are in the presence of the king. If they are careful with regard to His honor, they will be joyful, but if they defy him, woe to them more than to all other creatures, as they make war and they anger the king in his own palace.... It is taught in the *Sifra* (*Kedoshim* 11:14), "The Land of Israel is not like other lands; it does not sustain transgressors."

(Ramban, Leviticus 18:25; Homily on Rosh HaShana)

Further reading: For more on the heavenly Temple, see p. 161.

Although the Jewish people are the chosen people and they have a special connection to God, this connection is fully realized only in the Land of Israel. The Land of Israel is also where the prophets prophesy and where one can cleave to God. This is analogous to plants that require a certain type of soil in order to grow. They can grow properly only when they are placed in that soil.

Without the Land of Israel it is impossible to attain the special distinction of the Jewish people:

The special virtue comes first to the nation that is distinguished [by God] and is the nucleus.... Subsequently, the land also has a role regarding this virtue, as do the deeds and mitzvot that are dependent on the land, which are like the cultivation of a vineyard. But unlike a vineyard, which could produce grapes in another location as well, the chosen people can connect to the divine only in this land.

8. The two uses of the word "land" indicate that the Land of Israel is the physical manifestation of a spiritual realm.

Abraham and his descendants prophesied exclusively in the Land of Israel:

You see that the outstanding one of the distinguished people, Abraham, after he had advanced through the levels of perfection and became fit to adhere to the divine, was moved from his land to that place, the only place where he could reach complete perfection. This is what a farmer does when he finds, in barren land, the root of a tree whose fruit is good; he transfers it to cultivated land, as by its nature it will thrive there. He will tend to it there until it becomes a tree [like the other] trees of the garden. Until then, its growth was random, and its location was random. The same was true with regard to the prophecy of the descendants of Abraham in the Land of Israel. While they were in the Land of Israel, there were many who received prophecy, and there were many conditions that supported it: purity, Temple service, offerings, and above all, the closeness of the Divine Presence.

(Rav Yehuda HaLevi, *Kuzari* 2:12–14)

Further reading: For more on the factors that contribute to prophecy and the presence of the divine spirit, see p. 203.

Living in the Land of Israel

The Sages teach that one should live in the Land of Israel even if it means living among the gentiles, and one should not live outside of the Land of Israel, even if it means living among Jews. One who lives outside of the land, it is as though he worships idols, whereas dwelling in the Land of Israel is equivalent to all of the mitzvot. With regard to one who desires to settle in the Land of Israel, but who is compelled to remain abroad, God considers it as though he actually has done so.

One who lives in the Land of Israel demonstrates his faith in God:

Anyone who resides outside of the Land of Israel, it is as though he is engaged in idol worship. And so it says with regard to David: "For this day they have driven me away from cleaving to the inheritance of the Lord, saying: Go, worship other gods" (I Samuel 26:19). Who said to David: "Go, worship other gods"? Rather, this comes to tell you that anyone who resides outside of the land, it is as though he is engaged in idol worship (*Ketubot* 110b).

Because the mitzva of settling in the Land of Israel is so great, the one who lives there demonstrates his faith in God, and one who dwells outside of the land, it is as though he worships idols. The statement in the *Sifrei* is correct: "The mitzva of dwelling in the Land of Israel is equivalent to all the mitzvot in the Torah" (*Re'eh* 80). One demonstrates God's divinity through this mitzva, and not doing it is considered like idol worship, which is like a rejection of the entire Torah.

If one merely desires to settle in the Land of Israel, this causes God to regard his intent as though it were the deed itself:

The entirety of one's desire when he immigrates to the Land of Israel must be for the holiness of the place, for the sake of God's commandment.... Even if he cannot immigrate and is constrained for some reason, he must desire and yearn for the Land of Israel.... The Holy One, blessed be He, attaches a good thought to a deed [and considers it as though he has settled in the Land of Israel].

(Rabbi Ḥayyim Palagi, *Tokheḥat Ḥayyim, Ḥayei Sarah*)

Sanctity of the Land

The Land of Israel receives its holiness from the Jewish people, through whom God is glorified. Since God watches over the Jewish people, His eyes are always on the land. Even the air of this land makes people wise.

The holiness of the Land of Israel is due only to the fact that God watches over it; He is always taking notice of the Land of Israel, as it is written, "Always the eyes of the Lord your God are upon it, from the beginning of the year until year end" (Deuteronomy 11:12). Because of this, the Land of Israel is sanctified, and its air makes one wise (*Bava Batra* 158b).... But what spurs God to have it be as though His eyes are watching? It is because of the souls of the Jewish people [who live there], in whom God glories, as in the verse, "Israel, in whom I glory" (Isaiah 49:3).... This is why it is called the Land of Israel; it receives its holiness from "Israel, in whom I glory."

(Rabbi Naḥman of Breslov, *Likutei Moharan Tinyana* 40)

Since the Land of Israel is connected with the Jewish people specifically, before they entered the land it would devour its inhabitants, spewing out the nations that settled there. The land reveals its hidden good only when the Jewish people are settled in it. The superiority of the Land of Israel is not evident externally, but all blessings derive from the land.

The Land of Israel is designated only for the Jewish people, and the benevolent light that is concealed within it is revealed only to them.... Therefore, before the Jewish people arrived, its hidden good was not discernible, and the spies said that the land "devours its inhabitants" (Numbers 13:32). Based on this alone they should have understood that the Land of Israel is designated only for the Jewish people, and this is why it "spewed out the nation that was before you" (Leviticus 18:28).... Therefore, Caleb and Joshua said, "The land is exceedingly good. If the Lord is favorably disposed to us, He will bring us to this land and will give it to us" (Numbers 14:7–8), meaning, at that time the hidden good will be revealed.... The superiority of the Land of Israel is not evident externally, but the root of all blessings depends on the Land of Israel.

(Rabbi Yehuda Aryeh Leib Alter, *Sefat Emet, Shelaḥ* 5661)

Further reading: Read the story of the spies in *A Concise Guide to the Torah*, p. 372; *A Concise Guide to the Sages*, p. 187.

The Land of Israel, a place of sanctity and divine illumination, was given to the Jewish people so that they could truly serve God.

The intention of the Creator, blessed be He, was to give the holy land to the Jewish people because it is a land whose air makes one wise, as it corresponds to that upper land that is called the kingdom of Heaven. Therefore, one can easily come there to truly serve God.

(Rabbi Kalonymus Kalman Epstein, *Ma'or VaShemesh, Kedoshim*)

Further reading: For more on the Land of Israel and its holiness, see *A Concise Guide to the Sages*, p. 387.

My Heart Is in the East

By: Rav Yehuda HaLevi

My heart is in the east and I am in the farthest west.
How can I taste what I eat and how can it be pleasant?
How can I fulfill my vows and [self-imposed] prohibitions, when Zion is shackled by Edom [Rome, or the Church], and I am in the chains of Arabs?
It would be easy for me to leave all the delights of Spain,
An honor for me to see the dust of the ruined Temple.

An emissary from Safed came to the city of Rabbi Avraham Dov of Avritch and sang the praises of the Land of Israel. He described the air, the views, the greenery, and the fruit. In rich language he painted a picture of the beauty of the holy sites and the graves of saintly people. Finally, he became so moved that he cried out, "Even the stones in the Land of Israel are actually precious gems!" The rebbe, who for a long time had wanted to immigrate to the Holy Land, could not rest. He traveled to the Land of Israel and settled in Safed.

Some time later, the emissary returned home from his journey and asked the rebbe: "Did the rebbe find here what he had expected to see?"

"Yes indeed," replied the rebbe, "The land really is 'exceedingly good.' I have seen the holy sites and the graves of the saintly ones, the Western Wall and Rachel's Tomb, and the air of the Land of Israel truly does make one wise. But, when you said that the stones in the Holy Land are actually gems, that was a slight exaggeration."

The emissary responded emphatically, "Rebbe, those who are deserving see it!"

When the rebbe heard this, he stood up and went into his room without a word. He remained there for an entire year without emerging. After a year, he came out and invited the people of Safed to a feast.

Everyone assembled, longing to hear the reason for the rebbe's seclusion and for the gathering. The rebbe declared, "I have secluded myself, sanctified myself, and purified myself, and indeed my eyes have been opened! I bear witness before you that the stones of this land are shining, precious gems."

The Land of Israel is the *Shekhina* itself.

(Rabbi Menaḥem Mendel of Vitebsk, *Peri HaAretz*)

No matter where I go, I am always headed for the Land of Israel.

(Rabbi Naḥman of Breslov)

Israel among the nations, the Torah among the faiths, and the Land of Israel among the lands; these are the three epicenters where the treasures that nourish and sanctify the entire world are concealed.

(Rabbi Avraham Yitzḥak HaKohen Kook, *Orot* 151)

Free Will

A person cannot choose where he is born or how healthy he is at birth. Over the course of one's life, there are many matters that are out of his control. Nevertheless, we can choose whether to be righteous or wicked, whether to do good or to do evil. Likewise, we can choose what to do with what we have been given.

God does not decide whether a certain individual will be righteous or wicked; He grants each person the power to do as he chooses. Humans were created in the image of God; our free will comes from the divine image that is within us, and we are the only creatures that have free will. Before the sin of Adam and Eve, choosing evil meant choosing something that was external to human nature, but today, good and evil are mingled within us.

A related question concerns divine foreknowledge and free will. In Jewish thought, there is a significant amount of discussion surrounding the question: How can we say that an individual is making a choice, if God knows the future? Some distinguish between knowing the future and determining it, and others define divine knowledge differently, or limit the extent of our free will.

The Ability to Choose

Free will is unique to human beings; no other creature has it. If God determined whether an individual was going to be righteous or wicked, there would be no reason for the judgment of our actions, for reward and punishment, or indeed for the Torah itself.

Free will is unique to human beings:

Autonomy is given to every human being. If he wants to incline himself toward a good path and be righteous, it is possible for him to do so, and if he wants to incline himself toward a bad path and be wicked, it is possible for him to do so. This is what is written in the Torah, "Behold, the man has become as one of us, to know good and evil" (Genesis 3:22). This means that this human species is unique in the world, and there is no other species similar to it in that an individual possesses the ability in himself, by means of his own understanding, to know good and evil, and to do all that he desires, and there is no one who prevents him from doing good or evil.

Without free will there would be no place for reward and punishment:

This is a central principle and a foundation of the Torah and the mitzvot.... If God were to decree that an individual will be righteous or wicked, or if there were something that drew that person, by his essential nature, toward a particular path, branch of knowledge, attribute, or deed... what place would there be for the entire Torah? According to which law and which justice could a wicked person be punished or a righteous person be rewarded?

(Rambam, *Mishneh Torah, Hilkhot Teshuva* 5:1–4)

Further reading: For more on reward and punishment, see p. 256; *A Concise Guide to the Sages*, p. 164.

Even though God perceives all of our actions, He does not prevent us from doing wrong; rather, He allows us to sin. We have free will because we were created in the image of God, and just as God acts as He chooses, human beings are also able to act in accordance with their wills.

Because human beings were created in the image of the Holy One, blessed be He, He gave them autonomy to act as they will, and they are not compelled in their actions.... This is not the case with regard to the angels, who do not possess autonomy. They do what the Holy One, blessed be He, appointed them to do, and they cannot deviate from their mission. But humans, who were created in the image of God, are unique in that they are under their own authority. Just as God does what He wants, so too, people have a choice and can do what they want; they possess free will.

(Maharal, *Derekh Ḥayyim* 3:15)

God gave free will to humankind, yet He is also the One who gave us our power to make choices. The intention of creation was for everyone to know that our actions are the result of God's power.

God gave each of His creations the power to perform its [assigned] action: the fire burns and the tree grows. God did the same for the human; he has free will and can act as he chooses. The intention was that every creature would know that it is God who gives him his powers, and that even though a person acts of his own volition, he is like an ax in the hand of the woodchopper. This was the entire intention of creation.

(Rabbi Yehuda Aryeh Leib Alter, *Sefat Emet, Bereshit* 5632)

Further reading: For more on the meaning of being created in God's image, see p. 131.

Torah Concepts

When Do We Have Free Will?

There are three different types of situations: those where we have complete free will, events that are decreed by God and are therefore unavoidable, and those that combine free will and necessity.

Type one: Where one has complete free will:

Acts that are performed with absolute free will are those that are, by nature, optional. They are affected by diligence and effort, and one is praised or disgraced on account of them. Prohibitions and commandments are relevant to this type of action, and reward and punishment are received for them. The origin of such actions is in the individual; there is no obstacle or burden whatsoever to performing them.

Type two: Circumstances that are subject to necessity:

However, the actions that are completely necessary are those that are decreed, whether by the stars[9] or by God's providence, as we will see, and these are matters over which humans have no control at all. Putting effort into [changing] them is futile, because these matters, whether good or bad, are not contingent on free will.... In this way, unexpected evil may befall a person when he had not done anything to deserve it. It is clear that this type of good or evil comes as the result of a decree, regardless of one's choices.

Type three: Circumstances that combine choice and certainty:

Acts that combine the necessary, i.e., a [divine] decree, and free will, are like the case of one who digs a foundation and finds a treasure. If he had not made the effort to dig the foundation, he would not have found the treasure. It is clear that such matters are a combination of necessity and free will.... Most things that happen to people as a result of reward or punishment through God's providence occur in this way, namely, a combination of a decree, which is necessary, and free will.

(Rav Yosef Albo, *Sefer HaIkkarim* 4:5)

Good and Evil Inclinations Are Inherent

Free will changed after the sin of the tree of knowledge. Beforehand, we did not have any inner inclination toward evil; rather, evil needed to entice us from the outside. But after the

9. Most medieval thinkers considered astrological influence to be scientific fact. In modern terms, the equivalent would be physical necessity.

sin, good and evil mingled within us, and free will became a struggle between one's inner inclination toward good and one's inner inclination toward evil.

Before the sin of the first man, evil existed only outside of the human being:

Before the sin, the first man certainly had free will and could incline himself whichever way he desired, whether to do good or the opposite, God forbid, for this was the intention of creation. Moreover, this is apparent because he sinned. However, his free will was not due to the fact that there were forces of evil within him, for he was entirely righteous, and was composed only of forces of holiness. Everything in him was righteous, holy, and pure, absolute good, without any trace of the opposite. The forces of evil were a separate entity and external to him. He had free will, and he could enter into the realm of the forces of evil, God forbid, just like one may choose to walk into a fire. Therefore, when the "other side" wanted to cause him to sin, the snake needed to come from the outside to entice him.

Today, good and evil are intermingled, both in people and in the different dimensions of existence:

In contrast, nowadays, the evil inclination that entices an individual is within that individual. It seems to the individual that it is he himself who desires and is drawn to do the sin, and not that something outside of himself is enticing him.... This is the meaning of "the tree of the knowledge of good and evil" (Genesis 2:9); good and evil joined and became mixed together, one inside of the other, within [the individual] and dimensions of existence. [Consumption of the fruit of the tree brought this about] as the meaning of knowledge is connection.

(Rabbi Ḥayyim of Volozhin, *Nefesh HaḤayyim* 1:6)

Foreknowledge and Free Will

God knows what will happen, but He does not determine what will happen; He knows the future, yet He does not influence it. People make their own choices and God knows what they will decide. One cannot actually cause harm to another through his choices, as the harm that is to be brought upon that person has already been decreed by God. When an evil person kills or steals, it is due to his choice to act in an evil way. Nevertheless, even if he chooses not to engage in a particular act, the same damage will be brought about by one of God's many emissaries.

God knows what a person will choose, but does not compel him to do so:

Perhaps more may be said: If He knows what will occur before it occurs, then He already knows that a person will disobey Him, so it is impossible for that person to not disobey Him, for His knowledge is perfect... but we must consider that He knows the truth of what will happen. He knows the causes, and when something is caused, He already knows that it will be caused; and when it is caused by a person's choice, He already knows that that will be the person's choice.

It is important to distinguish between the person doing the deed, and its outcome:

It is further asked: When an individual, one of God's creatures, is condemned to be killed, whether as a punishment for sinning or as a [divinely decreed] ordeal, then when an evil person kills that individual, as Jezebel did to some of the prophets, what can we say about this deed, to whom do we attribute it? We conclude that the death is an act of God, while killing is the act of the evil person. If God's wisdom determined that someone deserves death, then if it had not been carried out by the evil person, the individual would have died from another cause. Likewise, this question is asked with regard to a thief, as financial loss is a decree of the Creator, either as a punishment or as a [divinely decreed] ordeal. How can we say, with regard to a theft, that it is an act of the Creator? The answer is that the loss is an act of the Creator, whereas the theft is the act of a person. If God's wisdom decreed the loss of a certain item, then if the thief had not stolen it, it would have been lost in a different way.

(Rav Se'adya Gaon, *Emunot VeDe'ot* 4)

Although nothing occurs in this world that is in opposition to God's will, human beings are able to do what they want, because God decided that we have free will. Therefore, when a person does as he chooses, this is God's will. This is not to say that a person's ability to choose impairs God's foreknowledge to any degree, since God's knowledge is not external to Him; rather, it is an intrinsic knowledge whose essence we are unable to comprehend.

God wants a person to be able to act in accordance with his own will:

Do not wonder and say: How is it that a person can do anything he desires and be in control of his actions, if nothing in this world can be done without the permission of his Master, and against His will?... Know, that everything that people do is in accordance with His will, even though our actions are in our hands. How? Because the Creator desires that fire and wind rise up, that water and earth descend,[10] that the sphere rotate circularly, and that the other creatures in the world behave in accordance with the nature He desired for them. So too, He desires that a person be autonomous and that he have control over all of his actions, that nothing compel or pull him, but rather, that he, on his own initiative and with his God-given understanding, will do anything that people are able to do.

God's knowledge is a spiritual knowledge, and we have no way to comprehend it:

Lest you say: Doesn't the Holy One, blessed be He, know everything that is going to occur; and before it occurs, doesn't He know that this person will be righteous or wicked? Or does He not know? If He knows that one will be righteous, it would be impossible for him not to be righteous. If you say that He knows that one will be righteous, yet it is possible that he will be wicked, this would mean that God does not have full knowledge of the matter. Understand, that the answer to this question is longer than the length of the land and broader than the width of the sea, and some major [theological] principles are connected to it. But you must understand what I say here.... The Holy One, blessed be He, does not know with a knowledge that is external to Himself as human beings do, for they and their knowledge are two entities. Rather, He and His knowledge are one, and human understanding cannot fully comprehend this. Just as a human does not have the ability to discover or to fathom the true [essence] of the Creator... so too, he does not have the ability to discover or to fathom the Creator's understanding.... That being the case, we do not possess the ability to know the way in which the Holy One, blessed be He, knows all creatures and all deeds. Nevertheless, we know beyond a doubt that a person's actions are in his own hands. The Holy One, blessed be He, does not lead him [to act in a particular way], nor does He decree upon him that he must do so.

(Rambam, *Mishneh Torah, Hilkhot Teshuva* 5:4–5)

According to our understanding of the world, we have free will. We are given this understanding so that we will worship God of our own accord. But in truth, everything is in the hands of Heaven.

On the deepest level, everything is in the hands of Heaven. A person's free will is as [inconsequential as] a garlic peel, and it is only what appears to

10. In accordance with Aristotelian physics, where there are four basic elements: fire, air, water, and earth.

him to be the case. For God conceals His ways from human beings because He desires them to worship Him, and if everything were revealed before a person, worship would not come from within him.

(Rabbi Mordekhai Yosef of Izhbitze, *Mei HaShiloaḥ, Koraḥ*)

Further reading: The principle of free will appears in the Bible: see *A Concise Guide to the Torah*, pp. 463, 503.

The Messiah

One of the foundations of Judaism is belief in the ultimate coming of the messiah. He will bring about the redemption not only of the Jewish people but of the entire world, and we await his arrival every day. The messiah will be wiser than King Solomon, and will be a great prophet whose level of prophecy will approach that of Moses. He will rebuild the Temple, gather in the Jewish people to the Land of Israel, and reestablish the Torah as the guiding constitution of the community. One who does not believe in the coming of the messiah is considered a heretic who rejects the Torah as well as Moses' authority.

In every generation there is a saintly person who is worthy of redeeming the Jewish people, but we do not know who he is, and even he does not know that he is to be the redeemer. When the time for redemption arrives, God will appear to him just as He appeared to Moses at the burning bush.

In the messianic age, the laws of nature will not change, but the physical properties of the world will be spiritually elevated. The entire world will be immeasurably good, and will be filled with the understanding of God. Those things that were already good during the exile will not cease to exist, but they will emerge from their pre-messianic state, and their true, inner essence will be revealed.

A Foundation of Our Faith

One of the foundations of Judaism is to believe in the coming of the messiah and to await his arrival, without predicting a particular time for it.

Believing that he will come:

The twelfth principle is that of the messianic era. This requires us to believe and trust that the messiah will come, and not think that he will come too late: "If it tarries, wait for it" (Habakkuk 2:3). We may not designate a [specific] time for his arrival, nor conjecture based on biblical verses to deduce when it will occur. The Sages say, "May those who calculate the end of days be cursed" (*Sanhedrin* 97b).

Believing that he will be greater than all kings who have preceded him, and that he is descended from the house of David:

We must believe that the messiah will be superior to, and more illustrious than, all other kings in history, as we see in the prophecies of all the prophets from Moses to Malakhi. One who has doubts about him or diminishes his stature rejects the Torah...This principle also includes the belief that the king of Israel may come only from the house of David, descended from Solomon. Anyone who opposes this family has rejected God and the words of His prophets.

(Rambam, *Commentary on the Mishna, Sanhedrin* 10:1)

Further reading: For more on the coming of the messiah, see *A Concise Guide to the Sages*, p. 391.

Belief in the coming of the messiah stems from belief in the prophetic texts, which itself is a Torah commandment. Nevertheless, one who does not believe in his coming, but does believe in divine reward and punishment of another kind, is not considered as one who rejects a fundamental principle of the Torah.

Belief in the messiah stems from belief in the prophetic texts:

Faith in the coming of the messiah is incumbent on all who accept the Torah of Moses. This is because the obligation to believe the statements of the prophets is explicitly stated in the Torah: "him you shall heed" (Deuteronomy 18:15), and the prophets spoke about the coming of the messiah. It is therefore clear that anyone who does not believe in his coming rejects the statements of the prophets and has violated a Torah commandment.

The importance of belief in divine reward and punishment:

Nevertheless, belief in the coming of the messiah is not a principle that amounts to a rejection of the entire Torah if one does not subscribe to it. Belief in [divine] reward is essential for every believing Jew and rejecting this principle is equivalent to rejecting the foundation of belief in God. Yet if one believes that reward is only for souls in the World to Come, or that it is physical, and [relates] to the resurrection of the dead, then even if he does not believe that there is [divine] reward in this world, he has not rejected the foundation, because he believes in the general principle of reward and punishment, although he disputes one type of reward.

(Rav Yosef Albo, *Sefer HaIkkarim* 4:42)

The Purpose of Creation

The purpose of Creation is for this world, a place of darkness and of forces of evil, to become a dwelling place for God, i.e., for God's light to shine and be revealed in the world. In the messianic era, and after the resurrection of the dead, Creation will be brought to its ultimate purpose and perfection. The physical body, and the physical world, will be refined, and we will be able to receive the revelation of the divine light. The way to bring about the purification of the world is through the mitzvot that we fulfill during the exile.

The purpose of Creation is for God's light to illuminate the darkness of this world:

The saying of the Sages is well known (*Tanḥuma, Naso* 24): The purpose of the creation of this world is due to the desire of the Holy One, blessed be He, to have a dwelling place in the lower world... so that God's infinite light will shine in place of darkness and of the "other side" [i.e., the forces of evil and unholiness], throughout this world.

During the messianic era there will be a perfect revelation of light:

It is known that the messianic era, and especially when the dead are revived, constitutes the purpose and completion of the creation of this world, and the reason it was originally created.... The physical aspect of the human body and of the world will then become refined and will be able to receive the revealed light of God that will shine upon the Jewish people through the Torah which is called "strength," [because it gives us the ability to receive this light]. Due to the abundance of light shining upon the Jewish people, the darkness of the nations will be illuminated as well, as it is written, "Nations will walk by your light" (Isaiah 60:3).

The future revelation of God's light depends on our actions in the present:

This final perfection that will occur in the messianic era and at the resurrection of the dead, i.e., the revelation of God's infinite light in this physical world, depends on our actions and our service of God throughout the duration of the exile.

(Rabbi Shneur Zalman of Liadi, *Tanya, Likutei Amarim* 36–37)

Awaiting the Messiah

One must internalize and contemplate how wonderful the messianic era will be. This is the way to fill a person with confidence in the redemption and anticipation of its arrival, so that he will desire it with all his heart.

One has only to instill in his heart the belief in the principle of the coming of the redeemer, which is one of the thirteen principles of faith. He should consider the salvation, the goodness, and the perfection, both spiritual and physical, which will come to the Jewish people in those days. Then he will desire it with great yearning, love, and devotion, saying, "If only the redemption would come soon and in my days!" He will be like a person who has a beloved and whose soul is bound to hers. All of his desire is for her, and all of his thoughts are upon her, without interruption. Such should be his deep desire for those days [i.e., for the messianic era], to attain perfection of the body and the soul, and to emulate his Creator by understanding the hidden mysteries of His Torah. In this way he will be considered as someone who anticipates the redemption all of his life.

(Rabbi Eliyahu HaKohen, *Shevet Musar* 51)

The Nature and Role of the Messiah

The messiah will be wiser than King Solomon. He will be a prophet whose prophecy will be on a level approaching that of Moses. He will build the Temple, gather in the Jewish people to the Land of Israel, and re-establish Torah law as the law of the land.

The messiah will teach the way of God:

That king who will arise from the descendants of David will be even wiser than Solomon, and a great prophet, close to [the level of] Moses, our teacher. Accordingly, he will teach the people and instruct them concerning the path of God, and all the gentile nations will come to hear him.

His task is to restore the Jewish royal dynasty, rebuild the Temple, and institute the observance of all Torah commandments:

In the future, the anointed king[11] will arise and restore the dynasty of David to its original sovereignty. He will rebuild the Temple and gather in the dispersed of Israel. In his days, all Torah laws will be restored to their previous state. Offerings will be brought, and sabbatical years and jubilee years will be observed in accordance with all the details set out in the Torah.

We will recognize the messiah, not through miracles that he will perform, but because of the role he will fulfill:

You should not think that the messiah will need to perform signs and wonders, create new physical phenomena in the world, revive the dead, or anything like that.... If a king arises from the house of David who studies Torah and performs mitzvot like his ancestor David did, in accordance with both the Written and the Oral Torah, and he compels all of Israel to walk in [the way of Torah] and to strengthen the breaches [in their Torah observance], and he fights the wars of God, he may be presumed to be the messiah. If he does all of this successfully and overcomes all the nations around him

11. The Hebrew word for messiah is *mashiah*, meaning anointed. The messiah is often refered to in rabbinic texts as *melekh hamashiah*, meaning the anointed king.

and builds the Temple on its site and gathers the dispersed of Israel, then he is certainly the messiah. If he does not succeed in all this, or if he is killed, it is clear that he was not the one promised by the Torah. Rather, he is like all the proper and worthy kings of the dynasty of David who have died.

(Rambam, *Mishneh Torah, Hilkhot Teshuva* 9:2; *Hilkhot Melakhim* 11:1–4)

Further reading: For more on the Third Temple, see p. 163.

The Messiah's Identity

The messiah will not be an angel, but a human just like anyone else. However, his character will be saintly, and he will grow even further in his righteousness. When the time comes, he will become the redeemer and will be given the unique soul of the messiah.

The messiah will certainly be human, a righteous person who is born from a man and a woman. But on that day he will grow in righteousness ... and then, on that day, at the very end, the soul of his soul, which has been kept in the Garden of Eden, will arrive and will be given to this righteous man, and he will then become the redeemer.

(Rabbi Ḥayyim Vital, *Arba Me'ot Shekel Kesef*, p. 78)

Just as Moses did not know that he would be the one to redeem the children of Israel, until the time for the redemption came, the messiah, too, will not know that he is the redeemer. In every generation there is one who is worthy to be the redeemer should the time for redemption come and should that generation deserve to be redeemed.

The messiah will not be aware of his role until the time of the redemption arrives:

Regarding the coming of the son of David, I must explain that Moses, our teacher, who was the first redeemer, reached the age of eighty years old and did not know or sense that he would be the redeemer of Israel. Even when the Holy One, blessed be He, said to him, "Go and I will send you to Pharaoh" (Exodus 3:10), he refused and did not want to accept it upon himself. So too will it be, God willing, for the final redeemer.

In every generation there is a Jew who is worthy to be the messiah:

Once the Temple was destroyed, an individual was immediately born who was worthy, due to his righteousness, to be a redeemer, so that if the time were to come, God would reveal Himself to him and send him, and then the spirit of the messiah, which was concealed above until the time for its coming, would awaken in him. This is what we saw with King Saul after he was anointed: The spirit of sovereignty and the divine spirit, which he had not felt beforehand, came over him. This is how it was for the first redeemer, and

Torah Concepts

this is how it will be for the final redeemer, and the righteous one himself will not know [until that time that he is to be the redeemer]. Due to our many sins, numerous potential redeemers have already died and, although they were worthy, we have not merited that the spirit of the messiah was awakened in them, because the generation was not worthy. But when the time comes, God willing, God will reveal Himself to him as He did to Moses at the burning bush, and He will send him [to redeem the Jewish people].

(Rabbi Moshe Sofer, *Responsa Ḥatam Sofer* 6:98)

What Will the Messianic Era Be Like?

In the messianic era, there will be no more war, hatred, or strife. There will be great abundance, which will enable everyone to engage in the Torah and its wisdom, and the knowledge of God will fill the earth. Nevertheless, there will be no change in the natural order of the world, and nothing new will be created.

The physical world continues as usual:

Do not think that in the messianic era any aspect of the world's physical nature will be negated, or that there will be anything new in creation. Rather, the world will continue in its normal way. When it says in Isaiah, "Wolf will reside with sheep, and leopard will lie down with kid" (11:6), this is a metaphor. The meaning is that the Jewish people will live securely with those who are wicked, and who are likened to the wolf and the leopard.... They will all return to the true faith and will not steal or destroy, but will, together with the Jewish people, peacefully eat that which is permitted, as it is stated, "A lion, like the ox, will eat straw" (Isaiah 11:7). The same is true of all other similar matters that concern the messiah; they are metaphors, and in the days of the messiah everyone will know what the metaphors were and what they alluded to.

In the days of the messiah, people will be free to study Torah:

The Sages and prophets did not yearn for the messianic era so that they could rule over the world, subjugate the gentiles, be praised by the nations, or eat, drink, and rejoice. Rather, it was so that they would be free to engage in the Torah and its wisdom, with no one oppressing or preventing them. This in turn is so that they would merit life in the World to Come...

The world will be filled with knowledge of God:

At that time there will be no hunger, war, envy, or rivalry. Prosperity will abound, and all delights will be as commonplace as dust. The entire world

Torah Concepts

will be occupied only with coming to know God. Consequently, the Jews will become exceedingly wise. They will know concealed matters and will attain an understanding of their Creator to the fullest extent that humans are able to do so; as it is stated (Isaiah 11:9), "For the earth will be filled with knowledge of the Lord, as the water covers the sea."

(Rambam, *Mishneh Torah, Hilkhot Melakhim* 12:1–5)

The meaning of the rectification of Creation is that there will be a tremendous amount of good, for both the body and the soul. Our inclination for good will grow stronger, and there will be no forces (physical or spiritual) that cause damage or loss. All hearts will be full of wisdom and everyone will receive the divine spirit.

During his days, and under his influence, the Jewish people will undergo a tremendous rectification, and all of creation will follow them. Good will abound on all sides, and evil will depart altogether, both from matters of the soul and matters of the body. The heart of stone will become a heart of flesh; people's inclination toward good will be heightened, and they will not be drawn after the physical at all. Rather, they will always turn toward service of God and toward the Torah, and they will be strengthened by it. At the same time, tranquility and prosperity will grow, and there will be no harm or loss...There will be no foolishness in the world; rather, all hearts will be filled with wisdom, and the divine spirit will envelop all flesh. Everyone will merit this without difficulty.

(Rabbi Moshe Ḥayyim Luzzatto, *Ma'amar HaIkkarim*)

We should not fear the coming of the messiah, as the redemption does not mean leaving behind the life and activities of the exile; rather, it is the liberation and redemption of that reality. Redemption, *geula*, is the same word in Hebrew as exile, *gola*, but with an additional letter *alef*, representing the revelation of divine truth. Redemption illuminates the existing world with a holy light.

Redemption is the revelation of the true, spiritual reality:

Redemption does not mean that by emerging from the exile we are abandoning life, the activities and the world that existed before, during the exile. On the contrary; redemption means that reality, which was suppressed by the exile, is... liberated.... All good things from the exile will remain in the future, but their exiled status will be removed; the concealment that covered up their true, spiritual states will be abolished.

Redemption, *geula*, is the revelation of the divine (the letter *alef*), in the exile, *gola*:

The idea of redemption is to elevate life in the exile by liberating all elements of the exile, and thereby creating redemption. By revealing within all the elements of exile, *gola*, the letter *alef* representing the master, *aluf*, of the world, we remove the concealment that covers up the reality and true purpose of the exile. We reveal the *aluf* [namely, the divine light] within it, such that redemption, *geula*, is created from *gola*. *Geula* is the revelation of the *alef* (*aluf*) in the *gola*. This means the revelation of the truth and spirituality of every aspect and activity of the exile, the revelation of the divine in all of the world's concerns.

Do not fear the coming of the messiah:

Based on what we saw above, there is an answer to all those who are alarmed and confused.... They ask what will happen, if the messiah suddenly comes, with regard to all the activities and interests they have engaged in during the many years of exile, e.g., the businesses they established, the property and assets they amassed, their friends and connections? The answer is that there is nothing to fear! Redemption does not mean the negation of the way we live in this world, i.e., the removal of the good things that we acquired (in accordance with the Torah) during the exile. On the contrary, the redemption includes all the good aspects of the exile, but they are elevated to a state of redemption, to their most true and complete state.

(Rabbi Menaḥem Mendel Schneerson, *Torat Menaḥem* 5751, vol. 3, p. 178)

Further reading: For more on the return of prophecy in the messianic era, see p. 210.

The followers of the Tzemaḥ Tzedek (the third Lubavitcher rebbe, Rabbi Menaḥem Mendel Schneerson, 1789–1866) were once sitting together at a gathering, discussing the idea of anticipating the arrival of the messiah. One hasid related that Rabbi Shneur Zalman of Liadi, the author of the *Tanya*, was once asked how the obligation to anticipate the arrival of the messiah could be consistent with the statement of the Sages that he will come when no one expects him. If we are indeed awaiting and expecting him at all times, how could we ever be distracted?

Rabbi Shneur Zalman answered, "These two things do not contradict each other. The messiah whom we wait for, and whom we imagine, will never come. The actual messiah who does come, is one that no one is expecting; therefore, the arrival of this particular anointed one will be entirely unexpected."

The redemption of Israel will occur like this: When the sun of redemption begins to shine on them, sorrow after sorrow will come upon them, and darkness after darkness. While they are in this state, God's light will shine upon them.

(*Zohar Ḥadash*, Genesis 6:1)

The messiah comes to cause the righteous to repent.

(*Zohar* 3:153b)

Since Creation, humans have been able to do as they wished, i.e., to be righteous or wicked...but in the messianic era they will naturally choose that which is good for them. Their hearts will not desire what is not proper; they will not wish for such things at all.

(Ramban, Deuteronomy 30:6)

[In the messianic era] gentiles will continually be arriving in Jerusalem. The gates of Jerusalem will therefore always be open, day and night; they will never close.

(Abravanel, *Mashmia Yeshua, Nevua* 12)

Trust in God

Trust in God frees a person from having to worry about worldly matters. It enables one to engage in Torah and the service of God. One who trusts in God knows that everything He does for human beings is for their ultimate good. Nevertheless, it is not enough merely to trust. We must put in effort and act to attain what we need, for example, we must work in order to make a living. Our efforts are not the true source of our livelihood, as everything comes from the hand of God, but they are nonetheless essential.

Even if one trusts in God, he must not expose himself to danger unnecessarily, because God desires that people keep themselves safe. Trust in God enables abundance to come from above at the time and place it is needed. It is precisely the fact that a person trusts in God that leads God to be good to him.

What Is Trust in God?

One who trusts in God does not worry about worldly matters, and does not go further than necessary to seek his livelihood. He does not need to perform exhausting labor. If something unfortunate occurs in his business dealings, he does not become too upset. One who trusts in God rejoices, because he trusts that everything God does is for his ultimate benefit.

The benefits of trusting in God:

The benefits of trusting in God include: (1) Mental rest from worldly concerns; relief from the anxiety and distress caused by the need to satisfy one's physical desires; having quiet, security, and serenity in life... (2) Rest from traveling far, which wears out the body and shortens life... (3) Rest for both the body and soul from performing difficult tasks and from work that exhausts the body; freedom from the need to serve kings, follow their bureaucracy, and their corrupt officials. One who trusts in God chooses a livelihood that brings greater rest for his body, a good reputation for himself, freedom for his mind, and that is best suited to fulfilling his obligations arising from the Torah and his faith. For his actions are not the cause and will not add anything to or subtract anything from his portion; rather, it is all by the decree of God... (4) Less worry with regard to business dealings, e.g., if one is left with [unsold] merchandise, or cannot collect a debt, or if he gets sick; for he knows that the Creator manages his concerns more than he does, and that He chooses better for him than that which he would choose for himself... (5) Joy at everything that comes to him [in life], even if it goes against his nature, because he trusts in God that He does only good for him in all things, like a mother who has compassion on her child as, against his will, she washes and diapers him, and tightens and loosens his clothes.

The nature of trust in God:

What is trust in God? It is spiritual tranquility for the one who trusts. His heart relies on the One in whom he trusts; he believes that He will do what is good and right for him in the matter of that trust, to the extent of his [limited] ability to understand what is [actually] good for him.

(Rabbeinu Baḥya ibn Pakuda, *Ḥovot HaLevavot* 4: Introduction, 1)

Further reading: For more on trust in God, see *A Concise Guide to the Sages*, p. 381.

Trusting in God means knowing that He can alter nature's course and change a person's lot in life. One must trust in God even when he is in distress, as God knows what is good for a person, even better than he himself does. Suffering occurs in order to bring people closer to God.

The Holy One, blessed be He, is all-powerful, and can deliver people from any situation:

Trust in God...means that a person should know in his heart that everything is in the hands of Heaven; it is in God's hands to change nature and to alter fate. Nothing can stop Him from an act of salvation, large or small. Even when misfortune is close by, God's salvation is at hand, for He is all-powerful. Even if one sees the sword upon his neck, he should not give up on the possibility of deliverance...

God sends us what is best for us:

One of the aspects of trust in God is that one should have no doubts with regard to his trust. Even if many evils and troubles find him, he should exert himself to serve God and to trust in Him absolutely, for his reward will be multiplied. God will choose good things for him, and the choice is not in his hands. For sometimes one thinks that he is choosing the right thing when it is in fact the opposite. In this way, every individual must relinquish all of his concerns to God's higher decision, because He, who formed the individual in his mother's womb, is the one who knows what benefits him and what harms him, even more so than he does himself. If a person sees that he has suffered misfortunes, he should consider this as a rebuke from God, for God rebukes those that He loves. Likewise, one should believe that everything is for his benefit, to bring him closer to God and to enlarge his portion in the world of reward.

(Rabbeinu Baḥya ibn Ḥalawa, *Kad HaKemaḥ*, *Bitaḥon*)

Torah Concepts

One who trusts in God engages only in Torah and mitzvot. He does not fear wicked people, nor does he do anything that conflicts with his service of the Creator. There are several ideas that strengthen us in achieving complete trust, including the knowledge that God has mercy on us and that all the good we have was sent by Him. We do not deserve the good that we have received, and we cannot add or detract from that which God has decreed. God can see whether or not a person has complete trust and it remains only for the person to fulfill the will of God.

One who trusts in God is not afraid of anyone:

If one believes in God with a full heart and trusts in Him firmly, that trust will enable him not to fear evil from any person, and likewise, not to serve or try to please another. Such an individual will not place his hopes on another, nor concede to him in a matter that goes against service of the Creator. He will not be afraid by the affairs of others, nor of [the possibility of entering into] disputes with them. If he rebukes others [for their bad deeds] he will not be over-cautious about their honor. If he [justifiably] shames them he will not be embarrassed before them or embellish lies for them.

Seven concepts that strengthen a person's trust in God:

One must study the ideas and concepts that strengthen his heart so that it maintains complete trust in God: (1) One should be fully aware that God has mercy on us more so than any human has. (2) All the good that comes to an individual from his father, mother, siblings, relatives, and friends is [actually] from God, and these people are emissaries of the Omnipresent. (3) One should be aware that all good comes as a result of God's kindness, and not because he is deserving of it. (4) One should be aware that all things in life have limits, and no one can add or take away from that which the Creator has decreed. If the Holy One, blessed be He, decreed that one will have little, he cannot increase the amount. Likewise, one cannot reduce the [amount if he receives] much. If God decrees that something is to occur at a later time, no one can hasten it, nor can one delay [something that is to occur in the near future]. (5) One should be aware that the Creator sees into his mind and knows whether his trust in Him is complete and without pretense. (6) One should accept upon himself to do all that God has commanded him, and to refrain from doing everything He has cautioned him not to do, just as he desires that the Creator will do what he trusts Him to do. (7) One should be aware that the Creator, blessed be He, created human beings with the ability to do many kinds of labor, and He created their sustenance for them, [which is obtained] through great effort and work.

(*Orḥot Tzaddikim, Sha'ar HaSimḥa*)

Faith, Trust, and Our Efforts

In order to trust in God, one must first believe that He is able to provide us with what we need and want. Nevertheless, trust in God is not always the result of having faith, since a person who has faith may still be afraid that he has sinned and that he is therefore unworthy of God's kindness.

Faith in God comes before trust in God:

With regard to faith and trust, one of them requires the other, whereas the opposite is not true. Faith precedes trust, although it does not [inevitably come] with trust, and does not need it in order to exist. On the other hand, the presence of trust indicates the presence of faith; trust cannot precede it or exist without it. Faith is like the tree and trust is like the fruit; one can trust in another only if he believes that the other is capable of fulfilling his requests.

The believer may fear that he is unworthy:

Not every believer has trust in God, because one may be afraid that he has sinned or that he has already received the reward for his good deeds, through miracles that the Creator has performed for him. When he finds himself sinning against the Creator, he does not dare to trust that He will save him or give him his heart's desire. Rather, he endeavors to escape from his troubles and to attain his desires using worldly means... Someone who believes in God may be afraid of the consequences of having sinned, but one who has trust in God is not afraid of the consequences of having sinned.

(Ramban, *HaEmuna VehaBitaḥon* 1)

If a person works and endeavors to sustain himself, this does not mean that he does not have complete trust in God. Taking action is necessary because, after the sin of Adam, God decreed that man would have to put in effort in order to eat. Effort is not the source of our success, but it is impossible to succeed without it. Once effort has been made, there is room for God's blessing, and one no longer needs to over-exert himself. Likewise, avoiding danger does not contradict trust in God, as God wants human beings to keep themselves safe.

One must put in effort to make a living, because this is what God has decreed:

The way to safeguard a person from these troubles is through trust, by casting his burden entirely upon God. One should know that it is impossible that what has been allotted to a person can be diminished in any way, and as our Sages said, "A person's entire livelihood is allocated to him from Rosh HaShana" (*Beitza* 16a). One could remain idle and this decree still would be fulfilled, were it not for the punishment that all mankind previously [received, at the sin of the tree of knowledge]: "By the sweat of your brow shall you eat bread" (Genesis 3:19). Consequently, one is obligated to put in some degree of effort for the sake of his livelihood, as this is what the heavenly King decreed; it is like paying a tax... But it is not that the effort is effective; rather, it is necessary. Once a person has made an effort, he has fulfilled his obligation; there is now room for the blessing of Heaven to rest upon him, and he does not need to spend his days continuing to over-exert himself.

God wants people to look after themselves:

God created human beings with sound intellect and good judgment so that they will follow the right path and guard themselves from harmful elements that were created to punish the wicked. When one does not act wisely and puts himself in danger, this is not trust, but foolishness. Such a person has sinned, as he has gone against the will of the Creator, who wants people to look after themselves.

(Rabbi Moshe Ḥayyim Luzzatto, *Mesilat Yesharim* 21, 9)

Our Trust Directs the Abundance from Above

Divine abundance is constant, but it is not defined in terms of time or place. Trust in God allows abundance from above to enter the limits of time and place, and to have an impact at the time and place where the individual needs it.

Abundance constantly descends from above, but it has no aspect of time. Sometimes, that which one needs now will come in two or three years. But viewing matters with trust in God gives a definition and a time to divine abundance so that it comes at the time and place that one needs it.

(Rabbi Naḥman of Breslov, *Likutei Moharan* 76)

Further reading: For more on earning a living, see p. 237.

Think Positively and Things Will Be Good

When one puts his fate in God's hands and relies, from the depths of his soul, only on Him, God treats him with generosity even if he is unworthy. This is the basis for the hasidic phrase, "Think good and it will be good."

One must cast his fate into God's hands:

The commandment to trust in God... is itself a service of God. It means that a person must rely on the Holy One, blessed be He, to the point that he casts his entire lot into God's hands, as it is written, "Cast your burden upon the Lord" (Psalms 55:23); and that he relies on nothing other than God.

When one relies on God, God is generous toward him:

This itself is the foundation of a person's trust in God – that the Holy One, blessed be He, will do good for him, palpable and revealed good, even if he is unworthy of this kindness.... If a person truly, from the depths of his soul, relies only on the Holy One, blessed be He, such that he is not concerned about anything, then this awakening itself causes the Holy One, blessed be He, to behave toward him in this manner, doing good for him (even if without this trust he is unworthy of it).

Think good and it will be good:

This is the meaning of the statement of the Tzemaḥ Tzedek, "Think good and it will be good." Trust in God itself brings about a positive outcome. This is not an incidental element of trust, but is the very definition of trust, concerning which we were commanded.

(Rabbi Menaḥem Mendel Schneerson, *Likutei Siḥot* 36, p. 1)

The Ba'al Shem Tov was once traveling with the saintly Rabbi Mendel of Be'er. During the journey, Rabbi Mendel became thirsty. The Ba'al Shem Tov said to him, "If you have complete trust in the Holy One, blessed be He, water will certainly appear."

And indeed, they immediately met a gentile, who told them that he had been searching for his escaped horses for three days. They asked him if he had any water, and he brought out a flask and gave some to Rabbi Mendel.

Rabbi Mendel was astonished, and asked, "It is clear to me that this gentile was brought here solely because of me, but why did he have to travel for three days prior to being here?"

The Ba'al Shem Tov replied, "The Holy One, blessed be He, prepared him for you in advance, so that if you had complete trust, your need would be fulfilled immediately."

The Temple

The Temple is the physical place where God's Presence is revealed. There, we serve God and bring offerings, and the *Shekhina*, the Divine Presence, is in a revealed state. At the time of Creation, God placed His *Shekhina* in the physical world, but because of the sins of humankind, it departed. After the Exodus, the children of Israel built the Tabernacle, and the *Shekhina* was present there to a limited extent. Only in the Temple does the *Shekhina* return to its place, and God reveals Himself plainly in this world.

The purpose of the commandment to build a Temple is for us to dedicate the best of our possessions to God, and for Him to reward us for this with revelations of prophecy and answers to our prayers. The act of building the Temple defies those philosophical approaches that maintain that God is distant from us. Due to His love for us, He is revealed to us in a physical space.

Why Does God Need a Temple?

The Temple is not for the Creator, but for us. The purpose of the commandment to build a Temple and to bring offerings is for us to give, to the extent that we are able, our best possessions to God.

People may wonder what the Creator has to do with the Tabernacle, curtain, lamps, and other such items. Logically, God does not require anything; rather, all creatures need Him. But the intention is that His servants will hand over to Him the best of their possessions: meat, wine, oil, incense, wheat, and other pleasant items. They will bring a little of these things, as much as they can, and He will reward them exceedingly, as much as He can.... He will reward them by granting them prophecy from that place.... Likewise, it will be the place through which He answers the prayers of the nation when any trouble befalls them.

(Rav Se'adya Gaon, *Emunot VeDe'ot* 3:10)

Further reading: For more on the Tabernacle and the Temple, see *A Concise Guide to the Torah*, pp. 196, 242, 464; *A Concise Guide to the Sages*, pp. 114, 320.

The Tabernacle and the Temple are where God dwells with us. The philosophical position that God does not oversee what happens in this world, and does not know what happens in it, can easily mislead those who are unlearned. In fact, God, in His kindness, behaves toward us in a manner contrary to that philosophy, dwelling in a specific place, in a tangible way.

The philosophers removed from God the knowledge of what happens in the world and awareness of our actions. Their statements became a stumbling block for the unlearned. Due to the kindness God has for His people, he acts toward them like a doctor who oversees the health of his patient, and He imposes certain actions upon Himself, like a pious and merciful king who sits among his people, in a tent or dwelling, and rejoices with them.

(Rav Yitzḥak Arama, *Akedat Yitzḥak*, Exodus 25:2)

The site of the Temple is the point of connection between this world and the divine abundance that comes from above. When they are worthy, righteous people possess the power to make this world, and their own souls, into a place where God can be present.

The earthly Temple corresponds to the heavenly Temple:

"They shall make for Me a sanctuary" (Exodus 25:8), for that is the gateway to heaven, from which divine abundance is brought down to illuminate the earth. Since the time of Creation, the *Shekhina* has rested in that place. Therefore, the Sages said, "If a person enters the earthly Temple and brings offerings in it, the Holy One, blessed be He, considers them as having entered and brought sacrifices in the heavenly Temple," for it is as though the heavenly Temple and the earthly one stand together.

God dwells in the souls of the Jewish people when they are worthy:

The Tabernacle was erected by Moses, who brought the *Shekhina* down to earth in his merit.... For saintly people have the power to make a spiritual, holy dwelling place in the lower realm, to the point that they become worthy of "And I will dwell among them" (Exodus 25:8), meaning a tangible [presence] and not only a dissemination of heavenly spirituality. The presence of the *Shekhina* is not within the wood or stone [of the Temple], but rather, "among them," if their deeds are worthy of this... God dwells principally in the souls of the righteous, and not in wood and stone.

(Alsheikh, Exodus 25:8)

Further reading: For more on the presence of the *Shekhina* in this world due to saintly people, see *A Concise Guide to the Sages*, p. 179.

Divine Revelation

God brought His *Shekhina*, the revelation of the Divine, into the lower realm. At the time of the Creation, the main presence of the *Shekhina* was on earth, but after the sin of Adam, the first human, it withdrew, and only once the Temple was built did it return to its place there.

When the world was created, the main presence of the *Shekhina* was in the lower realm:

One should know that at the Creation, the main presence of the *Shekhina* was in the lower realm. Everything was created with a clear order and priority – the upper realm [heaven] was allocated to the higher creations and the lower realm [earth] was allocated to the lower creations. When the *Shekhina* was infused into the lower realm, heaven and earth were united.... God was therefore present in perfect balance between the upper and lower realms.

After the sin of the first man, the *Shekhina* departed, and it was partially restored when Moses built the Tabernacle:

When the first human sinned, the presence [of the *Shekhina*] was damaged and the spiritual conduits [for receiving abundance from above] were broken. The *Shekhina* departed, and that which had been bound together [the upper and lower realms] was separated. Abraham, Isaac, and Jacob came and began to draw the *Shekhina* back toward the lower realm.... In their days, it hovered in the air [between worlds] but did not find a proper resting place on earth as it had at the time of Creation. Moses, our teacher, came along, together with all of Israel, and they made the Tabernacle and its vessels. They repaired the damaged [spiritual] conduits, restored the Divine Presence and reconnected to the abundance from above, drawing once again "living waters" from their sources [in Heaven], and returning the *Shekhina* to its dwelling in the lower realm. But this was now in a [mobile] tent, and not imbued in the earth as it had been at the time of Creation. This is the underlying mystical meaning of, "They shall make for Me a sanctuary, and I will dwell among them" (Exodus 25:8).

The building of the Temple by King David and King Solomon restored the *Shekhina* to its place on earth:

David planned the entire design of the Temple, and the significance of each and every item, according to the word of God. It was all in the image of the heavenly structure, [in order to create] a seat and dwelling place for the *Shekhina*. Subsequently, Solomon came and built the Temple, arranging the entire structure as David, his father, had planned, and the *Shekhina* descended and dwelled in the permanent Temple.... The *Shekhina* returned to its resting place on earth, in the permanent Temple. Consequently, the [spiritual] sources and conduits were restored, all pouring blessing into the Temple.

(Rav Yosef Gikatilla, *Sha'arei Ora* 1)

Offerings of the Soul

One of the central elements of the Temple service was the bringing of offerings and, through this spiritual service, people could express their closeness to God. The verse that introduces the section on offerings teaches that closeness to God is dependent only on the individual and his desire to be close; there is nothing external that prevents a person from becoming closer to God.

"When any man...brings [*yakriv*]," when a person comes closer [*yitkarev*] to the divine, then because "of you" [*mikem*] he will become "an offering [*korban*] to the Lord" (Leviticus 1:2). Becoming an offering to God, being close to Him, is dependent on you. For it is known that [the purpose of] offerings is to bring a person's faculties and senses closer [to God], and this verse comes to explain that when one wants to get closer to the Divine, it is "of you," dependent on you. One should not say: How can I become closer to the divine? He may know his own inner self, that he is sullied and degraded as a result of negative actions, and therefore feels extremely far from the Divine. But concerning [the question: How can I become closer to the Divine], it is stated, "of you," it depends upon you.

(Rabbi Yosef Yitzḥak Schneersohn, *Bati LeGani* 5710, ch. 2)

The Third Temple

Unlike the First and Second Temples, which were built by human beings, the Third Temple will be built by God, in Heaven. After bringing it into the world and standing it in its place, He will also build the walls of Jerusalem.

The deeds of the Holy One, blessed be He, are not like the deeds of human beings. When human beings built the earthly Temple, they first built the city walls, and in the end, they built the Temple. The city walls came first, in order to protect them, and afterward came the building of the Temple. The Holy One, blessed be He, is not like this. He builds the Temple first, and in the end, when he brings it down from heaven and puts it in its place, He will build the walls of Jerusalem, the city walls.

(*Zohar* 2:108b)

The Temple is like the heart, from which all other organs receive their vitality; the Temple gives life to the entire world. This is why the Temple is in the center of the world, just as the heart is in the center of the body.

(Maharal, *Gevurot Hashem* 71)

The World to Come

After a person dies, his soul leaves his body and ascends to the spiritual realm. The soul longs to enter the Garden of Eden, where it will be able to experience the radiance of the *Shekhina*, the Divine Presence. Is the Garden of Eden only for the righteous, or is it possible for wicked people to attain life in the World to Come as well?

There are souls that will immediately arrive at their place in the Garden of Eden, but there are others that will first require cleansing in Gehenna in order to later unite with God. Although the objective of this cleansing is one of compassion, it is nonetheless a difficult and painful process. Furthermore, a soul that did not fulfill its purpose on earth is required to return.

What Is the World to Come?

The World to Come is a place where we can comprehend God, and the greatest punishment possible is being denied this experience. There is nothing like this reward among the pleasures of the physical world.

The World to Come is eternal, spiritual life, reserved for the righteous:

The good that awaits the righteous is life in the World to Come. This is life without death, and good without evil.... The reward of the righteous is that they will receive this sweetness and live with this goodness. The punishment of the wicked is that they will not receive this life [in the World to Come]; rather, they will be cut off [they will cease to exist] and will die. Anyone who does not merit this life is truly dead; such a person does not experience eternal life, but is cut off due to his wickedness and ceases to exist, as happens to an animal.

In the World to Come there are no bodies or physical pleasures; rather, there is spiritual understanding and insight:

In the World to Come there are no bodies or physical forms, only the souls of the righteous, just like the ministering angels, who do not have bodies. Since there are no bodies, there is no food or drink, nor anything else that human bodies require in this world, and no physical experiences occur there, such as sitting, standing, sleeping, death, sadness, and laughter. The Sages said, "In the World to Come there is no eating, drinking, or sexual intercourse. Rather, the righteous sit with their crowns upon their heads, basking in the radiance of the *Shekhina*" (*Berachot* 17a)...What does "basking in the radiance of the *Shekhina*" mean? It means that they grasp the truth of the Holy

One, blessed be He, in a way that they were unable to when they were in the darkness of the lowly body.

The worst punishment is for a soul to be denied existence in the World to Come:

The greatest of all retribution is the soul being cut off, not meriting that life [in the World to Come]...This loss is what the prophets described metaphorically as "the pit of destruction" (Psalms 55:24), "oblivion" (Psalms 88:12), "inferno" (Isaiah 30:33), and "leech" (Proverbs 30:15). Terms of total destruction are used to refer to it, for it is a destruction without subsequent revival, and a loss that can never be restored.

Fools believe that the reward for performing mitzvot is physical pleasure:

This [reward of] goodness must not be regarded lightly. You should not imagine that, when a person lives entirely in the way of truth, there is no reward for their mitzvot, other than eating and drinking good food, engaging in sexual intercourse with beautiful people, wearing embroidered garments and those made of linen, living in dwellings made of ivory, and using vessels of silver and gold.... Wise and understanding people know that all these things are empty and worthless. They give great pleasure in this world only because we have bodies, and these are all physical needs. The soul desires them only because of the body's needs, so that its desires will be fulfilled and it will remain healthy. Once there is no body, all these things will be worthless.

There is no way that we, in this world, can truly comprehend the essence of life in the World to Come:

With regard to the tremendous good that the soul will experience in the World to Come, there is no way to grasp it in this world, as in this world we know only the pleasures of the body, which are what we desire. But that good [of the World to Come] is exceedingly great and cannot be compared to the good of this world except by way of metaphor. It is impossible to truly compare the spiritual good of the World to Come to the physical good of this world, e.g., food and drink, for the good [of the World to Come] is immeasurably greater; it is incomparable and inconceivable.

It is called the World to Come because we enter it after life in this world:

The Sages did not use the expression, "World to Come," to imply that it does not currently exist, or that this world is going to be destroyed and then that world will emerge. This is not the case since it does exist currently...They called it the World to Come because that life [in the World to Come] comes to an individual after life in this world, where we exist with both a body and a soul, and where everyone must live first.

(Rambam, *Mishneh Torah, Hilkhot Teshuva* 8:1–6)

Further reading: For the stages of the soul's departure from this world, see above, p. 26.

What Is Gehenna?

Suffering in Gehenna is not physical, but spiritual. When the soul yearns to join with its heavenly source but cannot yet because of its sins, it must undergo afflictions.

Punishment in Gehenna is not physical:

What is this judgment called Gehenna? If you say that the punishment comes to a person's body after his death, his body is as lifeless as a stone, and whether you burn his bones into lime or anoint them with balsam [oil]... which preserves them, it is of no difference to the stone. This is the same with regard to the body of a righteous person and that of a wicked person after their deaths. Furthermore, how could this body be in Gehenna, but that one in the good of the World to Come, when they are buried before you in one grave or concealed in a chamber in one coffin? Rather, the punishment is entirely spiritual.

The soul yearns to ascend and connect to holiness, and it is afflicted when it is unable to do so:

The punishment of Gehenna comes to a person immediately after death. As soon as the wicked person dies, his soul is tied to a wheel of fire, and it then joins the river of fire that emerges from beneath the heavenly throne of glory. The river descends to Gehenna, and the soul descends with it... In its essence, this soul, which returns to the element of fire and is attached to it, longs to ascend and to connect to the heavens, but the coarseness of the individual's sins separates [the soul] from its Creator, preventing this from occurring. Instead, the soul is pulled into the fire of Gehenna and joined to it. Having this wish denied is an affliction that brings immeasurable suffering, in addition to the suffering of Gehenna. This is what is meant by the excision of the soul; it is cut off from its root like a branch that is chopped from a tree.

(Ramban, *Torat HaAdam, Sha'ar HaGemul*)

The Sages called the suffering of sinners in Gehenna "the pocket of the slingshot." The soul is propelled in two different directions: toward the desires it became accustomed to in the [physical] world, which it is now unable to satisfy; and toward its yearning to connect to God, which it has not yet learned to do.

After death, the soul of the sinner longs for spiritual elevation but is unable to attain it:

This is the anguish and punishment of the soul: When a person is alive, he pursues his desires and physical concerns, and his soul is distracted from doing God's will and becomes accustomed to acting in accordance with the body's inclinations, which are the opposite of its own natural inclinations. When the soul separates from the body, it yearns for the things it was accustomed to, but it does not possess the means to attain them [because it no longer has a body]. By its own nature, it is inclined to embrace heavenly pursuits, which are [entirely] different from physical ones, and it yearns for them, but it does not have the basic ability, the education, or the experience of serving God, and someone who has not prepared and trained his soul for this cannot attain that pleasure.... Consequently, the soul yearns for two opposites simultaneously, the high and the low, one as a result of [the soul's] nature and the other as a result of [its] experience. It does not possess the means to attain the lower, nor the preparation to attain the higher.

The "pocket of the slingshot" refers to the affliction of the soul that yearns for two opposites:

This causes suffering that is more painful than any suffering in the [physical] world; more than any kind of broken bone, than being burned by fire, than the terrible suffering of the freezing cold, than being attacked with knives and swords, and than being bitten by snakes and scorpions...This is as our Sages said in tractate *Shabbat* (153b), "Rabbi Eliezer says, 'The souls of the righteous are preserved beneath the heavenly throne of glory...but for those of the wicked...one angel stands at one end of the world and another angel stands at the other end of the world and they sling the souls from one to the other, as it is stated, "The souls of your enemies may He cast away as from the pocket of a slingshot" (I Samuel 25:29).'" This alludes to [the soul's] two opposing desires.

(Rav Yosef Albo, *Sefer HaIkkarim* 4:33)

The sinner damages the root of his soul and strengthens the forces of impurity. While still alive, he is already in a state of Gehenna, which surrounds him while he sins.

With regard to the punishment of Gehenna, the sin itself is the sinner's punishment.... When a person does something that is prohibited by one of the negative commandments, the [resulting] damage and destruction is immediately inscribed above, heaven forbid, in the root of his [soul].... He [thereby] raises and strengthens the forces of impurity and spiritual negativity, may God protect us, from which he draws a spirit of impurity upon himself, and this enwraps him while he performs the sin. After he has performed the sin, the spirit of impurity returns to its place. As such during his lifetime, he is truly in Gehenna, which surrounds him when he sins, but he does not feel it until after he dies, when he will be trapped in the net that he has prepared: [A net] comprised of the forces of impurity and the demons that were created by his own actions.

(Rabbi Ḥayyim of Volozhin, *Nefesh HaḤayyim* 1:12)

The Function of Gehenna

The fire of Gehenna is in fact an act of kindness that is performed for the soul so that it will be able to receive a proper reward:

Even when [a soul] enters Gehenna and the fire purifies it, this is in order to cleanse and purify.... The Holy One, blessed be He, acts kindly toward the soul, washing away its stains in order to give it a proper reward. This is like a mother who, by washing off her child's dirt, is acting kindly toward him. If she leaves him in his filth, this is cruelty, as his body [his health] will deteriorate. Even though the child cries and is miserable, it is all for his own good.

(Rabbi Eliyahu de Vidas, *Reshit Ḥokhma, Sha'ar HaTeshuva* 3:38)

The afflictions of Gehenna are intended to rectify the soul so that it can ascend to the Garden of Eden:

It was said with regard to *Aher*,[12] "It is better that he be judged and [then] be brought into the World to Come [the Garden of Eden]" (*Ḥagiga* 15b). All the suffering of Gehenna is worthwhile so that the soul can take pleasure in the Garden of Eden. It is impossible for it to attain this delight until it has been cleansed by means of some amount of suffering.

(Rabbi Shneur Zalman of Liadi, *Torah Or*, Exodus 73:2)

---

12. This refers to Elisha ben Avuya, who learned Torah and then renounced his faith.

Gehenna achieves purification of the soul. Its purpose is to cleanse the soul from the evil that clings to it:

The purpose of Gehenna is to purify the soul from the filth of evil within it.... For the soul to receive the light of heavenly pleasure [in the Garden of Eden] and bask [in the radiance of the *Shekhina*], it first needs to undergo purification in the fire of Gehenna, which separates the evil from the good.

(Tzemaḥ Tzedek, *Or HaTorah*, Exodus 11)

Further reading: Read about the life and death of *Aher* in *A Concise Guide to the Sages*, p. 339.

A Respite from Gehenna

Shabbat is a day of rest in Gehenna as well, but only for those who observed it.

On Shabbat the wicked in Gehenna are allowed to rest:

Every Shabbat evening, once the day has been sanctified, the criers pass through all parts of Gehenna, [proclaiming,] "Let the punishments of the wicked cease, as the holy King has come and the day is sanctified, and Shabbat provides protection to everyone." The punishments immediately cease and the wicked ones receive a respite.

One who does not observe Shabbat will never have rest:

But the fire of Gehenna does not abate for those who never kept Shabbat. All the evil people of Gehenna ask about those [individuals], "In what way are these people, who have no rest, different from all the other wicked people who are here?" And the ones who inflict punishment answer them, "These are the wicked people who rejected the Holy One, blessed be He, and transgressed the entire Torah. Because they did not keep Shabbat there [in this world], they will never have any rest."

(*Zohar* 2:151a)

Reincarnation

If a person did not complete that which was assigned to him in this world, his soul must return to the world in a different body until his rectification is complete. A person stops being reincarnated only once all parts of his soul have been rectified.

If a person's *nefesh* [lowest level soul] was not entirely rectified the first time, and he passed away, that *nefesh* must return in a reincarnated form. This can occur several times, until all of its needs are entirely rectified. Then, even though it has been perfected, the *ruaḥ* [higher level soul] does not enter it unless there is a pressing need, due to the fact that the *nefesh* was rectified only through reincarnation.... Therefore, [the individual] needs to die, and his *nefesh* will then be reincarnated again and will receive its *ruaḥ*. Once the *ruaḥ* is rectified, he will [again] need to die and be reincarnated, and the *neshama* [highest level soul] will enter him, like the *ruaḥ* did. But if the *ruaḥ* was not rectified, the *nefesh* and the *ruaḥ* will need to be reincarnated together, perhaps several times, until the *ruaḥ* is rectified. The person will then die, and the *nefesh* and the *ruaḥ* will be reincarnated together with the *neshama*, [and this will be repeated] until all three are rectified. After this there will no longer be a need for reincarnation, because once the *nefesh* is rectified, the person is fully complete.

(Rabbi Yitzḥak Luria, *Sha'ar HaGilgulim*, Introduction 2)

Further reading: Regarding into which body an individual whose soul has been reincarnated several times will be resurrected at the resurrection of the dead, see p. 298.

Every Jew bears a mark from God. For this reason, God does not give up on any Jew. He will reincarnate a person many times until that person rectifies himself and merits life in the World to Come.

You know the mystical teaching with regard to reincarnation, that one can be reincarnated from mineral to vegetable [or from vegetable to animal, or from animal to human], until he is finally rectified. This is as the Sage wrote in the mishna, "All of the Jewish people [have a share in the World to Come]" (Mishna *Sanhedrin* 10:1). Although one person rectifies himself within a short period while another takes a long time, they will [both] ultimately be counted among the righteous. For this reason, the Holy One, blessed be He, troubles Himself, as it were, with [reincarnating] wicked people, to rectify them. The Sage explains [in the continuation of the mishna], "As it is stated, 'And your people, they are all righteous, they will inherit the land forever, the scion of My planting, My handiwork, to be adorned in splendor' (Isaiah 60:21)," That is to say, after their sins are rectified [they will enter the World to Come]. Why? Because they are "the scion of My planting." For He is eternal and they are the reflection of His essential light, and all who breathe, ultimately draw breath from God Himself.

(Rabbi Yitzḥak Luria, *Likutei HaShas, Avot*)

The punishment of Gehenna serves to cleanse the soul of the impurities that have stuck to it, but it does not rectify the soul itself. For this, one needs to be reincarnated.

Gehenna has the power only to eliminate contamination [due to sinful acts]...but not to perfect [the soul]. Therefore, with regard to one whose sins did not allow him to perfect his soul with Torah and mitzvot, Gehenna cannot help him to do this, as it can be done only through Torah and mitzvot. Therefore, after [going through] Gehenna, where the contamination is weakened so that [in future] he will not be caught up in the web of [his] previous sins, he will need to be reincarnated in order to complete his soul.... Without Gehenna, it would be impossible for sinners to be reincarnated, as [the cleansing process of Gehenna serves to halt] the continuation of their sins. Gehenna completes the rectification only for someone who has already perfected his soul in this or a previous reincarnation, but who has become contaminated due to his sins. Gehenna cleans these out entirely, and he ascends, cleansed and in peace, to his place [in the Garden of Eden].

(Rabbi Shmuel Bornsztain, *Shem MiShmuel*, Exodus 5672)

Rabbi Elimelekh of Lizhensk was known for his great humility. He would often denounce himself harshly. After his death, the *Maggid* (preacher) of Koznitz said that when Rabbi Elimelekh came before the heavenly court, he was asked about his deeds in this world, and he cried out, "I did nothing! I did not pray! I did not study! Nothing, nothing, nothing!"

They told him, "Then you must go to Gehenna."

He was given accompanying angels, who immediately brought him to the Garden of Eden, although he believed that they were bringing him to Gehenna. When he saw the Garden of Eden in all its splendor and glory, he exclaimed with excitement, "See how benevolent the Creator is! If this is what Gehenna looks like, imagine what the Garden of Eden looks like!"

A righteous person loves life in this world only because it is a step from which to ascend to the World to Come.

(Rav Se'adya Gaon, *Emunot VeDe'ot* 10)

The World to Come is immense and unending...a great light that does not resemble the light of this world.

(*Sefer HaYashar* 14)

Further reading: By saying Kaddish, those who are still alive can benefit the soul of the deceased in the World to Come; see above, p. 29; *A Concise Guide to Halakha*, p. 504.

Divine Providence

The fact that there is reward and punishment for our actions brings us to the realization that God extends His providence to us, in the sense of "an eye that sees, and an ear that hears" (Mishna *Avot* 2:1). Providence is not merely passive observation; if a person connects strongly to God, divine providence can save him from natural disasters. Even in a case where a divine decree is being imposed upon the entire world, an individual could potentially be elevated above it and saved from it.

Divine providence is not limited to human beings, but pertains to all elements of creation, as God is continuously creating the world. The Ba'al Shem Tov elucidated the principle of divine providence, asserting that God does not merely watch over the various species of animals and plants in a broad sense; rather, every miniscule event that occurs in the world is connected to His plan for creation as a whole. When we understand that in order to extend His providence to the upper worlds, God "lowers" Himself, it becomes clear that He also lowers Himself in order to govern each one of His creations on earth.

The Meaning of Divine Providence

The awareness that God extends His providence to the actions of human beings makes those who are devoted to Him rejoice in their good deeds, and likewise, it makes them ashamed of their evil deeds. In contrast to the handiwork of a human being, which exists even when it is separated from the one who produced it, creation is perpetually connected to God; this is divine providence. If God withdrew His providence from creation, the entire world would be destroyed.

An eye that sees:

A pious person does not perform one act, think one thought, or speak one word, without [considering] his belief that there is an eye that sees him, repays him for the good and for the bad, and calls him to account for anything objectionable in his speech or actions. Therefore, he walks and sits as one in awe. He trembles and is at times ashamed of his actions, just as he rejoices and delights, and his spirit is elevated, when he does good.... As a result of his faith, a pious person fulfills the saying of the Sages, "Keep your eye on three things, and you will not come to sin: Know what is above you: An eye that sees, and an ear that hears, and that all your deeds are recorded in a book" (Mishna *Avot* 2:1).

The difference between the handiwork of humans and the creations of God:

No part of creation is like the product of human labor. A person labors, for example, to build a mill. Even when he leaves it, the mill will continue to do the work it was designed for. The Creator, on the other hand, creates every organ and designates abilities to each one, and He also controls these abilities at every instant. Imagine Him removing His providence from them for one moment: The entire world would be lost.

(Rav Yehuda HaLevi, *Kuzari* 3:11)

Further reading: For more on the importance of reflecting on the fact that God is watching over us and sees all of our actions, see p. 192; *A Concise Guide to the Sages*, p. 367.

General Providence

God extends His providence to human beings and judges them in accordance with what they deserve. This is, however, the case only for humans; God watches over animals and plants in a broader, more general way. Divine providence is also proportional to the individual's degree of closeness and attachment to God, which is itself related to his intellect. Therefore, even with regard to humans, there are various levels of divine providence, and someone who is on a higher spiritual level merits a greater degree of divine providence.

Everything that happens to people is in accordance with divine justice:

Another fundamental principle taught by the Law of Moses is this: Injustice cannot be ascribed to God in any way whatsoever. All evils and afflictions, as well as all kinds of happiness of man, whether they concern one individual person or a community, occur in accordance with divine justice; they are the result of strict judgment in which there is no wrong whatsoever. Even when a person suffers pain from a thorn which pricks his hand, although it is immediately taken out, it is a punishment that has been inflicted on him for sin, and the slightest pleasure he enjoys is a reward [for some good action].

Individual providence is extended only to human beings:

I believe that divine providence in this low, or sublunary, portion of the world is concerned with details of the human species alone. It is only with this species that all that happens in life to individuals, their good and evil fortunes, are the result of divine justice, in accordance with the words, "For all His ways are judgment" (Deuteronomy 32:4). But I agree with Aristotle regarding all other living creatures, and *a fortiori* regarding plants and similar species. For I do not believe at all that [specific] divine providence is responsible for a certain leaf falling [from a tree], nor do I hold that when a certain spider catches a certain fly, it is the direct result of a special decree and the specific will of God at that moment.... In all these cases the action is, according to my opinion, entirely due to chance.... All this is providence over animal species [as whole units], and not to providence over individual animals.

Divine providence corresponds to the level that each creature has reached:

Understand thoroughly my position: I do not ascribe to God ignorance of anything or any kind of weakness. I believe that divine providence is related and closely connected to the intellect.... The more an individual has been able [to connect to] divine influence, due to his predisposition and his training, the greater must the effect of divine providence upon him be.... The level of divine providence is therefore not the same for all people.... Divine providence is very great in the case of prophets, and varies according to the degree of their prophetic ability, just as it varies in the case of pious and good people according to their piety and rightousness.... Ignorant and rebellious people fall into the category of animals; they are "like the beasts that perish" (Psalms 49:13).

(Rambam, *Guide of the Perplexed* III:17–18)

The world and the laws of nature are governed in accordance with what God has decided, and this cannot be altered by people's actions; that which has been decreed will indeed take place. Nevertheless, one who is devoted to God can be saved from such decrees and natural phenomena even though the divine decrees themselves are fulfilled.

The servants [the forces of nature] cannot change their nature or transgress the command that God has given them. Likewise, all heavenly and earthly creatures are affected by [these forces] in accordance with their nature]. Consequently, [the forces of nature themselves] cannot make it better or worse [for them]. If one bows down to the creations in the heavens [namely, the stars], this will not be effective. Rather, that which has been decreed upon the individual in accordance with the astrological constellation at his birth will happen to him, unless he believes in a power that is higher than that of the stars and devotes himself to it; then, he can be saved from decrees. For example, imagine an alignment of stars which determines that a certain river will flood a certain city, killing or carrying off its inhabitants. A prophet comes and warns them to return to God before this terrible day comes. They repent with all their hearts, and because they have devoted themselves to God, He puts into their minds the idea that all the residents of the city should leave the city in order to pray to God. They do so, and on that day, the river suddenly swells up and floods the entire city. God's decree was not removed, yet He saved them.

(Ibn Ezra, Exodus 33:21)

Further reading: For more on the stars and their influence on the Jewish people, see *A Concise Guide to the Sages*, p. 423.

Individual Providence

Even something that appears not to be controlled by God, or to have only general divine oversight, is in truth controlled by God. God determines the manner in which to extend His providence to the different species. While He oversees many species in a broad sense, He extends His providence to humans individually. Nevertheless, general providence also comes from God, since nothing can occur without His intervention. Therefore, ultimately, all things are dependent on God's will and intention.

Nothing is coincidental:

Before everything else, you must know that there is no act, small or large, that happens randomly, without divine providence. Rather, everything that takes place is conducted, in a concealed way, by the providence of the Infinite One, and His influence, which spreads from above to every level of all existence. Without Him, there are no actions or consequences, as He is the One who brings everything about and gives life to everything. Nothing exists outside of Him and independent of His power, intention, and will. [Nothing exists merely] by coincidence or out of necessity.... Nothing occurs by chance, without intention and providence, as everything comes from Him through divine providence. I have seen fit to divide the different types of providence, each with their own particulars and explanations into ten categories... as follows:

Ten types of providence:

(1) General providence that is extended to all creations that do not receive reward [or punishment for their actions]; these are divided into three categories: animals, plants, and inanimate objects. (2) Providence that is extended to human beings; every detail of each individual's life is governed by God. (3) General providence, which cancels out individual divine providence, [such as] a regional calamity. (4) Individual providence that is extended to animals or gentiles, bringing about their success or saving them, so that they will perform the function of being emissaries of God. (5) Providence

over forms of death. (6) Providence over afflictions of the human body [as punishment for sinning]. (7) Providence over afflictions due to God's love, [which purify the individual so that he will merit to enter the World to Come]. (8) Providence involving the testing of the righteous individual [as a result of which he experiences hardship in this world]. (9) Providence over misfortunes that occur to an individual due to his own foolishness; he brought adversity upon himself. (10) Providence involving God concealing His face [making it seem as though He is not attending to what is happening on earth, when in fact this is one of the modes of providence].

(Rabbi Yosef Irgas, *Shomer Emunim* 2:81)

One of the foundations of Hasidism is the recognition of divine providence and the knowledge that it is not only human beings who receive constant providence; rather, every single part of creation also does, whether animal, vegetable, or mineral. Divine providence is the life force that God bestows upon each creature. Delving deeper into this principle leads to the conclusion that everything that occurs in the world is connected to the plan for creation as a whole. Even regarding something that appears to have no bearing whatsoever on human life, everything that happens to it is part of the great plan for creation.

It is well known with regard to divine providence, as our teacher, the Ba'al Shem Tov, explains, that not only are all the slightest movements of all creatures under the governance of the Creator, and this providence comprises the creature's life force, which gives it existence, but also every tiny movement of each creature is also connected to the plan for creation as a whole. Take, for example, the movement of one blade of grass that grows deep in the forest, or on one of the highest mountains, or in one of the deepest valleys, where no human has ever passed. The movements of this blade of grass, throughout its days, to the right and to the left, forward and backward, are governed by God. He decreed that this particular blade of grass will live for a particular number of months, days, and hours, and that in this time it will turn and bend to its right and to its left, forward and backward, a specific number of times. Furthermore, each movement of this specific blade of grass is connected to the plan for creation as a whole.

(Rabbi Yosef Yitzḥak Schneersohn, *Sefer HaMa'amarim* 5696, p. 120)

Heaven and Earth Are Equal before God

Extending divine providence to every individual on earth does not in any way lessen or belittle God than extending divine providence to the angels and other heavenly beings. When we understand that God is higher than the greatest heights, and that He lowers

Himself even when influencing the upper [heavenly] realms is, it is not difficult to see that there is divine providence. God chooses to "descend" and observe both heaven and earth, and therefore, on earth, too, He watches over each individual, as for Him there is no difference between the loftiest spiritual being and the most insignificant physical being.

"Exalted above all nations is the Lord; above the heavens is His glory" (Psalms 113:4); [the other nations] extol the Divine by saying that His glory is above the heavens, whereas in the world below, it would be an indignity and diminishment [for God], and it is not His way to degrade Himself and govern that which occurs in the lower world. They claim that there is no specific divine providence.... But this is not the case. We say, "Who is like the Lord our God, who sits on high, who looks down to see what is in heaven and earth" (Psalms 113:5–6), both equally [in heaven and earth], for [supervision of] the heavens, too, is a total indignity for Him, just like earth is. Therefore, it is not correct to say that His glory is only above the heavens, since the heavens are equivalent to the earth... both are equal before Him.

(Tzemaḥ Tzedek, *Ma'amarei HaTzemaḥ Tzedek* 5615, p. 142)

One of the students of the Ba'al Shem Tov had difficulty accepting his teacher's approach to divine providence, i.e., the notion that God governs every one of his creations, from humans to grains of sand flying in the wind.

The Ba'al Shem Tov instructed him to go to the forest and stand near a tree, and to observe the course of the first leaf to fall from that tree. The student did so and began to follow the leaf. He followed it for a long while. Eventually, it blew across a field and landed between two stones. When the student reached it, he saw a worm emerge from between the stones and begin to eat the leaf.

He returned to his rebbe, and before he had even opened his mouth to describe what had happened, the Ba'al Shem Tov said, "The Holy One, blessed be He, who sustains the entire world, made that leaf come to that poor little worm, to provide it with food. The leaf's entire course was dictated by divine providence."

One must believe that even a piece of straw lying on the ground is there because God decreed that it should be there.

(Rabbi Pinḥas of Koritz)

Further reading: Read about divine providence in connection with one's livelihood on p. 237.

Marriage

When describing the formation of man on the sixth day of Creation, the Torah mentions that they were created as male and female, and that as a combined unit they are called Man: "Male and female He created them. He blessed them, and He called their name Man. . . ." (Genesis 5:2). The Torah directs the man to cleave to his wife and, together, to build a home through marriage. The man and woman help each other and complement each other.

True love between a man and his wife does not stem from physical desire, but from the shared will to build a home and fulfill the mitzvot, with each one helping the other. The longer a husband and wife live together and share their experiences, the more the love between them grows.

Marital intimacy transforms the couple into one body, but their ultimate connection occurs when both body and soul are one. Marital intimacy is referred to by the Torah as "knowledge" and it is specifically this area of life that indicates the loftiness of mankind. When the physical connection between the couple takes place in sanctity, a wondrous holiness rests upon the couple.

Marital Love

When Adam saw his wife for the first time, he expressed his love in a way that every man should toward his wife. The words that Adam used communicated to her that they are inseparable. All other women are only pale imitations of her. She is absolutely perfect, and he wishes to cling only to her.

See how pleasant are those words, how they are words of love: "[The man said: This time,] a bone from my bones, and flesh from my flesh" (Genesis 2:23), to show her that they are one and totally inseparable. Now he begins to praise her: "This shall be called woman." There is none other like her. She is the honor of the home. All other women compared to her are like a monkey alongside a human being. But "this shall be called woman" – absolute perfection. [This describes her] and no other.

All of Adam's words are words of love, as it is stated: "Many daughters have performed valiantly, but you have surpassed them all" (Proverbs 31:29). "Therefore, a man shall leave his father and his mother, and he shall cleave to his wife, and they shall become one flesh" (Genesis 2:24). All of what he said was aimed at lovingly drawing her close to him and uniting with her.

(*Zohar* 1:49b)

Further reading: For more on relationships, see *A Concise Guide to the Sages*, p. 376.

Complete love totally lacks any selfish motivation. It has only one goal – to do the will of the beloved. This is the most praiseworthy of all loves. A person's value can be perceived by how he loves.

The most complete love is when a person loves his beloved for the beloved's sake alone, with no other goal in his heart other than doing the will of the beloved, for he does not love his beloved for any other reason... This type of love, for the beloved's sake, only exists in wise and understanding people... And because this is the most praiseworthy of all types of love and is only found among people of wisdom and understanding, a person will be praised or criticized because of it. He therefore should not dilute it at all with any self interest.

(Rabbi Yosef Albo, *Sefer HaIkkarim* 3:36)

The wedding is merely the beginning of a couple's life together. The man and woman commit to sharing their lives. They are excited to fulfill the mitzvot together and help each other in performing them. The longer they are together, as days and years pass, both good and difficult, the connection between the couple strengthens and their love grows more powerful.

You see what the commitment of a Jewish marriage really is: Neither playful entertainment between a man and woman, nor imaginary infatuation that in reality ends up in disappointment, will connect a man and woman's hearts together. Instead, a husband and wife make a serious lifetime commitment. Their love stems from a joint excitement in fulfilling the mitzvot. The man gives his wife satisfaction when he helps her fulfill her mitzvot, she helps him fulfill his mitzvot, and together they diligently fulfill the mitzvot of their household. Their love therefore continually grows during their shared life; and the sanctity of their life increases as they take on many more roles and obligations. The day of the wedding is not the peak of their lives, but rather the springtime of their marital commitment. It is the day when the seed of their mutual love is planted. Therefore, it is impossible that a youth can love a young woman to the same degree as a Jewish man loves his wife or as an elderly man loves his elderly wife. For the bonds that tie their hearts and minds are only created and strengthened through the many good as well as difficult years.

(Rabbi Samson Raphael Hirsch, *BeMa'agalei Shana*, vol. 1, p. 203)

One and Only One Wife

God gave us a mitzva that serves to create a true and lasting connection between a man and his wife: "[The newly married husband] shall be free for his house for one year" (Deuteronomy 24:5). During the entire first year of marriage the husband and wife are not to be apart for any extended time. This enables him to get used to living exclusively with her.

One of the reasons for this commandment [of being "free for his house one year"] is that when God, blessed be He, thought about creating the world, He wanted it to be populated with good creatures, born of male and female, that would mate in a proper way – for He considers licentiousness abominable. He therefore decreed for us, the nation that He chose to associate with His name, that each man should live with the wife who is uniquely his and with whom he will have children for the entire first year of marriage, without interruption. The result of this will be that being with her will feel natural, and his attention will be drawn to her, causing her appearance and actions to enter his heart, until the actions of any other woman will naturally feel strange. For most people, by nature, will seek out and love that with which they are familiar. Through fulfilling this mitzva he will distance himself from other women and focus on his own wife.

(*Sefer HaḤinnukh,* Mitzva 582)

Uniting Opposites

Man and woman were created in a way that leaves them with only two options: They can either help each other or oppose each other. In fact, man and woman are opposites, and ought not to be able to connect. However, God makes peace between these two opposites and enables them to become connected to each other.

If he merits, she is a helper; if not, she opposes him:

[In Genesis 2:24, God refers to woman as] "*ezer kenegdo* (literally, a helper opposite him)." [The Talmud, building on the seeming contradiction between "helper" and "opposite him," states: "If he merits, she is a helper; if not, she opposes him" (*Yevamot* 63a)]. The explanation is that this help [of a husband and wife] is different from that of a father to a son or vice versa, for a father and son never truly oppose each other. In contrast, this helper [the wife] is "a helper opposite him (*kenegdo*)." The woman is equal to and as important as the man. She helps him, for the man brings [raw materials like grain or fabric] and she develops it [by making bread or clothing]. This is referred to as "a helper opposite him." However, if he does not merit, she is totally against him, whereas a father is never totally against a son. This seems to be the simple understanding of this passage…

Only God can connect two opposites like a man and woman:

There is a very lofty concept here, for male and female are two opposites, he a male and she a female. If he merits, they combine to make one totally united power. For each pair of opposites unites into one power when they merit. God, may He be blessed, makes peace between these opposites and connects and combines them… Therefore, when they do not merit, the fact that they are opposites causes them to be opposed to each other, for there is no combination and connection from Above.

(Maharal, *Ḥiddushei Aggadot, Sota* 17a)

Further reading: For more about the wedding, see p. 16; *A Concise Guide to Halakha*, p. 47.

Holy Intimacy

God is "one," and He determined that the nation of Israel would also be "one," and that every Jewish person can cling to God through transforming into "one." When is a person "one"? It is only when male and female join [in physical intimacy] with holy intentions. Their unity takes place with the desire of both of them, and then, when they are physically intimate, they are as one body, and then God grants them a spirit of holiness.

When is a human being called "one"? It is at the time when the male and female are physically intimate, sanctifying themselves with an elevated holiness, with the intention of sanctifying themselves. Come and see: When the human being is physically intimate as male and female and, as is appropriate, intends to sanctify himself, he is then complete, and called "one" and is without flaw. For this reason, a man has to make his wife joyous at that time, inviting her to become one with him, so both of them share this intention. When both of them are together, then all is one [they are united] in both soul and body. In soul, they cling together through their shared intentions. In body – it is, as we have learned, that an unmarried man is like one who is fragmented.

And when the male and female unite, they become one body. In this way, they are one soul and one body and are called "one person." Then, the Holy One, blessed be He, rests upon that "one" and deposits a spirit of holiness within that one.

(*Zohar* 3:81b)

Further reading: For more on man and woman as two parts of a whole, see p. 16.

The physical union between a man and woman is an elevated matter that the Torah refers to as "knowledge," because it causes knowledge and wisdom to descend to the world. This union, when performed with holiness, causes the Divine Presence to dwell together with the husband and his wife. But if their physical union is only powered by physical lust, the Divine Presence removes itself from them and they are left with only fire that devours them.

The physical union between a man and his wife is referred to as "knowledge":

Know that this union is sacred and pure when done in the proper way, at the proper time, and with the correct intentions. A person should not think that, God forbid, there is any shame or ugliness in appropriate marital intimacy. For marital intimacy is referred to as "knowledge." It is not for naught that the verse states: "Elkana knew Chana his wife" (I Samuel 1:19). This is the inner meaning behind the drop of seed that, when drawn from a holy and pure place, draws along with it knowledge and understanding, which is the mind. Realize that if marital intimacy were not a holy matter, it would not be referred to as "knowledge."

When marital intimacy is performed with holiness the Divine Presence is with the couple:

For the Sages, of blessed memory, said: "When a person is physically intimate with his wife in holiness and purity, the Divine Presence rests with them. But if they become lustful, the Divine Presence detaches itself from them and they remain 'fire and fire'" (*Kala Rabati* 1:7). This is similar to what the Talmud teaches: "Rabbi Akiva taught: If a man and woman merit, the Divine Presence rests between them. [But if] they do not merit, fire consumes them" (*Sota* 17a). Both statements can be explained as follows: When the Divine Presence is between them, the *yod* of the word *ish* (*alef-yod-shin*) and the *heh* of the word *isha* (*alef-shin-heh*) are still present, and the name of God (*yod-heh*) is between them. But if they did not intend to have a holy union but, instead, to merely fulfill their desire, and they became fired with lust and desire, the *yod* of the man's name and the *heh* of the woman's name, that together form the divine name *yod-heh*, depart from between them and two fires (*eish, alef-shin,* that remains when the *yod* is removed from the word *ish,* and *eish, alef-shin,* that remains when the *heh* is removed from the word *isha*) remain.

(Ramban, *Igeret HaKodesh*, chap. 2)

Further reading: For more on holy intimacy, see *A Concise Guide to Halakha*, p. 574.

Torah Concepts

One of the hasidim of Rabbi Moshe of Kobrin had a difficult time finding a husband for his daughter because his daughter was very exacting and kept rejecting the suggestions that were made to her. When he saw that his daughter would find fault with every boy that was suggested as a match for her, the father decided to travel to his rebbe and seek his counsel.

When the hasid entered the presence of the *tzadik* he said, "Young men of whom we thought very highly were suggested for her, yet our daughter rejects the suggestions one after another."

Rabbi Moshe heard the hasid's complaint. He smiled and said: "With regard to the daughters of Tzelofhad we find that the Holy One, blessed be He, said, 'To whomever is good in their eyes they shall be wives (Numbers 36:6). This teaches us that when suggesting a potential groom, he must be good in the daughter's eyes, as the verse says, 'their eyes,' referring to the daughters themselves, and it is not sufficient for him to be good in her parents' eyes."

For a man without a wife is half a body, and the Divine Presence does not rest upon him.

(*Zohar* 2, *Behar* 32)

One who truly loves another is always either afraid of doing something against his beloved's will or afraid that something will happen to his beloved. This is what they meant by "love is full of fear."

(Rabbi Yaakov Tzvi Mecklenburg, *HaKetav VehaKabbala,* Genesis 22:12)

For love is the uniting of the two lovers as if they were one entity.

(Rabbi Yitzḥak Arama, *Akedat Yitzḥak,* Genesis 2:18)

I always say to a couple at their wedding: "Take care, dear couple, to always strive to give each other satisfaction.... And know that the moment you start to make demands of one another, your bliss will evade you."

(Rabbi Eliyahu Eliezer Dessler, *Mikhtav MeEliyahu,* vol. 1, p. 36)

It is accepted practice that Jewish man consults with his wife in all of his affairs... both at home and outside the home. This is so that a wife should know about all of her husband's affairs and advise him about them, both at home and in his business affairs or his work. For her fate in life is bound up together with him and they share a common lot, and thus true peace in the home is established.

(Rabbi Ben-Tziyyon Meir Ḥai Uziel, *Hegyonei Uziel*)

Of all types of holiness, none compares to the holiness of marital intimacy, if it is performed with holiness, and he sanctifies himself.

(Shelah, *Sha'ar Ha'otiot, Kedushat Hazivug*)

Further reading: For the story of the daughters of Tzelofhad, see *A Concise Guide to the Torah*, p. 409.

Education and Parenting

God praised Abraham by saying: "For I love him, so that he shall command his children and his household after him, and they will observe the way of the Lord, to perform righteousness and justice" (Genesis 18:19). For a Jew, true praise comes from succeeding in educating his children and ensuring that future generations will also be educated.

The purpose of education is to eliminate bad habits while growing and developing by learning to do good. But education is not only training. The goal of education is to seek out the student's and child's soul. When we reach his soul, he himself will also want to do God's will.

Initially, a student should not be burdened with his studies. As he grows stronger it is worthwhile inspiring him to work hard at his studies in order to bring out the best in him.

An educator or parent needs to serve as a role model, as well as to establish a trusting relationship with a student or child. This will increase the chances that what they teach will actually be put into practice. Nevertheless, it takes time to see the results of education, and one should invest in education even if the results are not immediately apparent.

The Essence of Education

Over the course of our lives we advance and improve, but a change made during youth is easier and more impactful than one made at a more advanced age. A small sapling that begins to grow crooked can be strengthened with a little effort, but a tree that has grown crookedly and is now mature and old is very hard to straighten.

"[Hillel said:] If not now, when?" (*Avot* 1:14) Included in this statement is: If not now during youth, then when? If he leaves it until old age, he will not be able to do it. This is what King David said: "... so that our sons will be like saplings tended in their youth" (Psalms 144:12). When a sapling is still small, a person can cultivate it so it grows into a straight tree and does not become crooked. But once it has grown crooked, it is difficult to fix. Similarly, when a person is still a youth it is easy for him to grow on a good path and to avoid evil. But if one grew old in his wickedness, it will be difficult for him to change.

(Rabbeinu Yona Gerondi, Commentary on *Pirkei Avot* 1:14)

Further reading: For more on the importance of early education, see p. 15.

Education involves more than habituation, for an act done only out of habit is flawed. The Hebrew word for education, *ḥinukh*, means a new beginning, and in this sense means getting into the habit of personal renewal. If a person gets into the habit of renewing himself every day, he will continue to do so even in old age.

The mitzva of education is to become accustomed to doing mitzvot and learning Torah. Ostensibly, however, when a person becomes accustomed, his performance becomes "a commandment of men learned by rote" (Isaiah 29:13). As the mitzva of education necessarily involves habituation, he should be constantly advancing, viewing every day as new. This is [the meaning of the verse]: "Train the lad in accordance with his way; even when he grows old, he will not turn from it" (Proverbs 22:6). That is, he will not turn away from his training, for every day will be as a new beginning for him.

(Rabbi Shmuel Bornsztain, *Shem MiShmuel, Miketz* 5672)

Though it is possible for an educator to set a variety of different goals, King Solomon teaches us to focus on one main one. When he said that education must bring a youth to a state where he will retain his education even in old age (see Proverbs 22:6), he seems to define education as "revealing the soul of the student." When the student's soul is revealed, he himself will want the Torah and its mitzvot. In order to reveal the soul, the educator must penetrate into the child's own world with the knowledge that each person has a different inner makeup and different abilities – and he must work with those.

The goal of education is to reveal the soul of the student:

Since, even in his youth, a spirit from the Lord, a divine soul, is implanted and hidden within him, we must raise and educate him to bring it out, reveal it, and cause it to blossom, so he becomes a trustworthy Jew, a servant of God. He will want Torah from his inner being, and he will not veer from that path even when he grows old. But one who commands a youth, or even habituates him, cannot be sure that the child or student will continue to do what he was commanded when he grows up and is independent. Concerning this, Solomon commanded, "Educate the lad…." Educate him, penetrate his inner world and the Jewish holiness that is hidden within; reveal it, and only then "even when he grows old, he will not turn from it" (Proverbs 22:6).

The educator must "descend" to the student's level:

But the educator who wants to reveal the soul of the student that is buried and hidden within, to cultivate it and fan its flames so it burns with a lofty and holy flame so the student's complete being, even his physical powers, will grow in holiness and he will long for God's Torah, must bend himself down to the student he is educating. He must penetrate the student's childishness and lowliness, until he reaches the spark of his hidden – or even lost – soul and reveal it, cultivate it, and raise it.

Each individual student's education must be based on the student's own nature and personality:

Since this is so, education should not be identical for every youth. It is instead dependent on each youth according to his nature, mindset, and personality. And it is the educator's responsibility to get to know the student. The educator cannot suffice with knowing only his own mind and personality, for education is dependent on the one being educated. It is not only his own mind and abilities that the educator must activate and use in order to command and instruct. He must also grasp, activate, and use the student's mind and abilities. That which he commands and instructs one student should not be the same for another who is different from him in nature, will, and character traits. King Solomon has alluded this to us: "Educate the lad in accordance with his way" (Proverbs 22:6): each individual's own way.

The focus of education should not be on pedagogy, but on revealing the student's soul:

Our intent here is not to instruct in the art of pedagogy, how to work with the student's mind and abilities in order to increase his understanding of the straightforward meaning of the Torah. We are not now seeking the mind of the student, but rather, we seek the entire student: the soul, spirit, and *neshama* of the Jewish child.

(Rabbi Kalonymus Kalman Shapira, *Ḥovat HaTalmidim*, Introduction)

How Should We Educate?

Serving as a role model is the most important of all educational tools. When a parent does not act properly, how can he expect his child to act properly? In order to pass on proper values to a child the parent must also express his views about both the good and bad that other people do.

A person must be extremely careful not to speak, and certainly not to act, in a disgraceful manner in the presence of his child. And even though the speech or act itself is disgraceful whether or not he says or does it in front of his child, it is nevertheless worse in the child's presence, for his child might learn from him. For in such a case, if the father disciplines a child, saying,

"Why did you do such and such?" the child will respond, "But you did the same thing"... And if a father hears that someone else did something disgraceful, he should make it extremely clear to his children how terrible and disgraceful it is... This is in order that the child should consider the speech or behavior despicable and distance himself from it. If, on the other hand, a person hears that others did something praiseworthy, he should praise it exceedingly before his child, so his child will hear and desire to similarly do something good.

(Rabbi Eliyahu de Vidas, *Reshit Ḥokhma, Raising Children*, 49)

Education is a great responsibility that requires training and preparation of the educator. Not everyone is able to educate, and a person who is not appropriate for the task is likely to do harm. The results of education only become apparent much later in life.

The educator must be careful about how he speaks and should direct the student to focus on his service of God. Praising a student and giving him positive reinforcement enables him to advance, as a child who trusts his educator will also fulfill the educator's instruction.

Not everyone can educate:

An educator must be specially trained in order for his teaching and guidance to achieve its goals. Not everyone who is called a teacher or counselor can undertake this great responsibility, for someone who is not fitting for the task will not only be unsuccessful at educating, he will actually do harm and will be held responsible for the harm he does.

The results of education are apparent only after a long time:

The fruits of education do not grow overnight. Everything involved in education and guidance, certainly uprooting bad character traits and habits, demands much toil and a long time. In addition, the educator or counselor himself must work on [his own character and habits].

The educator must be careful about how he speaks:

The educator and counselor must know that in his instruction, not only is his choice of words important for effective teaching and counseling, but also the method of expressing those words. Whether he expresses himself with politeness and calm or with agitation and derision will affect the fundamental effectiveness of his teaching and counseling. If, when an educator or counselor speaks, even in general, about one of the greatest of human flaws, but uses inappropriate derisive terms, he will leave a negative impression on the one being educated or counseled. For one who hears derision from his educator or counselor, even when it is accurate, will lose his admiration for him.

The educator should set a path for and focus the student:

The educator and counselor needs to accompany the one being educated or guided little by little, just as one would teach a child to walk, step by step. He must also guide him wisely and carefully in setting priorities [in personal growth]. He should also be very careful about the student not getting involved in two things at once, whether it involves removing shortcomings or strengthening positive qualities.

Positive reinforcement:

Praise and compliments elevate one who is being educated or counseled. They remove him from his present state, and set him on a higher level than he was when he began. Positive reinforcement and rewards encourage and strengthen one who is being educated or counseled. They fill him with the spirit of aspiration for growth from one level to the next, both in scholarship and behavior.

One must weigh his words carefully before speaking to a student:

The educator or counselor must know very well what is fitting and what is improper. For what is fitting is not equally absolute and uniform for all people. Therefore, the educator or counselor must weigh each and every word carefully, especially whether it is fitting or improper, before he says it to the one being educated or counseled. He must then say it with love and affection, with wisdom and intelligence, for "the words of the wise are well received when said calmly" (see Ecclesiastes 9:17). [He must be cognizant of] what is fitting and needs to be done and what is improper and needs to be avoided.

The more an educator is trusted, the more those he is educating will following his direction closely:

To the degree that an educator or counselor knows what is fitting and what is improper, and to the degree that he is diligent in fulfilling the above three conditions of how to relate to those he educates or counsels, his words and instruction will be well received. This is not only for the sake of the discipline of the one educated or counseled, but because the student sees that the educator or counselor thinks everything out deeply. Then, even though he does not know the reason behind it, he will trust the educator or counselor and follow his direction with precision.

(Rabbi Yosef Yitzḥak Schneersohn, *Principles of Education and Counseling*)

One of the Chabad hasidim set out as an emissary of the Lubavitcher rebbe and became the principal of a school. When he once visited the rebbe and went in for a private meeting with the rebbe, the hasid complained that his educational work was taking up all of his time and he was learning much less Torah than he used to.

The rebbe responded: "Every mitzva has a set amount and measure, except for education. The influence of education is boundless: It influences the youth, his family, and his descendants for all generations."

If a youth finds constant diligent study too burdensome, you should placate him with small things that children love and desire, like honey, roast grain, nuts, and the like. You should say to him, "This is for you, in order that you go to school and study." When he gets older and no longer likes these, his father should say to him, "Go to school and learn and I'll buy you a beautiful belt and nice shoes." When he gets even older he should say, "I'll give you money so you'll learn *Birkat Hamazon* and prayers. He should buy him *tzitzit* and *tefillin* to educate him to do mitzvot…

(Rabbi Eliyahu de Vidas, *Reishit Ḥokhma, Raising Children*)

[The Talmud's statement,] "The power of the son is greater than the power of the father" (*Shevuot* 48a), [which in context deals with collecting loans,] alludes to the fact that the power of a son's Torah, good deeds, and proper character are the result of his father's educating him.

(Shenei Luḥot HaBerit, Sha'ar Ha'otiot, Ot Gimel)

Just as putting on *tefillin* daily is a mitzva from the Torah, incumbent on every Jewish man, with no distinctions made between a great Torah scholar and a simple man; it is likewise an absolute obligation, incumbent upon every Jew, to think for a half hour each day about educating his children. He must do all that is within his power, and even more, to see that his children actually end up going in the path in which he guides them.

(Rabbi Shalom Dovber Schneersohn)

Further reading: For more on parenting and education, see *A Concise Guide to the Sages*, p. 404. For more on the obligation to teach a child Torah, see *A Concise Guide to the Sages*, p. 487.

Fear of God

Fear of God [*yirat Hashem*] is one of the six constant mitzvot, and is the basis for fulfilling all of Torah and mitzvot. The most basic form of fear is fear of punishment in this world and in the World to Come. A higher level is fear of doing something against God's will. But the highest, most spiritual level of fear of God is awe that comes from being in the presence of God, the most exalted Ruler, who is constantly at a person's side. One who feels the constant presence of the Creator is not able to act as if he is alone.

A person cannot fulfill Torah and mitzvot without commitment, without having accepted "the yoke of the Kingdom of Heaven," and having a basic level of fear of God. Fear of God is also the perfection of the human species and the goal of the entire Torah. Each and every person can reach the lower level of fear, a cognizance that God watches him and sees his actions. But one who continues to serve God is able to reach the level of cleaving to God and a higher level of awe, knowing before whom he stands.

Basic Reverence for God

The development of fear of God, or reverence for God, is the purpose of the mitzvot and the ideal to which humanity must strive.

A person acts differently when he stands before the king:

A person does not sit, move, and occupy himself in the same manner when he is alone and at home as he does in the presence of a great king. His speech and cheer when he is among the members of his household and relatives are not the same as when he is in the presence of a king. If he therefore desires to attain human perfection, and to truly be a man of God, he should bear in mind that the great King who is over him, and is always close to him, is greater than any earthly king, even David and Solomon.

The consciousness that God is with us at all times brings on a feeling of trepidation and self-consciousness:

When the perfect ones bear this in mind, they are filled with fear of God, humility, and piety, with true, not [merely] apparent, reverence and respect of God...They understand that by these rules the above-mentioned idea will be firmly established in the hearts of men: That we are always before God, and it is in the presence of His glory that we go to and fro. The great men among our Sages would not uncover their heads because they believed that God's glory was around them and over them.

The goal of the entire Torah is fear of God:

What I have pointed out to you here is the object of all our religious acts. For by carrying out all the details of the prescribed practices, and repeating them continually, a few pious men may attain human perfection. They will be filled with respect and reverence toward God and, bearing in mind who is with them, they will perform their duty.

(Rambam, *Guide of the Perplexed* III:52)

When a person meditates daily that the Holy One, blessed be He, is found everywhere and observes all human actions, he will be careful not to do anything against God's will. A person should think deeply about this as he begins his day. Then, an additional small reminder during the rest of the day will help him act properly.

Any Jewish person, whoever he may be, who, for a considerable amount of time every day meditates on how the Holy One, blessed be He, truly fills the upper and lower levels of existence and the actual heaven and earth, and truly "that which fills the entire world is His glory" (Isaiah 6:3), if he observes, sees, and discerns his inner thoughts and feelings, actions and speech, and counts each of his steps, fear of God will be embedded within his heart for the entire day. When he later thinks about this, even for a short period of time at any point during the day, it will cause him to "turn away from evil and do good" (Psalms 34:15) in thought, speech, and deed, not to, God forbid, rebel against the watchful presence of He whose glory fills the entire world.

(Rabbi Shneur Zalman of Liadi, *Tanya, Likutei Amarim* 42)

A person only grasps the deeper level of fear of God, awe, when encountering God's greatness through intense meditation and great wisdom. However, when one first begins to come close to God he should strengthen his fear of punishment. He must remember that the Holy One, blessed be He, is even particular about details. Therefore, a person needs to be careful not to sin, even unintentionally, and to refrain from eating meat and drinking wine on weekdays, to avoid anger and strictness, and to pursue peace.

One who wants to purify himself and come close to God should first focus on fear of God and attain [the basic level of fear of God,] fear of punishment. For one can only come to the inner level of fear, awe, through great wisdom…Therefore he should be careful not to sin, even unintentionally, and should become totally detached from sin. One must be careful of minor sins, for the Holy One, blessed be He, is extremely particular with the righteous. A person should therefore separate himself from meat and wine on weekdays. He needs to heed the warning: "Turn away from evil and do good; seek peace" (Psalms 34:15). You must seek out peace and become one who pursues it. You must be careful not to be strict in your house about anything small or large, and certainly not to get enraged, God forbid.

(Rabbi Yitzchak Luria (Arizal), *Etz Ḥayyim*, Introduction)

The basic level of fear of God a person must acquire is accepting divine authority, to fear doing something against God's will. Fear of sin is the necessary basis for keeping all the mitzvot.

The type of fear that each and every person must necessarily have is fear of sin. This is being afraid to do something against God and God's will. It goes beyond actual sins, malicious or unintentional .... Therefore, this fear, that includes accepting divine authority, "the yoke of the kingdom of heaven," is necessary for every individual. It is impossible to be without it, for one who lacks fear of sin has thrown off the yoke of divine service and is open to all sorts of evil, God forbid.... This is what is referred to as "fear of heaven," for it is connected to accepting the yoke of the kingdom of heaven and fear of divine judgment. It is the preliminary stage of divine service and its foundation. As is well known, accepting divine authority is a prerequisite to all mitzvot, as our Sages say (*Mekhilta, Masekhta Baḥodesh, Parasha* 6): "Accept My kingship, then accept My decrees."

(Rabbi Shalom Dovber Schneersohn, *Kuntres HaAvoda* 2)

Further reading: For more on God's observation of all our actions, see p. 173; *A Concise Guide to the Sages*, p. 367.

Higher Reverence

Fear of God is called "the first mitzva" and is the gateway to belief and to keeping the rest of the mitzvot. There are a number of types of fear, including fear of the Holy One, blessed be He, that stems from fear of physical punishment or of spiritual punishment in the World to Come, that are not so praiseworthy. The main type of fear is the higher fear, awe of the Holy One, blessed be He, Himself, and His greatness.

Fear is the first mitzva:

Rabbi Shimon began speaking about the Torah's mitzvot, and said: All of the mitzvot that the Holy One, blessed be He, gave Israel are written in the Torah as a principle: "In the beginning, God created [the heavens and the earth]" (Genesis 1:1). This is the first of all mitzvot, and is referred to as fear of God, which is called "beginning"... This is the gateway through which one enters [the realm of] belief, and the world exists based on this mitzva...

The main fear is fear of God, not of sin:

Fear is divided into three types, two of them secondary and one of them primary. A person can be afraid of the Holy One, blessed be He, in order that his children will live [if he obeys God] and not die. He might also be afraid of physical or monetary punishment, and this might cause constant fear. People with those fears have not made the Holy One, blessed be He, their main focus. A man might be afraid of the Holy One, blessed be He, because he is afraid of punishment in this world or in Gehenna. These two are not the primary and fundamental types of fear. The primary type of fear is being in awe of one's Master, who is great and who controls, is the foundation and root of all of the worlds, and everything is as naught before Him.

(*Zohar* 1:11b)

There are internal and external types of fear. Internal fear is even higher than love of God. External fear is fear of rebelling against the Holy One, blessed be He, and getting punished. Internal fear, on the other hand, is what a person feels when he meditates on how great God is and how small man is in comparison. He feels unworthy of standing in His presence.

You should be aware of the statement of the kabbalists, that there are two types of fear, internal and external fear. External fear is lower than love of God and internal fear is higher than love. How is this possible? External fear is being afraid of transgressing the King's commandment lest he be punished and held accountable to the King's word. Internal fear is understanding the greatness of the Creator, may He be elevated, and the great spiritual delight, wealth, and honor in His palace. When a person appreciates this, he will be afraid and alarmed and say, "Maybe I am not worthy of standing in the King's palace. For considering my great potential and lowly state and shortcomings, perhaps He will find fault with me... This is the fear that is above love.

(Rabbi Menaḥem Recanati, *Vayera*)

Further reading: For more on reward and punishment, see p. 256; *A Concise Guide to the Sages*, p. 165.

The Greatness of Fear

Fear of God involves pain and effort, but a person who considers the good that can be gained from it will not be concerned about how much trouble he has. Nevertheless, fear of God does not bring about any physical damage or monetary loss. On the contrary, it will extend a person's life

The pain and effort involved in fear of God are insignificant when considering the benefits:

There is no doubt that if a person uses his judgment, he will realize that it is worthwhile to suffer great toil and trouble for a period of time in order to achieve an exalted goal or a great honor. This is the case even though, while he is going through the toil and trouble, he undoubtedly experiences pain and suffering. But when he considers the great honor or exalted goal he wants to attain through the trouble and effort, he will see it as insignificant when compared with the good he will attain. This is also true regarding fear of God, may He be blessed, as we have said. For when a person considers the elevated status he can attain through the fear, reflecting on God's great loftiness and exaltedness until it brings him to fear Him and tremble before Him, he will not worry about all of the trouble, effort, suffering, and anxiety that he experiences through fear.

Fear of God adds to a person's lifespan and does not cause damage:

For fear of God is unlike fear of flesh and blood. For someone who fears a man, a king, or a minister will always be in a state of fear and anxiety, and this will [take its toll on his health and] shorten his life. But the anxiety involved in fear of God will not only not shorten his life, but, as Solomon says: "The fear of the Lord will add days" (Proverbs 10:27). Similarly, even though it is natural for a faint-hearted person to have children who are likewise faint-hearted, and this trait will prevent him from becoming wealthy and holding on to his wealth, for because of his constant fear he will not do what he wants properly, yet David said: "Happy is the man who fears the Lord and who greatly delights in His commandments. His descendants will be mighty on earth" (Psalms 112:1-2) ... For fear of God does not shorten life or diminish wealth; nor does it bring about bad results, as does fear of flesh and blood.

(Rabbi Yosef Albo, *Sefer HaIkkarim* 3:36)

Further reading: For more on how covering the head is beneficial for bringing about fear of Heaven, see *A Concise Guide to the Sages*, p. 346.

When a person fears God he is able to stand up to the tests and difficulties that he encounters. God does not present anyone with a test unless it is for his benefit; and in order to pass a test, a person needs fear of heaven, which is evaluated through the test.

The foundation of fear of God is the experience of being tested. For the degree to which a person is God-fearing becomes apparent through the test... The Holy One, blessed be He, only has someone undergo a test when He wants to do something good for him. Then the accuser, identified with the attribute of strict judgment, comes before the Holy One, blessed be He, and says: "Master of the universe, You cannot possibly do good to him unless he passes a test." Therefore, a righteous person will take an oath that he will conquer his evil inclination.

(Rabbi Yehuda HeḤasid, *Sefer Ḥasidim* 13)

For the purpose of the entire Torah, including all of its commandments, prohibitions, promises, and anecdotes, is one thing: to fear Him, may He be elevated.

(Rambam, *Guide of the Perplexed* III:24)

An engaging mitzva and a great, high, and fortified wall up to the heavens that never abandons a person is fear of heaven, as it is stated: "Rather, be in fear of the Lord all day" (Proverbs 23:17). The sun of fear of God will shine on the soul and all that is hidden within it, dominating his thoughts day and night.

(Rabbeinu Yona Gerondi, *Igeret HaTeshuva*, chap. 2)

Further reading: The binding of Isaac was one of the most difficult of tests, and resulted in God giving Abraham the title "God-fearing." For more on the binding of Isaac, see *A Concise Guide to the Torah*, p. 45; *A Concise Guide to the Sages*, pp. 23, 30.

Torah Concepts

Self-Sacrifice

Throughout all of history, Jews have sacrificed their lives to sanctify the Divine Name. When confronted with the choice between a life that denies belief in God, and death that does not compromise belief, Jews stood up to the test and gave up their lives. The cry "Hear, Israel: The Lord is our God, the Lord is one" (Deuteromony 6:4) has accompanied us throughout all the generations, in all the countries of the Diaspora. In the past generation, a third of our people were exterminated merely because they were Jews. Theirs were also deaths that sanctified the Divine Name.

Every Jew recites the *Shema*, ["Hear, Israel...,] proclaiming his love for God, saying, "You shall love the Lord your God with all your...soul" (Deuteromony 6:5). If one says these words with intent, showing readiness to offer his life for God, it is as if he died sanctifying the Divine Name, even though he did not actually sacrifice his life. Mere willingness to give up one's life brings a person to the level of those who out of their love for God are willing to sacrifice their lives.

If, every time he sinned, a Jew sensed that he separates himself from God, he certainly would not sin. For how could a person, who was willing to give up his life so as not to be separated from God, think of sinning?

Love of God That Leads to Self-Sacrifice

There are righteous people who can be called "those who love God," because they are willing to give up their lives to sanctify His name. There are other righteous people who, even though they observe the mitzvot, cannot be included in this category.

"Those who love Him" [based on Exodus 20:6] refers to those who sacrifice their lives for Him. For those who accept the Lord's name and His exclusive divinity, denying any foreign god and refusing to serve them even if that endangers their lives, are referred to as "those who love Him." For this is the type of love to which we committed ourselves with our lives, as the verse states: "You shall love the Lord your God with all your heart, and with all your soul, and with all your might" (Deuteronomy 6:5). This means that you should give up your soul and your life out of your love of Him, not exchanging Him for any other god, and not serving Him in partnership with any foreign god...The rest of the righteous [who do not sacrifice their lives] are called "those who observe His commandments" [also based on Exodus 20:6 and Deuteronomy 7:9].

(Ramban, *Commentary on the Torah*, Exodus 20:6)

Further reading: For more on self-sacrifice, see the accounts of the deaths of Rabbi Akiva and Rabbi Hanina, *A Concise Guide to the Sages*, p. 364.

Readiness to Give Up One's Life

Every Jew can, in effect, sacrifice his life when he recites the daily *Shema*. Love of God "with all your soul" is a boundless love, loving Him to the degree that it means sacrificing one's life for Him. For one who reads the *Shema* with this intention, it is as if he has died each day to sanctify the Divine Name.

When a person recites the *Shema*, and reaches the verse: "You shall love the Lord your God with all your heart, and with all your soul, and with all your might" (Deuteronomy 6:5), he should think about what the Sages said: "'With all your soul' – even if He takes your soul" (*Berakhot* 54a). He should submit his soul to God, may He be blessed, and decide to sacrifice his life for the sake of the sanctity of the Divine Name, and be willing to die for Him. This will be considered as if he was actually killed to sanctify the Name. This secret has been revealed to us through what the Sages said in the *Sifrei* (*Va'etḥanan* 7): "'With all your soul' – this is what the verse states: 'For we are killed all day long for You' (Psalms 44:23). Is it possible for a person to be killed every day? Rather, these are the righteous, who the verse considers as having been killed every day."

(Rabbeinu Yona Gerondi, *Igeret HaTeshuva* 11)

Even someone who is not actually called upon to die sanctifying God's Name can reach that level of martyrdom through deciding to sacrifice his life for God.

Many Jews were killed at the time of the decree [the pogroms during the Crusades], and many decided to give up their lives but were then saved. A Jew whose name was Rabbi Shabtai saw in a dream another Jew named Rabbi Shabtai who had been killed. The murdered Rabbi Shabtai said: "All those who decided to die in sanctification of God's Name share our reward in the afterlife."

(Rabbi Yehuda HeḤasid, *Sefer Ḥasidim* 222)

Self-Sacrifice for Any Mitzva

The willingness to give up one's life to sanctify the Divine Name stems naturally from the nature of the Jew, who cannot separate from God. If a Jew were conscious of how any sin separates him from God, he would never sin. It is the evil inclination that deceives a person into thinking that he will be able to sin yet still remain connected to God.

A Jew cannot be separate from God:

Part of the nature of the Jewish soul is that it cannot be separate from God – "For You are our Father" (Isaiah 63:16). Because of that, even the most frivolous people or the sinners of Israel give up their lives to sanctify the Divine Name. They will not worship idols, God forbid, even if gentiles take their lives away, for they are unable to separate themselves from the unique, one God, may He be blessed.

If a Jew sensed the import of every sin, he would give up his life rather than transgress:

If he knew that through a particular evil act he would become separated from God, there is no way he would do it. However, the evil inclination entices him to think that he will nevertheless not be separated from God and will remain like any other Jew who is faithful to God. It also assures him that things will be good for him as it is written: "He will bless himself in his heart, saying: Peace will be with me, as I will follow the desire of my heart" (Deuteronomy 29:18). Even if he follows the [sinful] desires of his heart, nevertheless peace will be with him. In this manner he transgresses in various ways.

(Rabbi Shalom Dovber Schneersohn, *Kuntres UMa'ayan* 2:1)

Further reading: For more on the meaning of the words "with all your soul," see *A Concise Guide to the Sages*, p. 232.

Self-Sacrifice during the Holocaust

During the Holocaust, the Nazis tortured the Jews before murdering them. The rabbi of the Ukrainian town Lanovitz spoke publicly with his community moments before they were all taken to the cemetery, where they were murdered. He told them to accept death with joy, for theirs is a death sanctifying the Divine Name, dying for being Jews.

Dear brothers, we are passing into the kingdom of heaven... After the great suffering and the hell on earth that we have experienced, you are assured of reaching the inner realms of paradise... Therefore, do not be worried; go to your fate with joy. We are fortunate that we have the merit of being able to die as Jews. This type of death is considered dying to sanctify the Divine Name, for our only crime is our being Jewish.

(Rabbi Areleh Rabin)

Rabbi Elhanan Wasserman was murdered with other rabbis and students from the Kovno Ghetto. When they were taken to the place where they were to be murdered, the rabbi turned to his students and told them that they were now fulfilling the greatest mitzva of all – sanctifying the Divine Name. The fire that burns in our bones, he said, is the fire that will renew the Jewish nation.

Apparently, in heaven they view us as righteous people, for they want us, to atone for all of Israel with our lives. We must now repent, immediately, right here, for not much time is left.... We are now fulfilling the greatest mitzva: sanctifying the Divine Name. The fire that will blaze within our bones is the fire that will reestablish the Jewish nation.

(Rabbi Elḥanan Wasserman)

Before Rabbi Yisrael of Grodzisk and his community entered the extermination area in Treblinka, the rebbe turned to his followers and told them not to question God's actions, not to hesitate, and not to cry when they go to the furnace. The community fulfilled his request. Singing "*Ani Ma'amin*" [I believe with perfect faith in the coming of the messiah – a paraphrase of the twelfth of Rambam's thirteen principles of faith] and reciting the "*Shema*," they publicly sanctified God's Name.

Listen brothers and sisters, nation of God... We must be joyous that we have merited that our ashes will be like the ashes of the red heifer, and will purify the entire nation of Israel.[13] We must see ourselves as fortunate that it is our destiny to pave the way for the redeemer who approaches, and to accept, with love, our *akeda*[14] for the sanctification of His Name, may He be blessed. I command you not to hesitate and not to cry as you go to the furnace. On the contrary, be joyous; and while singing *Ani Ma'amin* and, like Rabbi Akiva did, reciting *Shema Yisrael* leave this world saying the word "*eḥad*."[15]

(Rabbi Yisrael of Grodzisk)

Torah Concepts

Rabbi Yosef Yitzḥak Schneersohn was imprisoned by the Soviet regime, accused of spreading Judaism throughout Russia. He was later miraculously freed.

Before his imprisonment, on the 19th of Kislev of that year, many hasidim gathered in his house, and they included spies for the Yevsektsiya (the Jewish section of the Soviet Communist Party). The rebbe knew of their presence, yet nevertheless spoke forcefully and passionately of the need for self-sacrifice in observing Judaism under the Soviet regime.

13. The red heifer was used to purify one who came into contact with a corpse. See Numbers 19.
14. The binding of Isaac; see Genesis 22.
15. The last word of "Hear, Israel: The Lord is our God, the Lord is one [*eḥad*]."

During that talk he said the following: "Jews! Grab self-sacrifice, grab it! This period of the need for self-sacrifice will pass. Soon a time will come when there will be complete religious freedom, and then you'll seek out the opportunity for self-sacrifice and you won't find it. Soon a time will come and you will speak laudingly of someone who sat in jail for being a Torah teacher or for opening up a *heder* [school], a yeshiva, or a *mikva* [ritual bath]. You will be jealous of them and regret that you did not merit this yourself. Jews – grab self-sacrifice!"

Further reading: For more on the belief in the redemption and the coming of the anointed one, see p. 145; *A Concise Guide to the Sages*, p. 391.

Prophecy

When the Torah was given at Mount Sinai, all of Israel experienced direct prophecy. However, that revelation was too powerful for them, and they requested that Moses serve as an intermediary between them and God's word. Following that model, God sent us other prophets to communicate His messages. Prophecy continued until the beginning of the Second Temple period. Since then, we have received God's word with less clarity. One of the indicators of the future redemption will be the return of prophecy to Israel. When the glory of God will be revealed in the future world, all will prophesy, young and old.

A person who possesses the highest intellectual and moral virtues can receive prophecy if he purifies himself and is free of sin. Nevertheless, prophecy is not automatic; God might still withhold prophecy from someone who is fit for it.

Prophecy is communicated through imagery and metaphor and the prophet did not necessarily receive the specific wording of his message. During prophecy, a prophet became detached from the physical world. If someone who is recognized as a righteous person gives us a miraculous sign or wonder indicating that he is a prophet, God commands us in the Torah to treat him as a legitimate prophet.

The Prophet

If a person is of excellent mind and character, separates himself from the behavior of the masses, and attaches his mind to the Holy One, blessed be He, a spirit of holiness rests upon him. Some character traits, like anger and sadness, prevent prophecy; and sometimes God decides to withhold prophecy from a person even though he would have been worthy of it.

Prophecy: A fundamental principle of faith:

Knowing that God grants prophecy to human beings is a principle of faith.

Characteristics of prophets and preparations for prophecy:

Prophecy only rests upon a person who is extremely wise, has mastery over his inclinations so that his drives do not overcome him in any way, rather, he always overcomes his natural drives, and upon one who possesses an extremely broad and sound mind.

A person who has all of these characteristics and is sound in body, when he enters the orchard [*pardes*][16] and is drawn after those great and obscure matters and has a mind that can understand and grasp them, he becomes continuously more holy and separated from the ways of the masses who walk in the darkness of temporal life. He constantly energizes himself and trains himself not to think about any useless matters, frivolities, or schemes. Instead, his mind is always free to be connected above, bound up with the heavenly throne, striving to understand pure and holy forms. He views the world through all of the Holy One, blessed be He's wisdom, from the primordial form until the core of the earth,[17] and from there recognizes His greatness. Immediately, the spirit of holiness rests upon him.

The prophet is elevated and transformed into a different person:

When that divine spirit of holiness rests upon him, his soul merges with the level of the angels who are referred to as *ishim*[18] and he transforms into a different type of person. He understands that he is no longer as he was, but has risen above the level of other wise men.

Things that prevent prophecy:

Some character flaws, like anger, totally prevent prophecy. The Sages said: If a prophet gets angry his prophecy abandons him (*Pesaḥim* 66b).... Anxiety and anguish [likewise prevent prophecy].... Our Sages expressed it this way: "Prophecy does not rest upon one who is in a state of laziness or sadness. Instead, it rests upon one who is in a state of joy" (*Shabbat* 30b).

Those who are precluded from prophecy:

We believe that there are those fit for prophecy, but when they prepare themselves for it do not prophesy, and this is in accordance with the divine will. In my view, prophecy is similar to miracles and functions like them. For if it was a natural phenomenon, then anyone who was fit for prophecy by nature, and trained himself based on how he was educated and instructed, would necessarily experience prophecy.... However, it is impossible, in our opinion, that one of the ignoramuses among the masses could experience prophecy any more than a donkey or frog could. Our principle is: Training

16. The orchard, or *pardes* in Hebrew, is the term used in the Talmud for a mystical state in which one is capable of receiving prophecy.
17. i.e., from the most abstract to the most concrete.
18. One of ten types of angels; see *Mishneh Torah, Hilkhot Yesodei HaTorah* 2:7.

and personal perfection are necessary, and then it is possible that the divine ability will be manifest in him.

(Rambam, *Mishneh Torah, Hilkhot Yesodei HaTorah* 7:1; *Shemoneh Perakim*, chap. 7; *Guide of the Perplexed* II:32)

Further reading: For more on anger and how problematic it is, see p. 194; *A Concise Guide to the Sages*, p. 421.

Preparing for Prophecy

After a person has refined himself and is free of sin, he is able to receive prophecy on condition that he prepares himself to do so. Prophecy does not involve the soul actually leaving the body, for that would merely be a dream like any other, but, instead, takes place when the soul is still within the body. During prophecy the prophet disconnects himself from his physical body and connects to his spiritual self.

Prophecy comes to a person after he has refined himself and is free of sins:

This explains the phenomenon of prophecy. For when a person is within a spiritually refined body, free of the filth of the evil inclination, of the drives of his foundational soul,[19] and with no sin that pollutes any of the roots of his soul, he can, if he focuses on it, connect to his upper spiritual source and cling to it.

The soul detaching from the body: Total focus on the spiritual:

However, even though one is fit to [prophesy], he must strip his soul entirely and separate his soul from physicality. Then his soul will be able to reconnect with its spiritual source. But this separation, spoken about in the mystical works dealing with prophecy and the spirit of holiness, is not actual separation, in which the soul leaves the body, as it does in sleep. If that were the case, prophecy would be no different from a normal dream. In truth, when the spirit of holiness rests upon a person, his soul is within his body and he is awake; it does not leave the body. The separation is that the prophet totally detaches himself from his thoughts and his imagination, which stem from his foundational animal soul. He stops [his animal soul] from imagining, thinking about, or pondering any matter related to this world, as if his soul left him. Then the power of imagination within him transforms, rendering an image as if he has ascended to the higher levels of existence, climbing stage by stage to the roots of his soul until he vividly imagines his

19. i.e., his ordinary physical drives.

upper source. All of the lights that he sees with his imagination are embedded in his consciousness in a way parallel to the way he imagines this world even though he does not apprehend them through sight, as is known by the science of nature.[20]

(Rabbi Ḥayyim Vital, *Sha'arei Kedusha* 5)

Further reading: For dreams and their meaning, see *A Concise Guide to the Sages*, p. 415.

Prophecy

All prophets experience prophetic visions while asleep. During prophecy they lose control of their bodies, and that opens up their minds to understand their visions.

There are many different levels of prophets. Just like one wise man might be wiser than another, so one prophet might be greater than another. All of them have their prophetic visions either at night in a dream or during the day after having fallen into a deep sleep, as it is stated: "I will reveal Myself to him in a vision; in a dream I will speak to him" (Numbers 12:6). When all of them prophesy their limbs shake, their physical strength is weakened, and their thought processes are interrupted, leaving their minds free to understand what they see.

(Rambam, *Mishneh Torah, Hilkhot Yesodei HaTorah* 7:2)

Prophecy is not communicated through direct speech, but through allegory and imagery. Prophecy is a vision the prophet sees, not speech that he hears. Some of the prophecies in the Bible are accounts of the interpretation of their visions, and others include a description of the vision as well as its interpretation.

The message the prophet receives through prophetic vision is given in the form of an allegory. The interpretation of the allegory is immediately clear to him and he knows what it means. Examples of this are the patriarch Jacob's vision of the ladder with angels ascending and descending upon it (Genesis 28:12) which alluded to the kingdoms throughout history that would enslave his descendants, the animals Ezekiel saw in his vision (Ezekiel 1), the boiling pot and almond branch that Jeremiah saw (Jeremiah 1:11-13), and the *ephah* measure Zekhariah saw (Zekhariah 5:6). The same is true for the rest of the prophets. Some of the prophets, like these, stated both the allegory and its interpretation, some only the interpretation, and some, like

20. It is a scientific fact that the visions one receives in this state are not visions of the physical world.

a portion of Ezekiel's and Zekhariah's prophetic messages, only the allegory without stating the meaning. But all of them prophesied through allegory and imagery.

(Rambam, *Mishneh Torah, Hilkhot Yesodei HaTorah* 7:3)

Not only does the prophet receive a message from God, but he is also given the specific words he should use. During prophecy, the prophet's free choice is removed; he is merely a channel to pass on the prophecy.

During prophecy, the prophet does not have any free choice at all – neither with regard to its contents nor its extent. He is merely a vessel to pass it on, like a glass mirror that reflects whatever sunlight shines on it. The spirit of God comes with specific words and the order with which he should convey them. The prophet does not choose words to express the meaning he received, as David said: "The spirit of the Lord spoke through me, and His word is on my tongue" (II Samuel 23:2), i.e., that statement came to him through the spirit of God, may He be blessed, and was not merely the intended message with a mandate to improvise words that express the message. Rather, the words themselves were also placed on his tongue by God. He had no choice in the matter; he was merely a vessel: The light of prophecy is seen through him and through him divine speech is heard.

(Rabbeinu Nissim of Gerona, *Derashot HaRan* 5)

In some prophecies the prophet receives only the content of his prophecy, and he must himself choose the words with which to communicate his message. There are also prophecies in which the prophet is also given the specific words to say to the people. Sometimes the prophet is also commanded to do a prophetic act, which arouses higher powers connected with the prophecy.

There are two aspects of prophecy: its content and the specific words [by which the prophet communicates the prophecy]. There are instances where the prophet grasps the content of the prophecy but is not constrained with regard to the words he uses, and can choose the words himself as he wishes. There are other instances, like the prophecies of Isaiah, Jeremiah, and the rest of the prophets whose prophecies are written for subsequent generations, where prophets are also constrained with regard to which words they can use. [The words were chosen] to incorporate multiple meanings. Even in this case, different prophets have different styles, in accordance with their character, their natural language, and style of speech. There are many times when prophets are asked to perform demonstrative acts along with their prophecy, as with Jeremiah's belt,[21] Ezekiel's brick,[22] and many similar cases. The point was to arouse, through those actions, whatever higher powers were needed in those matters the prophecy was about, in all its aspects. These powers had been made available and were appointed by God to be manifest at the appropriate time.

(Rabbi Moshe Ḥayyim Luzzatto, *Derekh Hashem* 3:4:8)

Levels of Prophecy

There are a number of ways in which God communicates with people: by a voice from heaven; by means of the Urim and the Tumim[23] that functioned during the earliest period of Jewish history; by the holy spirit, where a person would say words that God caused him to say without being aware of their origin; and by prophecy, in which a person's senses would be numbed and he would see visions from above.

A voice from heaven:

There are four levels of divine communication: a voice from heaven, the Urim and the Tumim, the holy spirit, and prophecy. These are increasingly higher levels of revelation… I will now explain these four levels to you: The first, the voice from heaven…was always heard by the Sages of the Talmud and pious people of the generations during the Second Temple era. They would make use of the voice from heaven when prophecy had ceased and the Urim and the Tumim no longer operated.

The Urim and the Tumim:

The second level was the Urim and the Tumim, which, through its holy names, conveyed an indirect divine revelation.

The holy spirit:

The third level was the holy spirit…in which a person would find that he experienced expanded consciousness, and wonderous words would come out of his mouth, speaking about future events. His feelings would not be affected at all; he would say words placed in his mouth through the spirit of holiness and he would not know the source of those words.

21. Which he hid under a rock and then uncovered (Jeremiah 13).
22. On which he etched an image of Jerusalem (Ezekiel 7).
23. The letters etched into the breastplate of the High Priest could be used by him to ask questions of God. The messages were transmitted through illumination of the letters.

Prophecy:

The fourth level was prophecy; in prophecy a person would speak of future events when all of his feelings were numbed. He would remain separated from physicality and anything connected with it, totally and exclusively uniting with his pure mind. Then he would see clear light with visions, perceiving things through a dream or while awake.

(Rabbeinu Baḥya ibn Ḥalawa, *Commentary on the Torah,* Deuteronomy 33:8)

The Obligation to Obey the Prophet's Message

Sometimes a prophecy's message is for the prophet himself, and at other times for others, who are commanded to heed his instructions. There is no obligation to heed just anyone who shows a wondrous sign and says words; we are only obligated to heed one who we recognize as fit for prophecy.

A prophecy might be for the prophet himself, to expand his mind and to increase his knowledge, so he knows of lofty matters he hasn't known about previously. A prophet could also be sent to one of the world's nations or to the people of a city or kingdom, to prepare them for the future and to tell them what to do, or to stop them from doing evil. When the prophet is sent, he is given a sign or wonder [to perform before them], so the listeners will know that God truly sent him. Not everyone who performs a sign or wonder is to be believed to be a prophet. Rather, [this is how we identify a true prophet]: If he is a person we previously knew to be fitting for prophecy through his wisdom and actions that are superior to that of his contemporaries, and if he follows the ways of prophecy, its holiness and asceticism, and he then proceeds to perform a sign and wonder and says that God sent him, it is a mitzva to heed him. This is stated in the verse: "[A prophet from your midst, from your brethren, like me, the Lord your God will establish for you;] him you shall heed" (Deuteronomy 18:15).

(Rambam, *Mishneh Torah, Hilkhot Yesodei HaTorah* 7:7)

What Is the Source of the Prophet's Power?

The prophet expresses Israel's essence and also transmits messages from the Holy One, blessed be He. The prophet's power is dependent on the children of Israel, and he needs them more than they need him.

The prophet serves as Israel's mouth [expressing the truths that make up their spiritual essence]. The prophet's abilities are therefore dependent on the children of Israel's service of God. As it is written: "A prophet from your midst...the Lord your God will establish for you" (Deuteronomy 18:15). More than Israel needs the prophet, the prophet needs them.

(Rabbi Yehuda Aryeh Leib Alter, *Sefat Emet, Balak* 5649)

The Restoration of Prophecy

Divine speech enters the world in different ways. There was a time when it came through prophecy, later it was through a voice from heaven to the Sages, and now God's word comes to people through dreams.

In ancient times, people would be inspired to prophesy, and they would know and experience the glory of the Highest. Once prophecy ceased, they would experience a voice from heaven. Now that both prophecy and the voice from heaven have ceased, people only [hear divine messages] through dreams.

(*Zohar* 1:238:1)

There was a tradition that prophecy would be restored to the Jewish people in the year 4976 (1216 CE):

We have a great and wonderful tradition, which I received from my father, who received it from his father and grandfather, who received it at the beginning of the exile from Jerusalem... that the verse, stated by Bilam, "Now, what God has wrought is what shall be said of Jacob and of Israel" (Numbers 23:23), contains a hint [to when prophecy will be restored]. First, calculate how much time elapsed from the six days of Creation until the time of Bilam's prophecy. Then, add an identical amount of time and you will arrive at the year when prophecy will return to Israel. Then, they will be told by prophets what God has wrought. This prophecy [of Bilam] was said in the fortieth year after the exodus from Egypt. You will find that from the beginning of the calendar [namely, the six days of Creation] until then, 2488 years elapsed. Based on this calculation and this interpretation of the verse, prophecy will return to Israel in the year 4976 after Creation (1216 CE). Undoubtedly, the return of prophecy will be a portent of the coming of the anointed one.

(Rambam, *Igeret Teman,* chap. 3)

Since the destruction of the First Temple there have been no prophets in Israel.[24] But during the age of the redemption, prophecy will return to those who are properly prepared to receive it.

Even though there have no longer been prophets since the First Temple was destroyed and the Ark of the Covenant was hidden by the prophet Jeremiah, and during the Second Temple period no one at all experienced prophecy, and all the more so, no one has received a prophetic vision during the exile, nevertheless, during the time of the redemption, prophecy will return to the Jewish nation. That is to say, to those people who are prepared for prophecy. This never applied to the other nations and never will.

(Don Yitzḥak Abravanel, Commentary on Joel 3:1)

Prophecy, in the future, will involve divine revelation for all, not only for prophets who are prepared for it. The prophecy of the future will be natural; even boys and girls will prophesy.

In the future, there will be a revelation of the actual divine light of the infinite. It will be visible and revealed to all, as the verse states: "The glory of the Lord will be revealed, and all flesh will see..." (Isaiah 40:5). There will be a similar prophetic revelation to each and every individual, as the verse states: "Thereafter it will be that I will pour My spirit upon all flesh, and your sons and your daughters will prophesy... also upon the slaves and upon the maidservants in those days" (Joel 3:1–2). This [prophecy of the future] is different from the prophetic revelation the prophets experienced, where a number of conditions were required to prophesy... In contrast, in the future, prophetic revelation will be part of the natural order; even boys and girls will experience it.

(Rabbi Shalom Dovber Schneersohn, *Sefer HaMa'amarim*, Continuation of 5672, part 2, p. 936)

The *Hozeh* (Seer) of Lublin was famous for his prophetic vision, and many would consult with him, even about day-to-day matters of their livelihood. Once, a butcher came to him and asked whether to slaughter his animals or sell them, because he was worried that they might be

24. The Bible actually records three prophets, Hagai, Zechariah, and Malachi, who prophesied during the early years of the rebuilding of the Second Temple.

treifot.[25] The saintly man instructed him to make a list of his animals and indicate each one's identifying marks.

When the list was presented to him, the *Hozeh* began to declare, "This one is kosher; this one is not," and so on. When he got to one animal he said, "This one, I don't know."

When the butcher asked the *Hozeh* for an explanation, the saintly man replied, "This animal has an internal condition that will present a halakhic question. They will bring it before a rabbi to decide whether it is kosher. I do not know what that rabbi's ruling will be, for 'Torah is not in heaven.'"

25. Animals that are physiologically damaged in a way that renders them non-kosher, e.g., having a hole in a lung.

Miracles

Our world is subject to the laws of nature. We are used to thinking that the sun that rose today will do the same tomorrow, and that the law of conservation of energy or the laws of gravity will continue for all time. However, every now and then miracles occur, and the nature that we are familiar with takes on a new look.

Many miracles happened to the Jewish people during the exodus from Egypt. Those miracles proved that God was watching over us and directing history. The wondrous survival of the Jewish people over the ages likewise strengthens our belief in God.

Alongside these revealed miracles are hidden ones. In truth, even the natural order is a miracle, reflecting how God's will expresses itself through nature.

Miracles Establish the Truth of Faith

The miracles that God performed during the exodus from Egypt were meant to strengthen belief in God and His prophets. God's hand is evident in the miracles that He has performed for the people of Israel throughout the generations.

The greatest of the Creator's benevolences to humanity, and the strongest proof of His existence, is the Torah, given to Moses His prophet, of blessed memory, as well as the signs He performed through him, and the way he changed nature showing awesome wonders, in order that we would believe in the Creator, may He be blessed, and His prophet. As it is written: "Israel saw the great power that the Lord wielded against Egypt and the people feared the Lord and believed in the Lord [and in Moses, His servant]" (Exodus 14:31). And it states: "You have been shown in order to know that the Lord, He is the God; there is no other besides Him" (Deuteronomy 4:35). If a person seeks nowadays to see something similar to those matters, he should take a truthful look at our survival among the nations since we went into exile and how our affairs have been while among them, notwithstanding that we do not agree with them, both with regard to the esoteric and the revealed, and they know it.

(Rabbeinu Baḥya ibn Pakuda, *Ḥovot HaLevavot, Sha'ar HaBeḥina* 2:5)

Further reading: For rabbinic stories of wonders and miracles, see *A Concise Guide to the Sages*, p. 347.

The miracles that took place in Egypt, like the ten plagues, establish the belief that God providentially oversees everything that happens in the world and He has unlimited control.

The goal of the miracles of the exodus from Egypt was to implant within us belief in God:

The Torah says with regard to the wonders [in Egypt]: "...so that you will know that I am the Lord in the midst of the land" (Exodus 8:18). This refers to divine providence, indicating that He hadn't left the world to happenstance – as is their opinion.[26] He also said: "... so that you will know that the earth is the Lord's" (Exodus 9:29), to teach that the world is created, [not eternal,] and it is His, for He created it *ex nihilo*. He also said: "... so that you will know that there is none like Me on the entire earth" (Exodus 9:14), to indicate His omnipotence, that He controls all and no one can in any way limit His activities. For the Egyptians either denied or doubted all of these truths. We see from here that great signs and wonders are reliable witnesses for belief in the Creator and the entire Torah.

Remembering the exodus from Egypt and the miracles that accompanied it is a way to transmit belief to subsequent generations:

Since the Holy One, blessed be He, will not perform a sign or a wonder in every generation before any wicked person or scoffer, He commanded us to make a constant reminder and sign for what our eyes saw, to pass it on to our children, they to their children, and to continue until the last generation.

(Ramban, *Commentary on the Torah*, Exodus 13:16)

Miracles and Nature

Miracles were already predetermined during the six days of Creation. The prophets did not actually perform wonders and bring about a change in nature. Rather, the Holy One, blessed be He, told prophets in advance when a miracle would take place, and they in turn told the people.

For when God created this reality and set the laws of nature into motion, He included that these miracles would take place at an appointed time. The sign that a prophet would give was that God would tell him what would take place at the time the prophet claimed it would. But what would actually happen [was not brought about by the prophet,] but was placed in nature from the outset.

(Rambam, *Guide of the Perplexed* II:29)

26. Perhaps referring to the Aristotelian notion that the individual events and physical beings are outside of God's direct purview.

 **Further reading:** For more on the great miracles that accompanied the exodus from Egypt, see *A Concise Guide to the Torah*, pp. 148, 169; *A Concise Guide to the Sages*, pp. 85, 97.

Hidden Miracles

Some miracles are revealed: It is easy to see how God interferes in nature and changes it. But there are also many hidden miracles, where the world looks as if it is behaving naturally, while, in truth, God is interfering in it.

Miracles can be divided into two categories: revealed miracles and hidden miracles. Revealed miracles are those great signs and wonders that are performed before the nations, like the signs of Egypt, the ten plagues, the splitting of the Red Sea, the manna and the quails, and bringing water out of a rock, that all involve changing the nature and regular behavior of the world. Hidden miracles include the events and occurrences that happened to Abraham, Isaac, and Jacob, like Abraham's war against the four kings and his victory. Even though it looked natural, it was really a hidden miracle. Similarly, the extension of the lives of the righteous and the shortening of the lives of the evildoers are all hidden miracles. Concerning this, King Solomon said, "The fear of the Lord will add days, but the years of the wicked will be shortened" (Proverbs 10:27). For even though worry and fear would naturally tend to weaken a man's strength and hasten his death, Solomon said that one who fears God and is worried about his sins will have a long life. All of this is a hidden miracle.

(Rabbeinu Baḥya ibn Ḥalawa, *Commentary on the Torah*, Exodus 30:12)

Torah Concepts

There are many miracles we do not know about even after they take place. God performs wonders for us that only He knows about. A person might wake up in the morning, without even knowing that a snake had tried to strike him and he was saved from its bite; a person traveling may not even be conscious that robbers had wanted to harm him and he was miraculously saved.

Rabbi Pinḥas opened the discussion: "To Him who alone does great wonders, for His kindness is forever" (Psalms 136:4). How many are the favors that the Holy One, blessed be He, does for people, and how many are the miracles that he performs for them every day, and one is unaware; He alone knows about them! A person wakes up in the morning not knowing that a snake had come to kill him and he unknowingly steps on the snake's head. No one except for the Holy One, blessed be He, knows about it. Behold, "To Him who alone does great wonders!" A person walks on a path and bandits are waiting to kill him. Someone else is taken instead of him [the bandits kill that other person,] and the traveler is saved, not knowing the favor that the Holy One, blessed be He, did for him and the miracle that He performed for him. He alone knows. Behold, "To Him who alone does great wonders!" He alone did it and knows about it. No one else knows.

(*Zohar* 3:200b)

Further reading: For more on Abraham's war against the four kings, see *A Concise Guide to the Torah*, p. 28.

In general, God chooses to guide events through hidden miracles in order to elevate the entire natural world.

It is understood that for Israel, in order to elevate them above all the nations of the earth, it would have been better, with more honor and a more glorious name, if God had related to them in an exclusively miraculous way. However, from the divine perspective, more is gained through hidden miracles that are cloaked in nature. This is analogous to the way that the soul must come to this world cloaked in a physical body in order for even the physical body to be elevated, refined, and transformed into something spiritual. Similarly, we can say that miracles cloaked in nature elevate even the physical world and refine it…

(Rabbi Shmuel Bornsztain, *Shem MiShmuel, Devarim* 5673)

In the days of the Ba'al Shem Tov there was a philosopher who reached the conclusion that the miracle of the splitting of the Red Sea was not a miracle. Instead, he thought that exactly when the children of Israel left Egypt a rare physical phenomenon took place, namely, the receding of the sea. He visited a number of the great rabbis but did not hear a response to his claim that satisfied him.

When the Ba'al Shem Tov became famous, the philosopher decided to visit him and ask his question. The Ba'al Shem Tov told him: "Even if what you say is true, the very fact that the Creator of the world timed events just so, and the sea receded just at the moment when the children of Israel were leaving Egypt and the Egyptians were chasing them, is that not an awesome miracle?!"

The man left extremely impressed and declared that for the first time he had received an answer to his question.

All that Israel experiences during the period of the exile are miracles that are performed for them. No one knows about them except for the Holy One, blessed be He, Himself, as it is written: "To Him who alone does great wonders" (Psalms 136:4). They are being recorded in heaven and in the future will become a book.

(Rabbi Menaḥem Mendel of Kotzk, *Emet V'Emuna*)

Further reading: For more on Purim as an example of a hidden miracle, see p. 86.

The Soul

Man is composed of soul and body. Man's soul gives him his special status as the pinnacle of creation. Man's body, on the other hand, is physical and, as such, his physical life is similar to that of an animal. The soul is referred to by a number of names – *nefesh*, *ruah*, *neshama*, *haya*, and *yehida* – each one reflecting one of its different levels.

The more a person gets to know his own soul, the more he can appreciate the Creator, for man was created with divine wisdom, "in Our image, in Our likeness" (Genesis 1:26). Through studying his human soul, a person can get to know the Creator of the world; and through understanding his character, a person can connect with the depths of his soul and understand his purpose in the world.

According to the kabbalists, a person has two souls. One soul gives vitality to the body, and the other, higher-level, soul is a fragment of the Most High and is the person's direct connection to the Divine. These two souls struggle for control over a person's life. The higher divine soul's victory comes when the body totally submits to the soul.

What Is the Soul?

The soul is the way we refer to a person's abstract spiritual dimension. The human being, created in the image and likeness of God, is the most intelligent and sophisticated of all creations, and possesses a mind and spirit that is totally independent of his body. The soul, which is eternal, is the medium whereby a person is able to perceive and experience spirituality.

The soul is man's spiritual dimension:

The soul of any being is its God-given spiritual form.[27] The superior mind that is characteristic of the human soul is the [special] spiritual form of a person whose mind is developed. Concerning this spiritual form the Torah states: "[God said], 'Let Us make man in Our image (*betzalmeinu*), in Our likeness (*kidmuteinu*)'" (Genesis 1:26). This means: Mankind will have a spiritual form that can perceive and grasp non-material spiritual beings, like angels that have a purely spiritual form, without any physical

27. The Hebrew word used by the Rambam is *tzura*, which is usually translated as "form," although it does not in this context imply any physical shape. Form and matter are concepts rooted in Aristotelian philosophy and express the distinction between the physical substance of an object and its more abstract identity. In this sense "form" can refer to the object's purpose, designation, and other abstract qualities. The soul and the body are specific examples of form and matter.

component – and a human can eventually become similar to them. This verse does not refer to man's visible physical form, such as a mouth, nose, jaws, and the rest of the body's makeup. That would be referred to as the *to'ar* [rather than the *tzelem* and *demut* mentioned in the verse]. This also does not refer to soul which is the life force present in every animal, through which it eats, drinks, reproduces, feels, and thinks. Rather, it refers to man's mind, which is the [special] spiritual form of his soul. That is what is meant by "in Our image, in Our likeness."

The soul is eternal:

The spiritual form of the soul is not composed of physical elements, which would result in it eventually decomposing. It is also not a product of the life force (*neshama*),[28] which would make it dependent on the *neshama*, just as the *neshama* is dependent on the physical body. Rather, it is from God, from heaven. Therefore, when the material body, composed of the physical elements, decomposes, and the *neshama*, which only exists in combination with the body, ceases to exist, that spiritual form [of the soul] remains intact, for it does not depend on the *neshama* in order to function. Rather, it perceives and understands those spiritual beings which are entirely non-physical [i.e., the angels], it perceives the Creator of all things, and it is eternal. This is what Solomon said, in his wisdom: "And the dust returns to the earth as it was, and the spirit returns to God who provided it" (Ecclesiastes 12:7).

(Rambam, *Mishneh Torah, Hilkhot Yesodei HaTorah* 4:8–9)

The Soul's Components

The soul is referred to by a number of names, each one corresponding to one of its different functions. The five ways of referring to the soul are *nefesh*, *ruah*, *neshama*, *haya*, and *yehida*. The first three names refer to those aspects of the soul corresponding in turn to: our desires and drives (*nefesh*), our anger and emotions (*ruach*), and our mental understanding (*neshama*). The other names, *haya* (alive) and *yehida* (unique), correspond to the aspects of the soul which are eternal and incomparable to any other creation.

28. There are different levels of a person's spiritual life force. The Rambam uses the term *neshama* for the lower-level spiritual force which animates and combines with the physical body during its life but ceases to exist after death. He uses the term *nefesh* for the higher-level spiritual form which lives on after the death of the body. Note that other commentators (see, for example, Rav Se'adya Gaon below) use these expressions in entirely different ways.

The meaning of the names *nefesh*, *ruah*, and *neshama*:

The soul only functions together with the body, for, in order to function, every creation requires the means with which to act. When the soul is connected to the body [during a person's lifetime], three of its properties are evident: cognition, anger, and desire. This is why we have three different names for the soul: *nefesh*, *ruah*, and *neshama*. The name *nefesh* indicates that the soul has desires.... The name *ruah* indicates that it can become angry.... The name *neshama* indicates its intellectual abilities.

The meaning of the names *haya* and *yehida*:

The terminology relating to the soul includes two additional names: *haya* and *yehida*. It is called *haya* because the Creator gave it eternal life. The name *yehida* indicates that this aspect of the soul is unique in the universe.

(Rav Se'adya Gaon, *Emunot VeDeot* 6)

Even though a person has only one soul, that soul has a number of components and different faculties. Just as a doctor who wants to heal a person's body must know the different parts of human anatomy, so too, in order to heal a person's soul and help him improve his character one must be familiar with its different components. The soul has five components: (1) the nutritive component that maintains the body and is responsible for everything connected with nutrition and growth; (2) the sensory component, responsible for the five senses; (3) the imaginative component, responsible for everything connected with memory and imagination; (4) the emotional component, connected with drives and will; (5) the intellectual component.

These are the components of the soul: (1) The nutritive component is the source of the ability for ingestion, retention, digestion, excretion, growth, reproduction, and separating between fluids that are important for nutrition and those that are to be expelled.... (2) The sensory component is responsible for the well-known senses: sight, hearing, taste, smell, and touch. This component is present throughout the body.... (3) The imaginative component is the ability to remember sensory impressions even when no longer experiencing the sensation. It can connect some sensations and disassociate others. This imaginative component can also connect certain ideas which a person has experienced to ideas which he has not experienced at all, and even those which cannot be experienced, such as where a person might imagine a ship made of iron sailing through the air.... (4) The emotional component is the faculty whereby a person either desires something or is repelled by it. This drives a person to either seek something or avoid it, to choose it or reject it. [It is the source of] anger and desire, fear and strength, cruelty and mercy, love and hate, as well as many other similar emotions and character traits. This faculty expresses itself through all the body's limbs. (5) Man's intellectual component is the faculty with which he understands and where his insight lies. Through it he acquires wisdom and distinguishes between appropriate and inappropriate actions.

(Rambam, *Shemoneh Perakim*, chap. 1)

Knowing the Creator through Knowing the Human Soul

The more a person gets to know his soul, the better he is able to recognize his Creator. The soul is derived from the divine and therefore takes pleasure in the good actions of a person and is pained by the bad ones.

A wise man said: "My son, know your soul and you will know your Creator".... We see that the soul is happy and rejoices over good acts, and worries and feels sad about evil acts. It is natural for a person to be happy with something which is similar to them and to be uncomfortable with something which is their opposite. As such, given that the soul is divine, it is happy and rejoices over good acts that are similar to its nature – for all Godly acts are good – and is sad about evil acts because they go against its nature and are opposed to it.

(Rav Yosef Albo, *Sefer HaIkkarim* 3:6)

A person knows for certain that he has a soul, an internal spiritual identity, even though he has never seen it with his physical eyes. Likewise, with his mind's eye, a person can grasp belief in God, even though seeing God's essence is impossible.

A person is certain that he has a living soul – that a soul exists within his body and animates it – for his body cannot live independently. For his body, alone, is as inanimate as an animal's flesh and bones sitting in a pot or in a stew. Rather, the body is animated by the life force of the spiritual soul within it – a living spirit that is tied to the blood, as the verse states: "For the blood is the life [literally, the soul]" (Deuteronomy 12:23). A person is certain about this even though he never saw the essence of the soul, how it functions and what it is. Nevertheless, its existence is clear to him through his intellect. This is something he sees through his mind's eye and this verification is as reliable as something he sees with his physical eyes.

(Rabbi Menaḥem Mendel Schneersohn,
Derekh Mitzvotekha, Ha'amanat Elokut 45a)

Healing the Soul

When a person's soul is sick he must turn to those who heal souls, much as one would go to a doctor if his body were sick. People tend to ignore their souls because they are too preoccupied with their bodies. A righteous person, in contrast, recognizes the soul's supremacy over the body, accepts physical suffering with joy, and knows that it comes because of his sins.

When the soul is sick it also needs a doctor:

People mistakenly think that sickness only applies to the physical body and that when the soul lacks something it is not "sick," but only has a spiritual deficiency. They will therefore go to great lengths to consult with doctors about a physical illness but will not do the same concerning a spiritual problem. The opposite is really true, though, for the [body's] limbs are the "clothing" of the soul. If [healing] the "clothing" requires so much effort, all the more so should a person [whose soul is sick] seek out doctors [for the soul], which is the essence of a person.

Most people are focused on their bodies, whereas the righteous treat the soul as central and the body as secondary:

Most people love only their bodies, not their souls. For they have no way of appreciating the pleasures of the soul, but when a person's body is suffering, he really feels it because he loves his body so much. To go to a wise man to ask him to pray on his behalf is considered something that a person will go to great efforts to do on behalf of his body – for out of love for the body people go to great extents. To sum up: A person sees any deficiency in his physical health as a great misfortune, but that is not the case for his soul.... For a righteous person the opposite is true. He does not love his body, which is of lesser importance but prefers his soul, which is more special. If, God forbid, something happens to him, he will assume it happened because of his many sins, saying: "Everything that the all-merciful One does – without a doubt – He does for the best" (*Berakhot* 60b). He accepts [physical suffering] with joy, and understands well that because "You are children [to the Lord your God]" (Deuteronomy 14:1), a father knows what is best for his young child more than the child himself. If he is saved from distress he will be very happy – as opposed to the less refined person we mentioned earlier – for the righteous person experiences a close relationship with the all-powerful and merciful Father and has found favor in His eyes.

(Rabbi Simḥa Zissel Ziv, *Ḥokhma UMusar* 1:122)

The Body-Soul Connection

One of the great wonders of Creation is that God merged a spiritual soul with a physical body and made them interdependent:

Observe and consider the fundamental connection of man's soul to his body. You will see that a person's body is made up of various elements of disparate natures. The Creator, may He be elevated, combined them through His power and connected them in His wisdom, making them into a body that is unified in its appearance yet diverse in nature. To that He combined an ethereal spiritual entity which is similar to the higher spiritual beings [the angels]. This entity is a person's soul which He bound together with the body in a manner appropriate for these two extremely [different elements]: the spirit of life [of the soul connects with the body's] natural heat, blood, sinews, nerves, and arteries. He also gave these a means to preserve and protect them from harm: The flesh, bones, tissue, skin, hair, and fingernails all protect, cover, and guard [a person from harm].

(Rabbeinu Baḥya ibn Pakuda, *Ḥovot HaLevavot* 2:5)

Two Souls

Every Jew has two souls: a good soul and an evil soul. The good soul enters the evil soul, and both of them dwell within the body and its limbs.

A person has a good soul and an evil soul:

When man sinned through the tree of the knowledge of good and evil, he caused this mix [of good and evil] in all of the worlds [levels of existence]. There is nothing that does not contain a mixture of good and evil.... It turns out that even in a person's soul this is the case, for he is hewn from the four spiritual elements from which all elevated beings were made, the four letters of the divine name.... This is man's essential soul, from the side of goodness. But "God made this [good] corresponding to that [evil]" (Ecclesiastes 7:14). This [corresponding evil soul] is called *adam beliya'al* (the wicked man), and is composed of the four major types of destructiveness, the four types of appearance of leprosy, and, likewise, the four evil elements. From there the evil soul is drawn toward man and is referred to as the *yetzer hara* (evil inclination). When this soul overcomes a person's good soul, harm, plagues, and sicknesses of the soul come upon him. If it overcomes [his good soul] even more it will kill him.

Further reading: For more on the body-soul connection and healing the soul, see p. 119; *A Concise Guide to the Sages*, p. 400.

Torah Concepts

The good soul is "clothed" in the evil soul, and both of them are "clothed" in the body's limbs and sinews:

The pure soul, which is the "fruit"[29] is made up of 613 limbs and sinews which are "clothed" within 613 corresponding limbs and sinews of the impure soul. This impure soul is called the "husk of the fruit."[30] Both souls, together, are clothed in the 613 physical limbs and sinews of the body. It turns out that the limbs of the pure soul are within those of the evil soul, and the limbs of the evil soul are within the limbs of the body.

(Rav Ḥayyim Vital, *Sha'arei Kedusha* 1:1)

Every Jew has two souls, one, called the animal soul, stemming from negative spiritual sources – referred to in kabbalistic literature as the *kelipot* (husks) and *sitra ahra* (the "other side") – and a second soul which is referred to as the divine soul. These two souls battle each other, each trying to gain control of the body, which can be likened to a small city that a powerful king is trying to capture. Victory, for the divine soul, means that the body is totally negated and subjugated to the divine soul. One must remember that the negative soul was also created by God, and He gave it the mandate to challenge and fight the divine soul. It is, therefore, happy when the divine soul overcomes it.

The second, higher soul in a Jew is a fragment of the Most High:

The second soul in a Jew is a fragment of the Most High … Although there are a myriad different levels of the soul, one above the other endlessly… nevertheless, the root of all aspects of the soul[31] in its entirety, from the highest of all levels to the lowest level, which is clothed in the body of the simplest and least-refined person, is drawn from the divine mind, which constitutes supernal wisdom, so to speak.

The structure of the Godly soul:

And so, every aspect and level of these three [components of the soul], *nefesh, ruah,* and *neshama,* is comprised of ten aspects, corresponding to the ten supernal *sefirot* from which they emanated, namely: *hokhma, bina,* and *da'at,* as well as the [*sefirot* known as] "the seven days of construction": *hesed, gevura, tiferet* [*netzah, hod, yesod,* and *malkhut*]. The [ten qualities of the] human soul are also divided into two categories: the intellectual and emotive

29. This is a classic kabbalistic reference to the essential and primary soul.
30. The husks are secondary to, and surround, the fruit but are eventually discarded. So too, the lower, impure soul is secondary and ultimately discarded.
31. The text refers here explicitly to *nefesh, ruah,* and *neshama* – different levels of the soul which have been described in more detail in previous sources.

attributes.... Furthermore, each divine soul has three "garments," namely: thought, speech, and action, [aspects of] of the 613 mitzvot of the Torah.

The structure of the soul from the "other side":

And so, God made this correspond to that. For just as the divine soul [of a person] is comprised of ten holy *sefirot* and is clothed in three holy garments, this is also [the case with] the soul originating from the *sitra ahra*[32] of *kelipat noga*[33] and which is infused in the [person's] blood. It too is comprised of ten crowns of impurity, which are [divided into] seven evil character traits, stemming from the four base elements mentioned previously, as well as the intellect engendering them, which is comprised of three components: *hokhma* (wisdom), *bina* (understanding), and *da'at* (knowledge). These are the source of the character traits.... When a person thinks or speaks about these [ten impure faculties], or acts on them, then the thought of his mind, the speech of his mouth, and the force of action in his hands and other limbs are referred to as "garments of impurity."

The battle of the two souls over control of the body:

It is analogous to two kings waging war over a city. Each wants to conquer it and rule over it, which means making the inhabitants follow his will, so that they obey anything he decrees upon them. So too, the two souls, the divine soul and the vital, animalistic soul from the *kelipa*, battle each other over the body and all its limbs. The divine soul seeks and desires to be its sole ruler, so that all the limbs will be subject to its discipline. [They will then become] a totally subjugated platform for the [divine soul], expressing its ten qualities and three garments, mentioned previously, until they are all clothed in the limbs of the body, such that the body will be infused exclusively with them and nothing foreign will mingle with them, Heaven forbid .... However, the animalistic soul from the *kelipa* desires the exact opposite, for the [ultimate] good of the person, so that he overcomes it and defeats it.

(Rabbi Shneur Zalman of Liadi, *Tanya, Likutei Amarim* 2–9)

Further reading: For more on the meanings of the terms *nefesh*, *ruah*, and *neshama*, see p. 219.

32. *Sitra ahra*, literally the "other side," is the evil spiritual force (see sources above).
33. *Kelipat noga*, literally "the husk of the aura," is a kabbalistic term referring to forces or aspects of the world that contain a mixture of good and evil that can be redeemed for good.

The Soul's Descent to This World

The soul must descend to this world into a coarse physical body. This descent causes the soul tremendous anguish and suffering. However, the soul ignores the anguish and suffering because the goal of its mission is to illuminate the body and its environment with holy light and to transform the physical body into a dwelling place for God.

The soul's descent into the body causes tremendous suffering:

The statements of our Sages, of blessed memory... strongly emphasize something that is clear and self-evident – the soul's purity and pristine clarity. [The soul] is purely spiritual and is intrinsically totally unconnected to physical and material matters, and certainly not to physical desires and the like, [for they] only come about through the body and the animal soul. Nevertheless, the Holy One, blessed be He, wanted this soul, that is directly connected to the divine, to descend and be clothed within a physical and material body and to be connected and united with it for a number of decades. This means that for a number of decades the soul will be in a state totally antithetical to its own nature.

It is impossible to imagine how much suffering the soul endures while fulfilling its mission:

This [process of the soul's descent into this world] is in order to fulfill the mission [it was given by] its Creator, i.e., to purify the body and illuminate a person's this-worldly physical existence with the light of the Endless One,[34] making it a sanctuary and dwelling place for the Divine Presence, may He be blessed. Then, the soul views all of the torture and suffering it endured while in the body and the physical world as totally insignificant. [On the contrary,] the eternal reward and pleasure it will merit through fulfilling its mission are immeasurably valuable compared to the [mere] fleeting suffering of this world.

(Rabbi Menaḥem Mendel Schneerson, *Igrot Kodesh* 8:2:292)

Rabbi Shalom Dovber Schneersohn had a hasid [disciple] who was a successful dealer in precious gems. That hasid once noticed that the Rebbe was paying special attention to, and showing great kindness toward, extremely simple people, which surprised the hasid greatly.

34. The Hebrew expression *Ein Sof* (lit., "Infinity") is the term used in kabbalistic thought for the ineffable, transcendent God who is the source from which the *sefirot* emanate.

When the opportunity presented itself he asked the Rebbe to explain his behavior. "These people have especially great qualities," the Rebbe replied. The hasid responded: "Excuse me, Rebbe, but I don't find anything special about them." The Rebbe did not respond.

Before the hasid traveled home, the Rebbe surprised him by asking him to show him some of his precious gems. The hasid gladly took out his case of diamonds and began to describe to the Rebbe the different qualities of the various stones. The hasid praised one stone in particular and called it a "wonder of wonders."

The Rebbe reacted by saying, "I don't see what you find so special about that stone."

The hasid, slightly offended, said, "You have to be an expert to appreciate them."

The Rebbe smiled, and said, "You also have to be an expert to appreciate a Jewish soul."

Further reading: For more on the simple Jew who saved the Jewish people from a heavenly accusation, see p. 70.

Suffering

This world – as opposed to the World to Come – contains suffering and evil. A believing person, who knows that God is good, asks himself the reason for all the world's suffering and evil. The answer to this question cannot be that it is God's revenge for wrongdoing since God loves the world He created and the people He created within it. If so, how do we explain the existence of suffering?

One of the explanations offered for the existence of suffering is that, through suffering, God gives people an opportunity to atone for their sins in this world, saving them from the more difficult hardships of Gehenna and healing their soul in this world. Another explanation is that suffering is sometimes a test. The righteous who undergo trials and tests willfully accept suffering with joy. All types of suffering are expressions of God's love – not revealed love, but a hidden one from a deep and hidden divine source.

How are we to react to the hardships we experience? One straightforward answer is to focus on bettering ourselves, given that hardships come upon us in order to fix our internal flaws. We should avoid excessive rumination over the goal and purpose of evil in general, and instead focus on how to better ourselves as a result of the suffering.

As human beings, we cannot understand the goal of evil and suffering in this world because of our inability to see more than a tiny portion of existence. Our vantage point is like that of a person with no knowledge of modern medicine observing a surgeon performing an operation. He would most likely think the surgeon cruel, or even a murderer. From our perspective on the world, we likewise see only a tiny part of the picture and do not begin to understand the countless factors involved in divine justice and providence.

Suffering and Divine Love

Suffering has replaced the offerings that the Jewish people would bring when the Temple in Jerusalem was standing. The goal of suffering is to cleanse a person of his sins in this world and save him from punishment in the World to Come. There is an additional reason for suffering. If someone did not suffer at all in this world, it would be as if he received, in this world, the full reward for his good deeds. God therefore brings lower intensity suffering in this world so we can receive our true reward in the next.

Suffering brings atonement now that the Temple is destroyed and we no longer bring offerings:

Why are they referred to as "sufferings of love" (*Berakhot* 5a)? Did we not explain above that suffering [in this world is understood as] punishment for the few sins he did [and therefore should be considered "judgment" and not "love"]?... Even so, one who sinned unknowingly does not deserve to be punished in Gehenna and in the "well of destruction"[35] for his error. Rather, he must be cleansed of that sin, and sanctified and purified, in order to make him fit for the level in the World to Come that is appropriate for his good deeds. Therefore, the Holy One, blessed be He, had mercy on His nation and His pious ones, and gave them [the commandment to bring] offerings to atone for sins done unknowingly. When, [as in our times,] the Temple is not standing, He sends them suffering in order to cleanse them of those unknowing sins.... As such, this suffering is an expression of God's love and compassion for a person.

Minor suffering comes to save a person from losing his reward in the World to Come:

Our Sages also mentioned another approach to suffering. They said: "In the academy of Rabbi Yishmael they taught: Anyone who went forty days without suffering has [already] received his [reward in this] world [as opposed to the World to Come]" (*Arakhin* 16b). The explanation is as follows: There are things that naturally happen to a person, like occasional inconveniences, bodily pain from eating spoiled food, or getting a headache from exposure to the sun. These are bothersome parts of life that even happen to kings. The only person who is saved from these [minor troubles] is the evil person who is destined for Gehenna and receives his reward in this world. Heaven makes sure that such a person is able to get whatever he wants in this world [in order to be punished fully in the next].

(Ramban, *Torat HaAdam, Sha'ar HaGemul*)

God wants the best for man. As such, when He brings man suffering His intent is to heal the sickness in his soul and to remind him to change his evil ways. If a person does not internalize this message, he ends up being punished twice, once in this world and once in the next. But when he is receptive to the divine message, he should be happy and thankful for the suffering he experienced.

You should know that God's reproof [through suffering] is for man's good. For if a man sins before Him and does something wrong in His eyes, God's reproof accomplishes two things: One is to atone for his sins and remove his iniquity.... It is through the body's sickness that the soul's sickness is healed, for sin is a sickness of the soul.... The second [goal of divine reproof] is to remind a person to repent from his evil ways. But if he does not internalize

35. This expression *be'er shahat* is taken from Psalms 55:24 and is used as a description of the place of punishment in the afterlife.

the reproof, nor humble himself as a result of the rebuke, and does not make a true internal transformation, woe to him and woe to his soul. For he endured suffering and bore punishment for his sin, yet his sin was not atoned for – and he ends up receiving double the punishment [in this world and the next]. But when a person is receptive to the divine reproof and improves his character and behavior [as a result], he should be happy about his suffering, for it benefited him immensely in many lofty ways. The suffering is a cause to thank God, may He be blessed, just like any other success [in life].

(Rabbeinu Yona Gerondi, *Sha'arei Teshuva* 2:3–4)

Further reading: For more on reward and punishment, see p. 256.

Suffering is also divine goodness which comes from above. In fact, it stems from a higher spiritual level than revealed goodness. Suffering, which appears in this world to be darkness, actually comes from a hidden lofty divine revelation, an extremely high divine light.

The Sages offer sound advice to clear one's heart of any sadness or nagging worries about mundane matters, or even [difficulties with] children, health or livelihood.... [Accept with joy] that this is also good. Its benefit is just not apparent to mortal eyes, since it emanates from the concealed world, which is higher than the revealed world.

(Rabbi Shneur Zalman of Liadi, *Tanya, Likutei Amarim* 26)

Every individual must connect with God through his own personal type of spiritual service. As such, the suffering a person endures is connected to his own spiritual level. Suffering also illuminates a person's soul and diminishes the importance of his body and materialism in his life. So one who undergoes suffering is purified and cleansed, and can be a positive influence on many others.

The suffering each person experiences fits his own particular soul and the way he as an individual is supposed to serve God:

Everyone experiences suffering according to his own soul and his own particular divine service. One person suffers because of his children or a parent or neighbor. Another, on a higher level, suffers [even] from distant neighbors. Another, even greater, suffers from anywhere in the city. And there are those who are very great who suffer from the entire world.

Suffering empowers the soul:

Anyone who suffers from particular people [in a sense] "carries" those people, for when he suffers from them he carries them upon himself. But how can a [limited] physical being carry so many people? [The process is as follows:] Through suffering his body becomes submissive – for all suffering is referred to as *tzarot* (troubles) because it constricts (*metzirin*) and oppresses the body. When the body is crushed through troubles, the soul shines and grows – for when [man's] physical [side] is subdued, his spiritual form (*tzura*[36]) grows.... The word *tzara* (trouble) is related to the word *tzura* (spiritual form), for through *tzarot* (troubles) the *tzura* (spiritual makeup) grows. It follows that through suffering and troubles a person's spiritual form – his soul – grows. [Because it grows] it is now able to carry on it a large number of people.

(Rabbi Naḥman of Breslov, *Likutei Moharan* 170)

Further reading: For more on the value of suffering, see *A Concise Guide to the Sages*, p. 256.

Reacting to Suffering

A person who suffers should react with joy and not become angry about the divine decree. The greatness of the righteous, who withstood the trials and tests they were put through, was in that they accepted them willingly and graciously. Suffering might be a punishment for sin or it might be a divinely orchestrated trial or test. No matter what its source, the suffering should be welcomed and accepted willingly.

A person should endure suffering with joy:

When a person encounters difficulty, whether [it affects] his body, his property, or any other matters, he should accept it all from his God with joy. He should endure the suffering willingly, accepting divine judgment, as opposed to suffering in anger over the decree.... Know, my brother, that we would not have praised Abraham for enduring the ten tests that God put him through if he had not accepted them all from God willingly and graciously. This is what the verse states [about Abraham]: "You found his heart faithful before You" (Nehemiah 9:8).

36. See footnote 27 above concerning the concept of *tzura*.

There are three types of suffering, with two divine goals:

You should distinguish in your mind between three different types of suffering: (1) suffering in order to serve God; (2) suffering in order to avoid rebelling against Him; and (3) suffering due to unfortunate events of this world. This third category can be subdivided into two: (a) suffering due to losing something [important]; and (b) [suffering due to the] lack of something much desired. Whichever type it is, the suffering may come upon you as punishment in order to bring forgiveness for sin; or it could be initiated by God as a trial or test so that God will increase your reward through the suffering and magnify your portion [in the World to Come]. Whichever of these two types it is, you should accept what God brings you willingly and graciously.

(Rabbeinu Baḥya ibn Pakuda, *Ḥovot HaLevavot* 8:3)

One who thinks that suffering comes to him "by chance" will evoke a negative divine reaction. God will relate to him as if "by chance," without special protection. There is certainly a reason behind suffering and a goal that it accomplishes. When a person experiences suffering, he should examine his actions carefully. In that way, the suffering can be an impetus for positive transformation and repentance.

When a person sees he is beginning to experience suffering he should not think that it came by chance. For someone who believes that is the case will be punished measure for measure. He will be left unprotected by God and subject to chance occurrences, as the Torah states: "And if you walk recalcitrantly with Me…so I also will walk with you recalcitrantly" (Leviticus 26:21–24). This is a great punishment, for the world is full of so many random occurrences that blow about [like winds], and one who is abandoned by Heaven has no protection at all.… But if a person experiences suffering and [yet] he thinks he did not sin, he should pay close attention to his behavior and he will find a reason for the suffering. He should carefully examine his actions and repent.

(Rav Yitzḥak Abuhav, *Menorat Hama'or* 5:3:1:1)

Further reading: For more on divine providence, see p. 173.

When a person experiences suffering he should not ask, "Why did God do this?" He should rather ask himself, "How should I react?" The reason for asking this question is because the purpose of suffering is to repair man's flaws. Through suffering a person must experience a spiritual crisis, an inner shock This crisis can then be a source of growth.

The question of the man of destiny:

When the "man of destiny"[37] suffers, he says in his heart, "There is evil, I do not deny it, and I will not conceal it with fruitless casuistry. I am, however, interested in it from a halakhic point of view, and as a person who wants to know what action to take. I ask a single question: "What should the sufferer do to live with his suffering?" In this dimension, the emphasis is removed from causal and teleological considerations… and is directed to the realm of action. The problem is now formulated in the language of a simple *halakha* and revolves around a daily task. The question of questions is: What does suffering obligate a man to do? This problem was important to Judaism, which placed it at the center of its *Weltanschauung*.… We do not wonder about the ineffable ways of the Holy One, but instead ponder the paths man must take when evil leaps up at him. We ask not about the reason for evil and its purpose, but about its rectification and uplifting. How should a man react in a time of distress? What should a man do so as not to rot in his afflictions?

The purpose of suffering is to repair flaws in man's personality:

The halakhic answer to this question is very simple. Suffering comes to elevate man, to purify his spirit and sanctify him, to cleanse his mind and purify it from the chaff of superficiality and the dross of crudeness, to sensitize his soul and expand his horizons. In general, the purpose of suffering is to repair the imperfection in man's persona.

Suffering without experiencing transformation is pointless and spiritually dangerous:

How pitiful if man's sufferings do not bring him to a spiritual crisis, and his soul remains frozen and bereft of forgiveness. How pitiful is the sufferer if his soul is not warmed by the flame of suffering, and if his wounds do not spark "the candle of God" (Proverbs 20:27) within him. When pain wanders in the wide world as a blind force without purpose, a stinging indictment of the man who squanders his suffering issues forth.

(Rabbi Yosef Dov Soloveitchik, *Kol Dodi Dofek* 7–9)

37. As contrasted with the "man of fate" who is helpless in the face of events, the "man of destiny" seeks to respond constructively, and in accordance with *halakha*, to life's challenges.

The Existence of Evil

The world is, for the most part, good, but because of our distorted perspective we sometimes perceive it to be predominantly evil. Most of the bad things in this world are not caused by external events, but are the result of human action. People often suffer because of their own character and personality flaws – for instance, due to the uncontrollable preoccupation with physical desires.

Those who think the world is mostly evil are mistaken:

People often think that there is more evil in the world than good; many sayings and songs of the nations dwell on this idea. They say that it is rare to find a good event, whereas evil events are numerous and lasting. Not only do common people make this mistake, but even many who believe that they are wise.... The reason for this error is that this ignorant man, and those like him among the common people, judge the whole world by looking at only one single person. For an ignorant man believes that the whole world exists only for him; as if he is the only relevant factor. If, therefore, anything happens to him that he does not like, he at once concludes definitively that the whole universe is evil. If, however, he were to just consider all of existence and comprehend what a small part of the universe he actually is, the truth would become clear. For this misconception has become widespread in that people see [only] the multitude of evils in the world... Their only focus is on certain individuals in the human species. What we actually have to consider is this: Every individual in mankind that is alive at present, and *a fortiori*, those of every other species of animals, are of infinitesimally small value in the context of the universe as a whole.

What are the causes of evil in the world?

The first type of evil is that which happens to people due to the natural reality of creation and decay; namely, that they possess a physical body.... You will, nevertheless, find that the evils of this kind that befall man are very few and only happen rarely.... The second type of evil consists of the harm that people cause to each other.... The causes of this are numerous and well known; this kind of evil is nevertheless not widespread among people in any country of the world. On the contrary, it happens rarely.... This type of evil does affect many people in the course of great wars, but even these are not frequent in the world as a whole. The third type of evil consists of that which a person causes to himself by his own actions. This is the largest group.... All people complain especially about this type of evil.... This evil stems from man's vices, such as excessive desire for eating, drinking, and sexual activity, over-indulgence and bad habits in these areas, or poor-quality food.

(Rambam, *Guide of the Perplexed* III:12)

External appearances can be deceiving, and can even evoke the exact opposite interpretation of what is really happening. To someone who does not understand medicine, a surgeon might appear to be torturing an innocent and helpless person, cutting into his flesh with a sharp knife. But the moment we explain to him that he is watching a sensitive and humane, experienced surgeon trying to save the life of a patient, his interpretation of the entire scene transforms. A superficial view of suffering and misfortune likewise can evoke a gross misconception of what they really are, and create a mistaken picture of a painful world. Suffering is certainly meant for man's good.

Man sees the external picture:

To clarify this idea I will use an analogy from the world of medicine: A person without any proper knowledge of medicine enters the operating room of a hospital. He sees in front of him a naked and helpless man lying on a table, surrounded by masked people who are holding lethal weapons (knives and other instruments). The masked men cut, poke, and extract this hopeless man's blood, ignoring the groans of their drugged and immobilized victim. The stranger's instinctive reaction would be to call for help: "Sadists are attacking a helpless man and mercilessly torturing him!" From his limited perspective and based on his "understanding" of medicine there is no doubt in his mind that he is witnessing first-degree murder.

The inner meaning of what he witnessed:

Had the stranger known that what he was witnessing was, in fact, a vital medical operation to save the life and health of the sick patient, he would easily have understood that those few hours of suffering on the operating table were not only tolerable but essential. The stranger would have been able to see and even to prove that the surgeons were not only not murderers, but exactly the opposite, deeply humanitarian people doing a great service to a sick man. He would maintain this impression even though [he knows that] the doctors are only human, cannot guarantee the success of the operation or the patient's complete recovery, and do not know how long the patient will live even if the operation succeeds.

The divine plan:

From all of this you can understand that during a person's lifetime in this world it is possible that [he will experience] periods of pain and suffering (either real or imaginary). But we know and can bear witness that all of this is [guided by] divine providence. It is clear to us that things do not "just happen" in our world. Painful events like these are part of the divine plan that takes into account the individual, his family, all other people [affected by it], and whatever happens to them. A person who thinks rationally will understand that the things that happened to him are, in truth, part of a system of divine providence at work in the world. [Our inability to understand suffering] is because we do not accept the [divine] promise of the Doctor or the Surgeon that great benefit will come from the temporary pain and suffering.

(Rabbi Menaḥem Mendel Schneerson, *Emuna UMada*, p. 84)

When Rabbi Shmelke of Nikolsburg visited the *maggid* (preacher) of Mezritch for the first time, he complained that he did not understand the meaning of the rabbinic statement: "One is obligated to recite a blessing for the bad [that befalls him] just as he recites a blessing for the good" (*Berakhot* 54a).

The *maggid* answered him: "Go to the study hall and you'll find my student Rabbi Zusha (of Anipol), and he'll explain the matter to you."

Rabbi Zusha was poor and needy his entire life. When he heard that the *maggid* had sent Rabbi Shmelke to him he was amazed, and said, "Why did our rabbi send you specifically to me? This question should be asked of one who at least once experienced suffering, whereas nothing bad has ever happened to me during my entire life. Thank God, I have only experienced good. How would I be able to understand the concept of accepting bad things with joy?"

Then Rabbi Shmelke understood the answer.

Livelihood

As opposed to the animals, who find their food readily available, human beings have to work for their livelihood. Adam, the first man, was already told: "By the sweat of your brow shall you eat bread" (Genesis 3:19). Nevertheless, a person who trusts in God believes that God will provide for his needs, just as He does for all the rest of His creatures. All he needs is for God to open his eyes so he can realize that.

Every day a person should pray to God to provide for his needs in a way that he can easily receive them. Even as he works to earn a living, a person should keep in mind that it is God who gives him the ability to be successful.

God Provides for All of Creation – as Well as for Man

God is concerned to provide for all of His creatures, and a person who trusts in God believes that He also provides for his own sustenance.

This person who trusts in and casts his lot upon God, may He be blessed, must think about the following: God is the one who gives food and sustenance to the bird flying in the sky and the chick developing in an egg. Even though they are in places where food cannot be brought, they nevertheless do not lack their sustenance because of God's loving-kindness, may He be blessed. All the more so [is this true for] man. God will certainly not withhold sustenance from man, who has an intelligent soul, and because of his intelligence is the recipient of divine providence.

(Rabbeinu Baḥya ibn Ḥalawa, *Kad HaKemaḥ, Parnasa*)

Man's Sustenance Is Prepared for Him

God has already prepared for man whatever he needs, but this is not always apparent. God must open up a person's eyes so he can see that this is indeed the case.

"Everyone is considered blind until the Holy One, blessed be He, opens up their eyes" (*Bereshit Rabba* 53:14). My teacher and grandfather (Rabbi Yitzḥak Meir of Gur), of blessed memory, explained as follows: Every need of every creature is prepared for him at all times and in all places, yet it is hidden from one's physical eyes. When the Holy One, blessed be He, opens up his eyes, a person sees that everything [he needs] is before him.

(Rabbi Yehuda Leib Alter, *Sefat Emet, Ḥukat* 5659)

How Prayer Affects Livelihood

At the beginning of each year, God grants each person his yearly portion of divine loving-kindness, but it remains on a high spiritual plane in the upper worlds. How that divine loving-kindness flows into his day-to-day existence in this temporal world is dependent on daily prayer.

Our [daily] prayers for health and sustenance and the like can be understood as follows: Even though [our yearly portion of sustenance] is fixed by God on Rosh HaShana and Yom Kippur, that divine decision only applies to the expression of divine loving-kindness in a general way, before it takes any concrete physical form. However, every day we request [in our prayers] that the loving-kindness set aside for us, and drawn from the highest spiritual levels, should take the concrete physical form [of good health and livelihood].

(Rabbi Shalom Dovber Schneersohn, *Kuntres UMa'ayan* 19:2)

Rabbi Levi Yitzḥak of Berditchev was once walking in the marketplace and saw a Jew wildly running through the streets, agitated.

The righteous rabbi asked him, "Where are you running?"

"For sustenance, for livelihood," replied the Jew, throwing his hands in the air. "I'm running after livelihood."

The righteous rabbi then asked, "How do you know that your livelihood is in front of you and you're running to find it? Maybe it is behind you and you're running away from it!"

I learned from my teachers, may God protect them, that anyone who is diligent about saying the blessing after a meal will be assured of having his livelihood provided for honorably for his entire life.

(*Sefer HaḤinnukh*, Mitzva 430)

Even with the greatest exertion, it is impossible to earn even one penny more than the Holy One, blessed be He, set for how much an individual will earn [in a particular year]. One must do all that is necessary to earn a living. But one must remember that all of the work we do is only secondary to God's blessing, may He be blessed, which is the main source of livelihood. We merit [such blessing] by acting as a Jew properly should.

(Rabbi Yosef Yitzḥak Schneersohn, *Hayom Yom*, 4 *Menaḥem Av*)

Further reading: For more on trusting that God will supply all of a person's needs, see p. 154.

The Righteous

Every generation has its righteous individuals and Torah scholars, extraordinary individuals who connect themselves intensely to God. All of Israel is one entity, likened to one body whose "head" is the *tzadik* (righteous person). Through him spiritual vitality reaches every individual. Someone who clings to and connects with the *tzadik* taps into his essence, the source of his soul, thereby connecting himself to God.

The *tzadik* influences his environment by setting an example. He intends that everything he does should be for God's sake. He seeks to find out what God's will is concerning everything he encounters. The *tzadik* can pray concerning a sick person with the same intensity with which he prays for himself, and this prayer can have a beneficial effect on the sick person. A *tzadik* can understand things through the divine inspiration which rests upon him, and in his face one can discern the light of the divine presence.

Even after a *tzadik* dies one can cling to the soul of the *tzadik* and connect with the belief in God and fear and love of God that were the focus of his life. People go to the grave of a *tzadik* to pray to God to receive divine influence, as well as to be able to connect to the spirit of the *tzadik*.

The Wise and the Righteous

Through divine inspiration the wise are able to access hidden knowledge.

The wise are always superior to the prophets. For divine inspiration sometimes rests upon the prophets and sometimes it does not. But divine inspiration has not left the wise even for one moment. They know "what is above" and "what is below" [in the upper and lower levels of existence] but have never wanted to reveal it.

(*Zohar* 2:6:2)

The Divine Presence shines on the faces of the righteous, and their natural countenance is one of awe, humility, and contrition.

The righteous are called "the face of the Divine Presence" (Jerusalem Talmud, *Eiruvin* 5:1). The light of the Divine Presence shines on their faces and they feel contrite [and are filled with] humility, awe, and serious-mindedness. This is what is meant by the verse: "So that His fear will be on your faces" (Exodus 20:17). The word "fear" alludes to the Divine Presence that is referred to as "fear," and that illuminates their faces.

(Rabbi Elazar Azkari, *Sefer Ḥaredim, Mitzvot Hateluyot Ba'aretz,* chap. 4)

Further reading: For more on the images of the wise man and the righteous man in talmudic and rabbinic anecdotes, see *A Concise Guide to the Sages*, p. 317.

The Righteous Man's Behavior

The secret of the Torah scholar's powerful positive influence on others is not his great knowledge, but his outstanding behavior and the example he sets. When Torah learning leads a person to love of God, integrity, righteousness, and control over his desires and drives, he becomes a role model for others.

It is not his vast knowledge that causes one to be recognized as a Torah scholar. His vast knowledge is also not that which draws others to Torah. It is rather his way of life that attests to his knowledge, and the personal example he sets in how he lives his life that draws others' hearts and souls to Torah. For if his [own] learning did not lead him to love of God, how could he influence others in this? If he is not ready to offer up his drives and desires on God's altar, if his lifestyle and actions are not in synchrony with his knowledge, who will accept such a Torah – that he himself abandons in his own life?

(Rabbi Samson Raphael Hirsch, *BeMa'agalei Shana*, part 4, p. 48)

The righteous know how to direct all their desires to God, who then reciprocates by directing His will toward them.

How fortunate are the righteous, who know how to direct their will to the lofty and holy King. All of their yearnings are not focused on this world, with its worthless desire. Instead, they know and try to direct their will and cling [to God] on high, in order to draw their Master's will to them, from above to below.

(*Zohar* 2:134b)

Further reading: For more on educating through setting an example, see p. 188.

The righteous have goals and intentions for all of their actions, even when, superficially, they seem to be involved in mundane activities. It is therefore meaningless for simple people to try to emulate the external aspects of how the righteous act.

When a simple person sees good and pious people involved in day-to-day matters, similar to the way we observe that our forefathers [Abraham, Isaac, and Jacob] were mostly involved in agriculture and livestock... he says to himself, "I'll do the same." Woe to people who see but do not realize what they see, for they only see the superficial aspect of things but do not appreciate their inner content. For the righteous do what they do with good and proper intentions, whereas others [do the same activities] but for meaningless purposes.

(Rabbeinu Nisim Gerondi, *Derashot HaRan, Derush* 7)

God's will is all-pervasive in creation, and the righteous are constantly seeking out what is the will of God.

The *tzadik* (righteous person) is always seeking out and searching to reveal God's will, may He be blessed. For the divine will is everywhere in creation, both in a general way – that God willed to create the entire world – and in all of the details of creation. In each and every detail God's will, may He be blessed, is present.... The *tzadik* constantly searches for and seeks out all of these [manifestations of] divine will. [He strives] to grasp and know the divine will, may He be blessed, in every thing. For instance: [He asks himself,] "Why is it God's will that the lion should have so much might and strength?"

(Rabbi Naḥman of Breslov, *Likutei Moharan* 17)

Connecting to the Wise and the Righteous

The Torah commands us to cling to God. Our Sages, of blessed memory, explained that clinging to Torah sages enables us to cling to God (*Ketuvot* 111b). One who connects with Torah sages learns Torah from them, and learns their outlook on life, for the righteous are the foundation of the Torah's continuity and give support to the souls of the nation.

We have been commanded to connect with and cling to Torah sages in order to learn from them the important mitzvot of the Torah and so that they can teach us the true understandings of Torah which are received [through tradition] from them.... For the Torah sages enable the Torah to endure, and they create a strong foundation to save the souls [of Israel]. For anyone who regularly associates with them will not easily sin. King Solomon said: "He who walks with the wise will become wise" (Proverbs 13:20). Our Sages, of blessed memory, said: "Sit in the dust of their [the Sages'] feet" (*Avot* 1:4).

(*Sefer HaḤinnukh*, Mitzva 434)

The nation of Israel is like one body with many limbs. The life force of all of the limbs is dependent on the brain in the head, and the brain of Israel is composed of the righteous and wise of each generation. One who clings to them is connected fundamentally to the source of his soul.

The souls of the simple people receive their sustenance and life force from the souls of the righteous and the Sages, the leaders of the Jewish people in that generation. This explains the statement of our rabbis on the verse,

"To cleave to Him" (Deuteronomy 30:20), that whoever cleaves to Torah scholars is considered by this verse as though he is actually cleaving to the Divine Presence (*Ketubot* 111b). By clinging to Torah scholars, the souls of the simple people are bound and united with their original essence and their [spiritual] roots in the supernal wisdom.

(Rabbi Shneur Zalman of Liadi, *Tanya, Likutei Amarim*, chap. 2)

The *Tzadik*'s Prayer

We do not pray to God through angels or other intermediaries from the upper worlds; instead, we pray directly to God. Nevertheless, it is permissible to request that the righteous pray on our behalf. This does not raise a concern about people praying to the righteous person himself, for he is only human and it is clear to all that he is not the source of anything good or bad.

It is permissible to request that the righteous pray on our behalf:

It is prohibited to pray to angels or other higher spiritual powers to act as intermediaries between us and our Creator. But there is no prohibition [to request that] the righteous – whose prayers are fitting to be answered – [pray on our behalf, for they] are creatures of this lower world.

The righteous are human beings, so there is no danger that people will serve them as opposed to God:

There are two reasons for this: One is that because of the high level of that middle world [of the angels and other purely spiritual beings] people are liable to mistakenly worship them through praying to them to be intermediaries. People will then come to think that the angels can cause good or harm and that it is appropriate to pray to them as independent entities. But it is impossible for them to make such a mistake with regard to creatures of this low world.... A second reason is that the lofty heavenly beings are not subject to occurrences and shortcomings of this world.... Therefore, if people pray to them, they will mistakenly think that, just as the [higher beings] are not subject to chance and weakness, so too, they have the ability to fulfill everyone's wishes and save people from random accidents and problems. But human beings, as righteous as they are, are subject to the misfortunes of this world and its occurrences. Therefore, when people come to the righteous and ask them to pray on their behalf, there is no concern that those people will make the mistake [of thinking the righteous have independent powers], since the same unfortunate event that happened to them can also happen to the righteous person.

(Rabbi Moshe of Trani (Mabit), *Bet Elohim, Sha'ar HaTefilla* 12)

A Torah sage who prays for another person does not approach his prayer as an outsider, for he feels the other's pain as if it were his own. He is not simply like an independent agent or a separate person serving as a go-between, but he prays, in a broad sense, for himself. There is actually an advantage to the righteous man's prayer. Because he is considered like the "head" of the Jewish people, it is natural that he should be the one to stand before God.

All of Israel are partners, as one body with one soul, and when one is in pain, another feels it and shares his pain. This is the source of Rava's statement: "One who prays for another must make himself ill on his behalf" (*Berakhot* 12b). The explanation is as follows: He should realize that he himself is sick [because all of Israel is as one body and soul]. Since both of them are in pain, it is better that the head should enter [before God to pray] rather than, for instance, the foot. The Torah scholar is the head, and the one [originally] in pain, who is now experiencing divine judgment and is being somewhat rebuked by Heaven, is like the foot. [Since that is the case,] it is better that the "head" enter [before God instead of the "foot"], since both are the relevant parties [who need to pray] and the Torah scholar is not merely a negotiator on behalf of another.

(Rabbi Moshe Sofer, *She'elot UTeshuvot Ḥatam Sofer, Oraḥ Ḥayyim* 166)

Any physical deficiency or need a person has is the result of some spiritual deficiency within him. The connection between the *tzadik* (righteous person) and the sick person that takes place when the *tzadik* prays on his behalf enables the sick person to repair his sin. It naturally follows that the need for punishment is removed and the sick person is able to recover.

We need to understand [the mechanism of how] a *tzadik* prays and his prayer is answered. This seems like a change [in the divine plan], yet God, in His ultimate Oneness, cannot change, heaven forbid. The matter can be explained as follows: When a *tzadik* prays for a person he does it with all of his 248 limbs and 365 sinews, without any external thoughts, and he connects the person he is praying for with his own 248 limbs, thereby elevating him. That is why he is answered. For where does the original deficiency come from? Certainly it is a punishment for a sin [the sick person] did with one of the limbs of his body. When the *tzadik* enwraps and covers him [through prayer], the limbs of the sick person become one with those of the *tzadik*, and that naturally repairs his sin. Once the sin is repaired, the punishment passes and leaves him.

(Rabbi Elimelekh of Lizhensk, *Noam Elimelekh, Parashat Emor, "Eleh Mo'adei Hashem"*)

Connecting with the Righteous after Their Death

While the *tzadik* is alive in this world, his influence is restricted by the limits of his physical existence. However, after his passing, anyone can draw from the *tzadik*'s true life – his belief, awe and love of God – without any physical limitations.

The *tzadik*'s true life is belief, awe, and love:

The holy Zohar states, "A *tzadik* is present in all the worlds even more after his death than during his lifetime" (*Zohar* 3:71b). This requires explanation. Granted, he is more present in the upper worlds since he has ascended there; but how can he be more present in this world? The answer is based on the explanation I received of the phrase used by our Sages, of blessed memory, "[the deceased] has left his life to all the living." As it is known, the life of the *tzadik* is not physical, but rather a spiritual life, comprised of faith, awe, and love of God.

After his death, the *tzadik*'s spiritual influence is not bound by the body:

And so, when the *tzadik* was living on this earth, these three attributes [of faith, awe, and love of God] were contained within their "vessel" and "clothing" in a physical location, in the sense of the soul bound to his body. All of his disciples could receive only the illumination and radiance of those qualities which could shine forth from this vessel – through his holy speech and thoughts.... However, after his passing, the aspect of his soul that remains in the grave separates from his spirit residing in the Garden of Eden, which is comprised of these three attributes. Therefore, all who are close to him are able to receive a measure from his spirit in the Garden of Eden, since it is not contained in a vessel nor confined to the dimensions of a physical location.

(Rabbi Schneur Zalman of Liadi, *Tanya, Igeret HaKodesh* 27)

Further reading: For more on visiting the graves of the righteous, see *A Concise Guide to the Sages*, p. 187.

The *tzadik* influences his disciples even after his passing. His students include not only those who actually came into contact with him during his lifetime, but even those who drew from his Torah and were strengthened through it in their own service of God.

A person can be considered a disciple of the *tzadik* even if he did not know about the *tzadik* nor come into contact with him while he was alive, but only learned of the holy books he wrote and left as a blessing after he passed away, and benefited from the illumination and radiance of his Torah, being strengthened in their service of God by those books which teach him how to serve and walk in the ways of God. Such a person is also connected with him for he believes in [the greatness of] the *tzadik* and receives from him the light of his Torah.

(Rabbi Shalom Dovber Schneersohn, *Kuntres HaHishtatḥut*, p. 28)

The Graves of the Righteous

Divine influence is present in the world, and during the *tzadik*'s lifetime it affects his very body. Even after the *tzadik*'s passing, the divine influence is present at his grave and it is worthwhile praying at the grave and tapping into that divine influence.

Not only during the lifetime of the righteous, but even after their death, the divine influence stays with them and is present in some way at their graves. For their bones, which [during their lifetime,] were already vehicles for the divine influence to take hold, still retain within them sufficient distinction to bestow that kind of influence. This is the reason why our Sages, of blessed memory, said that it is worthwhile prostrating oneself at the graves of the righteous and praying there to God. Prayer there is more readily accepted [than in other places], given the presence of the [physical] bodies which had already been affected by divine influence.

(Rabbeinu Nisim Gerondi, *Derashot HaRan* 8)

There are five levels of spiritual achievement when visiting graves of the righteous. The highest levels include the contrition and self-negation a person feels when encountering the soul of a righteous person, as well as connecting one's own spirit with the spirit of the *tzadik*.

A person feels contrition when encountering a *tzadik*:

People may visit the grave of a *tzadik* that they knew and were familiar with during his lifetime... when he was within a physical body. But now that the *tzadik*'s soul is in its pure spiritual state, this can bring the visitor to experience great contrition and actual self-negation, for he feels extremely ashamed by all of his actions and thoughts until now – since they are all revealed. For even while he was alive the *tzadik* knew people's thoughts and plans, as is well known. This is certainly the case for the soul of the *tzadik* after he passed away, which is purely spiritual.

Clinging to the soul of the *tzadik*:

Furthermore, through a powerfully connecting belief in the [greatness of the] soul of the *tzadik* [which comes] from the innermost part of a person's heart, and through using one's spiritual powers of imagination and creativity, and through great self-negation, a person's soul can cling to some aspect of the soul of the *tzadik* who dwells there [in the grave].... This is the concept of belief in the righteous, whereby people can travel to visit their graves even though they do not grasp the *tzadik*'s spiritual level at all.

(Rabbi Shalom Dovber Schneersohn, *Kuntres HaHishtatḥut* 8)

Rabbi Yitzḥak of Neskhiz had opponents who would annoy him in various ways. Once, when they intensified their pursuit of the rabbi, one of those close to the *tzadik* was unable to hold back and cursed them.

Rabbi Yitzḥak said: "The Holy One, blessed be He, doesn't listen to the curses of someone who loves a shot glass of liquor and enjoys a good sleep."

The disciple responded: "If that's the case, let the Rebbe himself – who doesn't enjoy a shot of liquor and doesn't enjoy a good sleep – curse him."

The rabbi responded: "Such a person loves to bless and not to curse."

In every generation sparks descend from the soul of our teacher Moses, may he rest in peace, and they clothe themselves in the bodies and souls of the sages of that generation, the "eyes" of the community, to teach the people so that they may know the greatness of God and serve Him with their heart and soul.

(Rabbi Shneur Zalman of Liadi, *Tanya, Likutei Amarim*, chap. 42)

Through his holy actions a *tzadik* can cancel all [negative heavenly] decrees against Israel. When the *tzadik* issues a decree, the Holy One, blessed be He, fulfills it. As the Sages state: The *tzadik* decrees and the Holy One, blessed be He, fulfills (see *Ta'anit* 23a).

(Rabbi Elimelekh of Lizhensk, *Noam Elimelekh*)

The *tzadik* always stands between God and the world, connecting the mute and dark world with divine speech and divine light.

(Rabbi Abraham Isaac Hakohen Kook, *Orot HaKodesh* 3:229)

The pure *tzadikim* do not complain about evil – they instead add righteousness. They do not complain about heresy – they instead add belief. They do not complain about ignorance – they instead add wisdom.

(Rabbi Abraham Isaac Hakohen Kook, *Arpelei Tohar,* 39)

Further reading: For our Sages' comments about the great levels the righteous reach, see *A Concise Guide to the Sages*, pp. 44, 179, 211, 337.

Charity

Concern for the weak and unfortunate is a theme that runs through many mitzvot. Keeping Shabbat includes a special emphasis on the servant and maidservant resting; we separate tithes from produce and give them to those who do not own land; every seven years there is a sabbatical year, when the poor freely eat of the field's produce. In addition to all of those mitzvot, there is a specific mitzva to give charity, money given to support the poor.

Supporting a person so he does not need to collect donations is an especially high level of charity. However, someone who does not want to work need not be given charity. The underlying concept behind the Jewish view of charity is expressed through the Hebrew word *tzedaka* – which derives from the root *tzadi-dalet-kof* – meaning that which is just and correct. The act of giving charity involves all aspects of the person, and the giver also gains through giving charity, not only the receiver. One who gives charity to the poor merits protection during times of strict divine judgment, and purifies his soul to make it more fitting and receptive to divine goodness. The giver receives ultimate and eternal goodness in the World to Come.

How Should Charity Be Given?

There are many ways to give charity. Even though all gifts to the poor are considered charity, there are nevertheless different levels of giving. The best of all is to help a person who lost his livelihood to find work, or to lend him money so he can build up his own livelihood and not need to collect donations. The lowest of all levels is to give begrudgingly.

There are eight levels of charity, each higher than the other: (1) The highest level of all is to help a Jew who became poor by giving him a gift or loan, entering into a [business] partnership with him, or finding him work to strengthen him so he will not need to ask others [for donations].... (2) A level below this is giving charity to the poor without knowing to whom one gave and without the poor person knowing from whom he received, for this is a mitzva [done] for its own sake.... Putting money in a *tzedaka* box is similar to this.... (3) Lower than this is where the giver knows to whom he is giving, but the poor person does not know from whom he received.... (4) Lower than this is where the poor knows from whom he received but the giver does not know to whom he is giving... to avoid the poor becoming embarrassed. (5) Lower than this is giving the poor person before he asks. (6) Lower than this is giving him after he asks. (7) Lower than this is giving less than appropriate, but giving it with a pleasant smile. (8) Lower than this is giving begrudgingly.

(Rambam, *Mishneh Torah, Hilkhot Matnot Ani'im* 10:7–14)

Further reading: For more on the greatness of charity, see *A Concise Guide to the Sages*, pp. 240, 245, 426, 457.

The best type of charity is to support the poor with dignity. Even though it does not appear to be charity, finding a job for someone who is having difficulty finding work, or buying merchandise from someone having difficulty selling it is a high level of charity. However, if someone can work but just does not want to, there is no need to feel sorry for him and give him charity.

There is a type of charity that does not appear like charity, but, before the Holy One, blessed be He, it is considered an excellent form of charity. One example is if a poor person has an object for sale or [is selling] a book that people don't want to buy – and a person buys it from him. Another example is if a poor person wants to write [a *mezuza, tefillin,* or a *sefer Torah*] but people do not want to hire him – and someone hires him. There is no better charity [than this]: He works at writing and you give him profit. But if you see a person who could learn and understand, or a scribe who could write, but they do not want to learn or write – if you give them charity, I would consider this [a fulfillment of the verse]: "[He hoped for justice, but behold, corruption;] for righteousness (*tzedaka*), but behold, outcry (*tze'aka*)" (Isaiah 5:7).

(Rabbi Yehuda HeḤasid, *Sefer Ḥasidim* 1035)

There are two complementary types of charity. One is fixed and organized, and another stems from compassion. God gave us many mitzvot to perform acts of kindness so the poor are not dependent on generosity of the rich alone. However, a rich person must also open up his heart and give out of compassion, not only because he is commanded to give. The Torah ensures that the needs of the poor are fully taken care of through a combination of two elements: (1) fear of God, which arouses a person's feelings to give to the poor; and (2) a sense of obligation and acceptance of the "the yoke of Heaven," which requires a person to give, irrespective of his feelings. When charity is given as a holy obligation, a poor person will not experience a feeling of shame, for he receives the gift from God Himself.

The advantage of fixed, obligatory charity:

This type of charity, where a person regularly donates a tenth of his income, becomes for the donor a holy obligation, rooted extremely deeply in his

Torah Concepts

consciousness. Its value is immeasurably greater than an act of kindness done out of spontaneous inspiration, that is fleeting and abrupt.

Further reading: For the laws of tithing income and charity in general, see *A Concise Guide to Halakha*, p. 615.

Fixed and regular charity, anchored in a variety of mitzva obligations, is a comprehensive response to the needs of the poor:

It is obvious that [donating a tenth of one's income] is not sufficient to fulfill "the commandments of the Lord are clear" (Psalms 19:9).[38] Indeed the Torah writes: "You shall open your hand to him" (Deuteronomy 15:8) – that you should open it and open it again[39] [when new needs arise]. You should never be stingy and close your hand and heart to your impoverished brother! But the Holy One, blessed be He, in His great mercy, did not leave the fate of his poor, widows, and orphans in the hands of these fleeting feelings of kindness. Through [a number of halakhic obligations] – the laws of the Jubilee Year, the Sabbatical Year, the prohibition against charging interest on a loan, tithes given to the poor, the unharvested portion of a field left to the poor, and the forgotten sheaves and dropped stalks [likewise] left to the poor – the Holy One, blessed be He, mixed kindness with fear of God and transformed the concern for taking care of the unfortunate and tending to their needs into an unavoidable holy obligation. Only through both of these together, combining fear of Heaven with acceptance of the yoke of Heaven, will it be possible to provide proper relief from poverty, suffering, and destitution.

One who gives charity as a mitzva actually gives his gift to God and the poor receives it from God:

Just as the combination of love mixed with fear [of Heaven] ensures that charitable donations are not dependent on personal inspiration or limited to the giver's passing mood, so too, the recipient is also protected through this from the shame and indignity of having to stretch out his hand [and collect charity]. When a Jew receives charity from his fellow Jew, the gift doesn't demean him – for it is not his gift to the poor.... The poor does not

38. Rabbi Hirsch understands this verse as a requirement that the mitzvot should be clear and instructional, not ambiguous and confused.
39. The Hebrew verse repeats the word "open," which the Sages explain as an injunction to give repeatedly.

receive his sustenance from the human giver, but, rather, directly from the full and open hands of the Holy One, blessed be He.

(Rabbi Samson Raphael Hirsch, *Bema'agalei Shana*, part 2, p. 100)

Charity [*Tzedaka*] Is Just [*Tzodek*]

Charity is correct and just. First of all, it is just (*tzodek*) that the receiver should get what he appropriately needs. But there is a second meaning [of *tzedek*] that appears in the Prophets: What is justly done for the soul of the giver. One who performs good deeds gives to his own soul the good that it deserves.

The word *tzedaka* (charity) is derived from *tzedek* (justice). It denotes the act of giving to each person what they are due, and showing kindness to each person as they deserve. In the books of the Prophets, however, the expression *tzedaka* is not used in the first sense, and does not apply to the payment of what you owe to others. When you give a hired worker his wages, or pay back a debt, this is not called *tzedaka*. But when you fulfill duties toward your fellow man out of moral virtue, such as healing the wounds of those who are injured, this is called *tzedaka*.... When you act according to moral virtues, you do justice to your rational soul, giving it what it is due.

(Rambam, *Guide of the Perplexed* III:53)

The Giver Gains through Giving Charity

Supporting the poor not only helps the poor person, but also the giver. Before strict heavenly judgment comes to the world, God grants a gift to someone he loves – the opportunity to support a poor person. Then, when the judgment does come, this mitzva serves as a protection and shield from harm.

When the Holy One, blessed be He, loves a person He sends him a gift. Who is that? It is a poor person, so the one God loves can gain merit through him. Once he gains the merit [of giving to the poor], he draws special divine favor from the "right side" [of divine loving-kindness], God spreads it over his head and marks him [for good]. When strict divine judgment comes into the world, the destroyer [sent by God] will be careful not to harm him, for the destroyer will raise his eyes, see that mark, and leave him [unharmed]. This is why the Holy One, blessed be He, presented him in advance with the poor person so as to be able to gain merit through him.

(*Zohar* 1:104a)

The Torah commands us to lend money to the poor. The world seems to have those destined to lend money and others destined to borrow. Why isn't wealth distributed equally? Why doesn't God give the poor their sustenance directly? In fact, in this way God acts toward us with great kindness – for someone who lends money to the poor has the opportunity to develop a loving and giving character. This makes him fitting to receive divine goodness.

God wanted the people He created to learn and become accustomed to the praiseworthy traits of kindness and mercy. By improving themselves with good character traits they become worthy of receiving divine goodness.... If not for this goal, He, may He be blessed, could have provided for the poor without involving us. Rather, it was out of His kindness, may He be blessed, that we were made His agents [to help the poor] in order to bring us merit.

(*Sefer HaḤinnukh*, Mitzva 66)

Further reading: For the anecdote about Rabbi Akiva's daughter, who gave charity on the night of her wedding and was saved from death, see *A Concise Guide to the Sages*, p. 426.

The rich person who gives charity gains more than the poor person receiving it. The poor benefit in this world through receiving charity, but the rich, by giving, benefit through reward in the next world.

How much greater is the benefit that the rich receive through giving charity to the poor than anything that the poor can receive from the rich! For what the poor receive from the rich only lasts during their time in this world, but the rich benefit through their merit in the World to Come.

(Rabbeinu Baḥya ibn Ḥalawa, *Kad HaKemaḥ*, *Tzedaka*)

When a person gives to another he merits receiving a flow of [divine] influence from above. God is the source of all goodness, and He grants wealth to all who give charity and bestows upon others that which was given to them.

Giving charity involves directing a flow of generosity toward other people. Anyone who does this is assisted by God, may He be blessed, from above. How does the Holy One, blessed be He, help him? Through giving him money that he can direct in a flow [of generosity toward others]. This is because one who bestows on others is like a spring. For just as a spring sends forth its waters far away, so too, a person bestows a flow of goodness on others. Therefore, God, may He be blessed, who is the [ultimate] source sending His flow of goodness to all life, directs that flow toward this person who will then direct it onward to others. Just like the waters of a spring flow outward, and the source of the spring sends forth more so there will be no lack of water – and the further out it sends water, the more water will be replaced – [so too, the more charity one gives, the more wealth God will send toward him]. But if the spring does not flow outward, the source will not give water.

(Maharal of Prague, *Netivot Olam, Netiv HaTzedaka* 1)

The Greatness of Charity

As opposed to all other mitzvot, which involve only certain aspects of a person, the mitzva of giving charity involves one's entire being. In order to earn money a person uses all of himself, and with the money he earns he is able to buy all of his needs. Therefore, charity elevates the entire person. There is an additional advantage to the mitzva of giving charity – that each and every act of giving charity adds to the refinement of a person's soul and strengthens his divine life force.

Giving charity involves one's entire being:

Charity is the principal mitzva [performed with bodily] action, and it surpasses all others. For all mitzvot are only intended to elevate the vital soul of the person toward God, since it is that vital soul which performs the mitzvot and "clothes itself" in them, thereby merging with the light of the Infinite One, blessed be He, which permeates them. You can find no mitzva in which the vital soul is more invested than the mitzva of charity. In all other mitzvot, only one faculty of the vital soul is invested, and then only at the time of the particular mitzva. However, with the mitzva of charity, a person gives money earned through his efforts, and all faculties of his vital soul were invested in doing his work or other activity through which he earned this money. When he gives that money to charity, his vital soul in its entirety is elevated to God. Even someone who does not earn a living through his own labor is nevertheless giving his soul's sustenance to God with his charity, since he could have used that money to purchase sustenance for his vital soul.

The more times one gives charity, the more the soul becomes refined, which in turn strengthens the life force of the Divine Presence:

Indeed, we have also found concerning the mitzva of charity that it is particularly beneficial – indeed, incomparably great – to perform the act of giving many times. The more times one gives, the better, as opposed to [giving a larger sum] once, even if the total amount is the same. This is in accordance with the Rambam's commentary on the Mishna, in which our Sages taught,

"And everything is [judged] according to the amount of action" (*Avot* 3:15). Apart from the Rambam's clear explanation that the reason for giving many times is to refine the soul through multiple actions, Scripture [also] gives a [different explanation in the] verses, "The act of...charity brings life" (Proverbs 10:16, 11:19). This means that the spiritual effect and mystical properties of giving charity draw supernal life from the infinite Source of life, blessed be He, down to the "land of life," which is the *Shekhina* (Divine Presence) which gives us strength. Regarding this the verse states, "You sustain them all" (Nehemia 9:6).

(Rabbi Shneur Zalman of Liadi, *Tanya, Likutei Amarim*, chap. 37; *Igeret HaKodesh* 21)

They once asked Reb Anshel Rothschild of Frankfurt, the founder of the Rothschild dynasty, what his net worth was. Reb Anshel quoted a figure that seemed lower than expected, given the scope of his business and his possessions.

Rav Anshel saw the puzzled look on the face of the person he was speaking with, and explained: "I cannot be certain that all of the wealth in my possession is really mine, for it might all be lost. The only thing that is truly mine is what I gave to charity. That is something no one can take away from me."

Holding on to [and strengthening] the character trait of kindness is the reason for performing all of the mitzvot. Once [the urge to perform acts of] kindness is deeply rooted within a person he will not transgress any mitzva, so that no evil should come to the world through his actions.

(Rabbi Eliyahu HaKohen, *Shevet Musar*, chap. 30)

The main focus of our service of God in these times leading up to the coming of the messiah must be the service of giving charity, as the Sages of blessed memory stated, "The Jewish people will be redeemed only through charity."

(Rabbi Shneur Zalman of Liadi, *Igeret HaKodesh* 9)

Through charity – and it is obvious that spiritual charity is included in this – a person's brain and heart become refined a thousand-fold.... This is not an exaggeration but a simple [truth]. What through normal service of God would take a thousand hours to achieve and succeed in, one can accomplish through one hour of involvement in giving charity.

(Rabbi Menaḥem Mendel Schneerson, *Igrot Kodesh* 6:1564)

Reward and Punishment

God promises reward for those who fulfill His commandments, and punishment for sinners. The primary reward is granted to the soul in the World to Come, and the main punishment is likewise after death. Nevertheless, the Torah refers many times to reward and punishment that will be meted out in this world to those who observe or trangress God's will. A variety of answers have been offered as to why the Torah mentions only reward and punishment in this world and not reward and punishment in the World to Come.

Reward and punishment are both expressions of God's love for us. Even punishment – divine rebuke – is an expression of divine love, but one who does not love God will certainly not love His rebuke. When we receive a blessing we do not deserve, it is meant to help us understand the depth of our rebellion when we sin. Punishments do not come because God wants to harm us; they are, instead, a natural result of sin. By sinning, one removes himself from God's protection, and therefore naturally experiences suffering. One who achieves a deep understanding of spiritual reality will recognize that the ultimate reward is divine service itself, the very fact that God accepts our service.

Why Is There Reward and Punishment?

God rebukes us so that we will follow the proper path. When He causes us to suffer it is because of His love for us. One who does not love God will ignore His rebuke.

Rabbi Yosei opened [his discourse with the following verse]: "Do not despise the admonition of the Lord, my son, and do not loathe His rebuke" (Proverbs 3:11). How beloved is Israel before the Holy One, blessed be He! The Holy One, blessed be He, wants to rebuke them and lead them along the straight path, like a father who loves his son. Because of his love [for his son], he always holds the staff in his hand, to lead him on the straight path, not veering to the right or to the left. This is the meaning of the [next] verse, "For he whom the Lord loves He rebukes, and He reconciles like a father with a son" (Proverbs 3:12). But one who does not love the Holy One, blessed be He, but hates Him, will disregard [divine] rebuke and disregard the staff.

(*Zohar* 3:114b)

Not only are punishments meant to inspire the nation to repent; the same is true of blessings. When we receive goodness from God and recognize His greatness, we realize how severe it is when we rebel against Him.

The creative punishment a king gave to the simple man who rebelled against him:

This can be likened to a villager who rebelled against the king by striking and throwing stones at the king's statue, or the like. The king promptly appointed him to an official post, and elevated him from position to position until he became viceroy. The more the king showered goodness upon him, the greater the position to which he was elevated, and the more he saw of the king's grandeur, attendants, and customs – the greater was the remorse that [the official] who had been a [simple] villager felt when he remembered how he had rebelled against this great and merciful king, who showered goodness upon him when he was deserving of punishment. The king did all of this intentionally, for had he put the villager to death, the latter would have experienced pain for only a short time. But in the manner described above, the villager felt remorse his whole life. [In fact, his remorse] constantly increased. As he reached more elevated positions he experienced greater remorse over his audacity in rebelling against such an honorable [king].

Punishment is given in a merciful way:

This is the meaning of the verse: "God of vengeance, Lord" (Psalms 94:1). God's vengeance is via His attribute of mercy,[40] unlike a king of flesh and blood. The reason is [as the end of the verse states]: "God of vengeance, appear," meaning that the vengeance is [carried out] by showing [the sinner] His greatness. When [the sinner] sees the King's greatness and remembers that he sinned against this King, there is no greater pain.

(Ba'al Shem Tov, *Keter Shem Tov* 108)

Further reading: For more on reward and punishment, see *A Concise Guide to the Torah*, pp. 329, 453, 494, 500; *A Concise Guide to the Sages*, p. 165.

Reward: Physical or Spiritual?

Although there is spiritual reward in the World to Come, this reward is not mentioned explicitly in the Torah. However, reward in this world for the fulfillment of mitzvot is

40. "The Lord" is the name of God associated with the attribute of mercy. The verse is therefore linking the God of vengeance with the attribute of mercy.

mentioned explicitly. There are several reasons why the Torah does not mention reward in the World to Come.

The Torah mentions only reward in this world but not reward in the World to Come:

His main point is to remove any criticism and complaint from our holy Torah by those who would say: "I have room to claim that since the reward for the soul is not mentioned in the Torah, [performing] these commandments certainly cannot give those who do so any spiritual reward in the World to Come. The goal of performing [mitzvot] is only to receive reward in this lowly world."

According to the Rambam, material bounty makes possible the study of Torah and the fulfillment of its mitzvot. The true reward for mitzvot is not mentioned in the Torah, so that it does not become the motivation for keeping the mitzvot:

The Rambam's approach is that the [worldly] rewards mentioned in the Torah for observance of the mitzvot are not the true reward. They are mentioned merely in order to indicate that when people fulfill mitzvot, God will remove all disturbances such as war, illness, famine, and other calamities, so that they can continue to serve God wholeheartedly and without distraction. However, the true, spiritual reward and punishment are not mentioned, so that people will serve God unconditionally and not in order to receive that reward or in order to avoid that punishment.

According to Ibn Ezra, spiritual reward is an abstract concept that is difficult for the simple masses to grasp:

The approach of Rav Avraham ibn Ezra is that it is difficult to imagine [the true] reward, because a physical being cannot grasp a spiritual concept. Therefore, the Torah hid that deep matter from the masses, because of their inability to understand it.

According to Rabbeinu Baḥya, the Torah focuses on physical reward because it is more miraculous than spiritual reward:

The approach of the venerable Rabbeinu Baḥya [ibn Pekuda]... is that all of the rewards that the Torah promises are supernatural, for it is not natural that rain should fall when people observe mitzvot, and be withheld from the earth when people do not act in accordance with the will of the Omnipresent, blessed be He. However, the fact that the life force returns to its source [through one's mitzva observance] is a natural phenomenon for the soul, and is not miraculous.

According to Rav Yehuda Halevi and Rabbeinu Nisim, the Torah's account of physical reward includes an allusion to the core of the spiritual reward: Cleaving to God:

Since it is stated: "I shall walk in your midst" (Leviticus 26:12), and "I will place My dwelling in your midst" (Leviticus 26:11), meaning that the Divine Presence will cling to Israel even in this world, where the soul is entwined with physicality, all the more so is it true that [the soul] will cling to the Divine Presence after it separates from physicality (after death). Everything the false religions promise after death the Torah promises us even in this worldly life, and [the fact that] prophecy exists in our midst proves this. This approach is also found in the response of the Sage to the king of the Khazars in the end of Section 1 of his book, and Rabbeinu Nisim takes this approach in his new [collection of] sermons.[41]

According to Rav Yosef Albo and the Ramban, the Torah mentions the physical reward for mitzvot because it is common to all, and the Torah addresses everyone:

All of the rewards mentioned in the Torah are for the nation as a collective, for the world is judged according to the majority of the people, and the rewards of rain, produce, peace, and the like will come to all of Israel as one. But the reward of the soul in the World to Come is not given to the nation as a collective; rather, each person is judged individually according to his actions.... This approach appears in *Sefer HaIkkarim* and in [the writings of] Ramban.

(Rabbi Shlomo Ephraim Luntschitz, *Keli Yakar*, Leviticus 26:12)

Further reading: For more on spiritual reward and punishment in the afterlife, see p. 165.

Reward and Punishment as a Natural Consequence of One's Actions

God does not punish a person directly, for He is the source of only good and lovingkindness. However, when a person sins, he thereby creates a barrier between himself and the divine goodness coming from above. This leaves him vulnerable to misfortune and calamity. According to this understanding, punishment is a natural result of man's own actions.

Man is treated in accordance with his actions:

The general principle in all matters is that "a person is measured according to the measure that he measures" (Mishna *Sota* 1:7). The explanation of this principle is not known by many, for they attempt to explain this matter with

41. The references here are to Rav Yehuda HaLevi's *Kuzari*, and Rabbeinu Nisim's *Derashot HaRan*.

regard to God, blessed be He, in a manner similar to the way people repay [others for their deeds]; each one repays his friend according to the good or bad that he did to him. But this is not the case with regard to God, blessed be He, God forbid. For with God, blessed be He, there is nothing other than everlasting goodness, loving-kindness, and mercy.... What [the Sages] of blessed memory meant when they said with regard to Him, blessed be He that "a person is measured according to the measure that he measures," is that a person will be repaid in accordance with his actions, whether good or not. For exactly corresponding to the manner of a person's thoughts and actions will he draw upon himself blessing or the opposite.... But it is man himself who causes himself to be liable [for misfortune] when he strays from the upright [path], and he [thereby] removes from himself the prerequisites that dispose him to receive goodness.

All misfortune that happens to a person comes about because the Divine Presence is hidden:

This is analogous to one who walks on a path that is straight and free of stones or other impediments, but is bordered on both sides by a thorny fence. If one passed by and scraped against the fence and was injured, it cannot be truthfully said about this person that God wanted him to be injured, but rather that he was the cause [of his own injury] because he was not careful to walk straight. Similarly with regard to a sinner, the attribute of strict judgment holds him accountable for his sin no matter what, but it cannot be said that the good God wants him to be held accountable. Rather, when goodness is withheld from him due to his sin, harm will find him. [The Sages] of blessed memory said similarly: "No evil comes from above" (*Bereshit Rabba* 51:3). The principle we are expressing is that any negative occurrence that comes upon a person occurs because the face of God is hidden from the person.

(*Sefer HaḤinnukh*, Mitzva 171)

Blessing and punishment are the natural results of the performance of mitzvot or sins, not externally imposed punishments. A good act brings about a flow of divine goodness in the upper spheres to the source of Jewish souls, resulting in blessing in the lower world. Conversely, sin blocks the channel through which divine goodness flows, and the results are felt in this world as misfortune.

Reward and punishment are a natural result of man's actions:

Know that the blessings and curses written in the Torah are not merely reward or punishment. Rather, they are truly natural [results of man's actions], like the fact that one who sows will reap, as the verse states: "He who works his land will have bread to satisfaction" (Proverbs 12:11). In the opposite [case of one who sins, the result is] the opposite.... This is the concept that all of the Torah's blessings are natural.

Sin affects the channels of the divine flow of influence:

When people sin, the channels of grace decrease and those of strict judgment increase. The entire world then experiences pain and lack. The worst of all is when the highest channels are completely blocked, and evil forces and foul waters are drawn from outer channels. Then there is destruction of countries, upheaval, and harrowing exiles. The admonitions written in the Torah refer to this state of affairs. In summary, in accordance with [the divine abundance] drawn by the community of Israel[42] above, so is the fate of the Jewish people below, so that different events causing death or life come about corresponding to the power that is drawn from upper levels.

(Rav Menaḥem Recanati, *Commentary on the Torah, Beḥukotai*)

Further reading: For more on the concept of "no evil comes down from above," see *A Concise Guide to the Sages*, p. 229.

The Reward for a Mitzva Is a Mitzva

The greatest reward is the understanding that despite man's lowliness, God desires his service and derives satisfaction from it, and the actions of man are extremely significant.

This is the ladder firmly planted in the ground to ascend the mountain of God and stand in His holy place. For it is through [first performing mitzvot] not for their own sake that one comes [to perform them] for their own sake, as he will understand in his heart that it is fitting to serve God not in order to receive reward, but rather to bring Him satisfaction. For there is no greater reward in this world than the fact that the great, lofty, elevated, terrifying, and awesome King consents to man, who is like nothingness and vapor, serving Him, and that a man's actions are considered desirable and satisfying before His throne of honor. What honor and greatness a man attains when a flesh and blood king desires him and lifts him up from the dirt to stand and serve him, finds satisfaction in his service, and enjoys [his company]! How infinitely and immeasurably greater it is when the King of all kings, the Holy One, blessed be He, desires us, derives satisfaction from

42. The community of Israel is understood as a metaphysical entity that is the soure of Jewish souls.

our actions, and builds entire worlds from our good deeds! If this were our only reward it would be more than enough.

(Rabbi Eliezer Papo, *Peleh Yo'etz, Sekhar Mitzva*)

When Rabbi Yisrael of Rizhin was incarcerated in a Kiev prison, he was greatly aided by two Jewish jailers. They had been drafted into the Russian army in their youth and considered it meritorious to help the *tzadik*. When he was freed, he wanted to bless them and asked them how they wanted to be blessed. One of them said: "I know that I have not been involved in either Torah or mitzvot, but, Rebbe, please bless me that in merit of what I did I should have a share in the World to Come."

The Rebbe blessed him and turned to the second man, who said: "I do not want a share in the World to Come as a free gift. The Rebbe should bless me that I should merit to perform good deeds in this world and reach the World to Come on my own merit." The Rebbe greatly enjoyed his request and blessed him. The Jew lived to a ripe old age and performed many good deeds.

"The reward of a mitzva is a mitzva" (Avot 4:2). This means that the greatest possible reward for a mitzva is the mitzva itself, the connection and attachment with the Holy One, blessed be He. (The word mitzva is related to the word togetherness [*tzavta*].)

(Rabbi Menaḥem Mendel Schneerson, *Torat Menaḥem* 2, p. 124)

Joy

Being joyful is not a mitzva per se, but it has the ability to facilitate the fulfillment of all mitzvot. Joy and a positive mindset give a person energy and allow him to overcome obstacles. Joy enables one to actualize his potential. Performing mitzvot with joy opens a person up to the gates of wisdom and divine inspiration. The Divine Presence rests with Israel only through joy.

What can one do to achieve joy? First of all, it is important to understand that the more difficult it is to be joyful, the greater the reward for being joyful. In addition, we should internalize the fact that serving God is such a great privilege that all the troubles in the world are insignificant in comparison. It is always possible to see the positive, and one should rejoice over whatever positive exists in a particular situation. Finally, even going through the motions and acting the way happy people act can bring on actual heartfelt joy.

Further reading: A proper view on human suffering makes it easier to experience joy; see p. 228.

The Greatness of Joy

The joy of serving God is itself a very important aspect of divine service, to the point that one who does not serve God with joy is liable for punishment. Joy in the performance of mitzvot sometimes necessitates humility and self-abnegation, which are praiseworthy. One whose concern for his personal honor prevents him from serving God with wholehearted joy is considered a sinner and a fool.

The joy that a person experiences when performing mitzvot and in loving God, who commanded them, is a great [aspect of divine] service. Anyone who withholds himself from this joy deserves punishment, as the verse states: "Because you did not serve the Lord your God with joy and with gladness of heart" (Deuteronomy 28:47). Anyone who is haughty, concerned with his honor, and who views himself with self-importance in these areas is a sinner and a fool. King Solomon warned about this, saying: "Do not glorify yourself before a king" (Proverbs 25:6). Anyone who lowers himself and treats himself lightly in these areas is a great and honored person who serves with love. This is what King David said: "And I would be demeaned even more than this, and I would be lowly in my eyes" (II Samuel 6:22). The only greatness and honor is to rejoice before God, as it is stated: "King David was leaping and dancing before the Lord" (II Samuel 6:16).

(Rambam, *Mishneh Torah, Sefer Zemanim, Hilkhot Lulav* 8:5)

Joy opens up all the gates of wisdom and divine inspiration. The joy that accompanies fulfilling God's commandments is greater than all of the pleasures of this world.

Each and every mitzva that one encounters is a gift sent to him by the Holy One, blessed be He, and the greater his joy [in performing the mitzva], the greater will be his reward. This is what the pious rabbi, the kabbalist, our teacher, Rabbi Yitzḥak Ashkenazi [the Arizal] of blessed memory, revealed to his confidant: That all that he had achieved, that the gates of wisdom and divine inspiration that had opened for him, was as a reward for being infinitely joyous over each mitzva that he performed. He said that this is the meaning of the verse [which states that Israel will be punished] "because you did not serve the Lord your God with joy and with gladness of heart, due to abundance of everything [*merov kol*]" (Deuteronomy 28:47). The explanation of the phrase *merov kol* is: More than all the pleasures of the world, and all the gold, precious stones, and pearls.[43]

(Rabbi Elazar Azikri, *Sefer Ḥaredim*, Introduction)

Judaism does not advocate a life of sadness and sorrow. On the contrary, one of Judaism's lofty goals is to live joyfully. Joy is a necessary precondition for divine revelation, and it is also a natural result of contemplating the truth of God's Torah and mitzvot.

Judaism has never advocated pain and mourning, abstinence and sorrow, as being among its lofty goals, and certainly not as the height of its aspirations. On the contrary, happiness and joy, exuberance and gladness are its loftiest goals. The Divine Presence does not rest among Israel through lethargy and pain, sadness, depression, or frivolousness. Only where joy has sought to dwell is an appropriate setting for God's presence. Frivolousness distances a person from the seriousness that characterizes the divine law, while the truth inherent in Torah is exciting, and chases away sadness, pain, and depression. It instructs and accustoms us to live a rich life full of exuberance and bliss [while still] on earth.

(Rabbi Samson Raphael Hirsch, *Bema'agalei Shana* 2, p. 98)

The Benefits of Joy

Joy leads a person to act energetically and it opens his heart, whereas sadness brings on heaviness and laziness. When people struggle, the energetic person will nearly always

43. The Arizal did not translate *merov kol* as "due to abundance of everything," indicating that Israel was led astray by abundance, but rather "more than everything," meaning that Israel's joy for mitzvot was not greater than its joy in all of the world's treasures.

emerge victorious over the lazy but strong person. Similarly, we can triumph in our struggle against the evil inclination only with the energy that flows from true joy.

It is necessary to state a fundamental principle: Just as in victory over something physical, such as when two people struggle to knock each other down, and one of the combatants fights with laziness and sluggishness, it is easy to defeat him and he will fall, even if he is stronger than his opponent, so too, in achieving victory over the [evil] inclination. It cannot be defeated with the laziness and sluggishness that stem from sadness that seals his heart like a stone. Rather, [victory is achieved] only through alacrity, which stems from the joy of an open heart, purified of any nagging worry or sadness.

(Rabbi Shneur Zalman of Liadi, *Tanya, Likutei Amarim* 26)

Joy brings out a person's hidden strengths, and thereby allows him to overcome ordinary limitations. While experiencing joy, a person can rise above his weaknesses and limitations.

We see that, in general, the nature of joy is to break barriers, any barrier or limitation on the soul.... When a person is in a state of great joy, such as at his child's wedding, abilities that are generally concealed and buried become manifest. For instance, consider someone who is naturally shy and sensitive and is embarrassed to stand in front of people or to speak in public, especially in the presence of people greater than he. When he experiences joy, he becomes like one who is naturally strong and confident. He is able to speak before people who are greater and better than he. He will not be embarrassed at all and will not feel lowly or downtrodden, and he will act like someone who is naturally self-confident.... This is because joy brings out one's latent, inner strengths to the point that it breaks the barriers of his normal limitations.

(Rabbi Shalom Dovber Schneersohn, *Sameaḥ Tesamaḥ*, 5657)

The Danger of Sadness

The evil inclination strives to make a person sad, thereby preventing him from serving God. One must understand that the evil inclination is deceiving him, and one must strive to the best of his ability to avoid being sad.

The evil inclination sometimes misleads a person into thinking that he has sinned:

The evil inclination sometimes misleads a person by telling him that he has committed a terrible sin, when in reality he merely ignored a stringency or did something that is not a transgression at all. The evil inclination's intent is to cause him to be sad and, due to his sadness, to cease serving the Creator, may He be blessed.

It is critical for one's service of God to avoid sadness:

A person must understand this deceit and tell the evil inclination: "I am not paying attention to the stringency you are telling me about, for your intention is to stop me from serving Him, may He be blessed. You are speaking falsehood. And even if it is a bit of a sin, my Creator will be more satisfied with me ignoring that stringency you are telling me about, causing me sadness while serving Him. On the contrary, I will serve Him with joy, which is an important principle. For my service is not for my own sake but to give Him satisfaction, may He be blessed. Therefore, even if I do not pay attention to the stringency you tell me about, my Creator will not be strict with me about it, because the only reason I ignore it is to avoid ceasing to serve Him. How can I cease serving Him even for a moment?" This is a great principle in the service of God, to take care [to avoid] sadness as much as possible.

(Ba'al Shem Tov, as cited in *Tzava'at HaRivash* 44)

How Is It Possible to Be Joyful?

The more difficult it is for a person to be joyful, the greater the reward for achieving joy. A person must recognize that the privilege of serving God is like earning a great fortune, and he will thereby pay no attention to the minor troubles of life.

It is known that for each and every mitzva, the reward [one receives] corresponds to the pain [experienced in fulfilling the mitzva] (*Avot* 5:22). So too with regard to joy. A man who is bitter due to the travails of life, if when he is involved in Torah study, prayer, the recitation of blessings, the performance of mitzvot, or on Shabbat, he clears his mind, forgets his sadness and anger, and rejoices in what he is doing, he will receive more reward than someone who is [naturally] relaxed and serene. The joy of an Israelite man in the service of God, may His name be blessed, should be comparable to that of one who earned a million gold dinars and in his joy ignores the pain of one small *peruta* that he lost. The joy of serving God, may He be blessed, outweighs the travails of life in this world even more than [earning a million dinars outweighs losing a *peruta*]. Even with regard to distress of the soul, such as over the destruction of the Temple and over one's sins, about which one is required to feel pain and to mourn, not all times are equal. Times of sadness should be separate from times of joy, and no foreign element should interfere with his joy.

(Rabbi Eliezer Papo, *Peleh Yo'etz, Simḥa*)

The way to achieve constant joy is to identify one's positive points and to be happy about them. Focusing on the positive is uplifting.

A person must search for and find his good points:

A person must be very careful to always be joyful and to keep himself very, very far away from sadness. Even when he begins to examine himself and sees that he has no goodness and he is full of sins, and the evil inclination wants to thereby cause him to fall into sadness or depression, God forbid, it is forbidden for him to fall in this way. Rather, he must seek and find within himself some good, for how is it possible that he has not performed any mitzva or good deed in his life? Even if he begins to examine that good point and finds that it too is flawed and incomplete, meaning that he sees that even the mitzva or the holy deed that he merited to perform was [performed when his mindset was] full of ulterior motives, extraneous thoughts, and [it therefore has] many defects, nonetheless, how is it possible that there was not a little good in that mitzva or holy deed? For despite it all, somehow, there was some good point in the mitzva or good deed that he performed. For a person must search and try to find in himself a little bit of good in order to revive himself and to achieve joy, as stated above.

Finding even a small amount of good in oneself can allow a person to overcome the bad:

By seeking and identifying a little bit of good within himself, a person actually tips the scales from being liable to being meritorious, and he is able to repent.[44]

(Rabbi Naḥman of Breslov, *Likutei Moharan* 282)

A person's emotions are affected by his actions and behavior. Even when a person is experiencing sadness, he should behave as though he is happy, and this will help him actually become happy.

One should not, God forbid, speak about depressing matters. On the contrary, he should always act in a happy way, as though his heart is full of joy. Even if he does not actually feel that way at the time, he will eventually feel that way. This is because the actions and activities that a person does will eventually find a permanent place in his heart.... The principle that emerges

44. It is as though there are two sides of a scale, one containing the person's merits and one containing his demerits. When he identifies the good in himself, he moves himself over to the plate with the merits.

is that one should be careful in his thought, speech, and actions, to avoid focusing on worry and fear. On the contrary, he should speak and act [joyfully], as mentioned above, and then he will internalize those character traits. In that way God will bestow upon him from above a spirit of joy and goodheartedness.

(Rabbi Menaḥem Mendel Schneerson, *Igrot Kodesh* 324)

An elderly Jew who appeared stooped over and dejected came to the Gerer Rebbe, Rabbi Yisrael Alter, the author of *Beit Yisrael*.

The rebbe asked him what was bothering him, and the Jew sighed and said: "I feel that all of my Torah and service of God is for nought. As the years pass it is clear to me that I am still the same coarse and materialistic person I once was, and that the Torah I have learned and the mitzvot I have performed have not elevated or refined me."

The Gerer Rebbe replied: "Isn't the mere fact that you are a Jew who merited receiving God's Torah and its mitzvot sufficient to fill your heart with infinite joy? Where is there any room for depression or sadness when we have merited the greatest source of bliss – to be Jews engaged in Torah and mitzvot?"

To the degree that a person cultivates true inner joy and goodheartedness he will merit the upper light. If he does this constantly, he will undoubtedly experience divine inspiration.

(Rabbi Yitzḥak Luria (Arizal), *Sha'ar HaMitzvot*)

It is a great mitzva to constantly be in a state of joy.

(Rabbi Naḥman of Breslov)

The joy of performing a mitzva and song negate all strict judgment and heavenly accusation, with regard to both the spiritual and the physical.

(Rabbi Menaḥem Mendel Schneersohn, *Igrot Kodesh Tzemaḥ Tzedek* 368)

Joy is a natural inclination. A person who is healthy in spirit and body will always be cheerful and joyous. This is the natural state of a healthy spirit.

(Rabbi Avraham Yitzḥak HaKohen Kook, *Ein Aya*)

Further reading: For more on joy, see *A Concise Guide to the Sages*, p. 441.

Torah

The Torah was given to us by the Creator of the world, and it contains numerous layers of meaning. The Written Torah is like a treasure chest, into which the Sages of each generation have placed the diamonds and jewels of the Oral Torah. Fools might think that the Torah is limited to its superficial meaning, but the Sages understood that it has inner layers of meaning. Every word of the Torah contains wondrous mysteries.

Torah study enables a person to unite with God's wisdom and will, a unity that is unparalleled [elsewhere] in this world. The performance of mitzvot can cause a person to be illuminated with a divine light, but even mitzvot do not create the unity with God that can be achieved through Torah study. Despite all of its side benefits, Torah should be studied for the sake of Heaven. All levels of existence are dependent upon and sustained by our Torah study. The Torah is constantly being renewed. The more a person exerts himself in Torah study, the greater the extent to which he connects to God and brings renewal to all levels of existence.

Before a person learns Torah he should contemplate the fear of God. Fear of God enables one to internalize the Torah he studies.

The more one learns, the better he is able to understand the Torah. However, a human being cannot grasp the full depth of the inner essence of Torah. Consequently, even one who is very advanced in his studies can always deepen his understanding of Torah.

The Ba'al Shem Tov gave us a path to understanding the inner aspects of Torah as they are relevant for every individual's service of God. Learning hasidic thought is a "tree of life," because in it, the Torah is not concealed in physical imagery but rather is the direct expression of love and fear of God and clinging to Him. Consequently, everyone, including women, is able and required to study the deeper meanings of the Torah.

The Divine Origin of Torah

One of the fundamentals of Jewish belief is that the entire Torah is of divine origin. Moses merely served as a scribe who transcribed God's word, to which he did not add at all. This applies to the entire Torah. Even verses that seem to include only technical tidbits of information were given by God and include deep layers of meaning.

The entire Torah comes from God:

The eighth foundation is that the Torah is from heaven; to wit, it [must] be believed that the whole of this Torah which is in our hand today is the Torah that was brought down to Moses our teacher; that all of it is from God [by] the transmission which is called metaphorically "speech"; that no one knows the quality of that transmission except he to whom it was transmitted, peace

be upon him; and that it was dictated to him while he was of the rank of a scribe; and that he wrote down all of its dates, narratives, and laws – and for this he is called the legislator.

This applies, without exception, to all parts of the Torah:

There is no difference between "the sons of Ham were Cush, Mitzrayim, Fut, and Canaan" (Genesis 10:6) and "the name of his wife was Meheitavel, the daughter of Matred" (Genesis 36:39) on the one hand, and "I am the Lord your God" (Exodus 20:2) and "Hear O Israel, the Lord our God the Lord is One" (Deuteronomy 6:4) on the other hand. Everything is from the mouth of the Almighty; everything is the Torah of God: whole, pure, holy, [and] true. One who says that Moses himself was the author of these verses and told these stories is considered by our Sages and prophets as being more of a heretic and misinterpreter [of the Torah] than all of the [other types of] heretics, for he views the Torah as having a core and a shell[45] .... Rather, each and every word of the Torah contains wisdom and wonders for those who can comprehend them, and the extent of their wisdom cannot be fully grasped.

(Rambam, *Commentary on the Mishna*, Introduction to *Ḥelek*)

The Torah has a soul, a body, and an external layer of clothing. The external layer of the Torah is its superficial meaning, and there are those who mistakenly think this is the entire Torah. However, the Torah also includes allusions to the measures necessary for man to achieve perfection. The greatest Sages contemplate the soul of the Torah, its most hidden teachings.

The holy Torah exists in both a limited and expansive form. It is written in the holy Zohar that the Torah has its clothing – the narratives of the Torah and the like; it has its body – allusions from its narrative [about how to achieve] the perfection of man; and the Torah also has a soul, its hidden [layers of meaning]. The fools say that [the Torah contains] only its external cloak, God forbid, for they see no further. The wise man recognizes the Torah's body, its allusions; and those who are even wiser examine the soul, the secrets of the Torah. The Torah was in fact given to Moses our teacher in a

45. Those who believe that some verses in the Torah were composed by God and some were composed by Moses are considered heretics for viewing the Torah as containing a core material of divine authorship as well as a less important "shell" of human authorship. In fact, the entire Torah is of divine authorship and contains deep layers of meaning.

form that incorporated various [layers of] limited and expansive meaning. Moses transmitted it to Israel, and everything is included in it.

(Rabbi Ḥayyim Halberstam, *Divrei Ḥayyim LeḤanuka*, s.v. *BeGemara Shabbat*)

Further reading: For more on the comparison between the different components of the Torah, see *A Concise Guide to the Sages*, p. 150.

The Written Torah and the Oral Torah

We received from God both the Written Torah and the Oral Torah. The Sages of every generation are responsible to find the words of the Written Torah that allude to the content of the Oral Torah. The Written Torah has been compared to a special chest in which each drawer and compartment must be filled with something specific. The wise son must find a place in the chest for each item.

The Torah – the wonderful treasure chest:

The Written Torah is like a beautiful and ornate chest, with hundreds and thousands of compartments and sub-compartments. Each compartment is unique in its length, width, and height, and each is crafted with wondrous wisdom. Each is constructed to hold various types of rings, bracelets, and earrings made with precious stones and pearls, as well as to hold different types of royal treasures; everything according to its dimensions, quantity, and value. The king gave his only son the wonderful chest to study, so he would come to understand the proper use of each and every compartment. He also gave him various types of jewelry crafted with precious stones and pearls, and many different types of royal treasures, so his son would analyze on his own how to place each type [of treasure] in its proper compartment.

The Sages of the Oral Torah fill the compartments of the Written Torah:

So too God, may He be blessed, first gave the Written Torah to His nation Israel, and with great wisdom He crafted various compartments and storage places within each and every verse. Then He conveyed to them the Oral Torah, which is the received transmission that is more expansive than the sea. He commanded them to toil very hard in order to discern an appropriate place within the Written Torah for each and every part of the Oral Torah, such that all of the compartments and storage places that he crafted in the Written Torah would be filled with the Oral Torah.

(Rabbi Yosef Ḥayyim, *Ben Ish Ḥai*, Year 1, *Aḥarei-Kedoshim*)

Why Study Torah?

The mitzva to study Torah is a mitzva to know God's ways. A person engaged in Torah study is engaged in the most elevated manifestation of faith. God will permantly rest His Presence on such a person.

It is a mitzva to study Torah every day, for Torah is the essence of the highest form of faith, which is to know the ways of the Holy One, blessed be He. For anyone who invests himself in Torah study is deemed meritorious in this world and in the World to Come, and he is saved from all the accusing angels. For the Torah is the secret of faith, as one who is engaged in it is engaged in the highest form of faith, and God rests His Presence within him such that it will never depart from him.

(*Zohar* 2:134b)

God gave us the Torah so that through its study we can unite our souls with His holiness. If one studies Torah only for some tangible benefit rather than in order to cling to God and bring His light into the world, then the land will remain bereft of sanctity. This is a cause of destruction, as the Sages taught that the Land of Israel was destroyed "because they did not recite the blessing over the Torah" (*Bava Metzia* 85b), meaning that the Jewish people did not have the proper intention when studying Torah.

Further reading: For more on the Torah and its sanctity, see *A Concise Guide to the Sages*, p. 449.

We study Torah in order to cling to God:

God's intent was always that we should engage in Torah study so that our souls would be empowered by the essence, spirituality, and sanctity of the Torah's source. Therefore, the Holy One, blessed be He, gave the Torah of truth to Israel as a gift that will never be forgotten, so that all 248 limbs and 365 sinews of our souls and bodies[46] should cleave to the Torah's 248 positive mitzvot and the 365 negative mitzvot. If the Jewish people were to study Torah with this intent, they would become a chariot and sanctuary for His Presence. The Divine Presence would literally rest within them, as they are a sanctuary of God, and the Divine Presence would establish a permanent dwelling within them. The land would shine with His glory. This would

46. Man has 248 limbs and 365 sinews in his body, and the soul is likewise divided into an identical number of parts. These correspond to the 248 positive mitzvot and 365 prohibitions of the Torah.

connect the heavenly entourage with the entourage of the lower spheres, and the sanctuary would be unified.

Studying Torah for ulterior motives leads to destruction:

But then[47] they transgressed this instruction and they engaged in Torah study only [to fulfill] their physical needs, for their benefit, in order to know the laws for the sake of business and to be haughty and to display their wisdom. They did not intend to be empowered and to cling to the sanctity and spirituality of the Torah and to draw the Divine Presence down to this earth so that their souls could be elevated to a great level after their deaths. Through this they caused a separation, for the Divine Presence was removed from the world and went up on high, and the land was left in its physicality, without sanctity. This caused its destruction and loss.

(Rabbi Yoel Sirkis, *Bayit Ḥadash, Tur, Oraḥ Ḥayyim* 47)

God is completely beyond human comprehension, but He inserted His light into the Torah. When a person studies Torah and internalizes its knowledge, he contains within him the divine light and thereby achieves an unparalleled unity with God.

God can be grasped only through Torah and mitzvot:

God is referred to as the Infinite One, [as it is written,] "His greatness is unfathomable" (Psalms 145:3), and "The mind cannot grasp Him at all" (*Tikkunei Zohar*, Introduction 17a). The same is true regarding His will and His wisdom, as it is written, "There is no scrutinizing His understanding" (Isaiah 40:28), and it is written, "Would you discover the mystery of God" (Job 11:7), and it is written, "My thoughts are not your thoughts" (Isaiah 55:8). Regarding this, the [Sages] taught, "Wherever you find God's greatness, you find His humility" (*Yalkut Shimoni, Ekev* 856). [This means that] God constricted His will and wisdom within the 613 mitzvot of the Torah and in their laws, as well as in the letter sequences of the Tanakh, with their homiletic explanations in the Sages' commentaries. This enables any aspect of the soul residing in a human body to comprehend them with its mind and fulfill them with action, speech and thought, to the greatest extent possible.

When a person understands a *halakha* he unites with God and His wisdom:

When a person comprehends a certain ruling with his intellect, as a *halakha* set forth by the Mishna, Talmud or halakhic authorities, he thereby

47. This is a reference to the First Temple era.

comprehends, grasps, and encompasses God's will and wisdom with his intellect. The mind cannot grasp God Himself, or His will and wisdom, unless they are concretized in the *halakhot* outlined before us. Moreover, his intellect also becomes encompassed by them. This constitutes a wondrous unification, which is totally unparalleled in the physical world, actually achieving complete union and unification.

The advantage of learning and knowing Torah over fulfilling other mitzvot:

The mitzva of studying and comprehending the Torah has an infinitely great and wondrous advantage over all the [other] mitzvot [performed by bodily] action, including even the mitzva of speaking [words of] Torah. For in all mitzvot of speech and action, God enclothes and envelops the soul from head to foot in divine light. [However,] through the study of Torah, not only is the intellect enveloped in [the light of] divine wisdom, but the divine wisdom is also [contained] within him – what the intellect is able to comprehend, grasp, and encompass in the knowledge of Torah, according to each person's intellect, and his ability to know and comprehend the literal, allusive, homiletic, and esoteric [meanings of the Torah].

(Rabbi Shneur Zalman of Liadi, *Tanya, Likutei Amarim*, chap. 4–5)

All of existence is dependent on our Torah study. If there were no Torah study in the entire world for even one moment, the entire universe would cease to exist. When we study Torah, God's light is abundant in the world; when we decrease our study, God's light in the world also decreases.

The life force and continued existence of all of the worlds is dependent upon our speaking and thinking about Torah. It is undoubtedly true that if the entire world, from one end to the other, were devoid of our engagement and contemplation in Torah even for a moment, God forbid, then all of the upper and lower worlds would be instantly destroyed and would turn into nothingness, God forbid. Similarly, the abundance of their [divine] light is dependent only on the extent of our engagement in Torah study.

(Rabbi Ḥayyim of Volozhin, *Nefesh HaḤayyim* 4:11)

Torah study is beneficial to a person in many ways. However, a person's motivation for studying Torah should be his love for Torah and for God. The Sages said: "Envy, lust, and honor drive a man from the world" (*Avot* 4:21). If one studies Torah because he is jealous of others or in order to receive benefits or honor from others, that study will drive him from the world.

One should study Torah only due to his love for it and not for any other reason. If he intends to study for any one of these three reasons [envy, lust, or honor], they will drive him from the world. Sometimes a person studies out of jealousy of another, as "jealousy among scribes increases wisdom" (*Bava Batra* 22a), and not out of love for the Torah itself.... Sometimes a person studies to fulfill his desires, for he knows that most people tithe their money and donate it to a Torah scholar, and therefore their desire brings them [to study]... The [mishna also] mentions "honor," referring to one who studies for the honor he will receive, [such as that people allow him to be] the first to enter and the first to depart. Concerning [one who studies for any of] these three motivations, [the mishna] states that they "drive a man from the world," for this is not Jacob's portion; rather, one must study out of love for God, may He be blessed.

(Rabbi Shmuel de Uçeda, *Midrash Shmuel*, *Avot* 4:21)

Further reading: For more on studying Torah properly, see *A Concise Guide to the Sages*, p. 454.

New Torah Insights

When a person applies himself in Torah study, he thinks of new insights. These new insights stand before God, who creates from them a new heaven and a new earth. Through Torah the entire world is renewed, and it is from these new Torah ideas that God constantly creates the heavens and the earth.

New insights into Torah are referred to as the "new heavens and new earth":

Rabbi Shimon began: How much must a man engage in Torah study day and night, for the Holy One, blessed be He, listens to the voices of those who are involved in Torah study, and from any new insight gleaned from the Torah by the one engaged in its study, He fashions a [new] firmament.... Similarly, each and every matter of wisdom stands in its entirety before the Ancient One, and He calls them "new heavens," renewed heavens, hidden, of the secrets of the higher wisdom. All those other new Torah insights stand before the Holy One, blessed be He, and they ascend and become the land of the living, then descend and crown one land, and everything becomes renewed and a "new earth" from that new Torah insight.

From new Torah insights God fashions a new heaven and earth:

Concerning this it is written: "For just as the new heavens and the new earth that I make will remain before Me – the utterance of the Lord – so your descendants and your name will remain" (Isaiah 66:22). It is not written "I made," but "I make." He constantly creates [a new heaven and earth] from the new insights and secrets of the Torah.

(*Zohar*, Introduction 4:1)

No day is like the one that preceded it. Every day God renews the Torah, through which He creates the entire universe. One is therefore always able to establish a new connection to Torah that never existed before.

The Holy One, blessed be He, renews the act of creation every day, and the Torah is called "the act of creation," for through Torah the worlds were created, as is known. The Holy One, blessed be He, is constantly creating anew. It follows that no day is similar to another. Every day [brings the possibility of] clinging and connecting to a new Torah, namely, the new Torah insights that were created today and were not present yesterday. The uniqueness of today has never yet existed.

(Rabbi Menaḥem Naḥum of Chernobyl, *Me'or Einayim, Ki Tisa*, s.v. *vayiten el Moshe*)

How to Study Torah

Although it is permitted to learn Torah for ulterior motives, it is highly preferable to study Torah for its own sake, without seeking external benefits. However, the enjoyment a person has while learning does not detract from his purity of purpose, and he is not considered one who is studying not for its own sake. This is because the enjoyment itself connects a person to Torah, and that is the main goal of Torah study.

I have heard some people straying from the path of logic with regard to the study of our holy Torah. They say that if one studies, perceives new insights, and rejoices and delights in his study, that study is not undertaken for its own sake to the same degree as it would be if he studied superficially, did not derive enjoyment from his study, and did so only for the sake of the mitzva. [This is because] one who enjoys his study mixes his own pleasure into his study. In fact, this is a well-known mistake. On the contrary, the primary aspect of the mitzva of Torah study is to rejoice, delight, and enjoy his study, and then the words of Torah will become absorbed in his blood. Once he enjoys the words of Torah, he becomes attached to Torah.... I agree that if one studies only because he enjoys his study and not for the sake of the mitzva, that is considered study not undertaken for its own sake.... But if one studies for the sake of the mitzva and enjoys his study, that is study for its own sake, and is entirely sacred, for the enjoyment is also a mitzva.

(Rabbi Avraham Borenstein, *Eglei Tal*, Introduction)

Before a person begins to study Torah he should spend at least a short time contemplating the fear of Heaven. Fear of Heaven is like a storehouse which is necessary for the storage of grain. If one studies Torah without fear of Heaven, the Torah he studies goes to waste.

Torah needs a proper receptacle that can contain it:

It is certainly impossible to say that there is no need for purity of thought and fear of God in order to engage in Torah study, God forbid. For we have learned in an explicit mishna: "If there is no fear, there is no wisdom" (*Avot* 3:17). For fear of God is the storehouse for the holy Torah that allows man to retain it. If he does not first prepare a storehouse of fear of God, the abundant produce of the Torah will be as if it is lying in the field, accessible to be trampled by the feet of oxen and donkeys, God forbid, and he will not retain it at all.

Before Torah study one should consciously intend to connect to God:

Whenever a person prepares himself to study, he should spend at least a short time in contemplation, with fear of God and a pure heart, confessing his sinfulness from the depths of his heart. This is so that his Torah study will be holy and pure. He should intend to cleave to the Torah through his study. In this manner he cleaves to God, as it were, for God and His will, expressed through *halakha*, are one.

(Rabbi Ḥayyim of Volozhin, *Nefesh HaḤayyim*, 4:4–6)

When a person exerts himself in his Torah study he becomes completely connected to Torah. If one invests great energy in his study, the Torah will remain with him and will teach him its ways.

"It is first called 'God's Torah,' but when he toils in it, it is called 'his Torah'" (Rashi, Psalms 1:2). It can be explained that it is called his Torah because it will instruct him and teach him.[48] This is because one firmly acquires the Torah that comes to him through toil, effort, and exertion. He will cling to it tightly, to the point that the Torah itself will teach him all of its ways. This is not the case if he studies without toil, in which case none of his learning

48. The word Torah is related to the word *hora'a*, which means instruction or teaching.

will remain with him. This is what the Sages of blessed memory meant when they said about the verse: "My wisdom too (*af ḥakhmati*) stood by me" (Ecclesiastes 2:9): "The Torah that I learned with anger (*af*) remained with me"

(*Midrash Zuta*, Ecclesiastes 2:9). This refers to the Torah one studied with effort, exertion, and suffering.

(Rabbi Menaḥem Mendel of Kotzk, *Ohel Torah, Vezot HaBerakha*)

One who studies Torah must remember that as much as he learns and understands, there are always deeper levels that he does not yet comprehend. Consequently, one who understands only the superficial meaning of what he studies but knows that there is additional depth, or even one who reads without any comprehension of the material, will receive reward for his Torah study on the condition that he constantly tries to increase his knowledge and understanding.

When a person comes to study Torah, his intent must be that he is studying divine words whose deep meaning is hidden from him. In this way all the Torah that comes out of his mouth will be more pleasing to God than sacrifices.[49] But even if all he comprehends is the superficial meaning of the story, or even if one does not understand at all because he is not fluent in the language and he merely reads the words, he will receive good reward for his efforts. With regard to people like these it is stated: "He meditates on his Torah day and night" (Psalms 1:2). The Sages explained that it does not say "the Torah" but "his Torah," meaning according to the level of his understanding. Even if one does not know how to connect the words, if he is involved in it day and night he will receive his reward and his actions are deemed significant, provided that he constantly increases [his Torah study].

(Rabbi Yeshaya Horowitz, *Shenei Luḥot HaBerit, Bayit Aḥaron*)

There are those who expend great resources on traveling the world and they pride themselves on having visited many different places. Similarly, it is proper for a person to have at least a superficial familiarity with a wide range of works of Torah, such that he can say, "I was there." In the World to Come he will be reminded of what he learned in this world.

It is fitting for a person in this world to peruse all the sacred works and learn them all so that he will have been everywhere, just as there are great aristocrats who expend great resources traveling through countries so that

49. See Psalms 69:32.

afterward they can proudly say that they were in those countries. Just as it is common for aristocrats to proudly say, "I was in Warsaw" and the like, it is similarly fitting for a person in this world to see every place in the holy Torah so that in the World to Come he can proudly say that he was everywhere, meaning in all of the holy books, as mentioned above. In the World to Come he will be reminded of everything he learned in this world.[50]

(Rabbi Naḥman of Breslov, *Siḥot HaRan* 28)

The Mystical Side of Torah

In the Garden of Eden there were two trees: the tree of life and the tree of knowledge. Adam ate from the tree of knowledge, and God expelled him from the garden so that he would not also eat from the tree of life. The Zohar explains that the Torah is the tree of life, and one who connects to Torah is connected to life. Involvement in worldly endeavors is considered involvement with the tree of knowledge, which ends in death. It is primarily through the deeper layers of the Torah and hasidic thought that the Torah serves as the tree of life.

The Torah through which the divine light is experienced is the tree of life:

The Written Torah is called the tree of life because it was not so enclothed in material expression,[51] and the divine light is felt in it.... How much more so with regard to the mystical side of Torah, which was not enclothed at all in physical clothing, for it speaks of spiritual matters, the process of divine emanation, and divine matters in general. Comprehension of this [side of Torah] is spiritual cognition, and the divine light is felt in it. Its focus is to know God and to thereby come to love and revere Him.... This is especially true of the teachings of the Ba'al Shem Tov, of blessed memory, which our fathers, our holy rabbis, of blessed memory, may their souls rest in peace, have passed on to us. They reveal and explain the greatness and exaltedness of God, and all divine matters that lead to love and reverence of God. They teach us to know God and how to serve Him with love and reverence as is required of us, as well as the paths leading to it.... Therefore, the mystical side of Torah is considered the tree of life, for it reveals the divine and allows one to develop a complete heart, meaning love and fear of Heaven, which is the primary goal of all involvement in Torah and mitzvot.

50. One who studies a wide range of books will not be able to delve deeply into all of them. Nonetheless, it is valuable for him to study a wide range of books so that he will have a superficial familiarity with them. Even if he does not remember what he learned, he will be reminded of it in the World to Come.
51. The Written Torah does not focus so much on the mundane world, and therefore its divine light is more easily felt.

It is a mitzva to study the mystical side of Torah:

Therefore, it is a mitzva and obligation for each and every person to study the mystical side of Torah.... One who does not study the inner Torah is responsible for the loss of his own life, for one can fall even through the study of Torah.... This is certainly the case for one who does not want to engage in this type of study and to study only the revealed aspect of Torah. He will cling to the "place of death"[52]... and only with and through [the mystical side of Torah] will he merit the light of life, for it is the tree of life and through it he will come to love and fear of God.

(Rabbi Shalom Dovber Schneersohn, *Kuntres Etz HaḤayyim*, chap. 11)

The Arizal (Rabbi Yitzḥak Luria) revealed many aspects of the inner Torah, and the Ba'al Shem Tov explained them and revealed how they are relevant for every individual's service of God. Since every Jew has a divine soul, he can illuminate the darkness in his heart with divine light.

The main way that the Ba'al Shem Tov's Torah sheds light is relevant only to the greatest sages in the world, for his teachings are a commentary on the mystical teachings that were earlier revealed by the Ari. The Ari spoke of matters dealing with the upper worlds and the holy spheres, whereas the Ba'al Shem Tov added and explained that all of this is relevant to the service of God of a Jew in this lowly world.... But since the Torah of the Ba'al Shem Tov is a holistic system, just as it is above all the worlds it is also below all the worlds. [It belongs to] every Jew simply because he is a Jew, since he has [within him] a portion of the divine. It can lift him from his lowliness and light up the darkness of his heart with the light of God, may He be blessed. The Torah of the Ba'al Shem Tov teaches us the way to raise up the light of the soul, hewn from the throne of glory, even in the simplest of Jews.

(Rabbi Shalom Noaḥ Berezovsky, *Netivot Shalom*, Part 1, *Ḥasidut* 1)

Torah Study for Women

In the past the Sages said that women should not study the Oral Torah (e.g., Talmud). This was due to the fact that women did not receive any formal education. Nowadays, when women receive a general education comparable to men, they should also study the Oral Torah. This change is related to the fact that the final redemption is drawing closer.

52. Studying the revealed Torah without the inner Torah is dangerous, for it can degenerate into learning Torah without connecting to the Torah's holiness.

Women learn the *halakhot* applicable to them, and the teachings of Hasidism are included in this:

First of all: "Women are obligated to learn the *halakhot* applicable to them in order to know them, such as ... all positive mitzvot that are not time-bound, and all prohibitions from Torah law or rabbinic law, in which they are obligated like men" (*Shulḥan Arukh HaRav, Hilkhot Talmud Torah* 1:14). This includes the vast majority of the Torah's laws; if only all the men would be fluent in all of this. Another important principle is with regard to studying the inner layers of the Torah through hasidic thought, where all matters of belief in God and His unity, and love and fear of God are explained, as the verse states: "Know the God of your father and serve Him with a whole heart" (I Chronicles 28:9). This study is pertinent to fulfilling the "six commandments whose obligation is constant[53] and does not lapse for even a moment during a person's entire life" (*Sefer HaḤinnukh*, Introduction). Women are obligated in them just as men are.

Nowadays women have to study the Oral Torah as well:

Even with regard to studying the Oral Torah in general (in addition to studying the laws pertinent to them), since women and girls study various subjects as it is ... they are not only permitted to learn the Oral Torah, but it goes much further. Based on the very reason for this law, it is necessary to teach them the Oral Torah, and not only halakhic rulings without reasons, but also the reasons for the *halakhot* and even the give-and-take dialogue of the Oral Torah. It is natural (for a man or a woman) to desire and enjoy this kind of learning, and in this way their intellectual development ("cleverness"[54]) will be in the spirit of our holy Torah .... It can be said that the reason we have merited an increase in Torah study for women specifically in recent generations is that preparations for the time of redemption are accelerated at the end of the age of exile. For "in those days knowledge, wisdom, and truth will increase" (*Mishneh Torah, Hilkhot Teshuva* 9:2).

(Rabbi Menaḥem Mendel Schneersohn, *Hitva'aduyot* 5750, vol. 3, p. 172)

53. The six constant mitzvot are: belief in God, the prohibition of idolatry, belief in the unity of God, love of God, fear of God, and the prohibition to stray after one's eyes or heart.

54. The Sages stated that it is preferable that a woman not study the Oral Torah lest she develop a spiritually unhealthy "cleverness" (*Sota* 21b). However, that was because women at that time did not receive any formal education. Now that women do receive a formal education, it is necessary for them to study the Oral Torah so that their intellectual development takes place in the spirit of Torah.

Further reading: For more on every individual's obligation to learn Torah, see *A Concise Guide to Halakha*, p. 509.

When the great Rabbi Bunim of Zikhlin came to Rabbi Menaḥem Mendel of Kotzk, he was immediately swept up with the hasidim's ecstatic service of God, and his diligence in Torah study declined somewhat. The Rebbe noticed and addressed him with the following question: "They say that a learned scholar is one who has filled his belly with the Talmud and the Codes. Why do they say "belly" instead of "head"?

Rabbi Bunim remained silent. The Kotzker Rebbe responded: "Just as the stomach is filled every day but the hunger immediately returns, so a scholar must hunger every day for Torah study. One whose learning wanes has no place with me."

Our nation exists only because of its [Written and Oral] Torahs. Since the Creator said that the nation will remain as long as heaven and earth continue to exist, by definition its Torahs will remain for as long as heaven and earth continue to exist.

(Rav Se'adya Gaon, *Sefer HaEmunot VehaDe'ot, Ma'amar* 3)

"Good" refers to none other than Torah. For if people were to feel the sweetness and pleasantness of the Torah's goodness, they would be crazed and wild in their pursuit of Torah. An entire world full of silver and gold would not be considered significant at all in their eyes, for the Torah includes all the goods in the world.

(Rabbi Ḥayyim ben Atar, *Or HaḤayyim, Ki Tavo* 26:8)

By engaging in Torah study, one calls to God to come to him, so to speak, like a person who calls his friend to come to him, or a small child who calls his father to come and be together with him, and not leave him by himself, God forbid.

(Rabbi Shneur Zalman of Liadi, *Tanya, Likutei Amarim* 37)

"Do not cast me off in old age" (Psalms 71:9). The words of Torah should not seem old to you. Rather, every day they should be new in your eyes.

(Ba'al Shem Tov, *Keter Shem Tov, Hosafot* 66)

Every person has a special portion in the holy Torah that was allotted to him at Sinai. A subject matter that one has a strong desire to learn is the portion that he was allotted at Sinai.

(Rabbi Menaḥem Mendel of Kotzk, *Ohel Torah Nedarim*)

Exerting effort in Torah study is not only a means to an end, so that one will thereby attain a high level of comprehension of Torah. It is an end in itself, as it is through exertion in Torah study that one merits the light of Torah and to cling to God. Without exertion in Torah study, even if one is intellectually gifted, he will not merit the hidden light that is concealed specifically for those who exert effort in Torah study.

(Rabbi Shalom Noaḥ Berezovsky, *Netivot Shalom*, Part 1, *Torah* 4)

Just as a father buys a *Humash* for his young son and also hires him a tutor, so God, may He be blessed, both gave us the Torah and also, Himself, teaches each one of the children of Israel. This is [the meaning of] the blessing we recite: "The one who teaches Torah to the nation of Israel."

(Rabbi Yitzḥak Meir Alter, *Ḥidushei HaRim*)

It is the Torah of life – the Torah that gives instruction to each and every person about his day-to-day life.

(Rabbi Yosef Yitzḥak Schneersohn)

"That you make us accustomed to Your Torah." [This phrase in the prayers] is difficult. Didn't the prophet rebuke Israel and say: "Their reverence of Me has become a commandment of men learned by rote" (Isaiah 29:13), which proves that habituation is not good?

Apparently it is only for mitzvot that it is not good, but for Torah study habituation is good.

(Rabbi Menaḥem Mendel of Kotzk)

One who has not achieved the capacity to taste the World to Come, but his soul still longs and thirsts for God, pining for Him all day, and yet he does not quench his thirst in the waters of Torah available to him, is analogous to someone who is standing at a river but screams, "Water, [bring me] water to drink." [Against this,] the prophet protests, "Ho, everyone thirsty, go to water" (Isaiah 55:1).

(Rabbi Shneur Zalman of Liadi, *Tanya*, *Likutei Amarim* 40)

Further reading: The path to attaining excellence in Torah study is often not easy. Read anecdotes about great Torah figures and their path to Torah in *A Concise Guide to the Sages*, p. 330.

Torah and Other Forms of Wisdom

The Torah is divine wisdom, and we cling to it and believe in its truthfulness. God also granted man the intelligence and wisdom to think independently and to examine the world. How does the Torah view human wisdom and what is the relationship between the two?

Involvement in the natural sciences can deepen a person's awareness and appreciation of the Creator. Certain types of wisdom can contribute to a person's livelihood, and there are those who also know how to use human wisdom in their service of God. But one who delves into human wisdom without a strong foundation of belief in God can get caught up in heretical ideas and can eventually lose his faith entirely.

What about contradictions between the Torah and scientific findings? Not every verse of the Torah is meant to be understood literally, and it is important to remember that the Torah has multiple layers of meaning that we must uncover. However, it is also important not to blindly accept every scientific theory. Often, theories are advanced to explain certain findings but are later updated or rejected on the basis of new evidence.

Torah and the Natural Sciences

Knowledge that is rooted in clear, incontrovertible evidence can be relied upon and used, regardless of who discovered or formulated that knowledge.

The reason for all of these calculations,[55] why we add this number [of minutes or hours to the month] or why we subtract, how we know each of these matters, and the proof for each of them, is [all based on] the wisdom of astronomy and geometry about which the wise men of Greece compiled many books and these are now in the hands of the Sages. But the books that the wise men of Israel, descendents of the tribe of Issachar, composed during the days of the prophets did not reach us. Since all of these matters have clear, conclusive, incontrovertible proofs, it is inconsequential whether these books were authored by prophets or gentiles. With regard to any matter whose reason is known and whose truth is confirmed through

55. The reference is to calculations of when the moon will become visible at the beginning of the new month.

conclusive proofs, one is not relying on the particular individual who said or taught [this information], but rather upon the proof that has been discovered and the reason that has become known.

(Rambam, *Mishneh Torah, Hilkhot Kiddush HaḤodesh* 17:24)

Further reading: For more on the mitzva of sanctifying the new month, see *A Concise Guide to Halakha*, p. 237.

People invest time and energy in attaining human wisdom. However, even those who study logic, mathematics, physics, astronomy, and music yearn to understand that which is beyond the physical world. Through Torah study, especially if one learns from a teacher who has been trained in the wisdom passed down by Jewish tradition, one can come to know much about the spiritual world and the divine.

It is clear that the primary benefit of other types of wisdom is only to serve as a stepladder to [Torah] and to the wisdom they call knowledge of the Creator. For when they spend their time studying logic so they will not make a mistake in their inferences, and then they come to [study] mathematics, including complex calculations and geometry, the benefit these [studies] provide is that one will be able to say the height of a wall or the depth of a pit. If they then move from these [studies] to astronomy, which has great benefit [in allowing one] to know the movements of the constellations, the closeness and distance [of the heavenly bodies to the earth], the inhabitable earth, and eclipses, the benefit still does not match the effort. If they move to the study of music, the effort is even greater and the benefit less. They themselves admit that the great benefit of all of these comes when they reach in their research the wisdom they call metaphysics, which is wisdom of the divine. They research and acknowledge incorporeal intellects, which are angels, and that there are different levels of them in existence, until they reach the Prime Cause, may His kingship be blessed and exalted, and they research how creations came from Him.... But a Jewish child has read more about creation [than these scholars], for he sees in the Torah what was created on the first day and what was created on the second day. If he analyzes this and thinks wisely about it, or [learns] from a teacher who has received the oral tradition, he will know that whatever comes first in creation is more fine and more lofty than what comes next, and he will derive the number of primary elements that exist.

(Ramban, *Torat Hashem Temima*)

The natural sciences are the product of human thought and comprise a significant body of wisdom. Human wisdom can aid one to attain divine wisdom, and natural sciences can bring one to appreciate the greatness of God, who created the natural world. However, when scholars promote views that run counter to belief in God, one should pay no attention other than for the purpose of knowing how to respond effectively.

Natural sciences are fundamentally correct:

"If a person tells you, 'There is wisdom among the nations,' believe him" (*Eikha Rabba*, 2).... These are the words of the Rambam in his work: Concerning whatever the scholars of the nations said about what is beneath the sphere of the moon, one should accept their [wisdom], for they were wise with regard to the natural world. But what they said about what is above the sphere of the moon, which goes beyond nature, one should not accept [their wisdom]. For they were wise concerning the natural world, but with regard to that which is above nature, which is divine wisdom, one should not listen to them (based on *Guide of the Perplexed* II:22).

(Maharal of Prague)

Learning natural sciences is part of appreciating the greatness of the Creator, and leads to a deeper understanding of the Torah:

What they have formulated is bona fide wisdom, for there is no difference between Jewish wisdom and the wisdom of the nations.... Consequently, one should study the wisdom of the nations, for why should one not study wisdom that is from God, may He be blessed? It is illogical to say that although it is bona fide wisdom, one should not stray from the Torah, as it is written: "You shall ponder it day and night" (Joshua 1:8).... For this wisdom is like a ladder upon which to ascend to the wisdom of the Torah.... For one should study anything that [aids one to] comprehend the nature of the world, and one is [even] obligated to do so, for everything is created by God and one should appreciate it and thereby recognize his Creator.

One should disregard human wisdom when it contradicts Jewish belief:

The principle that emerges from what we have written is that one should examine their words so that he can respond to them, to a questioner, as the Sages said (Mishna *Avot* 2:14).[56] If he finds that they said something proper that strengthens belief, he should accept it. However, if he finds something, even a small thing, that contradicts Jewish belief or that [contradicts]

56. The mishna states: "Know what to respond to an apostate."

anything said by the Sages, God forbid that he should listen to them. But he should think, in his mind, how to respond to their words according to his ability.

(*Netivot Olam, Netiv HaTorah*, chap. 14)

Human wisdom can serve as an aid for Torah study, but only Torah is absolute, objective truth. One should engage in other areas of study from a Torah perspective. Torah and other subjects are not of equal value. Other subjects are human wisdom, whereas Torah is divine wisdom, the objective standard for all other areas of study.

All types of wisdom can serve as aids to Torah study:

Torah is primary and absolute. This does not mean that we should refrain from gaining any exposure to other realms, but we must make these secondary to Torah study. The Torah is the yardstick [by which we assess] them. God's Torah is the sole authority, whereas the others are human wisdom, and are therefore imperfect.... We should consider that which we learn from the Torah to be absolute fact. Other areas of wisdom should be merely auxiliary. One should engage in their study only if they can aid his study of Torah and they are viewed as secondary to the primary [goal of Torah study]. The truth of Torah should be to us an unconditional axiom.

The Torah is the point of departure, and the yardstick by which to measure other disciplines:

Our sole focus should be [Torah. In this way,] whatever we absorb or create in the spiritual realm will be from a Torah perspective. We will not absorb things that are inconsistent with it, and we will not accept things that emerge from a different set of assumptions and mix them with Torah. The Torah should not be considered equal to other disciplines, as though it is one discipline among many others. It should not enter one's mind that there is Jewish wisdom and truth, and along with it, with the same degree of authority and importance, there is non-Jewish wisdom and truth.... Just as we are certain that the Torah is from Heaven and disciplines developed by mankind are just the wisdom of the human mind, and they include conclusions based on one's limited understanding of nature, so too, we are certain that there is only one truth, and one discipline that serves as our yardstick by which to measure all else.

(Rabbi Samson Raphael Hirsch, *Commentary on the Torah*, Leviticus 18:4)

A Jew may study the wisdom of the nations only in order to be able to earn a good livelihood, or if he knows how to use this knowledge in the service of God. Otherwise, such involvement constitutes a sin of neglecting Torah study. It is even worse than other manners of neglecting Torah study, as it defiles the intellectual aspect of a Jew's divine soul.

One who studies the wisdom of the nations is considered to be engaged in idle chatter [and thereby violates] the sin of neglecting Torah study, as we stated in *Hilkhot Talmud Torah* (3:7). Moreover, the impurity of the wisdom of the nations is even greater than the impurity of idle chatter. [The latter] envelops and defiles only the emotional attributes [that stem] from the holy element of air within the divine soul, with the impurity of *kelipat noga* (the glowing husk) associated with idle chatter, which derives from the evil element of air within this *kelipa* (husk) of his animal soul, as stated previously. [The idle pursuits] do not defile the aspect of his soul's wisdom-understanding-knowledge, [i.e., the intellect], since these are foolish and boorish matters that fools and ignoramuses can also speak of. However, the wisdom of the nations envelops and defiles also the aspect of his divine soul's wisdom-understanding-knowledge with the impurity of the *kelipat noga*.... [Engaging in this wisdom is permitted] only if it is utilized as an instrument to earn a gainful livelihood, enabling him to serve God, or if he knows how to apply it to the service of God or His Torah. This is the reason Rambam and Ramban, and their peers, studied this [wisdom].

(Rabbi Shneur Zalman of Liadi, *Tanya, Likutei Amarim*, chap. 8)

Torah Concepts

Exposure to human wisdom can lead a person to heresy. Consequently, only a righteous person, whose faith is strong, can and must be involved in [pursuing] human wisdom.

In truth, it is a great prohibition to be a philosopher, God forbid, and to study books of [human] wisdom, God forbid. Only a very righteous individual can begin to study the seven types of wisdom,[57] for one who enters these types of wisdom can fall, God forbid. For each and every type of wisdom has a stumbling block, an expression of [the spiritual legacy] of Amalek, and through that stumbling block one can fall, God forbid. Amalek was a philosopher and an intellectual and he denied God, as it is written: "He [Amalek] was not God-fearing" (Deuteronomy 25:18). He conducted himself based only on [human] wisdom and did not fear God at all. But when

57. In the Middle Ages wisdom was divided into seven categories: logic, mathematics, geometry, physics, astronomy, music, and metaphysics.

the righteous individual enters [the study of] these seven types of wisdom he steadies himself and stays secure in his position through faith, an expression of the verse: "The righteous will live by his faith" (Habakkuk 2:4).

(Rabbi Naḥman of Breslov, *Likutei Moharan* 2:19)

The Information and Technology Revolution

According to a statement of Rav Katina cited in the Talmud (*Sanhedrin* 97a), this world lasts for six thousand years, corresponding to the six days of creation, and then the seventh millennium corresponds to Shabbat. Near the end of the sixth millennium the world prepares for Shabbat and there is therefore an explosion of scientific knowledge and technological development.

In the six-hundredth year of the sixth millennium[58] the gates of wisdom will open above and the springs of wisdom below. The world will prepare to enter the seventh [millennium], like a person who prepares for Shabbat on Friday afternoon.

(*Zohar* 1:117a)

The development of science and technology greatly aids the service of God. An example is the invention of the telephone, radio, and satellites, which enable a person to see what is happening on the other side of the world. This serves as a vivid image that fosters appreciation of how God observes everything man does and constantly judges his actions.

The telephone, radio, and satellite serve as an illustration of the fact that God sees our every action:

The real purpose of any item in creation is for it to be used by the Jewish people in the service of God.... For example: One of the forces of "nature" that was revealed and developed in recent years is the ability for a human voice speaking in a particular place to be immediately heard in another place, on the other side of the world or on the moon, through a telephone or radio. Additionally, it has recently become possible to see this person and all his movements [somewhere else in the world]. This worldly innovation, the ability to hear each and every sound that comes out of a person's mouth, at that exact moment, all over the world, and to see him, gives a vivid illustration to the concept of "an eye sees and an ear hears" (Mishna *Avot*

58. This is the year 5600 from Creation, corresponding to the year 1840 CE, which is near the beginning of the ongoing technological revolution that led to the development and use of electricity and steel, and the automobile, telegraph, radio, telephone, and light bulb.

2:1).... With regard to everything that a person does, even in the innermost chambers, at that precise moment, "an eye sees, an ear hears, and all of your actions are written in a book."

This thought is accessible and inspiring:

Once a person has a vivid illustration of this matter, his comprehension of the fact that "God stands over him... and He scrutinizes him, examining [the thoughts of his] innards and [the emotions] of his heart to determine whether he serves Him properly" (*Tanya, Likutei Amarim* 41), will not be a merely intellectual understanding, but it will be more visceral. It will naturally have more impact on his character, such [that it will be expressed in his] thought, speech, and action.

(Rabbi Menaḥem Mendel Schneerson, *Likutei Siḥot*, Part 15, 58b)

Further reading: For more on meditating on God examining all of our actions, see pp. 173, 192; *A Concise Guide to the Sages*, p. 367.

Torah and Science

The Torah's description of Creation contains mystical secrets; not all of it is meant to be understood at face value. Therefore, the Sages taught that the secrets of Creation are transmitted from teacher to disciple privately rather than publicly (*Ḥagiga* 11b).

The Torah's account of Creation is not meant to be taken literally in its entirety, as the masses believe. If it were [entirely true in a literal sense] the Sages would not have been concerned about [publicizing] it, they would not have attempted to keep it hidden, and they would not have objected to discussing it in public. The superficial meaning [of the account of Creation] can lead to significantly inaccurate concepts, the assimilation of false ideas about God, or even to total abandonment and denial of the foundations of Torah.

(Rambam, *Guide of the Perplexed* II:29)

The Torah tells of the creation of the world approximately six thousand years ago. However, according to the Sages this process was preceded by the creation and destruction of a number of other worlds. This rabbinic statement can help explain the fact that geologists have dated the world as much older than it is according to our tradition. Their findings pertain to items left from previous worlds.

"This teaches us that the Holy One, blessed be He, repeatedly created worlds and destroyed them, saying: 'These are worthwhile to me and these are not worthwhile to me'" (*Bereshit Rabba* 3:7).... Now, my dear brothers, look at the foundations upon which our holy Torah rests. This secret was transmitted to our fathers and teachers, and they revealed it to us hundreds of years ago, and now, in our age of clarity, it has been found in nature. From all that has been stated, it is clear that what the kabbalists transmitted to us hundreds of years ago, that there was a world that once existed and it was destroyed, and then [a new world] arose, [and this happened] four times, and each time the world was more perfect than before, has all been confirmed to be true in our day and age.[59]

(Rabbi Yisrael Lipschitz, *Tiferet Yisrael, Derush Or HaḤayyim*)

Knowledge of God is built on recognizing the unity of the Creation. When we notice that the natural world is a single, integrated system, built with incredible wisdom, this strengthens our recognition of God and His wisdom. The theory of evolution does not contradict Torah but is rather a possible interpretation of the Creation narrative. If wisdom requires the conclusion that the universe was formed over billions of years, that increases our recognition of the greatness of God, who invested so many years to reach the goal.

Evolution is one possible interpretation of the Creation narrative:

In summary, although the approach of modern-day philosophers and scientists has not been proven... we must clarify that even if these theories are proven correct, they do not at all threaten the foundations of Torah. They rather cast light on the esoteric narrative of Creation.... The kabbalists especially have already explained, relying also on the midrash that states that God created worlds and destroyed them, that creation has undergone several stages until it reached this state.

The theory of evolution only increases our admiration for the Creator:

The idea of an evolutionary process over billions of years is very distressing to the small-minded. They think that evolution leaves room for denying the living God, but they are very mistaken. Knowledge of God is built only on recognition of the unity [of creation]. When we how see the vast creation is organized with wisdom, and how living creatures have body, spirit, and intellect, and everything is integrated into one system, we recognize the great

59. The theories that state that the world is billions of years old and that there have been several catastrophic events or processes that have destroyed nearly all life on the planet are compatible with the statement of the Sages that God created and destroyed the world several times.

spirit that is here that gives life to all and sets a place for all. If the ways of wisdom necessitate that this develop over billions of years, we should be even more amazed at how great and lofty is [God], the eternal Source of life, such that billions of years of constant development toward achieving a particular goal are like an instant to Him.

(Rabbi Avraham Yitzḥak Kook, *Linevukhei HaDor*, chaps. 4–5)

Scientists formulate hyphotheses and theories and test them, whereas the Torah deals with absolute truths. Reconciling these two realms is inappropriate. We have no plausible ways of measuring the conditions at the time of the creation of the world. Therefore, there is no place for questioning the description that appears in the Torah with different theories of the age of the world.

Science formulates theories, whereas the Torah deals with absolute truths:

It was quite a surprise to me to learn that you are still troubled by the problem of the age of the world as suggested by various scientific theories which cannot be reconciled with the Torah view.... I underlined the word theories, for it is necessary to bear in mind, first of all, that science formulates and deals with theories and hypotheses while the Torah deals with absolute truths. These are two different disciplines, where reconciliation is entirely out of place.

Theories that deal with matters that cannot be proven in a laboratory are not true science:

We must distinguish between empirical or experimental science dealing with, and confined to, describing and classifying observable phenomena, and speculative science, dealing with unknown phenomena, sometimes phenomena that cannot be duplicated in the laboratory.... At best, science can only speak in terms of theories inferred from certain known facts and applied in the realm of the unknown.... In view of the unknown conditions which existed in "prehistoric" times, conditions of atmospheric pressures, temperatures, radioactivity, unknown catalyzers, etc., etc., as already mentioned, conditions that is, which could have caused reactions and changes of an entirely different nature and tempo from those known under the present-day orderly processes of nature...we have no conceivable measurements or criteria of calculations under those unknown conditions.

The "scientific" theories contradict each other:

It is no wonder that the different "scientific" theories about the age of the world not only do not fit with each other, but some of them even contradict and negate each other, where the maximum age according to one theory is less than the minimum age of another.

(Rabbi Menaḥem Mendel Schneerson, *Mind Over Matter*, p. 34)

Professor Velvl Greene, of blessed memory, was a well-known scientist in Minnesota who had begun returning to Judaism. He read an article that the Lubavitcher Rebbe had published about the faulty foundations of the theory of evolution and sent him a long letter with several critiques of his article.

The Rebbe replied with a letter that addressed other topics but did not pertain to his critiques. The exchange of letters continued, but the Rebbe did not respond to the professor's questions.

One day the Rebbe wrote him that he heard that the professor and his wife sent their daughter to a religious summer camp, and it is therefore time to repay an old debt. In the remainder of the letter he explained at length his position concerning evolution and responded to all of the professor's original critiques.

In one of his meetings with the Rebbe the professor asked why the Rebbe had delayed his response for so long. The Rebbe responded: "My mission in this world is to bring Jews closer to their Father in heaven, not to win arguments."

Other types of wisdom do not truly nourish the soul, for doubts will always remain, and every philosopher contradicts his predecessor.

(Don Yitzḥak Abarbanel, Commentary on Isaiah 55:2)

This is a principle in the war of ideas: When an idea is raised that contradicts something in the Torah, we do not necessarily need to disprove that idea. We can build the palace of Torah over it, and in this way we can be uplifted by it. It was for this very purpose that these ideas were revealed.

(Rabbi Avraham Yitzḥak Kook, *Igrot HaRa'aya*, *Igeret* 105)

Resurrection of the Dead

Belief in the resurrection of the dead is one of the fundamentals of Jewish faith, but there are differing opinions in Jewish tradition about what it entails. According to Rambam, the dead will be resurrected, live a long life, and then die once again. The ultimate end is spiritual existence, which is called the World to Come. According to Ramban, the World to Come is when the righteous will be resurrected and will receive their ultimate reward as eternal material beings.

Upon the resurrection of the dead, the body will receive all those parts of the soul that it had elevated while alive. This will not be a direct continuation of life in this world, as one's familial relationships are negated upon death. Nevertheless, since one's soul will continue to exist, one's relationship with his parents will also continue, as they are responsible for portions of a person's soul.

The resurrection of the dead will take place in the Land of Israel. The body of one who was buried elsewhere will be brought to the Land of Israel through subterranean tunnels, and only then will the soul be returned to its body, bringing the body back to life.

What Is Eternal Life?

The opinion of the Rambam is that while the resurrection of the dead is one of the fundamental principles of the Torah, the ultimate goal is life in the World to Come. After the resurrection, people will live a long life but will eventually die again. Their souls will live eternally in the World to Come, which is entirely spiritual.

Life after the resurrection of the dead is not eternal:

> The resurrection of the dead is a fundamental principle of the Torah, and one who does not believe in it has no portion in the Torah of Moses our teacher. But it is not the ultimate goal. That goal is the World to Come.... Those people whose souls will return to their bodies will eat, drink, engage in sexual relations, and have children, yet they will die after a very long life, like the lifespans of those living in the messianic era. The life that is not followed by death is the life of the World to Come, since that is a life without a body.

The messianic era will last for a long time, the anointed king will die, and his son will rule after him:

The anointed king (the messiah) will die, and his son will rule after him, and then his grandson. The prophet already told of the death of the anointed king: "He will not weaken and will not be broken until he establishes justice in the land" (Isaiah 42:04).[60] His kingdom will last for an exceedingly long time, and people's lifespans will also be very long, because when worries and sorrows will be removed, people's lifespans will increase. Do not be surprised if this kingdom will last thousands of years, for when a group of good people bands together it does not quickly disband.

(Rambam, *Igeret Teḥiat HaMetim*; *Commentary on the Mishna*, Introduction to *Ḥelek*)

The opinion of the Ramban is that after a person's death, the soul enters a spiritual world referred to as the Garden of Eden. Eventually, the messianic era will arrive, which will be an epoch in this world. Finally, the time for the resurrection of the dead will arrive. This is the time of the ultimate reward, and is referred to by the Sages as the World to Come.

After the dead are revived they will not die again:

We will therefore believe what [the Sages] said: "The dead that the Holy One, blessed be He, will, in the future, revive will not return again to their dust" (*Sanhedrin* 92b).... This matter is often repeated by the Sages, as they state in many places in the Midrash and Talmud: "The expression: 'That it may be well with you,' is a reference to the world where all is well, and the expression: 'That your days may be long,' is a reference to the world that is entirely long" (*Kiddushin* 39b). Their intent is that all who merit [to be resurrected] will have long life, for there will be no death.

The body will be like the soul and will never die again:

The place of reward of the souls and their continued existence in the world of souls is called by our Sages "the Garden of Eden." They sometimes refer to it as "ascension" or "the heavenly academy." Later, the messianic era will arrive, which will take place in this world. Finally, there will be the day of judgment and the resurrection of the dead, which is a reward that includes both body and soul. That is the great, primary [goal] for which all who place their hope in the Holy One, blessed be He, aspire, and that is the World to

60. The verse implies that the anointed king will weaken and die after he fulfills his mission of establishing justice in the land.

Come, where the body will become like the soul, and the soul will cling to the knowledge of the Most High, as it did when in the Garden of Eden, the world of souls. [The soul] will be elevated with even greater spiritual comprehension, and all of this will continue to exist eternally.

(Ramban, *Torat HaAdam, Sha'ar HaGemul*)

The goal of the creation of the world and of humanity is for this dark, lowly world to become a place where God's presence dwells and is openly apparent. Consequently, the final and lasting reward is specifically in this world.

God desired that His dwelling place be in the lower levels of existence:

The reason for the creation of the world in general and the creation of humanity in particular, and their purpose, is that the Holy One, blessed be He, desired a dwelling place specifically in the lower spheres. Meaning, the lower spheres… [which include all of] physical existence, should be in a state of negation [relative to God]. In this manner, the light of the infinite God, may He be blessed, will rest on them and be revealed through them…. This is why the Torah and commandments were given below and apply to physical entities and to a soul resting specifically within a physical body. This is so their performance can transform independent existence into negation, making it a vehicle for Godliness.

Man's perfected state will come through the resurrection of the dead, when his soul will rest within a physical body:

In the world after the resurrection, God will totally remove the spirit of impurity from the world; there will no longer be sin or death in the world. For the Holy One, blessed be He, will slaughter the evil inclination, which is also the angel of death. Humankind will then reach its absolute perfection, not only as a result of its [divine] service and the reward for it, but also through a gift given from above…. This reward will be received below specifically by a soul that is in a body. That will be the ultimate purpose and goal of this world, for the world was originally created so that God, may He be blessed, will have a dwelling place in the lower spheres.

(Rabbi Menaḥem Mendel Schneerson, *Igrot Kodesh* 2:200)

Further reading: For more on the idea that the goal of the physical world is to serve as an abode for God's presence, see p. 146.

Which Body Will Be Resurrected?

A person might descend to this world in several reincarnations, each time perfecting a different part of his soul. Each body will be revived along with the parts of his soul that he perfected while inhabiting that body.

If [a person descended to this world] once, and attained only the level of *nefesh*[61] but did not merit to fully perfect his soul before he died, then since that first body did not complete the improvement of all aspects of the *nefesh*, it will be resurrected only with the specific aspect of the *nefesh* that it did improve.... Then the aspects of the *nefesh* that were improved by the second body, along with the entire *ruah* and *neshama*, will be with the second body at the time of the resurrection. The first body will have no share in the *ruaḥ* or *neshama*, but it will share with the second body part of the *nefesh*, according to the parts of the *nefesh* that it improved. The other parts of the *nefesh* will be with the second body.

(Rabbi Ḥayyim Vital, *Sha'ar Hagilgulim*, Introduction 4)

Further reading: For more on reincarnation, see p. 170.

Will Family Relations Be Restored?

The only familial relations that will remain at the time of the resurrection are those based on the soul. Therefore, the relationships between parents and children will remain, and there will be an obligation to honor one's parents:

Nonetheless, the connection of children to their father and mother will not cease. Even after the resurrection, all will be obligated to honor their parents. This is because the bodies that will be revived include within them the aspects of the soul that remained in the grave hovering over the bones, as we said above. This is the soul of childhood, which was drawn down to a child by his father and mother. The obligation to honor parents is not specifically because [of their role in] the creation of the body, but because they drew down the child's soul through their union.

(Rabbi Yosef Ḥayyim, Responsa *Rav Pe'alim* II, *Sod Yesharim* 2)

---

61. According to kabbalistic thought, the soul comprises several parts, including the *nefesh*, *ruah*, and *neshama*. The *nefesh* is responsible for a person's physical desires and instincts and is the life force of the physical body. The *ruah* is responsible for a person's spiritual development, including emotion, inspiration, and the ability to negate one's ego in order to do good for others. The *neshama* represents the highest spiritual level, in which a person dedicates himself fully to spiritual development, and the materialistic world ceases to have any significance for him.

Rolling through Underground Tunnels

Though all dead people will eventually be resurrected, those in the Land of Israel will be resurrected first, and those outside the Land of Israel will roll there and be resurrected there.

The first to be resurrected will be those in the Land of Israel:

Rabbi Yohanan said: "The dead of the Land of Israel will come to life first. This is the meaning of what is written: 'Your dead will live' (Isaiah 26:19).[62] [The following phrase,] 'my corpses will rise,' refers to those outside the Land of Israel."

Corpses located outside the Land of Israel will receive their souls only in the Land of Israel:

The dead who are outside the Land of Israel will have their bodies reconstructed. Then they will roll underneath the ground until the Land of Israel; they will receive their souls there and not outside the land. This is the meaning of what is written: "Therefore, prophesy and say to them: So said the Lord God: Behold, I am opening your graves, and I will take you up from your graves, My people, and I will bring you to the soil of Israel" (Ezekiel 37:12). What is written afterward? "I will put My spirit into you and you will live" (Ezekiel 37:14).[63]

(*Zohar* 1:118b)

When Israel will rise up from the dust, there will be many lame and blind people among them. Then the Holy One, blessed be He, will shine the sun upon them to heal them, as it is written: "[But the sun of righteousness will shine for those who fear My name,] with healing in its rays" (Malachi 3:20).

(*Zohar* 1:203b)

62. The phrase "your dead will live" is interpreted as a reference to those in the Land of Israel. The continuation of the verse, "my corpses will rise," is interpreted as a reference to those outside the Land of Israel.
63. These verses appear in Ezekiel's vision of the dry bones.

Prayer

Three times a day, in the morning, afternoon, and evening, we stand before God in prayer. One is obligated by Torah law to pray and to request that God provide for him. At the beginning of the Second Temple period, the Sages arranged the formalized structure of prayer that forms the basis of the prayer books used today. The Talmud records a dispute about whether the three daily prayers were originally instituted by the forefathers, Abraham, Isaac, and Jacob, or whether they correspond to the daily offerings sacrificed in the Temple.

Prayer forms the structure and framework of a Jew's spiritual day, and it is referred to as the "service of the heart." But alongside structured, formalized prayer, there is also a form of prayer that bursts forth spontaneously from the heart, and which does not have a set text. Sincere prayer nourishes the soul. During prayer a person develops himself spiritually and thus becomes worthy of receiving divine blessing.

To prepare the heart for prayer one should meditate on God's greatness and one's own lowliness. When one turns to God with a broken heart it evokes a divine response. When one prays with joy, he draws to himself divine blessing, which is not the case when one prays in a state of sadness. Proper prayer requires concentration. It requires sufficient time for praying thoughtfully and meaningfully, and the synagogue provides an ideal setting for prayer.

Further reading: For more on prayer, see *A Concise Guide to the Sages,* p. 457; *A Concise Guide to Halakha,* p. 483.

The Obligation to Pray

Service of God is not limited to the sacrificial rites in the Temple; it includes the service of the heart, which is prayer. There are three essential stages of prayer: praising God, petitioning Him that He provide for one's needs, and thanking Him for the good one has received.

It is a positive commandment to pray every day, as it is stated: "You shall serve the Lord your God" (Exodus 23:25). The Sages learned through an oral tradition that this service is prayer. It is also stated: "To serve Him with all your heart" (Deuteronomy 11:13). The Sages said: "What is service of the heart? It is prayer".... The requirement imposed by this commandment is as follows: A person must pray and supplicate every day. He should recite praises of the Holy One, blessed be He; then request the provision of his needs, using [language of] request and supplication; and then give praise and thanks to God for the good that He has bestowed upon him. Each person [should pray in this fashion] according to his abilities.

(Rambam, *Mishneh Torah,* Laws of Prayer 1:1–2)

Despite its centrality in the prayer service, the text of the *Amida* prayer, also known as *Shemoneh Esreh* (literally, "eighteen," because it was originally formulated with eighteen blessings), is of rabbinic, not biblical, origin. Its importance is compared to that of the spinal cord, which, although it is not counted as one of the limbs of the body, is what allows the entire body to function. Similarly, prayer is the foundation and facilitator of all of the commandments.

The number of blessings in the *Shemoneh Esreh* prayer corresponds to the number of vertebrae in the spinal column:

For the eighteen blessings of the *Shemoneh Esreh* correspond to the eighteen vertebrae of the spinal column that house the spinal cord, as is known from the *Zohar* (*Tikkunei Zohar* 18) and from the Talmud in *Berakhot* (28b). By way of analogy, a person has 248 limbs, including the eighteen vertebrae of the spinal column. But the spinal cord itself, which runs through the vertebrae, is not counted among the number of limbs. Nonetheless, it is what supports and sustains all the limbs. The spinal cord runs from the head to the thighs, and the life force is drawn through it from the brain to all of the limbs. For the limbs are connected to the ribs, the ribs to the vertebrae, and the vertebrae to the spinal cord. The spinal cord is not one of the limbs, but it is what connects them, starting from the brain and spreading to the legs. Therefore, if the spinal cord is damaged, one's life is in danger.

Intent in prayer corresponds to the spinal cord:

This can be likened to the commandments, which are the 248 limbs of the King.[64] Our Sages, of blessed memory, said: "Fulfilling the commandments requires intent" (*Berakhot* 13a). "Intent" refers to the element of prayer, which serves as the "intent" and inner content of the commandments. Prayer is the primary [factor] that supports and stabilizes the 248 positive commandments. It is comparable to the spinal cord, which supports and sustains the limbs, even though it is not counted among the 248 limbs.

(Rabbi Shneur Zalman of Liadi, *Likutei Torah, Balak,* s.v. *Lo hibit aven*)

64. The 248 positive commandments are associated with 248 aspects of divine revelation.

Further reading: For more on the institution of prayer and its source, see *A Concise Guide to the Sages*, p. 469.

Fixed Prayer and Personal Prayer

The Torah obligation to pray does not include a fixed text. At the beginning of the Second Temple period, the Men of the Great Assembly established the formalized text of the prayer service that remains in use. Their goal was to make it easier to concentrate during prayer and to create a unified text for the entire nation. The prayer service was formulated with great precision, and much thought was put into both its themes and its wording.

From the days of Moses until the days of the Men of the Great Assembly, there was no uniform structure of prayer. Instead, each individual composed his own prayers according to his understanding and wisdom. It was so until the Men of the Great Assembly came and instituted this prayer, the *Shemoneh Esreh*, so that it would be formulated for all. They formulated it in simple, understandable language, so that the ideas therein would not be confusing due to the language and it would be uniform for all, both the wise and the simple-minded. Nevertheless, they formulated it with great intent and extreme care, in that it is arranged with three blessings of praise before the petitionary prayers, and three following them. In between are twelve blessings that include petitions for all of a person's needs. All of this was not just by chance, but done after long consideration.

(Rabbeinu Baḥya ibn Ḥalawa, *Commentary on the Torah*, Deuteronomy 11:13)

Torah Concepts

Prayer is service of the heart, and requires mental exertion – both in keeping extraneous thoughts at bay and in concentrating on the words of the prayer. In addition, the words of the prayer have mystical meanings, which are the soul of the prayers. Praying in this mystical manner involves meditating on the names of God that appear in the text of the prayers.

Thought during prayer:

A person must perform service of the heart with great dedication. He must be as mighty as a lion to be alert that no extraneous thought enters his mind. If he is not able to empty his mind of extraneous thoughts during prayer, he should seek out techniques and strategies [to avoid them]. For instance, he should think: The Creator, may He be blessed, is standing opposite me, hearing what comes out of my lips, and checking the thoughts of my heart. He will then tremble and be full of shuddering and agitation. He should employ whatever resources he can think of that will enable him to overcome and remove his foreign thoughts. After that, he should be as mighty as a lion in another way, contemplating the meaning of the words. He should pour forth his words and spirit before the King of all kings, the Holy One, blessed be He, who hears prayers and can do the impossible. In truth, doing so takes great effort.... This is the explanation of why our Sages, of blessed memory, called prayer "service of the heart" (*Mekhilta deRashbi* 23:25), for it is great work, holy service.

Intention is the soul of prayer:

The matter of prayer with intention, which is the soul of prayer, is the mystical aspect of prayer. For the revealed aspect of prayer is that it is about temporal life. Similarly, recounting the praises of the Holy One, blessed be He, and how He, may He be blessed, directs his acts, are revealed matters. But their inner and mystical element, that which touches on the loftiest matters in the world, is the soul of the words. This element is the mystical meaning of the divine names, and the names are the *sefirot*[65] through which the Lord is unified and through which the inner aspect of His unity, may He be blessed, is expressed. The Holy One, blessed be He, longs for this type of prayer.... The revealed aspect of prayer is analogous to the body and intention in prayer to the soul.

(Rabbi Yeshaya Horowitz, *Shenei Luḥot HaBerit, Masekhet Tamid, Ner Mitzva* 10)

A person should turn to God in his own language and converse with Him about whatever happens in his life. This type of prayer has the advantage of not being "recognized" by any negative spiritual forces that are trying to destroy prayer. Nevertheless, a person must continue to pray according to the fixed prayer text established by the Sages and not limit himself to improvised and spontaneous prayer.

Prayers, supplications, and requests that have already been formulated by the Sages are known to all of the destructive spiritual forces and accusers. They ambush these types of prayers because they already recognize them. An analogy: On a paved highway, well known to all, murderers and bandits always lie in ambush because it is a road they already know about. But one who travels by a new and unknown path does not need to worry about murderers and bandits, for they do not know it as a place where they can lie in ambush. Similarly, a conversation that a person has between himself and his Maker is a new path, a new prayer that one says from his heart in a new

65. The sefirot are ten aspects of divine emanation written about extensively in Jewish mystical literature.

way, so the accusers are not lying there in ambush for him. Nevertheless, he[66] warned about how important it is to also say the other fixed supplications and requests.

(Rabbi Naḥman of Breslov, *Likutei Moharan* 2:97)

There are prayers that flow from the heart and break out of the depths, and at other times it is the mind that arouses the heart to pray. For standard prayers, whose texts are fixed, inspiration generally stems from the mind, whereas prayers that spring forth from a person's heart are usually connected to personal experiences and have no fixed and ordered text.

Prayer [can come about] in two ways: Sometimes the heart is inspired to pray, as the verse states: "Their hearts screamed out to God" (Lamentations 2:18). As a result of one's troubles in his heart, prayer breaks forth from its deepest recesses. Prayer can also come about through thought and meditation, inspiring one to pray. Even though prayer is impossible without both mind and heart, nevertheless one type of prayer emerges because of the distress he feels in his heart and that inspires his mind to think thoughts of prayer, whereas the other emerges through meditating with his mind, and the mind arouses the heart – which is the soul – to pour forth to its source.... We can say that this is also the difference between the fixed prayers instituted for us by the Men of the Great Assembly and the prayers that individuals say because of the events that occur on a particular day.

(Rabbi Shmuel Bornsztain, *Shem MiShmuel, Va'etḥanan* 5675)

The Greatness of Prayer

Proper prayer is one said with complete intent, and functions as the core of a Jew's day. Prayer is spiritual sustenance for a person's soul, sustaining it until the next prayer.

Thoughtful prayer, said with concentration, is the focus of the day:

The prayer of a pious person[67] is not one of custom or habit, like the song of a starling or parrot. Rather, every word is accompanied by thought and concentration. In this way, for the pious one, the time of prayer forms the core and purpose of his time. Other times are like paths that lead to this time [of prayer], for he looks forward to its coming. Through such prayer, he

66. Rabbi Naḥman of Breslov: In the original, this passage began "I also heard in his [Rabbi Naḥman's] name."

67. In Rav Yehuda HaLevi's *Kuzari*, the pious person (the *ḥasid*) lives the ideal Jewish life, fulfilling all of the commandments properly and actualizing the divine ideal.

becomes similar to the spiritual entities and distances himself from animalistic tendencies.

Prayer is sustenance for the soul and sustains it from prayer to prayer:

The value of prayer for the soul is like that of food for the body. For a person's prayer is good for his soul just as food benefits his body. The blessing that results from each prayer rests upon him until the time of the prayer that follows, just as the energy from the meal he ate keeps him sustained until the evening meal.... During prayer a person purifies his soul from all that it went through in the interim [since the last prayer], and prepares it for the future.

(Rav Yehuda HaLevi, *Kuzari* 3:5)

Prayer has two central goals: First, God, who is good, wants what is good for us. He therefore gave us commandments so that, through fulfilling them, we can merit all good. He also tells us that the way to receive our needs is by praying to Him and requesting them, and this itself is also a commandment. In addition, prayer strengthens our consciousness and belief that the Holy One, blessed be He, is responsive to our needs and watches over us, and that He is omnipotent and nothing is beyond His ability.

[One] of the reasons for this commandment is what I have previously mentioned many times, that good things and blessings will be granted to people according to their actions, good-heartedness, and proper thoughts. The Master of all who created them wants what is good for them, and leads them and brings them success through His precious commandments that will bring them merit. He provided for them and informed them how to attain all of their positive desires – that is, through requesting of Him, may He be blessed, the One who has the ability and wherewithal to give them anything they lack. For He will respond from Heaven to anyone who calls to Him truthfully. Besides informing them of this [divine] quality, He commanded them to use it and to always request all of their needs and what they want. In addition to attaining what we want, through arousing our spirits and totally focusing our thoughts on His being the good Master who does good to us, we also merit that His eyes are open, [watching over] us everywhere we go. All the time, at every moment, He hears when we cry out to Him; "The Guardian of Israel neither slumbers nor sleeps" (Psalms 121:4). [Prayer also brings us merit through] believing in His kingship and His unquestionable and unlimited ability, that there is nothing that holds Him back or impedes Him from anything He wants.

(*Sefer HaḤinnukh* 433)

Torah Concepts

Prayer involves the needs of the person praying, but it also includes an element of service of God. This is because prayer is aimed at strengthening our recognition of our complete dependence on the Creator.

Prayer is God's will:

"The prayer of the upright is His gratification [*retzono*]" (Proverbs 15:8) – it is God's will,[68] may He be blessed. Even though prayer, where a person makes requests of God, may He be blessed, is for his own benefit, nevertheless, such prayer is the service of the upright. This refers to prayer, which is His will.

The service of prayer is to deepen belief in God:

Do not ask: How is it possible to say that prayer is service of God, may He be blessed? Do we not pray for the sake of reward?[69] If so, why is prayer referred to as "service"? We have already explained that the entire concept of service indicates that everything belongs to God, may He be blessed.... The same is true for prayer. When a person prays before God like a servant appealing to his master for his requested needs, this prayer indicates that man needs God. If it is so that man is dependent on God, may He be blessed, he is His – for one who is dependent on another is his, as will be explained later. Therefore prayer is completely [considered] service, for it indicates that a person is dependent on God, may He be blessed, and is therefore His.

(Maharal, *Netivot Olam, Netiv HaAvoda* 1)

Further reading: For more on divine providence over human behavior, see p. 173.

Every sickness has its own specific cure, but prayer works for everything. Prayer is effective for a sick person praying to get well, and also for someone sentenced to death who wants to be saved. It is a cure with no negative side effects.

The special quality of prayer itself is that it is effective for all things. For we find that prayer is effective for healing the sick, as it did for Hezekiah: "I have heard your prayer... behold, I am healing you; on the third day you will go up to the House of the Lord" (II Kings 20:5). It is also effective to save from death. For when Israel sinned through the Golden Calf, Moses was told, "Let Me, and I will destroy them" (Deuteronomy 9:14), and they were

68. The Hebrew "*retzono*" can also be translated as "His will."

69. Since requesting our needs is so central to prayer, is not prayer, almost by definition, for the sake of receiving our needs?

later saved through Moses' prayer.... If so, prayer is like an all-purpose balm that is effective for all sicknesses and all poisons, as opposed to other types of antidotes, which are effective only for specific sicknesses.

(Rav Yosef Albo, *Sefer HaIkkarim*, chap. 20)

Why Is Prayer Effective?

Prayer presents a philosophical difficulty. It seems to have the power to change what God already decreed for a person's life. But does that not involve the seemingly impossible function of changing God's will? Prayer does not change God's will but transforms the person. Through prayer a person becomes primed and fitting to receive the divine flow. Prayer transforms him from bad to good, making him deserving of divine goodness.

Does prayer change God's will?

What has brought people to doubt [the efficacy of] prayer... is that they say that the following possibilities are unavoidable: If some good was decreed by God for someone, there is no need for prayer. And if that good was not decreed, how can prayer be effective to change God's will, so He will [now] decree good that he hadn't decreed earlier? For God does not change from willing something to not willing it or from not willing it to willing it.

Prayer transforms a person:

This approach is incorrect. For influences from above will influence the one receiving them only when he is at a specific level and properly prepared to receive them. If a person does not prepare himself for receiving that flow of influence from above, he prevents the good from reaching him. If, for instance, it was decreed that a man's grain harvest should be successful in a certain year, but he did not plow or sow that year – then even if God sends powerful rains upon the earth, that man's harvest will not be successful, since he neither plowed nor sowed. He prevented the goodness from reaching him, because he did not prepare himself to receive it.... In a similar vein, the effectiveness of prayer or of proper action can be explained. The one who prays prepares himself to receive the flow of goodness or cancels the misfortune that was decreed upon him, by changing his own spiritual level.[70]

(Rav Yosef Albo, *Sefer HaIkkarim* 4:18)

70. Prayer transforms the person and thereby prepares him to receive goodness that he was decreed to receive. Alternatively, if some misfortune was decreed upon him because of his evildoing, his prayer or a change in his behavior transforms him into a good person – not the one the misfortune was decreed upon.

Torah Concepts

Preparing for Prayer

In order to prepare for prayer one must think about God's greatness and the kindnesses He does for the Jewish people in general and each individual in particular. He should also realize that the ability to stand before God in prayer is itself one of the kindnesses He does for us, for man by himself is not worthy of it.

How is the heart prepared? Before starting to pray one should sit silently for a while without doing anything. He should remove all other thoughts from his mind and think about the greatness of the One who spoke and the world came into being: His wonders, His awesome and mighty acts, and the kindness He did for His nation. One should also think about the good and kind things that God did for him.... He should think of his own deficiency and lowliness vis-à-vis his Creator.... He should think that he wants to now get up before the King, and to supplicate and request of him his requests and desires. The person is, in truth, unfit and unworthy to stand before Him, if not for the great kindness and perfection of the Creator who permitted and commanded him to pray, even though his service may fall short [of what it should be]. Then he should get up and pray.

(Rabbi Menaḥem di Lonzano, *Derekh Ḥayyim*, p. 49)

Further reading: For more on proper preparation for prayer, see *A Concise Guide to the Sages*, p. 457.

How Should One Pray?

Every aspect of service of God, including every prayer, has a particular appropriate intention. With the proper intent, a person can attain his spiritual goal. Yet, there is one general type of intent that breaks all barriers and attains whatever is needed – that is, approaching God with a broken heart. A broken heart enables a person to cling to God.

The main element of intent is [approaching God with] a broken heart, subjugating himself and clinging to God, may He be blessed. There is a parable for this matter: Every lock has a key that opens it precisely, a key that was fashioned with precision to fit a specific lock. There are thieves who open a door without a key; that is, they break the lock. This matter is the same. Every need has a key, which is the appropriate intention when praying for the fulfillment of that need. But the main way to open all doors is to be like a thief who breaks it all. That is, one has to thoroughly break his heart through great humility. This will break the curtain that separates the person from above and which was causing him to be closed off [from divine goodness].

(Ba'al Shem Tov, *Keter Shem Tov* 243)

Torah Concepts

Joyful prayer has an advantage over prayer out of sadness. God accepts both prayers, but whereas He gives the one who cries what he needs, He gives with great abundance to the one who prays joyously.

Prayer conducted with great joy is certainly more acceptable before Him, may His name be blessed, than prayer that is with sadness and crying. The parable for this is when a poor person supplicates before the king with great crying, the king gives him only a small amount. But when a minister presents the praises of the king joyfully, and then, through this, he also makes his request – the king responds to his request in an expansive way, in the way one gives to ministers.

(Ba'al Shem Tov, as cited in *Tzava'at HaRivash* 107)

In order to pray properly, to say every word and think about its meaning, one must dedicate a sufficient amount of time to prayer and not hurry.

When a person takes enough time for his prayer, an amount that is not too short for the needed time, so that he can say each request by itself, slowly, he will be able to concentrate. But if he does not have this amount of time or if he does not speak in a measured manner, but rather, hastily, he will not be able to concentrate.

(Rabbi Menaḥem di Lonzano, *Derekh Ḥayyim*, p. 49)

Prayer in the Synagogue

Praying in the synagogue enhances and intensifies the power of prayer. The sanctity of the synagogue elevates one's prayer, and praying with the community gathered in the synagogue creates a power that cannot be achieved when praying alone at home.

Since prayers are so awesome and lofty…that the upper spiritual worlds are dependent on them, and the future redemption – may it come speedily in our day, amen – is also dependent on them, it is therefore proper to try and take care to pray in a synagogue. The synagogue is like the Temple, and is referred to as a "miniature Temple,"[71] where the Divine Presence rests. A person can accomplish there through prayer ten times what he would be able to if he were to pray in his home. For there in the synagogue he will find two advantages [over prayer in his home]: the sanctity of the place and the many people assembled there.

(Rabbi Yosef Ḥayyim, *Ben Ish Ḥai*, Year 1, *Miketz*)

71. See *Megilla* 29a and Ezekiel 11:16.

The Rebbe of Munkatch, Rabbi Ḥayyim Elazar Shapira, author of *Minḥat Elazar*, was hospitalized toward the end of his life in a medical center in Budapest. On Friday, before Shabbat, he asked permission to have a *minyan*[72] near his sickbed. The hospital administration did not grant permission, but the doctor in charge of his treatment decided to take responsibility and allow it, provided that the prayer would be done quietly.

When the prayer began and Rabbi Shapira reached the words, "Let those the Lord redeemed say it, those He redeemed from the hand of the foe.... They cried out to the Lord in their trouble" (Psalms 107:2, 6), a scream broke forth from his mouth. After the prayers, the doctor asked the Rebbe why he didn't keep his promise. The Rebbe answered that he saw that other sick people cry out, even in the middle of the night.

The doctor objected: "The other sick people are crying out because of their pain and suffering."

The Munkatcher Rebbe answered: "Do you know what 'Jewish pain' is? How painful and bitter it is for the Jew who, for two thousand years, is still waiting for the messiah?"

72. A quorum of ten men for communal prayer.

Hope and Despair

We are filled with hope, both on a personal level and on a collective level – looking forward to the salvation of the entire nation of Israel. Prayer strengthens hope and enables a person to connect to a place where he recognizes God's unlimited power to fulfill his hopes.

Despair stems from a person's lack of trust in his ability to cause change and to become changed. The recognition that God always accepts us enables us to avoid falling into the clutches of despair. The basis of the Jewish nation's survival is the belief that we should never give up hope, in any situation. When a person has a kernel of belief, he does not despair.

Hope

God is omnipotent, and He will save the nation of Israel as well as each individual. When a person prays for what he hopes for, he shows that his hope is sincere. This will also enable him to receive that which he hopes to receive.

The [appropriate] hope and anticipation with regard to the collective is that a person should always express hope to God that He should save his nation as a whole and their lot should be positive.... As for the individual, he should hope that God, in His mercy and great kindness, will lead him on an upright path, save him from evil, and [help] him choose what is good and proper for himself.... When many difficult troubles present themselves to him, he should hold fast to his simplicity. He should increase his courage, and hope to God; thinking, knowing, and understanding that nothing holds God back from giving him what he asks for and fulfilling his request, for His abilities are limitless.... When a person prays for that which he hopes for, that indicates that his hope is sincere. He will then be able to receive the kindness for which he hoped.

(Rav Yosef Albo, *Sefer HaIkkarim* 4:48)

Further reading: For more on complete trust in God, see p. 154.

Do Not Despair

Hopelessness and despair sometimes creep into a person's consciousness because he does not sufficiently believe in the power of repentance. As the prophet taught us: As long as a person is alive, he can still return to God. There is therefore no reason for a person to despair as a result of of his sins.

"What shall a living man complain? Each man for his sins. Let us search and examine our ways" (Lamentations 3:39–40). This verse speaks about a living individual, [and tells us] that he has no reason to complain about his sins – saying that since he sinned he has no way to repair what he did and he will not be able to attain purity. For as long as he is still alive he should not give up hope, because despair is not justified unless a person died in his sinfulness. But while he is still alive, at any time or moment he is able to seek out and find a cure for his sickness, through something that applies equally to all of us. "Let us search and examine our ways, and return to the Lord" (Lamentations 3:39–40). "The gates of repentance are always open" (*Devarim Rabba* 2:12), and we are obligated to "lift up our heart with our hands" (see Lamentations 3:41), so that our hearts should be given and handed over to our hands[73] to direct it to the good path, directed toward Him, may He be blessed, who dwells in heaven.

(Rabbi Azarya Figo, *Bina LeIttim, Derush* 61)

There is no reason in the world for despair. No matter how low a person's spiritual level sinks, there is always hope for him.

The principle is that it is forbidden for a person to make himself lose hope. Even if someone is a simple person and does not know at all how to study Torah, or if he is in a place where he is not able to study Torah, nevertheless, even in his simplicity he must strengthen himself in fear of God and simple service [of God] appropriate for his level.... Even someone who is, God forbid, at the lowest level – the All-Merciful One should save us from this – even someone who is placed in the depths of hell – the All-Merciful One should save us from this – since he holds himself where he is, he should still have hope of repenting and returning to Him, may He be blessed.

(Rabbi Naḥman of Breslov, *Likutei Moharan* 2:78)

Further reading: Read the story of Rabbi Elazar ben Dordaya and his "last minute" repentance in *A Concise Guide to the Sages*, p. 464.

The nation of Israel was formed specifically after everyone had given up hope on the possibility that our patriarch Abraham and our matriarch Sarah would have a child.

73. That is, in our control.

Then Isaac was born, and from him came the nation of Israel. This teaches us to believe that we should never give up hope.

The entire formation of the Israelite nation was after complete despair, that "Abraham and Sarah were old" (Genesis 18:11),[74] and [in the words of Sarah herself], "Who would have said of Abraham that Sarah would nurse children, as I have born a son for his old age?" (Genesis 21:7). No one even considered believing that they would have a child. Even after the angel's promise, the righteous Sarah, who knew and believed that God, may He be blessed, is omnipotent, still laughed within, for it was so far removed [from reality] to believe in this, knowing of Abraham's old age... and her own old age. She also thought that if it was God's will that He would remember them [and they would have a child], He would have remembered them earlier. For it is preferable [for God] to minimize a miracle, and He does not perform an unnecessary miracle. But, in truth, this was from God, so that the building of the nation would specifically come about after complete despair, when no person – even Sarah – believed that they would be remembered by God. For this is the total essence of an Israelite, to believe that one should not at all give up hope. God, may He be blessed, can always help, and, as the verse states: "Is any matter beyond the Lord?" (Genesis 18:14). One should not investigate why God did it that way.

(Rabbi Tzadok HaKohen of Lublin, *Divrei Sofrim* 16)

The Essence of Jewishness

When a person remembers his essential Jewishness and his inner connection to God, he does not fall into despair. Sometimes God "hides His face" and man is drawn toward hopelessness, but this is only a way of testing the essential core of his Jewishness.

The main test is for there always to remain a point of Jewishness that can be held onto in times of failure. When Moses our teacher said, "Whoever is for the Lord, to me" (Exodus 32:26), the tribe of Levi gathered around him. Surely there were also great people among the rest of the children of Israel. But they had fallen into despair when they saw how concealed the Divine Presence was. All of this was so that they would overcome divine concealment.

(Rabbi Avraham Mordekhai Alter, *Imrei Emet, Behaalotekha*)

---

74. The verse ends: "It had ceased to be with Sarah the manner of women," indicating that she was no longer physically able to have children.

Further reading: For more on challenges and their significance, see p. 197, 231.

There is a story about Rabbi Yisrael Salanter, who went out to the streets of the city on one of the nights of the Ten Days of Repentance, and saw a faint light shining from a dilapidated house. Rabbi Yisrael entered, and saw a cobbler sitting by a dwindling candle, striking a shoe energetically with his hammer.

Rabbi Yisrael asked him: "Why are you so hasty, my fellow Jew?

The cobbler answered him: "Rabbi, as long as the candle is burning – it is still possible to repair!"

Rabbi Yisrael went out to the street and called:

"Jews! Listen my Jewish brothers! As long as the candle is burning it is still possible to repair!"

Hopelessness is one of the clever strategies of the evil inclination that wants to lead a person astray and push him away, God forbid, from serving his Maker.

(Rabbi Menaḥem Mendel Schneerson, *Igrot Kodesh* 12)

The theme of *Pesah Sheni*[75] is that no situation is lost. It is always possible to repair and complete. Even someone who was impure or distant, and even [if it was] "for you,"[76] namely, the impurity or distancing was willful, nevertheless he can correct it.

(Rabbi Yosef Yitzḥak Schneersohn, *HaYom Yom*, 14 Iyar)

Concerning strengthening oneself so that a person will not become depressed because of his many flaws and the great destruction he caused through his actions, [Rabbi Naḥman] said: If you believe you can destroy, believe that you can repair.

(Rabbi Naḥman of Breslov, *Likutei Moharan* 2:112)

75. On the fourteenth of the month of Iyar, those who were not able to bring the paschal offering at the normal time, the fourteenth of Nisan, because they were impure or distant from the Temple, have another chance to offer it.

76. Numbers 9:10 – "When any man shall be impure by means of a corpse, or on a distant journey, for you or for your generations, he shall offer the paschal lamb to the Lord."

This trait [of humility], seeing oneself as the lowliest of men – even though it is an incomparably good trait… nevertheless one must exercise great caution that it does not cause terrible despair, which is worse than all.

(Rabbi Shmuel Bornsztain, *Shem MiShmuel, Mo'adim, Sukkot*)

The voice of God calls to him, in contrast: There are in fact ways [to return to God], and do not say "despair, hope is lost." Despair is the product of laziness, and if you exert effort, you will find [your way].

(Rabbi Yaakov ben Shlomo Tavshonsky, *Imrei Haskel* 15)

Further reading: Read the story of King Hezekiah, who did not despair even when faced with a severe heavenly decree, in *A Concise Guide to the Sages*, p. 319.

Repentance

One who sinned against the Creator of the world should rightfully be punished and distanced from God. But God, in His mercy, allows us to repent and once again stand before Him. Repentance returns us to the state of serving God and being acceptable in His eyes. Repentance applies to all areas of our lives. Ideally, a person repents of his own volition, but even repentance as a result of afflictions is accepted. Even if one repents a moment before death, his repentance is accepted.

One type of repentance involves correcting one's actions, but there is another type of repentance, which focuses on thought and renewing our connection with God. This is a lofty type of repentance, inspired by love of God. This type of repentance transforms our sins into merits, for it was the distance from God that brought about the ultimate closeness.

In repentance a person stands before God by himself and receives forgiveness and atonement.

Further reading: For more on repentance, see *A Concise Guide to the Torah*, p. 502; *A Concise Guide to the Sages*, p. 461.

How Does One Repent?

Repentance is the way a person returns to the proper path after he has strayed from it. Both someone who transgressed negative commandments and one who failed to fulfill positive commandments are obligated to repent. The way to correct one's failure to fulfill positive commandments is to renew one's devotion to good and proper deeds. The way to correct transgressions is through being more cautious about sin and by distancing oneself from a sinful environment. Repentance can be compared to someone who was not following a proper diet and now needs to eat certain foods or avoid certain foods in order to get back on track.

Repentance is an act of repair:

The reason for repentance is to repair a person so he can serve the Creator, may He be blessed, after having abandoned divine service and sinning. Repentance involves bringing back what was lost, whether because of his foolishness about God and serving Him, or because his desires overcame his reason, ignoring what God obligated him to do, or because of connecting with bad friends who enticed him, sinning because of them, and the like.... The abandonment of service of the Creator can be in one of two ways: deserting what the Creator commanded him to do and ignoring it, or acting in a way counter to the divine will and thereby rebelling against one's Creator.

The repair must correspond to the damage:

If one abandoned the service of God through avoiding doing what the Creator commanded him to do, the way to repent for what he was deficient in is to strive to undertake proper activity.... But if his sin was doing that which God warned him against doing, the way to repair it is to avoid going back to that entire type of act and to try to do the opposite [of his sin].

Repentance is like correcting a nutritional imbalance:

An analogy for this in the natural world is someone who became sick because of malnutrition, either because of not eating what would have preserved his health or eating that which damaged his health and caused it to deteriorate. If he was sick because of not eating nutritious food, the way to return to proper health is by increasing the amount of foods and medicines that are appropriate for his nature until he returns to equilibrium. Once he returns to his healthy state he can eat as normal. But if his sickness came about because of eating foods that are dangerous [to his health], he will return to health by avoiding those and similar foods, and [by eating those that are] the opposite of its nature. When his body is once again healthy and reaches a state of normality, he can eat foods that are in between the two types of foods [the dangerous and its opposite], midway between the two types.

(Rabbeinu Baḥya ibn Pakuda, *Ḥovot HaLevavot, Sha'ar HaTeshuva* 7:1)

Repentance applies not only to sins, but also to personality traits:

Do not say that there is [a need for] repentance only from active sins, like promiscuity, robbery, and theft. Just as one must repent from these, he must also search through his bad character traits and repent from anger, enmity, jealousy, mockery, and from pursuit of money, honor, food, and the like. He must repent from all of these. These sins are more difficult than those that involve an action, for when a person is steeped in these [bad character traits], it is difficult to detach oneself from them.

(Rambam, *Mishneh Torah, Hilkhot Teshuva* 7:3)

Further reading: For more on anger, see p. 194; *A Concise Guide to the Sages*, p. 421.

The motivation to repent and change can stem from a number of sources. One person might come to it by himself, another might need criticism or rebuke from others or inspiration from the the Torah or the Prophets, and still others are moved to change after they experience misfortune. Even if someone repents on his deathbed, it is still considered acceptable. Nevertheless, repentance that is self-motivated is of a higher order and brings about greater reward than if the impetus to repent comes from external sources.

Self-motivated repentance:

Repentance is divided into different levels – the higher the level the greater the reward it brings ... The foremost level, higher than all others, is what our Sages, of blessed memory, spoke about when they said: Who is a penitent? It is someone who encountered sin but separated from it (see *Yoma* 86b) .... The second level is someone who is also himself inspired to repent, but is motivated by the masses who speak disparagingly about his evil deeds. The person senses this himself, knows that he has developed a bad reputation, and is therefore motivated to remove his bad trait .... The third level is one who is also self-motivated, but is inspired by the time dedicated to repentance – namely, the Ten Days of Repentance – knowing that his life is being weighed, his actions are written in the book,[77] and he will be judged on all hidden matters, whether good or bad.

One who repents after being rebuked:

The fourth level is one who did not inspire himself to repent but was instead rebuked about his evil deeds. He accepted the rebuke and repented because of it. That is also a good practice and comes from upright character .... The fifth level is when a person reads God's Torah and the words of the prophets, and understands the prophets' rebukes and parables, their warnings, and the destiny spoken about in their books. He takes the words of the Torah and prophets more seriously than the words of those who rebuked him. He was afraid and worried when he read about the serious punishments coming to "those who twist their crooked ways" (Psalms 125:5), and he returned to God. This is also a good practice and an upright character trait .... The sixth level is someone who was not himself motivated to repent, and also not by one of the [external motivations] we spoke about, but after constantly sinning saw that others were punished for the same sins he has. He was afraid he would die like the others and be punished for his evil deeds.

One who repents only when he feels there is no other choice:

The seventh level of repentance is someone who does not humble his heart because of any of the above reasons until he encounters misfortune and

77. Based on Avot 2:1: "All of your actions are written in a [heavenly] book."

is terrified – whether he encounters suffering through loss of property or the death [of people close to him], for one may be inspired to repentance from any damage or trouble that comes to him.... The eighth level is when a person is inspired to repent in his old age, when his natural drives and his strength have weakened. Also on this same level is anyone who repents because sin is unavailable or impossible.... The ninth level is someone who was not chastised by any of the above, but when the time comes for him to die, he senses that the cessation of his vain life is soon to come and he is afraid about the afterlife and worried about his sins, and he longs to return to God with all of his heart. His thought [to repent] will not be effective if he plans on returning to his old ways if he is healed of his sickness – for this is not included in repentance, as we have said repeatedly, repentance never works for one who intends to return to sin. But this person firmly decided to totally leave his evil path even if he lives [and is healed] from his sickness. Then, in this state of repentance, he leaves the world. Even though this repentance was done out of most extreme weakness, his repentance is acceptable and he receives atonement for his sins.

(Meiri, *Ḥibur HaTeshuva, Meshiv Nefesh*, 1:2)

Repentance: The Soul Returns to Its Source

The Hebrew word for repentance, *teshuva*, also means returning. God is the source of all creation, and when a person repents, he returns to the source of his creation. When one who distanced himself from God through sin then returns to Him out of love, he transforms a negative into a positive. Distancing himself from God, which was at first tragically negative, is ultimately a positive, because it brought him closer to God.

Repentance is when a person returns to God with all of his heart and soul. This is part of the world order, for this world returns to God. The world has no independent existence, and returns to God from where it came and where all in existence return to. This is what keeps them in existence, for they return to God... Because repentance is the return of elements of creation to God just as they came from Him, when a sinner returns to God, even his willful sins become as merits, for here there is a returning to God and a return to the proper order of the world. Therefore, when this sinner repents – he who distanced himself from God through his sin, and the distance necessitated returning to God, his distance becomes a merit,[78] for

78. His willful sins become merits, because his distance created a need to return to God, which is the movement of all of existence, for all came from God and return to Him.

there is now returning to God. This is the case only when the repentance was out of love, for love involves totally clinging to God.

(Maharal, *Netivot Olam, Netiv HaTeshuva* 2)

Man's soul is holy and connected to God, but sins conceal its light. When a person repents, his soul once again shines within him, as well as in its spiritual source above.

Every Jewish person has a point that is holy to God, and it is the living soul. It is through sins that the burden of materialism and physicality conceal the light of the soul and it cannot illuminate.... To the degree that he returns the power of his soul into his body, so will the power of his soul illuminate its spiritual source above.

(Rabbi Yehuda Aryeh Leib Alter, *Sefat Emet, Nitzavim* 5635)

Repentance is the return of the soul to its place. The mystics distinguished between higher and lower repentance. Lower repentance is repenting for improper acts and the soul returning to its source after having been distanced through sin. Higher repentance is when the soul clings to and comes close to the Creator, exactly as it was before it descended into a body.

Lower repentance:

So it is written: "Jacob the allotment [*ḥevel*][79] of His inheritance" (Deuteronomy 32:9). By analogy, [the soul is] like a cord with one end above and the other end below. If a person pulls the lower end, he will dislocate the higher end and pull it toward him as much as it is possible for it to be pulled.

It is literally the same with regard to the root of the human soul.... He pulls down its sustenance through his evil deeds and thoughts into the sanctums of the "other side," so to speak, from which he receives his sinful thoughts and deeds.... When a person repents properly, he then extracts from them the sustenance, which he channeled through his actions and thoughts.

For through his repentance, he restores the sustenance of the Divine Presence to its place.

Higher repentance:

Once the wind has passed and cleansed them, then their soul is able to return literally to Being, blessed be He, and ascend upon high to its source

79. The word *ḥevel* can also mean cord.

and cling to Him in wondrous union... This constitutes complete repentance. The aspect of this unification and repentance constitutes the aspect of higher repentance which follows lower repentance.

(Rabbi Shneur Zalman of Liadi, *Tanya, Igeret HaTeshuva*, 6–8)

The Power of Repentance and Its Unique Greatness

God has mercy on all of His creatures, and helps even evildoers return to Him through repentance. He removes them from darkness by implanting the path to repentance into their hearts and the path to healing into their souls. Even though a person caused ruin through sinning, nothing holds him back from repenting. God accepts all who repent and has mercy on them.

God accepts the repentance of all:

Nothing in the world stands in the way of repentance, and the Holy One, blessed be He, certainly accepts all penitents. If a person repents, the path to life is ready before him. Even though he caused damage through sin, all is repaired, and everything returns back to its repaired state.... Therefore, this person, even though he transgressed and caused damage where he should not have, when he repents before God He accepts him and has mercy over him. For the Holy One, blessed be He, is full of mercy and He is full of mercy toward all of His creations.

God helps the evildoer repent:

Come and see what is written: "He went waywardly in the way of his heart" (Isaiah 57:17). Afterward it is written: "I saw his ways and I will heal him; I will guide him and pay condolences to him and his mourners" (Isaiah 57:18). The verse states that "he went waywardly." Even though the evildoers do what they do purposely, for they went "in the way of their heart," and others warn them but they do not want to pay attention to them, nevertheless when they repent and choose the good path of repentance, healing is presented before them.... The Holy One, blessed be He, sees his ways, pointlessly going after evil. The Holy One, blessed be He, says: I must strengthen him. This is what is written: "I saw his ways," that they go in the darkness. The Holy One, blessed be He, says: I want to give him healing. This is what is written: "I will heal him." The Holy One, blessed be He, introduces the way of repentance into his heart and healing into his soul. "I will guide him".... The Holy One, blessed be He, guides him on the straight path, like one who holds another's hand and takes him out of the darkness.

(*Zohar* 2:106b)

The spiritual level of a penitent is greater than the level of the righteous, for the penitent tasted of sin yet abandoned it. It is forbidden to remind a penitent of his past. If he hears himself being belittled for his past, he should be humble and lowly and know that his level will be even higher.

Penitents are on a higher level than the righteous:

One who repents should not imagine that he is distant from the level of the righteous because of the transgressions and sins that he did. This is not the case. Rather, he is beloved and dear before the Creator as if he never sinned at all. Not only that, but his reward is great, for he tasted the taste of sin and separated himself from it and conquered his evil inclination. Our Sages said: "In the place where penitents stand, even the full-fledged righteous do not stand" (*Berakhot* 34b). This means: Their level is greater than those who never sinned at all, because the penitents conquered their evil inclination more than the righteous did.

The greatness of repentance:

How lofty is the level of repentance! Yesterday this person was separated from the God of Israel.... He would cry out to Him and not be answered... fulfill commandments and they would be torn up before him... and today he clings to the Divine Presence.... He calls out and is answered immediately... fulfills commandments and they are accepted with satisfaction and joy.... Furthermore, his actions are desired.

It is forbidden to mention to a penitent his past deeds:

The way of penitents is to be exceedingly lowly and humble. If fools scorn them about their previous deeds and say to them, "Yesterday you did such and such and yesterday you used to say such and such," the penitents should not concern themselves with these fools. They should just listen, be joyous, and know that this is a merit for them. For whenever they are ashamed of the acts they sinned through and embarrassed by them, their merit is great and their level grows. It is an outright sin to say to a penitent, "Remember your previous actions," to mention them before him to embarrass him, or to mention things or matters similar to them in order to remind him of what he did.

(Rambam, *Mishneh Torah, Hilkhot Teshuva* 7:4–8)

My Soul, Prepare Provisions

By: Rabbeinu Baḥya Ibn Pakuda

My soul, prepare plentiful provisions, do not hold back
while you are still alive and have the ability, for the way is long.
Do not say, "Tomorrow I will take provisions," for the day is passing,
and you do not know what the day will bring.
Know that yesterday will never return
and all that you did then is weighed, counted, and calculated.
Do not say "Tomorrow I will do it,"
for the day of death is hidden from all.
Hurry and do each day's amount
for death at any time can send its arrow or lightning bolt.
Do not delay from doing each and every day's amount,
for like a bird moves away from its nest, so a man moves from his place.

A hasid who was pursued by the Communist regime in Russia hid for a while with a family in a remote village. One night a terrible tragedy happened; the mother put her infant baby to sleep next to her in bed, and apparently smothered her during her sleep. The hasid recounted: "I was lying in my bed and heard how the woman was walking to and fro in the house and muttering to herself, 'What did I do! What did I do!' This lasted several hours. After that, she started to mutter: 'What do we do now? What do we do now?'"

"That night," said the hasid, "the two stages of repentance became clear to me: regret over the past – 'What did I do!' – and accepting improvement on ourselves for the future – 'What do we do now?'"

Do not give up hope about repenting. A person can still redeem his soul through repentance and good deeds even if he sinned over and over again and did much evil in God's eyes for his entire life. Despite [his sins], the gates of repentance are not locked.

(Rabbi Elimelekh of Lizhensk, *Noam Elimelekh, Emor*)

Further reading: For more on hope and despair, see p. 311.

Biographies

Kabbala

Kabbala refers to the concealed, mystical teachings of Judaism. These teachings constitute one of the four layers of Torah study: the plain meaning (*peshat*), allusion (*remez*), exegesis (*derash*), and the concealed meaning (*sod*). This last category touches on essential spiritual questions, such as: How did God create the world? What does it mean to be human? What is the significance of learning Torah and of observing mitzvot? How does one achieve prophecy? These concealed matters are mainly theoretical, but like other subjects in Torah, Kabbala contains practical instructions on how we can transform our behaviors and our lives.

The concealed Torah ("*sod*," literally meaning "secret") is so called because it was the established practice among the Sages not to teach it to everyone, out of concern that it would not be properly understood. Therefore, these lessons have traditionally been passed down from teacher to student. They are taught only when a student has been found who is able to comprehend them even when they are imparted to him in the most concise form and when there is no concern that his exposure to the spiritual reality will harm his ability to judge the physical reality.

The Ancient Concealed Torah

The most ancient Jewish sources discuss matters that concern Jewish mysticism, Kabbala. The Torah describes wondrous and miraculous events like the Creation, the splitting of the Red Sea, and the giving of the Torah. The books of the Prophets describe the revelation of God to human beings. Likewise, there are concealed traditions mentioned in the texts of the mishnaic era, e.g., *Ma'aseh Bereshit*, which is concerned with what occurred at Creation, and *Ma'aseh Merkava*, which is concerned with the revelation of the *Shekhina*, the Divine Presence. These ideas find expression in independent works such as *Sefer Yetzira*, which discusses the creation of the world via the letters of the Hebrew alphabet, and the *Heikhalot* (palaces) literature, which discusses the structure of the upper worlds and the role of the angels.

The ancient, concealed Torah reached its culmination with the *Zohar*, a work attributed to the mishnaic Sage Rabbi Shimon bar Yohai. The *Zohar* consists of a commentary on the Torah in accordance with its concealed meaning. The main subject of the *Zohar* is how God acts and is revealed in the world. The *Zohar* is full of unique terms that have become identified with Kabbala and are a hallmark of all later kabbalistic works.

Zohar

The *Zohar* is the fundamental book of kabbalistic wisdom. It is attributed to the mishnaic Sage Rabbi Shimon bar Yohai. The main body of the *Zohar* is composed of an exegetical, kabbalistic commentary on the Torah, the Song of Songs, and the book of Ruth, written in Aramaic. Some parts are structured as a dialogue between Sages, and others are written as stories about Rabbi Shimon bar Yohai and his students. Additionally, interspersed throughout the *Zohar* are a number of independent sections that concentrate on particular topics:

- *Tikkunei Zohar,* on *Parashat Bereshit,* on the meaning of the term *bereshit,* "in the beginning," and the secrets of Creation.
- *Saba deMishpatim,* which consists of lessons taught by an elderly Sage, an expert in the passage in *Parashat Mishpatim* that discusses Hebrew slaves.
- *Raza deRazin,* on *Parashat Yitro,* on the secrets concealed in a person's face and hands.
- *Sifra diTzniuta* and *Idra deVei Mishkena,* on *Parashat Teruma,* on various kabbalistic secrets.
- *Idra Rabba,* on *Parashat Naso,* on the human body.
- *Rav Metivta,* on *Parashat Shelah,* in which the head of the heavenly academy teaches about the World to Come.
- *Yenuka,* on *Parashat Balak,* which details an encounter with a child who is a master of the concealed Torah.
- *Idra Zuta,* on *Parashat Haazinu,* about the death of Rabbi Shimon bar Yohai.
- *Ra'aya Meheimena,* which is spread over several *parashot* and which contains explanations for mitzvot.
- Several other short essays.

Zohar Ḥadash is the name for texts that were first printed independently of the *Zohar* but were later incorporated within it. The *Zohar* emerged as a complete work only at the beginning of the fourteenth century, but it was known to the kabbalistic Sages prior to this time.

From the *Zohar*:

"The wise will shine like the radiance [*zohar*] of the firmament, and those who lead the multitudes to righteousness, like the stars, forever and ever" (Daniel 12:3). "The wise" are those who study the concealed wisdom; "will shine," meaning that they will glow with the brightness of the heavenly wisdom; "like the radiance" is a reference to the shining light of the river that emerges from the Garden of Eden. This is the secret of "the firmament," where the stars, planets, sun, moon, and all the other lights are found.

(*Zohar* 2:2a)

The Period of Rabbi Yitzḥak Luria (Ari)

In mid-sixteenth-century Safed, kabbalistic thought flourished. Kabbala was enriched by the theories and practices that developed, and its adherents experienced a unique religious life. Rabbi Moshe Cordovero (Ramak), Rabbi Yitzḥak Luria (Ari), and his student, Rabbi Ḥayyim Vital authored works explaining and expanding on the *Zohar*. Various kabbalistic customs were established, such as a version of the prayer liturgy that contained mystical intentions, the *Kabbalat Shabbat* service, Kabbala study groups, and prostration upon the graves of Sages in the Galilee region.

Emotionally, the Jews of Safed, some of whom had been expelled from Spain, felt they lived in a time close to the redemption, and this brought about a proliferation of creativity. Some figures wrote biblical commentaries and compiled collections of non-halakhic portions of the Talmud and *midrashim*. Poets composed such poems as *Lekha Dodi* (Rabbi Shlomo Alkabetz) and *Yedid Nefesh* (Rabbi Elazar Azikri). Large-scale works, such as the *Shulḥan Arukh*, were published. There were some, among them Rabbi Yaakov Beirav, who even tried to restore the traditional ordination of Sages, *semikha*, in order to reestablish the Sanhedrin.

This generation is known as the era of the Ari because he was the main proponent of kabbalistic thought in the period.

Rabbi Moshe Cordovero (Ramak)

Ramak (1522–1570) came from a family of Jews who were expelled from Cordova, Spain. He learned the revealed Torah from Rabbi Yosef Karo, and the concealed Torah from Rabbi Shlomo Alkabetz. He served as a judge in the religious court of Safed, and wrote several books: *Pardes Rimonim*, which addresses disputes concerning the *sefirot*, and *Eilima*, which summarizes and expands on the kabbalistic tradition of the *Zohar* and of the ancient Kabbala. *Or Yakar* is a commentary on the *Zohar* of which only part was published due to its length. *Tomer Devora* is a work of Musar that is written in accordance with kabbalistic principles. It teaches a person how to connect to God.

Rabbi Cordovero used to go with Rabbi Shlomo Alkabetz into "exile," secluding themselves in nature. On these walks, in their discussions or via mystical enlightenment, they achieved an understanding of difficult passages in the *Zohar*.

From Ramak:

At every moment a person is sustained and alive due to the heavenly power that flows to him.... Although the person sins with this power it is not withheld from him; rather, the Holy One, blessed be He, tolerates this affront. He has given this person power and the motion of his limbs, and he uses that power, at that moment, for sin and actions that cause God's anger. But the Holy One, blessed be He, tolerates it.

(*Tomer Devora* 1)

Rabbi Yitzḥak Luria (Ari)

The Ari (1534–1572) was born in Jerusalem, studied in Egypt with Rabbi Betzalel Ashkenazi, and secluded himself for many years on an island in the Nile Delta. At age thirty-six, he immigrated to Safed, where he gathered a small group of students. Foremost among them was Rabbi Ḥayyim Vital, who put the words of the Ari into writing. After two years teaching his insights to his close disciples, the Ari died at the age of thirty-eight. The book *Etz Ḥayyim*, written by Rabbi Ḥayyim Vital, consolidates the Ari's fundamental kabbalistic approach.

The Ari wrote songs for the Shabbat table: *Azamer BiShevaḥin* for Shabbat evening, *Asader LiSeudata* for the day, and *Benei Heikhala* for the third meal. He may also have written special intentions for one to have while reciting specific prayers. His writings have been edited by various individuals at different times. Multiple versions of the prayer book are attributed to him, and a number of halakhic rulings are cited in his name. The book *Shivḥei HaAri* praises his holiness and the wonders he performed.

About the Ari:

Everything the Ari attained, namely, that the gates of wisdom opened for him and that he received the divine spirit, was in reward for his boundless joy at the performance of each mitzva, as it is written, "Because you did not serve the Lord your God with joy and with gladness of heart, from abundance of everything" (Deuteronomy 28:47). "From abundance of everything" [means that serving the Lord is greater than] all the various pleasures of this world, such as gold and precious jewels.

(Rabbi Elazar Azikri, student of the Ari, *Sefer Ḥaredim*)

Rabbi Ḥayyim Vital

Rabbi Ḥayyim Vital (1542–1620) was the foremost student of the Ari. He was born in Safed, and served as a rabbi in Safed, Jerusalem, and Damascus, where he died. He recorded the lessons he heard from his teacher, and permitted very few individuals to read the manuscripts. The manuscripts were later copied illicitly, having been taken from the Safed *geniza*.[1] As a result, various editions and versions of the Ari's writings have been distributed.

Rabbi Ḥayyim Vital's son, Rabbi Shmuel Vital, reedited the Ari's work *Etz Ḥayyim*, arranging it into eight "gates," including the Gate of Kabbalistic Intentions, the Gate of the Mitzvot, and the Gate of Reincarnation.

Rabbi Ḥayyim Vital wrote *Sha'arei Kedusha*, a work of Musar written in accordance with kabbalistic principles. Another of his works is *Sefer HaḤezyonot*, a mystical diary of his dreams and his encounters with significant people.

From Rabbi Ḥayyim Vital:

It is known to wise people that the human body is not the person himself. The body is called mere human flesh.... The person himself is in fact a spiritual being. The body is a garment that the intelligent soul, which is the person himself, wears while still in this world. When a person dies, this garment is removed from the soul, and it will be encased in a pure, clean, spiritual garment.

(*Sha'arei Kedusha* 1:1)

Kabbala in Spain and Italy

In the Middle Ages and the early modern era, Spain and Italy were important centers of kabbalistic learning. Spain was the birthplace of the systematized Kabbala in the thirteenth and fourteenth centuries. There the well-known commentaries were written that developed Kabbala into a complete theoretical system. In later centuries, Italy took the place of Spain and became a hub of kabbalistic thought and creativity, chiefly following the school of the Ari, which originated in Safed.

Rav Menaḥem Recanati

Born in Italy, Rav Menaḥem Recanati (1250–1310) was one of the earliest Italian kabbalists. He wrote *Peirush Recanati LaTorah*, a kabbalistic commentary on the Torah that cites long passages from the *Zohar*, some of which would have been unknown today were it not for this work. He also

1. A storeroom or repository in a synagogue, used for discarded, damaged, or defective sacred books, papers, and items.

wrote the halakhic work *Piskei Recanati,* which contains concise halakhic rulings, and the book *Ta'amei HaMitzvot.* He was known to be an expert in Kabbala and philosophy, and his books influenced many scholars. Some of his works were translated into Latin, and as a result they influenced gentile scholars as well.

From Rav Menaḥem Recanati:

All wisdom is alluded to in the Torah, and there is nothing other than the Torah.... If so, the Holy One, blessed be He, is not separate from the Torah, nor is the Torah separate from Him; there is nothing extrinsic to the Torah. Therefore, the kabbalists said that the Holy One, blessed be He, is the Torah.

(*Ta'amei HaMitzvot*)

Rav Yosef Gikatilla

Rav Yosef Gikatilla (1248–1310) was born in Castile, Spain, and was a student of Rav Avraham Abulafia. His most influential work was *Sha'arei Ora,* which explains the names of God and the ten *sefirot,* the instruments of Creation. He also wrote other works of Kabbala and *aggada*: *Ginat Egoz,* on *gematriya,* the system in which each Hebrew letter is given a numerical value, which often highlights connections, sometimes mystical ones, between words; *Sefer HaNikkud,* which explains the Hebrew vowel signs in accordance with Kabbala; *Kelalei HaMitzvot,* a halakhic and aggadic explanation of the mitzvot, arranged alphabetically; and *Sefer HaMeshalim,* which teaches moral lessons through analogies, such as: "To what is the effect of drinking wine similar? If one drinks a little, this is like when a spy comes to a city, and the inhabitants sense what he is and they are cautious. If one drinks a lot, this is like an enemy conquering the city" (85).

From Rav Yosef Gikatilla:

The early Sages possessed the holy divine names, which they received from the prophets.... Through these names they could create signs and wonders. They did not use them for their own needs, but only when there was a decree against the Jewish people, and it was therefore necessary, or in order to sanctify God's name.... One must know that each one of these names is like a key, which can access anything a person needs in this world.

(*Sha'arei Ora,* Introduction)

Rabbi Yosef Irgas

Rabbi Yosef Irgas (1685–1730) was born and died in Livorno, Italy. His book *Shomer Emunim* is an explanation of the foundations of Kabbala. He wrote it in straightforward terms and intended it for the general community. It takes the form of a debate between two individuals: She'altiel, who learns the revealed Torah, namely, Talmud and *halakha*, and Yehoyada, who believes that one must also learn the mystical aspects of the Torah.

Rabbi Irgas publicly opposed Sabbateanism, a movement that began in the seventeenth century, whose followers proclaimed Shabbetai Tzvi as the messiah. Rabbi Irgas wrote short essays against that movement, called *Tokhaḥat Megula* and *HaTzad Naḥash*.

His explanation of *tzimtzum*, the notion that God contracted Himself in order to create the finite world, was that God's contraction was not a literal contraction. Rather, God can be found in the world after Creation just as He was found prior to Creation. This went against the explanation of Rabbi Irgas's teacher, Rabbi Emanuel Hai Ricci, who held that *tzimtzum* was an actual contraction. This dispute endured; it was even a point of disagreement, to a certain extent, in the famous dispute between the Ba'al Shem Tov and the Vilna Gaon.

From Rabbi Yosef Irgas:

It is true that the foundation of Kabbala is faith in the early Sages, whose wisdom, piety, and traditions we see to be true. But we must not, as a result, prevent ourselves from examining and challenging their words and assumptions. On the contrary; our way is to analyze kabbalistic matters just as we do halakhic matters.

(*Shomer Emunim* 1, p. 2)

Rabbi Moshe Ḥayyim Luzzatto (Ramḥal)

Rabbi Moshe Ḥayyim Luzzatto (1707–1747), a prolific writer, was born in Padua, Italy, and moved to Mantua, and later to Frankfurt, Amsterdam, and ultimately Akko. He is buried in Tiberias. His best-known works of Kabbala are: *138 Pitḥei Ḥokhma*, which discusses the foundations of Kabbala; *Da'at Tevunot*, written as a discussion between the mind and soul; and *Ḥoker UMekubal*, a proof of the truth of Kabbala.

His most famous works are *Mesilat Yesharim*, a book of Musar that teaches the reader how to progress from one level to the next in one's service of God and ultimately attain divine revelation; and *Derekh Hashem*, which is about the foundations of faith. He also wrote books of logic, rhetoric, and grammar: *Leshon Limudim* and *Sefer HaHigayon,* as well as plays written in the Italian dramatic style: *Migdal Oz* and *LaYesharim Tehilla.*

Some rabbis of his generation suspected him of heresy and Sabbateanism. He was excommunicated and made to take an oath that he would not study or teach Kabbala, and his works were even confiscated. He earned his living as a diamond cutter. He was eventually suspected of violating his oath, and he was compelled to immigrate to the Land of Israel. He settled in Akko, where he died in a plague.

From Ramḥal:

The foundation of piety, and the root of pure complete service of God, is that one clarifies and ascertains his obligation in this world, and determines where his gaze and purpose need to be directed in all his life's endeavors.

(*Mesilat Yesharim* 1)

Works Influenced by Kabbala

Kabbalistic literature mainly includes Torah commentary, Musar, or explanations of the mitzvot. There are many books that are influenced by Kabbala but are not actually kabbalistic works, as they do not serve to develop kabbalistic ideas; rather, they utilize those ideas to illustrate a concept, to reinforce a point of Musar, or to demonstrate the kabbalistic basis for original Torah ideas. Alternatively, they are simply influenced by the ideas and spirit of the kabbalistic worldview.

Rabbi Moshe Alsheikh

Rabbi Moshe Alsheikh (1508–1600) was born in Edirne (formerly Adrianople), Turkey, studied with Rabbi Yosef Karo, and served as a judge on the Safed religious court. He died in Damascus. His most famous work is *Torat Moshe,* popularly known as *HaAlsheikh HaKadosh,* a commentary on the Torah in accordance with Kabbala and Musar. He also wrote commentaries on the Prophets and Writings.

Due to its combination of commentary on the verses and Musar, his style became the model for preachers, and it became necessary to print the book because Alsheikh's ideas were being used without being attributed to him. It is told that the Ari refused to teach him Kabbala, yet Alsheikh engaged in his own kabbalistic learning. Rabbi Ḥayyim Vital was his student in matters of *halakha.*

Toward the end of his life, Alsheikh traveled to Turkey, Syria, and Persia, to collect charity for the poor of the Land of Israel. He even wrote a book on the decline of Safed's status that occurred at the end of the sixteenth century.

From Rabbi Moshe Alsheikh:

From my youth, engaging in Talmud study is what raised me.... My heart did not set out to make order of the various interpretations of the Torah; I engaged in this only when I rested from studying *halakha* on Fridays. For each week, on Shabbat, the people come to me to hear my sermons concerning the holy words of Torah that are read in their time, namely, the weekly *parasha*.

(Introduction to *Alsheikh on the Torah*)

Rabbi Ḥayyim of Volozhin

Rabbi Ḥayyim (1749–1821) was born in Volozhin, served as the rabbi of that town, and established the Etz Ḥayyim yeshiva there. He wrote *Ruaḥ Ḥayyim*, a commentary on tractate *Avot*; and a book of responsa, *Ḥut HaMeshulash*. His most significant work was *Nefesh HaḤayyim*, which describes, in accordance with Kabbala, the virtues of humankind, the nature of God, the importance of in-depth Torah study, and the necessity of scrupulously performing the mitzvot in order to connect to God. A student of the Vilna Gaon, he is considered by many to be the main representative of the non-hasidic (*mitnagged*) worldview. He emphasized the importance of Torah study for its own sake, without concern as to whether or not it brings about a perceivable connection to God.

From Rabbi Ḥayyim of Volozhin:

If, on the first night of Passover, a person troubles himself so much with regard to his intention when eating an olive-bulk of *matza*, as he wants to eat in sanctity, purity, and connection to God, and his preparations continue all night until after daybreak, when the time for eating *matza* has ended.... All his purity of thought is an abomination and is not desired by God. But one who ate an olive-bulk of *matza* within the prescribed time, even without excessive sanctity or purity, has fulfilled the positive commandment, as written in the Torah.

(*Nefesh HaḤayyim* 4)

Jewish Thought

Jewish thought refers to philosophical matters that are discussed in Jewish literature. Fundamental questions such as the purpose of the world and what it means to act in a moral fashion are found in the Bible and the words of the Sages, but not in a systematic fashion. The publication of books of philosophical and moral problems and their solutions, set out in an orderly manner, began in the Middle Ages, flourished in the Golden Age of Spain and later in Ashkenazic areas, and has persisted in recent generations until the present day.

Jewish thought is not monolithic. It adjusts in style and content in response to the changing questions that arise in the Jewish world in each generation. One could say that Jewish thought is the spiritual and intellectual reckoning of the Jews with the spiritual questions of the Jewish people. For this reason, the focus of Jewish spiritual thinking has always been internal, primarily through the interpretation of both the Written Torah and the Oral Torah. Nevertheless, one does find discussion of theological and spiritual matters that are relevant to any audience interested in religion in the most general sense. Each thinker offers a different viewpoint on such matters, and this is the source of the richness and the variety that is characteristic of this literature.

Jewish Philosophy

In the Middle Ages, Greek philosophy was highly influential among Arab scholars. Likewise, there were many Jewish scholars who together developed a similar, Jewish branch of philosophy. The defining factor of Jewish philosophy, in contrast to general philosophy, is the extent to which Jewish sources influence its content. Furthermore, Jewish philosophy is concerned with questions that are unique to Jewish life. It addresses matters that are pertinent in the realm of Jewish thought, such as providence, revelation, the chosenness of the Jewish people, reward and punishment, explanations for the mitzvot, and the divinity of the Torah. Nevertheless, Jewish philosophy was influenced by general philosophical thought as well, and adopts some of its theories.

Rav Se'adya Gaon

Rav Se'adya Gaon (882–942) was born in Egypt, studied in the Land of Israel, and was appointed as head of the academy in Sura, Babylonia. He was involved in a number of controversies in his day: He disagreed with the *geonim* of the Land of Israel concerning the fixing of the Jewish calendar, struggled against the Exilarch in Babylonia concerning matters of authority, and opposed the Karaites concerning the status of the Oral Torah.

He was a prolific writer, leaving us with many books in a variety of fields. He translated the Torah into Arabic, and wrote a commentary on the Torah and on several books of the Prophets and Writings. He also wrote a dictionary and a book of Hebrew grammar, arranged the ritual prayers in his *siddur* (prayer book), and wrote liturgical poetry. He created an organized, systematic theory of Jewish philosophy in his work *Emunot VeDe'ot* and in his commentary to *Sefer Yetzira*. He also wrote several important works of *halakha*, such as *Sefer HaShetarot* and *Sefer HaYerushot*.

Rav Se'adya was a groundbreaking leader who understood the issues facing his generation. Through his actions and innovations he shaped Jewish life at that time. His varied undertakings brought Torah to the people and strengthened Jewish traditions. His linguistic works enabled Arabic-speaking Jews, who did not have a strong grasp of Hebrew, to study Torah. His philosophical works demonstrated the biblical basis for Jewish philosophy. Additionally, he was a strong opponent of the Karaite position.

Rav Se'adya's works made their mark on later generations as well. Terms that he coined, such as the distinction between rational mitzvot [*mitzvot sikhliyot*] and mitzvot of compliance [*mitzvot shimiyot*], remain in use. Matters that he determined to be significant, such as the status of humankind in the world, are still discussed. His philosophical method, which relies on tradition on one hand, and on logic and understanding on the other, is still employed.

From Rav Se'adya Gaon:

The purpose of Creation is for our world. Look at all of its parts; the land and the water are both inanimate, and the animals do not speak. This leaves only humankind as its purpose.

(*Emunot VeDe'ot* 4)

Rav Yehuda HaLevi

Rav Yehuda HaLevi (1075–1141) was born in Tudela, Spain, and died in Jerusalem. A poet, philosopher, and doctor, he was an associate of the poets Rav Moshe ibn Ezra and Rav Avraham ibn Ezra. He wrote hundreds of poems, both religious and secular, which are published in the anthology *Diwan*. Some of his poems can be found in the prayer book, and some have even been set to music and are sung on Shabbat.

His philosophical work is called *The Kuzari*. Its purpose was to defend the Jewish faith from the criticisms of Christians, Muslims, and Karaites. It takes the form of a dialogue between a Khazar king and a rabbi. The latter explains the shortcomings of Aristotelian philosophy and the flaws in Christian and Muslim beliefs, demonstrating, by contrast, the merits of the Jewish faith. The frame story is based on the well-known legend that the king of the Khazars and his subjects converted to Judaism. The book asserts that Jewish faith is based on prophetic, spiritual revelation, and it understands Jewish history, and the longed-for redemption, on the basis of this assumption. The writer maintains that Judaism did not lose its prophetic, messianic vision, even while the Jews were living under Arab and Christian rule.

Rav Yehuda HaLevi ultimately fulfilled his dream of reaching Jerusalem. Legend has it that as he prostrated himself beside the Temple Mount, he was trampled to death by an Arab horseman.

From Rav Yehuda HaLevi:

Israel among the nations is like the heart among the organs; it is the sickest of them all and the healthiest of them all.

(*Kuzari* 2:36)

Rambam – Rav Moshe ben Maimon

Rambam (1135–1204) was born in Cordova, Spain, lived in Fustat, Egypt, and was buried, according to tradition, in Tiberias. He wrote several significant works of commentary and *halakha*. As a young man he began writing his commentary on the Mishna, which includes a number of important introductions: introduction to the Mishna, which is concerned with the relationship between the Written Torah and the Oral Torah; introduction to *Avot*, which deals with ethical and moral behavior; and introduction to *Ḥelek*, the final chapter of tractate *Sanhedrin*, which is about the interpretation of *aggadot*, i.e., non-halakhic statements of the Sages, and the basic principles of faith.

His *Sefer HaMitzvot* lists all the Torah commandments, and lists the principles for determining which are derived from the Torah and which are rabbinic law. His *Mishne Torah* is a code of Jewish law, and was the first of its kind. It contains final halakhic rulings drawn from the many disagreements found in the Mishna and in extensive discussions in the Talmud. It even addresses the mitzvot that are not applicable in our time. The work is intended for one who wishes to know the *halakha* without having to learn other sources beforehand.

Rambam also wrote a work of philosophy, called *Guide of the Perplexed*, which interprets the Torah and the mitzvot from the perspective of philosophy. One of the notions that he upholds is that of negative conceptions: One must not describe God in any positive terms, but only by negating descriptions, because one cannot attribute human qualities to Him. The book was widely criticized because of its attempt to provide purely philosophical justifications for the mitzvot. For this reason, some opposed Rambam and banned his works.

Rambam was a doctor, and in his medical writings he emphasized the importance of healthy eating as a way of preventing illness. He was the leader of the Jewish community in Egypt and provided support to the Jews of Yemen when they faced adversity. He also maintained strong ties with the rabbis of Lunel and Marseille, in the south of France. Rambam's influence on his generation was immense, and his works and ideas became prized assets for all future generations of the Jewish people.

From Rambam:

The perfection in which a person can truly take pride is attained by him when he has acquired, as far as it is possible for a human being, the knowledge of God, the knowledge of His providence, and of the manner in which it influences His creatures in their creation and continued existence. Having acquired this knowledge he will then be determined always to seek loving-kindness, judgment, and righteousness, and thus to imitate the ways of God.

(*Guide of the Perplexed* III:54)

Rav Yaakov Anatoli

Rav Yaakov Anatoli (1194–1256) was born in Provence, lived in Naples, and made his living as a translator, in addition to being a doctor. He was the son-in-law of the translator Rav Shmuel ibn Tibon. His work *Malmad HaTalmidim,* is divided into chapters following the order of the weekly Torah portions, and offers rationalistic, Maimonidean interpretations of the Torah. In this work, he encourages his readers to study philosophy, and interprets biblical verses in accordance with their philosophical significance.

Rav Anatoli maintained friendly ties with gentile scholars. He exchanged ideas with them and even cited some of them in his commentary on the Torah. He translated Aristotle's works on logic from Arabic into Hebrew.

From Rav Yaakov Anatoli:

One must examine a statement in and of itself, and not in relation to who said it. You see that Moses our teacher placed the section concerning Yitro before the section describing the giving of the Torah, because Moses valued Yitro's advice.

(*Malmad HaTalmidim,* Introduction)

Ramban – Rav Moshe ben Naḥman

Ramban (1194–1270), a physician by trade, was born in Girona, Catalonia, Spain, and died in Jerusalem. His commentary on the Torah is comprehensive and deep, giving original explanations on all four levels of interpretation: plain meaning (*peshat*), allusion (*remez*), exegesis (*derash*), and concealed meaning (*sod*). His Talmud commentary attests to his sharp analytical skills and to his mastery of both the Babylonian Talmud and the Jerusalem Talmud. He was the first to integrate into his commentary the explanations of the Babylonian *geonim*, of Rashi and *Tosafot* from the lands of Ashkenaz (western Europe), and of the halakhic authorities of Spain.

In the realm of *halakha*, Ramban's book *Milḥamot Hashem* defends Rav Yitzḥak Alfasi, known as Rif, from the criticisms of Rav Zeraḥya HaLevi. Ramban also wrote a criticism of Rambam's count of the 613 mitzvot in *Sefer HaMitzvot*. Ramban's main halakhic work is *Torat HaAdam*, which is concerned with matters of burial and mourning. His main philosophical work is *Sha'ar HaGemul*, about reward and punishment.

His writings do not contain many explicit kabbalistic ideas. He was careful to keep his kabbalistic wisdom concealed, revealing it only through allusions, which he generally prefaces with the phrase "in the way of the truth." Nevertheless, it is believed that he studied Kabbala and was in contact with the kabbalists of Girona. Ramban took part in the Disputation of Barcelona, debating a Jewish apostate named Pablo Christiani. After Ramban's decisive victory, documented in *Sefer HaVikuaḥ*, which contains the transcript of the debates, he was compelled by the authorities to flee, and he immigrated to the Land of Israel.

From Ramban:

Everything that occurred to the patriarchs is a sign for their descendants. This is why the verses provide a lengthy description of their journeys and their digging of wells and other incidents. One who reflects upon these passages may think that they are superfluous and insignificant, but they serve to teach about the future.

(Ramban, *Genesis* 12:6)

Sefer HaḤinnukh

This work enumerates the Torah commandments, arranged according to the weekly Torah portions. The book has been attributed to Rav Aharon HaLevi (1235–1303), or to his brother, Rav Pinḥas HaLevi, though not conclusively. The book's objective was to educate youngsters who had reached the age of mitzva observance to learn the 613 mitzvot. The work is based on Rambam's count of the commandments in *Sefer HaMitzvot*. For each mitzva, the writer lists its source in the Torah, its main *halakhot*, to whom it applies and when, and its reasons. The reasons for the mitzvot are called its "roots," because their objective is not to justify a particular mitzva, but to deepen its significance in the human experience. For example, when discussing the reasons for the many mitzvot related to the exodus from Egypt, the writer coined the phrase, "Our hearts follow our actions" (mitzva 16). Likewise, he often explains the reason for a mitzvah as being "to make a strong impression and affix a lesson in our minds." Although the book was ostensibly intended for educators, it is widely studied and has made a significant contribution to halakhic discourse.

From *Sefer HaḤinnukh*:

One must know and fully believe that everything that occurs to a person, both good and bad, comes to him from God. Even with regard to circumstances that are brought about by the hand of another person, by someone acting against another, nothing occurs that is against God's will.

(*Sefer HaḤinnukh* 241)

Rav Ḥasdai Crescas

Rav Ḥasdai Crescas (1340–1410) was born in Barcelona and died in Saragossa, Spain. He participated in numerous disputations, debating representatives of the church, and wrote a book refuting the principles of the Christian faith.

His philosophical approach is considered to be original and innovative. He maintained that faith in God stems from emotion rather than from the intellect, and that the notion of free will contradicts that of God's foreknowledge. He criticized Aristotelian science, which was accepted at the time, and it seems that much of his thinking was influenced by the Kabbala. His complex ideas are presented in his book, *Or Hashem*. Some see this work as a harbinger of the scientific revolution of the seventeenth century, and of the epistemology of the eighteenth century.

His son was killed in the 1391 Spanish pogroms, and evidently, this influenced Rav Crescas's worldview.

From Rav Ḥasdai Crescas:

It is incontrovertible that the One who acts is also One who knows, desires, and is able, and the one who is acted upon desires and makes choices.... It is incontrovertible that there is some relationship and connection between God and people, and this connection is prophecy.

(*Or Hashem* 2)

Rav Yosef Albo

Rav Yosef Albo (1380–1444) served as the rabbi of the communities of Aragon and Castile, Spain. His book, *Sefer HaIkkarim*, consolidates Rambam's principles of faith and those of Rav Ḥasdai Crescas, who was Rav Albo's teacher, into three central principles of faith: the existence of God, the divinity of the Torah, and reward and punishment. He asserts that it is possible to derive all other Jewish beliefs from these three. The book's clear and straightforward style led to its widespread reputation as an essential work on Jewish beliefs.

Rav Albo participated in the Disputation of Tortosa, defending the Jewish faith against representatives of the church. Unlike other rabbis, who were concerned about possible repercussions, he dared to criticize Christian theology.

From Rav Yosef Albo:

Though it is not the way of the bee, according to its nature, to have the understanding to build those cells of wax, where the honey is collected, in the shape of a hexagon, God gave it the understanding to build them in this shape, which is similar to a circle, which is the natural shape.... All this is found in the bee because it is God's work.... This is the pleasantness of work that is in fact brought about by the Divine.

(*Sefer HaIkkarim*, Introduction)

Rav Yitzḥak Arama

Rav Yitzḥak Arama (1420–1494) was born in Spain and lived in a number of different Spanish communities before settling in Calatayud. He died in Naples, following the expulsion of the Jews from Spain. His book *Akedat Yitzḥak* is a collection of sermons, each of which connects a verse from the weekly Torah portion with an idea from the *Zohar* and a philosophical concept. This work was widely praised, both for its content and for the structure of the sermons, which, for many generations, was considered the only acceptable structure for sermons. While the ideas in the book are based on those of Rambam and the *Zohar*, the use of a philosophical framework for the commentary recalls the style of the sermons given by priests in church, which every Jew was obligated to listen to according to Aragonese law.

From Rav Yitzḥak Arama:

The maidservant [i.e., philosophy] will accomplish as much as she can, and the mistress [i.e., Torah] will remain seated under her canopy. When the maidservant finds favor in the eyes of those who see her, and they elevate and honor her, and begin to believe that she is the one in charge, and they bring the mistress before the maidservant to do her work, then the Torah will fade away and there will be great crying out and grieving.

(*Ḥazut Kasha* 11)

Rabbi Moshe of Trani (Mabit)

Mabit (1500–1580) was born in Thessaloniki to a family of Spanish exiles, and moved to Safed at a young age. There he was appointed as a judge in the religious court of Rabbi Yaakov Beirav. He served in this role, alongside Rabbi Yosef Karo, for fifty-four years. His important works are *Responsa of Mabit,* which contains his answers to eight hundred questions in all areas of *halakha*; *Kiryat Sefer,* which discusses whether the sources of *halakhot* are from the Torah or the Sages; and *Beit Elohim,* which contains topics of Musar, Jewish thought, and prayer.

While Mabit and Rabbi Yosef Karo respected and admired one another, they disagreed with regard to many halakhic matters. Their dispute concerning the *halakhot* of the Sabbatical Year is well known. While Rabbi Karo was influential in Safed and the rest of the Land of Israel, Mabit was considered an important authority throughout the Ottoman Empire, and was asked to decide disputes and questions that were brought to him from far and wide.

From Rabbi Moshe of Trani:

The purpose of prayer is not to be answered, but to teach us that there is no one in the world to whom it is proper to pray other than to God. One must recognize that a person has nothing in this world, and that there is no one who can fulfill his needs other than God.

(*Beit Elohim, Sha'ar HaTefilla* 2)

Rabbi Yehuda Loew of Prague (Maharal)

Maharal (1520–1609) was born in Poznan, Poland, and served as the rabbi of Nikolsburg. Later he became the leader of the Jewish community of Prague, which is where he died. He was a prolific author, and his writing is methodical and comprehensive. His book *Gur Arye* is a commentary on Rashi's commentary on the Torah, *Netivot Olam* is a work of Musar, *Tiferet Yisrael* discusses the importance of the Torah, *Netzaḥ Yisrael* is concerned with exile and redemption, *Gevurot Hashem* is about the exodus and the festival of Passover, and *Ner Mitzva* is about Hanukkah. He also wrote a systematic commentary on the talmudic *aggadot*.

His writing is remarkable for its breadth, as it covers a wide range of subjects and covers each subject extensively; for its length, as it relates to every angle of the subject; and for its depth, as his thinking is original and daring.

Maharal represented the Jewish community to the authorities, and thanks to his knowledge of the philosophy and science of the time, he became friendly with Rudolf II, king of Bohemia, and possibly with Johannes Kepler as well.

Maharal sought to change the prevailing method of Torah study, which involved studying Talmud via the method of *pilpul*, i.e., intricate and at times exceedingly complex analysis. Instead, he favored an organized system of study that would lead to the mastery of Bible, Mishna, and Talmud. To this end, he instructed his student Rabbi Yom Tov Lipmann Heller to write the commentary on the Mishna, *Tosefot Yom Tov*. He also encouraged the study of Mishna in groups. In the nineteenth century, his name became associated with the legend of the Golem of Prague.

From Maharal:

Therefore, the name "Torah" is fitting for the Torah, as it comes from the term "teaching" [*hora'a*], and the Torah teaches a person the ultimate objective to which he should aspire.

(*Netivot Olam* 1)

Rabbi Menaḥem di Lonzano

Rabbi Menaḥem di Lonzano (1550–1626) was born in Italy or Turkey, lived in a number of different places, and immigrated to Jerusalem. He wrote the book *Shetei Yadot*, which contains two parts: *Yad Ani* and *Yad HaMelekh*. He divided each part into five separate sections, corresponding to the five fingers on each hand. These writings include linguistic materials, liturgical poetry, and Kabbala.

Some of the sections in the first part include: *Or Torah*, the Masoretic text of the Torah; *HaMa'arikh*, a completion of the dictionary *HeArukh*; and *Avodat HaMikdash*, a liturgical poem that describes the Temple service. The second part includes a collection of aggadic *midrashim*, which he published in accordance with manuscripts that he possessed.

He suffered greatly during his life. He was orphaned at a young age and lived his entire life in poverty. He suffered from personal attacks and had physical difficulties ranging from problems with his feet and blindness in one eye.

He was bold, and did not hesitate to disagree with Ramak, the Ari, and Rabbi Ḥayyim Vital in kabbalistic matters, nor to criticize Rabbi Yisrael Najara for not revealing that he borrowed entire passages from Arabic poetry that Rabbi Menaḥem di Lonzano considered inappropriate for religious poetry.

From Rabbi Menaḥem di Lonzano:

Although I am obligated to honor the ones with whom I disagree, both they and I are obligated to honor the truth.

(*Derekh Ḥayyim*, Introduction)

Rabbi Azarya Figo

Rabbi Azarya Figo (1579–1647) was born in Venice, served as the rabbi of Pisa, and died in Rovigo, Italy. He wrote the book *Giddulei Teruma,* a commentary on *Sefer HaTerumot* by Rav Shmuel of Sardinia, which deals with monetary cases in Jewish law. Rabbi Figo's prodigious scholarship is apparent from the fact that when he wrote *Giddulei Teruma,* he hardly had any books at his disposal. *Bina LeIttim* is a collection of his sermons on the festivals, in which his brilliance, mastery of the Bible, and exegetical skill are demonstrated. This book has continued to be popular among preachers throughout the generations. As was customary among Italian Jews, Rabbi Figo studied at the University of Venice and subsequently devoted himself to Talmud study.

From Rabbi Azarya Figo:

Freedom is, by nature, much yearned for, not only by humankind, but even by animals, which cannot speak. All creatures instinctively become distressed and afraid when they are enslaved by another, and it turns their joy into sorrow.... All the more so, humans cannot bear the burden of enslavement to others. For this reason, the hatred of Joseph's brothers toward him grew.

(*Bina LeIttim* 44)

Commentary on the Torah

Many of the earliest writings in the field of Jewish thought were written as commentaries on the Bible. Commentary was necessary due to the difficulties that arise in the attempt to understand biblical language, but each commentator chooses to explain the meaning of the text and present his understanding of the biblical worldview, while emphasizing the themes that are close to his heart. Consequently, Torah commentary weaves together simple explanations of terminology and concepts, with elucidations of the profound ideas that are embodied in the condensed biblical text. Such Torah commentary is fruitful and creative, making the Torah into a continuous stream of ideas that answer the reader's questions even before he asks them.

Rav Avraham ibn Ezra

Ibn Ezra (1089–1164) was born in Tudela, Spain, but was compelled to flee as a result of religious persecution. He wandered to Italy, France, and even England and North Africa. He never received communal support in his travels, and he lived in poverty.

He was a close friend of Rav Yehuda HaLevi, and like him, Ibn Ezra wrote hundreds of hymns, some of which are still sung today by Jews throughout the world, e.g., *Agadelkha Elohei Khol Neshama, Lekha Eli Teshukati,* and *Tzama Lekha Nafshi.* He wrote numerous works of grammar, including *Sefat Yeter, Safa Berura,* and *Tzaḥot,* as well as books on mathematics, including *Sefer HaMispar* and *Sefer HaEḥad.*

In his biblical commentary, he makes use of grammar to identify the straightforward meaning of the text, comparing the Torah's wording to that employed in the Prophets and Writings. Each brilliant linguistic analysis is condensed into just a few words and unlocks the true meaning of the text. In his commentary, he did not feel himself beholden to the interpretations of the talmudic Sages.

Ibn Ezra enjoyed word games and mathematical puzzles, and he also learned astronomy. There is a crater on the moon, Abenezra, which is named after him.

Biographies

From Rav Avraham ibn Ezra:

The fifth way, the interpretive approach that I will employ, is to explain each verse in accordance with its context, grammar, and straightforward meaning. Only with regard to mitzvot and statutes will I rely on our early Sages and I will establish our terminology in accordance with their words.

(*Ibn Ezra on the Torah,* Introduction)

Rabbeinu Baḥya ibn Halawa

Rabbeinu Baḥya (1255–1340), a student of Rashba, was born and lived in Saragossa, Spain. It is believed that his name derives from the term *ben Ḥiyya,* son of Hiyya. His book *Rabbeinu Baḥya on the Torah,* or just *Rabbeinu Baḥya,* was written in the style of aggadic midrash. At the beginning of each

Torah portion he cites a verse from the book of Proverbs and then explains the Torah portion in accordance with its plain, midrashic, philosophical, and mystical meanings. As the work quotes many aggadic *midrashim* that have since been lost, it is a valuable source of these texts.

Rabbeinu Baḥya's book *Kad HaKemaḥ* includes sermons on subjects of faith and Musar. Another of his works, *Shulḥan Shel Arba*, addresses the *halakhot* of mealtimes. It also discusses the celebratory feast, described in aggadic midrash, that will take place in the messianic era.

From Rabbeinu Baḥya ibn Halawa:

Our Torah consists of all wisdom; all other types of wisdom are maidservants to it. They are presented as matters for in-depth investigation, but our Torah is from the Holy One, blessed be He, and it is the foundation of everything.

(*Rabbeinu Baḥya on the Torah*, Introduction)

Don Yitzḥak Abravanel

Abravanel (1437–1508) was born in Lisbon, Portugal, but was forced to flee from there, and went to Toledo, Spain. He served as treasurer to the kings of Portugal, Castile, Aragon, and Naples. As a result of his close ties to the authorities, he was able to assist Jews who were in trouble. Nevertheless, he was unable to prevent the expulsion from Spain or the confiscation of his personal fortune. Following the expulsion of the Jews from Spain he lived in various areas of Italy, including Naples, Sicily, and Venice.

His biblical commentary is known for being thorough and methodical. At the beginning of each section, he lists all the questions that need to be addressed, and then he answers them one by one. In his books *Yeshuot Meshiḥo* and *Mashmia Yeshua*, he develops the themes of faith in the messiah and in the resurrection of the dead.

As befitted a member of the Abravanel family, a large family of financiers and politicians said to be descended from King David, he also wrote about the Torah's political approach: Who is fit to rule and the proper form of government.

From Don Yitzḥak Abravanel:

Look at the lands that are under the leadership of kings.... Each [king] does whatever is right in his eyes, and the land is filled with cruelty because of them. For who shall tell him what to do...? Today, the kingdoms of Venice...Florence...Genoa...Siena, Bologna, and others, have no king; rather, they have leaders who have been elected to lead from a fixed day until a fixed day. These are the righteous kingdoms; they are not crooked.

(Abravanel, I Samuel 8:6)

Rav Avraham Saba

Rav Avraham Saba (1440–1508) was born in Castile, Spain, and began writing his Torah commentary there. After the expulsion from Spain, he found refuge in Portugal, but a short while later the king of Portugal ordered forced conversions to Christianity and prohibited the possession of Jewish religious items. He was consequently compelled to hide his writings under an olive tree near Lisbon. From there, he fled to Fez, Morocco, where he managed to rewrite these texts from memory despite already being old and sick.

He wrote several books, including *Tzeror HaMor*, which combines interpretation according to the plain meaning of the text with kabbalistic interpretation, producing original ideas. Legend has it that while he was on a ship to Verona, Italy, Rav Avraham became ill. There was a terrible storm, and he told the sailors that if they agreed not to throw his body overboard in the event of his death, he would pray that the ship would not sink. He died a few days later, and the sailors fulfilled his wish, bringing his body to the Jewish community of Verona for burial in the city's Jewish cemetery.

From Rav Avraham Saba:

I trust in God that He will help me, and place a new song in my mouth, so that I may remember a little of what I wrote. For I know that the bulk of the original book is missing, because old age and forgetfulness have advanced within me.

(*Eshkol HaKofer*, Esther, p. 22)

Rav Ovadya Sforno

Sforno (1468–1550) was born in Cesena, Italy, and was the leader of the Jewish community of Rome and later of Bologna, where he died. His commentary on the Bible is concise, focused on the plain meaning of the text, and written in the philosophical style. It was well received and was printed in *Mikraot Gedolot*, a popular edition of the Torah with several commentaries, which caused it to become even more widespread.

Sforno had a thorough knowledge of mathematics and grammar, worked as a doctor, and was fluent in many languages. He translated books from Hebrew to Italian for the pope, the king of France, and numerous European scholars. In Rome, he faced anti-Jewish persecution and was ultimately forced to leave. In Bologna, he answered questions of *halakha* and Jewish thought that were brought to him. He also established a printing house there.

From Rav Ovadya Sforno:

It is proper that a person try to marry a woman who is suitable for him and who will become attached to him, even if he will need to leave his parents. There will not be true attachment between people who are dissimilar, but only between people who are similar, because they will have similar opinions.

(Sforno, Genesis 2:24)

Rabbi Shlomo Efrayim Luntschitz

Rabbi Shlomo Efrayim Luntschitz (1540–1619) was born in Luntschitz, Poland, served as the head of the yeshiva in Lvov, and succeeded Maharal as the rabbi of Prague. He was known as a charismatic and inspiring speaker.

His famous work, *Keli Yakar*, is a collection of sermons on the weekly Torah portion that he gave over the years. In it, he interprets the different layers of the Torah: plain meaning (*peshat*), allusion (*remez*), exegesis (*derash*), and concealed meaning (*sod*). He is known for his mastery of the Torah as well as his sensitivity to the social realities of his time. Many of the sermons are concerned with communal matters and with correcting injustice. He frequently points out the inequalities between the ruling class of powerful rabbis and wealthy leaders on the one hand, and the poor on the other.

He wrote the book after he recovered from a serious illness, having vowed while ill that he would write it if he survived (*Keli Yakar*, Introduction): "In God's mercy, He brought me out of turmoil, reviving me. On that day I vowed to God, 'I will complete this work in honor of God and His Torah, in order to uncover His essence.'"

From Rabbi Shlomo Efrayim Luntschitz:

I have seen something scandalous in the words of most of the commentators who come to explain the Torah: There is almost nothing new in their statements. In most cases where there is a simple explanation that is readily understood, it is found in several commentaries.... I decided to minimize my use of the words of others in order not to extend my book using words that I did not work on. All my words adhere to the plain meaning of the text.

(*Keli Yakar*, Introduction)

Rabbi Ḥayyim ben Atar

Rabbi Ḥayyim ben Atar (1696–1743) was born in Sale, Morocco, traveled to Fez and Meknes, lived in Livorno, Italy, and eventually immigrated to Jerusalem with many of his students and established the Keneset Yisrael yeshiva. He was a well-known preacher and charity collector. He wrote a number of books, including *Ḥefetz Hashem* on some tractates of the Talmud, *Peri To'ar* and *Rishon LeTziyyon* on *Shulḥan Arukh*, and *Or HaḤayyim* on the Torah.

He was greatly admired among Moroccan Jews, and hasidic leaders also recognized his greatness. They called his book "the holy *Or HaḤayyim*," and established special times when it was to be studied. In the book, each Torah portion is analyzed thoroughly, and various interpretations are considered on the levels of plain meaning (*peshat*), allusion (*remez*), exegesis (*derash*), and concealed meaning (*sod*). The book stands out for its deep spiritual focus, both in its literary analysis as well as in the passion that it seeks to instill for Torah study.

From Rabbi Ḥayyim ben Atar:

When it states, "You shall love your neighbor as yourself" (Leviticus 19:18), this means: Love him because he is like yourself. When he prospers, this will benefit you, and through him, you will perfect yourself. Consequently, he is not a separate entity; rather, he is like a part of you.

(*Or HaḤayyim*, Exodus 39:32)

Rabbi Yaakov Tzvi Mecklenburg

Rabbi Yaakov Tzvi Mecklenburg (1795–1865) was born in Leszno, Poland, was a student of Rabbi Akiva Eiger, and served as the rabbi of Koenigsberg, Germany. He was an active opponent of the Reform movement in Germany, whose leaders were making changes to the *halakha* and the prayer liturgy.

His main work was *HaKetav VehaKabbala*, a commentary on the Torah whose objective was to explain the straightforward meaning of the Written Torah, which he refers to as the *ketav*, in accordance with the traditional interpretation of the Oral Torah, which he refers to as the *kabbala*. He uses grammar and cantillation marks to support his interpretations, and also proposes his own original explanations. The first book of its kind, it spurred the growth of an entire genre of biblical commentaries that seek to reveal the connection between the text's straightforward meaning and the Midrash.

From Rabbi Yaakov Tzvi Mecklenburg:

The Written Torah, [i.e., the *ketav*] and the oral tradition [*kabbala*] will be united in the hands of the people of the covenant.... What does the *ketav*, the "body," have without the *kabbala*, the "soul"?

(*HaKetav VehaKabbala*, Introduction)

Netziv – Rabbi Naftali Tzvi Yehuda Berlin

Netziv (1817–1893) was born in Mir, now in Belarus, and died in Warsaw, Poland. He served as the head of the Volozhin yeshiva for almost forty years. He studied halakhic *midrashim* and geonic literature, and wrote the commentary *Ha'amek She'ala* on *She'iltot deRav Aḥai Gaon,* while producing a critical edition of that work based on original sources and manuscripts.

He also wrote *Ha'amek Davar,* a commentary on the Torah, based on his discourses on the weekly Torah portion, which he would deliver in the yeshiva. In the book, he explains the straightforward meaning of the verses in accordance with their grammar. The work stands out for its literary analysis.

Netziv supported *Hibat Tziyyon,* a proto-Zionist movement, and was in contact with some of its leaders. Toward the end of his life he was forced to close the yeshiva due to pressure from the Russian authorities to change the nature of the institution.

From the Netziv:

This book, the book of Genesis, is called "the book of the upright" by the prophets.... The Holy One, blessed be He, is upright, and He tolerates only righteous people who walk the straight path, including in their dealings with the world. They must not be crooked, even if this is for the sake [i.e., the fear] of Heaven.... This was the greatness of the patriarchs. This teaches that they were saintly and pious and loved God in every possible way, but they were also upright.

(*Ha'amek Davar,* Introduction to Genesis)

Jewish Thought in Works of *Halakha* and Custom

Halakhic literature is concerned with describing a person's obligations in accordance with the Torah's commandments. It encompasses all areas of life and behavior: between the individual and God, between the individual and others, and those that affect only the individual himself. Books on Jewish customs complement the halakhic literature, as they describe the customs that are traditionally accepted and practiced. These genres are full of extensive discussions concerning the details of the mitzvot. Through thorough analysis, these works seek to arrive at a more complete understanding of the reasons for the mitzvot.

This understanding is particularly significant. From a practical perspective, it allows halakhic rulings to accord with the purpose of the commandment and the nature of the custom; from a philosophical perspective, it reveals the ideas concealed within the *halakha* and the custom; and from an emotional perspective, it helps us to internalize the obligation and understand its true intention.

Rav David Abudarham

Abudarham (fl. 1340) was born in Seville, Spain. His major work is *Ḥibur Peirush HaBerakhot VehaTefillot,* but it is popularly known as *Sefer Abudarham.* It is a detailed commentary on the prayer book, and it cites the customs of the communities of Spain and France, in particular those of Seville and Toledo. In addition to his commentary on the various weekday and Shabbat prayers, the writer discusses many other liturgical matters such as the Passover haggada, the order of the weekly Torah readings and the *haftarot* (the weekly readings from the Prophets), the blessings recited before performing mitzvot, and the Grace after Meals. He even gives a detailed explanation of the calculation of the Jewish calendar. He cites the prayer books of Rav Amram Gaon and Rav Se'adya Gaon, as well as previously published books of customs. He devotes considerable attention to issues of spelling and vowelization, as well as to the different existing versions of the prayers. His surname is apparently derived from the currency called *dirham,* and it is believed that his family worked in commerce or tax collection.

From Rav David Abudarham:

Due to the length of the exile and the enormity of its hardships, the customs of the prayers have changed in the various lands. Most people raise their voices in prayer before the God of the Universe, and they are fumbling around like blind people in the dark; they do not understand the meaning of the prayers.... When I saw that the gates of prayer and service have been locked, and those who know and can teach about it are few, I thought to write this book, which provides valuable interpretations.

(*Sefer Abudarham,* Introduction)

Rabbi Moshe Met

Rabbi Moshe Met (1551–1606) was born in Przemysl, Poland, and served as the rabbi of Belz, Krakow, and Opatow. He was a student of Rabbi Shlomo Luria, and a member of the Council of Four Lands, the administrative council of the Jews of Poland and Lithuania. His book *Mateh Moshe* is a halakhic work written in the order of the *Oraḥ Ḥayyim* volume of *Shulḥan Arukh,* which deals with *halakhot* pertinent to the Jewish calendar, whether daily, weekly, or annual. It details *halakhot* and customs, and provides explanations given by contemporary rabbis, as well as *aggadot* and Musar ideas that are based on the same themes.

From Rabbi Moshe Met:

There is no person whom the Holy One, blessed be He, does not test. He tests the rich person to see if his hand will be open to the poor, and He tests the poor person to see if he can endure suffering without rebelling. If the rich person passes his test and acts charitably, he will enjoy his money in this world and the principal will remain for him in the World to Come. If the poor person passes his test, he will receive double reward in the future.

(*Mateh Moshe, Amud Gemilut Ḥasadim* 2:2)

Rabbi Yoel Sirkis

Rabbi Yoel Sirkis (1561–1640) was born in Lublin and served as the rabbi of Brisk, Belz, and Krakow, Poland. He was wealthy, and consequently was able to run a yeshiva and provide support for poor Torah scholars.

His greatest work was *Bayit Ḥadash* (*Baḥ*), a commentary on the *Tur* with notes on the *Beit Yosef*. The book traces the source of each *halakha*, in the Mishna, the Talmud, and the early commentaries, showing its underlying logic and analyzing the reasons for it. He also wrote *Haggahot HaBaḥ*, textual emendations to the Talmud in accordance with manuscripts as well as his own logical deductions. These were printed in the margins of the Vilna edition of the Talmud. His opinions with regard to the needs of the community are evident in his halakhic rulings.

Rabbi Sirkis also sought to form an education system where religious studies, Hebrew grammar, and mathematics would be taught. At age fourteen, each student would be examined to determine whether or not he was capable of learning Talmud, and anyone not suited to Talmud study would be taught a profession.

Some believe that Rabbi Sirkis's surname was Yafeh and that he changed it to Sirkis, meaning "of Sarah," after his mother or mother-in-law, which was customary in those days.

From Rabbi Yoel Sirkis:

I called this work of mine *Bayit Ḥadash*, which means new house, because I did not gather into my house, that is, I did not cite in this work, the statements of the great ones unless they contained something new, such as a new question, solution, interpretation, or ruling.

(*Bayit Ḥadash*, Introduction)

Rabbi David Frankel

Rabbi David Frankel (1707–1762) was born in Berlin. He served as the rabbi of Dessau and later as the chief rabbi of Berlin. His works *Korban HaEda* and *Sheyarei Korban* constitute his commentary on the orders of *Nashim, Moed,* and part of *Nezikin,* of the Jerusalem Talmud. His commentary completes the work of Rabbi Eliyahu of Fulda on tractates *Bava Kamma, Bava Metzia, Bava Batra,* and the order of *Zera'im*. Rabbi Frankel's commentary is influenced by the Babylonian Talmud, yet it has become, alongside Rabbi Moshe Margolies's *Penei Moshe,* the most influential commentary on the Jerusalem Talmud, on which relatively few commentaries have been written.

From Rabbi David Frankel:

"As water reflects a face to the face, so does the heart of a person to a person" (Proverbs 27:19). One looks into water and sees a face like his own; if he laughs, it laughs, and if he has a crooked nose, it has a crooked nose. The same is true with regard to the heart of a person, which mirrors that of another person; if one loves the other, the other will love him back.

(*Korban HaEda, Yevamot* 15)

Ḥatam Sofer – Rabbi Moshe Sofer

Ḥatam Sofer (1761–1839) was born in Frankfurt, Germany, and served as the rabbi and head of the yeshiva in Pressburg, Hungary. He wrote *Responsa Ḥatam Sofer,* which comprises thousands of questions and answers on every topic in Judaism. The book is considered a fundamental halakhic work because of its tremendous scope, its bold, original reasoning, and the writer's thorough command of Talmud and *halakha*. He also wrote *Ḥiddushei Ḥatam Sofer* on some tractates of the Talmud, and *Torat Moshe,* a collection of his sermons on the weekly *parasha*.

He was the foremost opponent of the Reform movement in Hungary, and he reshaped the face of Judaism in the region in light of the challenges of the time. He was in contact with many of the great scholars of his generation, and he taught hundreds of students in the Pressburg yeshiva, training them to serve as the leaders of the communities of Hungary.

The name Ḥatam Sofer is based on a talmudic expression (see *Gittin* 66b), and it alludes to the first letter of his name as well as to his family name, Schreiber, which means scribe [*sofer*]. Many of his descendants were rabbis, and they chose similar names for their works: *Ketav Sofer, Shevet Sofer,* and *Ḥatan Sofer*.

From Ḥatam Sofer:

Only if one studies Torah for its own sake, the Holy One, blessed be He, illuminates his eyes and he merits the truth, even if others refute him…God helps him to comprehend the truth. It is permitted to act in accordance with his words as though they came from Heaven.

(*Torat Moshe*, Deuteronomy 16b)

Ben Ish Ḥai – Rabbi Yosef Ḥayyim

Ben Ish Ḥai (1835–1909) was born and died in Baghdad. He had contact with Jewish communities from India to England, and was on friendly terms with the rabbis of the Land of Israel, especially the kabbalists of the Beit El yeshiva in the Old City of Jerusalem.

His book *Ben Ish Ḥai* is a collection of his sermons on the weekly Torah portion that he delivered to the congregation each Shabbat. The book weaves together *aggada* and *halakha*, and connects the halakhic rulings of Rabbi Yosef Karo with the words of other halakhic and kabbalistic authorities, both Sephardic and Ashkenazic. Due to its clear, didactic style, this work is considered, even today, the main work of *halakha* for Iraqi Jews.

Ben Ish Ḥai wrote on many different areas of Torah: *Ben Yehoyada*, a commentary on talmudic *aggadot*; *Torah Lishma*, a book of responsa; *Da'at UTvuna*, kabbalistic teachings; books of stories and parables; and even a book of mathematical puzzles, among many other books. He thoroughly understood Jewish life in his generation, and his books and sermons are filled with folk stories and parables that are pertinent even to the common people. His sermons were very popular; it is told that when he spoke at the Great Synagogue of Baghdad four times a year, the synagogue would be filled to capacity, but everyone would remain quiet out of reverence and awe for the rabbi, and consequently the entire congregation heard him clearly.

From Ben Ish Ḥai:

It is known that the hearts of most of the nation are not drawn to expounding *halakhot* alone; rather, the majority of one's sermons should be words of *aggada* and Musar.

(*Ben Ish Ḥai*, Introduction)

Rabbi Yeḥiel Mikhel Tukachinsky

Rabbi Yeḥiel Mikhel Tukachinsky (1871–1955) was born in Lyakhavichy, Lithuania, and was the head of the Etz Hayyim yeshiva in Jerusalem. He worked on calculating halakhic times, such as the exact times of sunrise and sunset; the correct time for reading the Megilla, the book of Esther, on Purim; and the halakhic issues surrounding the international date line. He published *Luaḥ Eretz Yisrael,* a calendar that contains the daily halakhic times as well as the customs of the Land of Israel. This calendar is still commonly used in synagogues today. Rabbi Tukachinsky also wrote books on the mitzvot of the Land of Israel, e.g., *Sefer HaShemita,* and a series on the sanctity of Jerusalem, called *Ir HaKodesh VehaMikdash.*

His book *Gesher HaḤayyim* deals with the topics of visiting the sick, burial, and mourning. It incorporates *halakha, aggada,* and Jewish thought with regard to the various aspects of death, including purification rites, accompanying the dead, burial, the customs of the seven-day mourning period [*shiva*], the thirty-day mourning period [*sheloshim*], the twelve-month mourning period, and the recitation of Kaddish. He characterizes life as "a bridge that connects between two worlds," and discusses the meaning of life and its transience, and the spiritual meaning of death and the life that follows it.

From Rabbi Yeḥiel Mikhel Tukachinsky:

Temporary life on this earth is nothing but a passageway to a life that is more abundant and bright. There is no conception of this when we are alive and are confined within a mere body, having limited understanding.

(*Gesher HaḤayyim* 3:1)

Jewish Thought in the Modern Era

In the face of dramatic changes in the structure of the Jewish community in the modern era under the influence of the Enlightenment, widespread abandonment of Torah and mitzvot, and nationalism, Jewish thinkers were required to respond to new questions and formulate original insights concerning the purpose of the Jewish people and the place of Torah in the new world. Modern Jewish thought contends with various changes that have taken place with regard to Jewish life. One change stems from the growing influence of external, non-Jewish elements, which necessitates a redefinition of Jewish identity and the delineation of the boundaries between sacred and secular, tradition and progress, and the Jewish people and the nations of the world. Another change relates to the physical circumstances of the Jewish people: Migration to the Land of Israel from the Diaspora and the need to assume responsibility for the renewal of Jewish settlement there, migration to the New World, and active participation in the development of science and culture. All of this necessitates a reconceptualization of the uniqueness of the Jew and his role in a changing world.

Rabbi Yisrael Lipschitz

Rabbi Yisrael Lipschitz (1782–1860) was the rabbi of Danzig. His main work was *Tiferet Yisrael,* a commentary on the Mishna that includes the translation of difficult passages into German. The commentary is divided into two parts: *Yakhin,* written in accordance with the text's straightforward meaning; and *Boaz,* novellae. It includes an introduction to each order of the Mishna in which he explains complex *halakhot,* e.g., the sanctification of the month, the setting of the Jewish calendar, the structure of the Temple, and leprous marks. He appended an essay, *Derush Or HaḤayyim,* to his commentary on *Nezikin.* In it, he discusses paleontological and geological discoveries made in his day, such as fossils, and explains them in the context of faith in Creation.

From Rabbi Yisrael Lipschitz:

In-depth study means that one should not move on from something he has learned until he has asked himself seven questions and answered them: who, what, to whom, when, where, how, and why. When one knows the answers to all seven of these questions, everything difficult and complex will become clear.

(*Tiferet Yisrael, Yakhin, Avot* 2:14)

Rabbi Samson Raphael Hirsch

Rabbi Samson Raphael Hirsch (1818–1888) was born in Hamburg, Germany, and served as the rabbi of various cities in Bohemia and Moravia, and then in Frankfurt, Germany. His books *Nineteen Letters* and *Ḥorev* are concerned with the revelation at Sinai, and they explain the Torah's commandments to the younger generation. He translated the Torah into German and also wrote a broad commentary on it, which emphasizes the symbolism of each mitzva. In his commentary, he uses creative etymological tools similar to those employed by the Sages.

He established schools in accordance with the motto: *Torah im derekh eretz,* Torah with the "way of the land." His outlook encourages the combination of Torah study and general studies, and views the Jew's integration into society in a positive light. Rabbi Hirsch opposed religious reformers, rejected the changes that they made due to the changing times, and emphasized the importance of religious action, and not merely having faith. At the same time, he believed that Jews are obligated to acquire an education and earn a livelihood, and to relate to the universal human experience. In this respect, Rabbi Hirsch is responsible for shaping the image of the Orthodox

German Jew, who is as careful about minor mitzvot as he is about major ones, works for a living, and is sensitive to societal etiquette and customs, as well as to those with whom he interacts.

From Rabbi Samson Raphael Hirsch:

In nature, phenomena are recognized as facts even if you do not yet comprehend their causes or interrelationships; their existence does not depend on the results of your investigations. The same is true with regard to the Torah's commandments; they are law for you.... Your fulfillment of a mitzva must not depend on your investigation of it.

(*Nineteen Letters* 18)

Rabbi Avraham Yitzḥak HaKohen Kook

Rabbi Avraham Yitzḥak HaKohen Kook (1865–1935) was born in Griva, Latvia, and served as a rabbi in Bauska, Latvia, and then in Jaffa and Jerusalem. Subsequently, he was appointed as chief rabbi of Palestine.

He wrote works of *halakha* and *aggada*. His halakhic works deal extensively with mitzvot that are dependent on the Land of Israel. The halakhic basis that he provided for the selling of land to gentiles during the Sabbatical Year is well known, as is his work *Halakha Berura,* which summarizes the *halakhot* in relation to their talmudic sources. In the domain of *aggada,* he wrote *Ein Aya,* a commentary on the *aggadot* in tractates *Berakhot* and *Shabbat.*

Most of his philosophy can be found in his work *Orot HaKodesh,* a collection of passages written in a poetic style, which describe the development and progress of humankind and of the world. He accorded theological-mystical significance to Jewish nationalism, although he criticized its pioneers and leaders for abandoning the observance of the mitzvot. He was strongly criticized for his positive attitude toward Zionism and boycotted by members of the ultra-Orthodox communities that had existed in the Land of Israel in the centuries prior to the waves of Zionist immigration. Nevertheless, he established the Central Universal Yeshiva and supported the Zionist enterprise in accordance with his worldview.

From Rabbi Avraham Yitzḥak HaKohen Kook:

The pure, righteous ones do not lament over evil; rather, they increase righteousness. They do not lament over heresy; rather, they increase faith. They do not lament over ignorance; rather, they increase wisdom.

(*Arpelei Tohar*)

Rabbi Ben-Tziyyon Meir Ḥai Uziel

Rabbi Ben-Tziyyon Meir Ḥai Uziel (1880–1953) was born in Jerusalem and was a rabbi in Tel Aviv, Jaffa, and Thessaloniki, after which he was appointed as the Sephardic chief rabbi of the Land of Israel.

His main works are *Mishpetei Uziel*, which consists of halakhic questions on many topics, and *Hegyonei Uziel*, on matters of faith and Musar. He was appointed as the *Ḥakham Bashi* at age thirty-one, representing the Jews before the Ottoman authorities, and later before the British commissions for partition. He was popular and tried to bring people together in peace.

He dealt with many contemporary issues: He worked to abolish the conscription of thousands of Jews to the Turkish army, and prevented harm from coming to the Jewish community when the Nili underground organization was discovered. He also worked to strengthen supervision of kosher food and the status of the rabbinate in the Land of Israel, and he established institutions for the study of Torah. Toward the end of his life he was appointed as a member of the Jewish National Council and a representative of the Jewish Agency.

From Rabbi Ben-Tziyyon Meir Ḥai Uziel:

Remove all causes of division and dispute from our camp and from our country, and replace them with all the causes of peace and of unity between us, and our camp will become pure and sanctified, fortified and unified.... God, who makes peace in His heights, will make peace for us and bless us.

(*Hegyonei Uziel*, Will 13)

Rabbi Yeḥiel Yaakov Weinberg

Rabbi Yeḥiel Yaakov Weinberg (1884–1966) was born in Russia, studied at the Mir yeshiva, and became acquainted with Rabbi Natan Tzvi Finkel, the Alter of Slabodka. Rabbi Weinberg, who was the head of the rabbinical seminary in Berlin, was imprisoned in work camps during the Holocaust. He died in Montreux, Switzerland.

He was a preeminent halakhic authority, and answered questions on a wide range of topics, including: stunning an animal with an electric shock before slaughtering it, disinterment of the remains of the dead, mixed-gender youth movements, bat mitzva celebrations, and the status of the children of a marriage between a Jew and a non-Jew. His book of responsa is called *Seridei Esh*, "the remnants of the fire," because most of his writings were destroyed during the Holocaust. Some of his other writings are collected in the book *Lifrakim*.

In his youth, he spent time among the followers of the Musar movement in Lithuania. Subsequently, he studied at university in Berlin, and was then appointed as the head of the rabbinical seminary. In addition to teaching and training rabbis, he was involved in talmudic research. Rabbi Weinberg managed to merge the approaches of Musar, academics, and classical rabbinical thought. Furthermore, his thinking was sharpened by a unique level of sensitivity due to the terrible suffering that he experienced during the Holocaust.

From Rabbi Yeḥiel Yaakov Weinberg:

We see in Judaism a lofty vision, filled with glory: The development of creativity within the framework of observance. Creativity is constantly being renewed, while observance remains unchanged. The contents are fluid, while the form is fixed.... Although the reasons for the mitzvot have changed, and will change again in every generation and in each spiritual era, their practical fulfillment has not changed, nor will they ever change.

(*Lifrakim*, p. 184)

Rabbi Yosef Dov Soloveitchik

Rabbi Yosef Dov Soloveitchik (1903–1993) was born in Pruzhany, Belarus. His father was his primary teacher of Torah, and he studied philosophy at the University of Berlin. He served as a rabbi and professor of philosophy in Boston and New York.

He wrote a number of influential philosophical treatises, including *Halakhic Man*, on the philosophy of *halakha*, and *The Lonely Man of Faith*, on the existential condition of the believer. Additionally, his Talmud lectures, given in the analytical style of his grandfather, Rabbi Ḥayyim Soloveitchik, have been published, as have other works on various topics in Jewish thought.

He was one of the leaders of American Jewry, and shaped the image of the Modern Orthodox American Jew. His works are considered to be among the most brilliant and challenging in the field of Jewish thought. He endeavors to conceal his passionate experience of Judaism beneath his rational and complex style.

From Rabbi Yosef Dov Soloveitchik:

Prayer is a vital need of a religious person. He cannot stop the thoughts and feelings that are in the depths of his soul, the doubts and hardships, the longings and yearnings, the despair and bitterness. In short, the great abundance that is concealed within his religious consciousness.... Prayer is essential. It is impossible for living, invigorated religious feeling to endure without it.

(*Ra'ayonot Al HaTefilla*, p. 245)

Musar

The Bible, Talmud, and halakhic literature all focus on the practical aspects of Jewish life. For the most part, they do not address an individual's spiritual and emotional experience; this is discussed in the literature of Musar, or moral conduct, beginning with the book of Proverbs. This branch of literature elucidates the moral principles according to which one should live, which apply even in circumstances that are not discussed in halakhic literature. These guidelines have been given a number of different names. They have been called "the way of the world [*derekh eretz*]," "the straight path," and "the fifth section of *Shulḥan Arukh*."[2] Another objective of Musar literature is to cause the individual's behavior to match his inherent desire to act with righteousness. This requires a person to examine his actions as well as his thoughts and feelings, to ensure that they give rise to the rectification of the soul and the enhancement of its strengths, rather than the reverse. On an even higher level, Musar aims to bring a person to perfect understanding and to the complete rectification of his actions, producing greater closeness and connection to God.

Musar writings are the part of the literature of Jewish thought that has developed a systematic approach to the principles of moral conduct. Musar is not only a moral theory; it sets a standard of behavior for both individuals and the congregation that goes beyond the letter of the law. Works of Musar frequently address Torah commandments such as loving God and repentance, considering them as practical commandments in all senses, and discussing all their particulars. Such works address the importance of having the correct mindset, and the spiritual significance of a person's every action.

Rabbeinu Baḥya ibn Pekuda

Rabbeinu Baḥya ibn Pekuda (1050–1120) lived in Saragossa, Spain. His book *Ḥovot HaLevavot* was the first work dedicated exclusively to Musar. It distinguishes between the spiritual duties of the heart and the duties of the limbs, namely, the practical commandments that one fulfills with his body. Rabbeinu Baḥya believed that one's spiritual obligations are limitless, because a person can always progress and enhance his spiritual strengths, directing them toward a more complete understanding of God.

The book outlines a gradual progression; the individual ascends from one spiritual level to the next, ultimately reaching the level of love of God. The book gained popularity, despite the rigorous religious demands it places

2. *Shulḥan Arukh* is the widely accepted work of *halakha* by Rabbi Yosef Karo, and consists of four sections.

on the individual, as a result of its literary style, which incorporates proverbs, parables, and folktales.

From Rabbeinu Baḥya ibn Pekuda:

One who trusts in God is he whose trust is strong that God will provide for him as He desires, and in the time and place He desires, just as He provides for the fetus in its mother's womb; for the chick inside the egg, where there is no opening through which to bring anything in from the outside; for the bird in the sky; for the fish in the water; for the ant; and for the worm, despite their weakness.

(*Ḥovot HaLevavot, Sha'ar HaBitaḥon*, Introduction)

Rabbeinu Yona Gerondi

Rabbeinu Yona (1210–1263) was born in Girona, Spain, and died in Toledo. His most influential writings on the Talmud are *He'arot Shel Talmidei Rabbeinu Yona al HaRif* on tractate *Berakhot*, and *Aliyot deRabbeinu Yona* on tractate *Bava Batra*. He is known for his masterful scholarship. His books of Musar, *Sefer HaYira* and *Sha'arei Teshuva*, were apparently written as sections of one work on Musar topics, called *Sha'arei Tzedek. Sha'arei Teshuva* deals with the fundamentals of repentance and its various levels and processes, as well as ways of achieving atonement.

Legend has it (although this lacks historical basis) that Rabbeinu Yona wrote this work as penitence for the boycott that the rabbis of Spain placed on the works of Rambam and on his followers.

From Rabbeinu Yona Gerondi:

One of the greatest benefits that God provided for his creations is that He gave them a way to ascend from the pit of their actions and escape the snare of their transgressions, thereby enabling them to hold back their souls from destruction and dispel God's anger. He cautions them to return to Him when they sin against Him, in His tremendous goodness and righteousness, for He knows their inclinations.

(*Sha'arei Teshuva* 1)

Rabbi Yehuda HeḤasid

Rabbi Yehuda HeḤasid (died 1217) was the leader of Hasidei Ashkenaz, a pietistic movement in Germany. He was born in Speyer and was the head of the yeshiva in Regensburg.

Although he did not claim authorship of any books, two well-known works are attributed to him. *Sefer Ḥasidim* is an influential book that describes supererogatory practices and behaviors both in interpersonal mitzvot and mitzvot between the individual and God. The book reveals particular sensitivity to social inequalities, perversion of justice, and intellectual pride among scholars who learn Torah without fear of Heaven.

Another work attributed to him is *Tzava'at Rabbi Yehuda HeḤasid,* Rabbi Yehuda HaḤasid's ethical will, which contains a list of around seventy precepts concerning marriage, birth, death, and dwelling places. These were accepted as binding in some Jewish communities.

Hasidei Ashkenaz placed particular significance on the liturgy, and they established exact texts of the liturgy based on mystical considerations. The hymn *Shir HaKavod,* also known as *Anim Zemirot,* which became part of the liturgy in many Ashkenazic communities, is also attributed by some to Rabbi Yehuda HeḤasid.

There are many stories told about him. For example, legend has it that when he was young he was an excellent archer, and only at the age of eighteen did he decide to devote his life to Torah.

From Rabbi Yehuda HeḤasid:

Sefer Ḥasidim was written for this reason: So that those who fear God and all those who return to their Creator with full hearts will read it. They will understand what they must do and what they must be careful of. But it was not written for the wicked; if the wicked read it, some of it will appear ridiculous to them.

(*Sefer Ḥasidim* 1)

Sefer HaYashar

Sefer HaYashar is a thirteenth-century work of Musar of unknown authorship. Some attribute it to an otherwise unknown Rabbi Zeraḥya the Greek. It deals with the topics of Creation, faith, worship, love and fear of God, the performance of good deeds, and prayer.

From *Sefer HaYashar*:

One who loves must possess wisdom, for if he does not possess wisdom, he will not recognize the qualities of his beloved. He will not recognize the other's intellect or other precious attributes, and if he does not know his attributes, then he will not know how to love him.

(*Sefer HaYashar* 3)

Rav Menaḥem HaMeiri

Meiri (1249–1315) lived in Perpignan, in the south of France. His major work is *Beit HaBeḥira* on the Talmud, which clearly reviews the views brought in the Mishna and the Talmud, and by Rashi and *Tosafot*, as well as the halakhic rulings of the Ashkenazic, Provençal, and Sephardic authorities including those of the author himself. He also wrote *Kiryat Sefer* on the *halakhot* of writing a Torah scroll, and *Magen Avot* on various halakhic topics.

He sought to reconcile the Torah with science and philosophy, and refused to take part in the boycott of the Rambam, arguing that his precious wisdom should not be lost.

Ḥibur HaTeshuva, which is concerned with repentance, includes sections on the Ten Days of Repentance, Rosh HaShana, fast days, and the *halakhot* of mourning. According to the introduction, Meiri wrote this work in response to a Christian scholar who claimed that the Jews do not engage in repentance.

From Rav Menaḥem HaMeiri:

"The testimony of the Lord is trustworthy, making the simpleton wise" (Psalms 19:8). "The testimony of the Lord is trustworthy," namely, it is proper to believe in it even without examination. But once there is trust, it is proper to delve into its wisdom, and to reach ultimate perfection through inquiry. Matters that are incomprehensible to those who oppose them will be revealed through study.

(*Beit HaBeḥira*, Introduction)

Ran – Rabbeinu Nisim Gerondi

Rabbeinu Nisim (1315–1376) was born in Barcelona, and was the spiritual leader of the Jewish community of Spain. His main works include a commentary on Rabbi Yitzḥak Alfasi's *Halakhot*, novellae on the Talmud, many responsa, and a commentary on tractate *Nedarim*. These works reveal his ability to elucidate complex ideas clearly and logically. He also wrote *Derashot HaRan*, twelve sermons that address numerous topics in Jewish thought, including ethics, prophecy, and the proper system of government. His vast knowledge of science, medicine, and philosophy is evident in this work.

Ran would rebuke the wealthy members of his community for their laxity with regard to mitzva observance. Apparently, they made a false accusation against him as a result, and he spent around six months in a Spanish prison. Ran was also a scribe, and a Torah scroll purported to have been written by him has survived until the present day.

From Rav Nisim Gerondi:

Every nation requires government. A wise man once said that even thieves agree that there must be honesty among them. The Jewish people need this just like the other nations. Additionally, they need it in order to enforce the Torah's laws.

(*Derashot HaRan* 11)

Rav Yitzḥak Abuhav

Little is known about the life of the fourteenth- and fifteenth-century scholar Rav Yitzḥak Abuhav, although he was apparently of Spanish origin. His most influential work is *Menorat HaMaor,* which combines *halakha, aggada,* and Musar taken from the rabbinic literature and the biblical commentaries. The book is divided into seven sections, called "lamps." These sections are: self-restraint, speech, mitzvot, Torah study, repentance, peace, and humility. The work emphasizes aggadic literature as a significant part of the development of good character traits and behavior. *Menorat HaMaor* is significant in that it is one of the first works of Musar intended for readers of all levels, men, women, and children, and is written in a style that is clear and accessible. For this reason, it continued to be popular in later generations as well.

From Rav Yitzḥak Abuhav:

Heaven is my witness that my only intention in writing this work was for the honor of God, and it was not for the honor of my name. For I know that there is no wisdom, knowledge, understanding, or intelligence within me, and I do not know how to express myself well.

(*Menorat HaMaor,* Introduction)

Orḥot Tzaddikim

This book was written in the fifteenth century by an unknown author. It is a compilation of adages, rebukes, and Musar taken from the writings of the Sages and others. It is based on earlier Musar works such as *Sha'arei Teshuva* by Rabbeinu Yona. The content of the book is organized in terms of opposing character traits, such as extravagance and miserliness. The writer instructs the reader to control his character traits, and advises when to apply each one. The book makes expert use of aggadic materials. It has been published in many editions and is considered one of the fundamental works of Musar due to the fact that it depicts human nature so well.

From *Orḥot Tzaddikim*:

One who has many different types of coins, both small and large, and does not know their value, does not know what he can buy with each one until he learns its value.... But the fool, who does not weigh them or consider their value...will certainly suffer considerable harm. My son, accept that this is a metaphor concerning the many traits within you, both large and small. Use your wisdom to assess each trait so that you know the value of each one, and so that you know which traits the great King has "put out of circulation." Guard yourself against them so that they will not be found within you in a way that will cause you ruin or punishment. Through this, you will achieve perfection; you will be a craftsman with your tools at the ready.

(*Orḥot Tzaddikim*, Introduction)

Early Modern Musar

Topics related to Musar are scattered throughout the Bible and the literature of the Sages, often in the form of stories with an implicit moral lesson. The Musar literature systematized and ordered these concepts and produced a complete moral worldview. Musar literature illustrates, via the Torah's commandments and stories, the positive and negative qualities of human beings, and defines proper and improper behavior. Close examination of the message of each story reveals what is proper and improper behavior.

This branch of literature became popular among all classes of the Jewish people because of its similarity to aggadic literature. It also addresses topics that are not well developed in aggadic literature but rather in mystical literature, such as the reward and punishment received for keeping or transgressing the mitzvot. This fits the biblical sense of the term *musar*, which means chastisement or punishment. These texts are today mainly learned by devotees of Musar. Some call such works "books of awe" due to the fear that they evoke in the reader.

Later Musar literature returned to the world of *halakha*, and applied Musar ideas to the day-to-day challenges of the Jew, whether in the synagogue or in the marketplace.

Rabbi Elazar Azikri

Rabbi Elazar Azikri (1533–1600) was born in Safed and is buried next to Rabbi Yitzḥak Luria (Arizal) in the old cemetery of Safed. He studied under the great halakhists and kabbalists of his generation. He wrote commentaries on several tractates of the Babylonian and Jerusalem Talmuds. His most famous work is *Sefer Ḥaredim*, which arranges the mitzvot according to the parts of the body: hands, feet, nose, ears, eyes, trachea, esophagus, and heart. He emphasizes love of God as well as of humankind, and stresses the importance of harmony and fellowship between people. He established the *Sukkat Shalom* group, whose objective was to bring its members together and rouse them to devote themselves to God. The book is called *Sefer Ḥaredim* due to the great fear [*harada*] one should feel for improper behavior. The song *Yedid Nefesh,* which was later included in the prayer book, first appeared in *Sefer Ḥaredim.*

From Rabbi Elazar Azikri:

You must be aware that the mitzvot are all one. It is impossible to have one without another. This is like a woven garment; each thread is attached to another and participates in [the garment's] existence.

(*Sefer Ḥaredim,* Introduction)

Rabbi Shmuel de Uçeda

Rabbi Shmuel de Uçeda (1545–1604) was born in Safed. He established a yeshiva where Talmud and *halakha* were studied alongside Kabbala. His book *Midrash Shmuel* is a collection of commentaries on tractate *Avot,* along with his own explanations of various topics in the tractate. He also wrote commentaries on the books of Ruth and Lamentations. He was a student of the Arizal, and he signed the letter recognizing Rabbi Ḥayyim Vital as the Arizal's successor.

From Rabbi Shmuel de Uçeda:

Why is it the custom in all places to study tractate *Avot* between Passover and *Shavuot,* one chapter each Shabbat? Because at that time, the days become warmer. Physical desires are stirred up, and the evil inclination begins to rule over us. This tractate is full of words of rebuke. It encourages a person to pursue his good traits. This way, the good inclination overcomes the evil inclination. Therefore, it was decreed that tractate *Avot* should be studied at this time.

(*Midrash Shmuel,* Introduction)

Rabbi Eliyahu de Vidas

Rabbi Eliyahu de Vidas (sixteenth century) was born in Safed and studied with Rabbi Moshe Cordovero. He apparently served as the chief rabbi of Hebron, which is where he died. His book *Reshit Ḥokhma* is a collection of passages and stories from the Talmud, Midrash, and *Zohar.* The aim of the book is to instruct the individual on how to serve God. It is divided into five sections: fear, love, repentance, holiness, and humility. The book was published during the writer's lifetime and has been printed in several editions.

A number of abridged versions have also been written, demonstrating the work's popularity.

From Rabbi Eliyahu de Vidas:

The essence of Torah for its own sake is learning Torah in order to fulfill it. . .that the wisdom of the Torah should impart understanding of fear of Heaven to the individual.... One's wisdom will endure through this, as this wisdom was obtained only in the service of advancing fear of Heaven, which is the fulfillment of the Torah.

(*Reshit Ḥokhma,* Introduction)

Shelah – Rabbi Yeshaya HaLevi Horowitz

Rabbi Yeshaya HaLevi Horowitz (1558–1630) was born in Prague and served as the rabbi of Frankfurt, Poznan, and Krakow. He moved to Jerusalem at an advanced age. His major work, *Shenei Luḥot HaBerit* (abbreviated to *Shelah*), contains customs, Kabbala, *halakha*, Musar, sermons, biblical commentary, talmudic commentary, and an encyclopedia of talmudic terms. It is unique in its incorporation of such varied subjects in one work.

He had a significant influence on the hasidic movement. He also compiled a prayer book, called *Siddur Sha'ar HaShamayim*, and composed prayers to be recited on particular days. He suffered persecution at the hands of the Ottoman authorities in Jerusalem, and was even imprisoned for a short time. Subsequently, he was forced to flee to Safed. Later, he moved to Tiberias, where he died.

From Rabbi Yeshaya HaLevi Horowitz:

This was the wisdom of Adam the first man; he gave a name to each thing so that it would be known by that name.... Every creation in the lower realm has a source in the upper realm. If this were not so, how could the elements of this world connect [to the upper worlds], if their foundations have no source above? If creatures have no source above, how would the abundance and providence of the Master of everything spread over them? This was his wonderful insight; he perceived the source of each thing and named it in accordance with its true essence.

(*Shenei Luḥot HaBerit, Toledot Adam, Bayit Aḥaron* 14)

Rabbi Moshe Ḥayyim Luzzatto (Ramḥal)

Rabbi Moshe Ḥayyim Luzzatto (1707–1747) was born in Padua, Italy. He moved to Mantua and later to Frankfurt, Amsterdam, and ultimately Akko. He is buried in Tiberias. He was a prolific writer. His best-known works of Kabbala are: *138 Pitḥei Ḥokhma,* which discusses the foundations of

Kabbala; *Da'at Tevunot,* written as a discussion between the mind and soul; and *Ḥoker UMekubal,* a proof of the truth of Kabbala.

His most famous works are *Mesilat Yesharim,* a book of Musar that teaches the reader how to progress from one level to the next in one's service of God and ultimately attain divine revelation; and *Derekh Hashem,* which is about the foundations of faith. He also wrote books of logic, rhetoric, and grammar: *Leshon Limudim* and *Sefer HaHigayon,* as well as plays written in the Italian dramatic style: *Migdal Oz* and *LaYesharim Tehila.*

Some rabbis of his generation suspected him of heresy and Sabbateanism. He was excommunicated and made to take an oath that he would not study or teach Kabbala, and his works were even confiscated. He earned his living as a diamond cutter. He was eventually suspected of violating his oath, and he was compelled to immigrate to the Land of Israel. He settled in Akko, where he died in a plague.

From Ramḥal:

The foundation of piety, and the root of pure complete service of God, is that one clarifies and ascertains his obligation in this world and determines where his gaze and purpose need to be directed in all his life's endeavors.

(*Mesilat Yesharim* 1)

Rabbi Eliyahu HaKohen

Rabbi Eliyahu HaKohen (1659–1729), who was born and lived in Izmir, Turkey, was a rabbinic judge and kabbalist. His most famous work is *Shevet Musar,* which discusses asceticism in this world, and reward and punishment in the World to Come. He was wealthy, and he strongly believed that the wealthy are obligated to care for the poor, rebuking the wealthy members of his congregation about this. His book was known to inspire fear and awe as a result of the castigations and punishments described in it. It is told that Rabbi Simḥa Bunim of Peshisḥa said that he once encountered someone who insulted and accused him, but Rabbi Simḥa Bunim then kissed him. When asked who it was, he explained that he was referring to the book *Shevet Musar.*

From Rabbi Eliyahu HaKohen:

One must take to heart the fact that the Holy One, blessed be He, made him wealthy in order to make him a guardian of the poor.... One must place before his eyes the fact that by providing the poor with what he has, he can profit, by acquiring his place in the World to Come.

(*Shevet Musar*, Introduction)

Musar in the Sephardic World

Ḥida – Rabbi Ḥayyim Yosef David Azulai

Rabbi Ḥayyim Yosef David Azulai (1727–1806) was born in Hebron and traveled to Africa, Asia, and Europe to raise money for the poor and those learning Torah in the Land of Israel. He settled in Livorno, Italy, and died there, and in 1960 his remains were brought to the Mount of Olives for burial.

He was a prolific writer and wrote more than one hundred books, on a wide range of Torah subjects. His most significant halakhic works are a book of responsa called *Ḥayyim Sha'al* and *Birkei Yosef* on *Shulḥan Arukh*. He also wrote a historical work, *Shem HaGedolim*, which contains rabbinic biographies as well as a bibliography of rabbinic literature. In writing it, he became an expert at identifying manuscripts. He also wrote books of exegesis, Musar, Kabbala, biblical commentary, and novellae on the Talmud.

He recounts his journeys collecting charity as an emissary of the Jewish community in his autobiography, *Ma'agal Tov*. There he describes his encounters with kings and other prominent individuals, and his visits to famous sites such as Versailles, the British library in London, and the Amsterdam Zoo.

From Rabbi Ḥayyim Yosef David Azulai:

One who cheats everyone and steals from everyone is considered by the masses to be a sharp trader and is praised for knowing how to profit. His theft becomes permitted as it is called a profit.... One who fears God will open his eyes and mind to the fact that for a tiny trace of theft, one requires reincarnation in order to repay that which he stole.

(*Lev David* 19)

Rabbi Eliezer Papo

Rabbi Eliezer Papo (1786–1827) was born in Sarajevo, Bosnia, and served as the head of the Jewish community of Silistra, on the border of Romania and Bulgaria. His book *Peleh Yo'etz* is concerned with subjects of Musar and faith. It is arranged alphabetically, advising the reader with regard to every area of life in a clear and accessible style. Rabbi Papo was also a kabbalist, and was known for his fasting and adoption of other ascetic practices.

He was greatly revered by his community as a miracle worker, and there are many legends about him. For example, it is told that he accepted upon himself death at the hand of Heaven in order to stop a plague in his city. Each day, he would pray, "May it be Your will, Lord our God and God of our ancestors, that You have mercy on every man and woman, both small and great, of Your people Israel." He would consult his wife on Musar matters.

From Rabbi Eliezer Papo:

I beg all who are knowledgeable in matters of faith to read my work and teach my words in public, in synagogues and study halls. Perhaps God will reconsider with regard to me and bestow merit upon me because my words bear fruit, and through this my soul will rejoice in God.

(*Peleh Yo'etz*, Introduction)

Rabbi Ḥayyim Palagi

Rabbi Ḥayyim Palagi (1788–1869) was born in Izmir, Turkey, and was appointed the *Ḥakham Bashi* (chief rabbi) of Izmir. A prolific writer, he wrote around eighty books, on topics of Musar, Bible, *halakha*, and Kabbala. The title of each work contains his name, Ḥayyim. His book *Tokheḥat Ḥayyim* contains Musar insights derived from the Torah.

He worked tirelessly for the good of the community and enacted decrees benefiting the poor. For example, he ruled that the communal tax on kosher meat be distributed to the indigent. He also established compulsory education for children until they knew how to read and were proficient at using the prayer book. He endeavored to build a medical center for the Jewish community of Izmir with help from Baron Edmond James de Rothschild and Sir Moses Montefiore, and assisted in saving the Jews of Damascus during the "Damascus affair" blood libel.

He was popular with the Ottoman authorities and was buried in a state funeral attended by representatives of the army and government, and even by foreign diplomats.

From Rabbi Ḥayyim Palagi:

This is the character of [my wife,] the beauty of my home, who is blessed among women: Whenever there is any rejoicing or celebration in our home that involves making a meal for the poor, she does not give food to any of the invited guests until she has arranged the tables for the poor. After this, she prepares the tables of food for the invited guests.

(*Tzedaka LeḤayyim*, p. 55)

The Lithuanian Musar Movement

The Musar movement, founded by Rabbi Yisrael Salanter, proposes a way of serving God that emphasizes the shaping of a person's character. It is a practical approach that spiritually prepares the individual to serve God.

Over time, the movement split into different schools of thought that emphasized particular foci: stringency and self-discipline (Kelm), the greatness and honor of humankind (Slabodka), emotional experience and spiritual refinement (Mir), and avoiding self-deception (Novardok). The goal of all of these approaches is to be motivated by the fear of Heaven. They all emphasize caution with regard to the evil inclination, which tries to lead people astray. They teach that one must seek to understand his own character thoroughly and learn how to guide it. In practice, a follower of the Musar movement would periodically listen to Musar discourses to rouse his soul so that he would not sink into routine and neglect his moral obligations.

The Musar movement captured the hearts of many Lithuanian Jews because it constituted a clear stance against the Enlightenment, and because, like the discipline of psychology, which developed at the same time, it examines the mind of the individual with a critical and sensitive eye.

Rabbi Yisrael Salanter

Rabbi Yisrael Salanter (1810–1883) established the Musar movement. Born in Zagare, Lithuania, he disseminated his ideas in Lithuanian cities such as Vilna and Kaunas, as well as in western Europe. Later in life he served as the rabbi of Konigsberg, Prussia, which is where he died. While he did not write any books, his students collected some of his letters and summarized some of his sermons in the book *Or Yisrael.* He spread his approach by establishing Musar study groups as well as small study halls where Musar was learned. Likewise, he spoke publicly about the importance of Musar. Later, he published the journal *Tevuna*. The essence of his approach is that the internalization of Musar ideals strengthens one's service of God. In addition, one must work to subdue the evil inclination. It is important to know that there are times when the evil inclination obscures a person's understanding. Therefore, one should be aware of his own nature, including his strengths and weaknesses. One must not deny or repress dark urges; rather, one must confront them with the belief that he can overcome them.

From Rabbi Yisrael Salanter:

In order to achieve fear [of God], one must study the books of Musar with enthusiasm, with a true heart, a sorrowful voice, and with lips aflame. The ideas must be expanded upon with clear imagery, because the imagination is invaluable to Musar. It awakens the soul with regard to the feelings of the limbs. It can draw imagery from matters that are known concerning the suffering of the body and soul. We see the power of the imagination with regard to the power of musical instruments and song, which transport the soul to joy or to sorrow.

(*Or Yisrael, Sha'arei Or*, p. 17, 3)

The Alter of Kelm – Rabbi Simḥa Zissel Ziv

Rabbi Simḥa Zissel Ziv (1827–1898) was one of the founders of the Musar movement. He was born in Kelm, Lithuania, and traveled to towns in Lithuania, Germany, and Russia to spread his teachings. He died in Kelm.

He established a yeshiva called *Talmud Torah*, and after it closed, he gathered his foremost students and formed a group called *Devek Tov*, whose members dedicated themselves to the study of Musar and to one another. His book *Ḥokhma UMusar* is a collection of letters written to the members of the group.

The Alter of Kelm advocated self-discipline, order, and meticulousness with regard to every detail of life. He strictly oversaw the course of study that was undertaken in the yeshiva. He taught his students never to act without prior thought, and to always behave with integrity.

From Rabbi Simḥa Zissel Ziv:

Socrates, the philosopher, said that there are some who believe that one must know the answer to every question they are asked, for if they do not, they are not wise. [Socrates continues,] "But I do not say so; rather, all my wisdom is in knowing that I know nothing".... This is why the Sages of the Talmud were called, "students of Sages [*talmidei hakhamim*, they were like students, who]".... All their lives are still studying.

(*Ḥokhma UMusar, Igeret Kevod Talmidei Ḥakhamim*)

Biographies

Rabbi Yosef Yehuda Leib Bloch

Rabbi Yosef Yehuda Leib Bloch (1860–1929) was born in Lithuania and was the rabbi of the city of Telz, as well as the head of the Telz yeshiva. Rabbi Bloch established numerous educational institutions in Telz, including a preparatory school for the yeshiva, a training college for teachers, a rabbinical college, and a girls' secondary school.

The classes he taught in the yeshiva are compiled in the work *Shiurei Da'at*, in which he presents his outlook on numerous topics of Jewish thought, e.g., miracles and the laws of nature, prayer, and others. This work earned him a reputation as the philosopher of the Musar movement. He dealt with strong opposition to the study of Musar from some of the yeshiva heads and students.

From Rabbi Yosef Yehuda Leib Bloch:

The stature of a great person is great. He begins here, below, and he continues to rise until he reaches the higher, loftier realms. But the stature of a lowly person is lowly. He begins here and ends here, and even his head does not reach above his lowly world.

(*Shiurei Da'at, Shiur Koma*)

Rabbi Elḥanan Wasserman

Rabbi Elḥanan Wasserman (1874–1941) was born in Lithuania, was a close disciple of the Ḥafetz Ḥayyim, and was head of the Ohel Torah Yeshiva in Baranowicze. Some of his novellae on the Talmud were published in the book *Kovetz Shiurim*, and are still studied today. He was one of the leaders of *Agudat Yisrael* and opposed the Zionist movement because of the outspoken secularism of many of its leaders. When the Germans invaded Lithuania he was offered a chance to escape but chose to remain and continue to teach his students about the sanctification of God's name. He was murdered in the Kovno Ghetto together with his students.

From Rabbi Elḥanan Wasserman:

After liberalism waned, people turned to democracy, socialism, communism, and the numerous other "isms" that have inundated our generation. Major sacrifices [*korbanot shel damim*], in both senses of this word [*damim* means both blood and money], were made to these objects of idol worship, i.e., both money and lives were sacrificed. But they all disappointed; none of these ideologies fulfilled the hopes that people hung on them.

(*Ikveta deMeshiḥa*, p. 18)

Rabbi Yeruḥam Levovitz

Rabbi Yeruḥam Levovitz (1876–1936) was born in Lyuban, Belarus, and served as the *mashgiah*, the spiritual guide, of the Radin Yeshiva and the Mir Yeshiva. He was responsible for establishing the Musar approach of the Mir Yeshiva. His sermons were compiled in the books *Da'at Torah* and *Da'at Ḥokhma UMusar*. He emphasized the uniqueness of each individual, and was known for his sensitivity toward every one of his students, even during the times when there were several hundred young men learning in the yeshiva. He exhorted people to free themselves from the shackles of society, which conceal the individual's personality and unique virtues. He would chastise the yeshiva students for their behavior in order to help each one fulfill his personal potential.

From Rabbi Yeruḥam Levovitz:

A farmer who heals a sick person places cold water upon his head. But a doctor heals in a different manner. When one's head hurts, he gives him drops for his heart. Because the doctor understands where the illness is coming from, this is what he heals. It is astounding how our holy Sages understood spiritual illness, and the prescriptions [i.e., spiritual advice] they gave to combat it.

(*Ma'amarei HaMashgiaḥ* 35, p. 72)

Rabbi Eliyahu Eliezer Dessler

Rabbi Eliyahu Eliezer Dessler (1892–1953), a descendant of Rabbi Yisrael Salanter, was born in Homel, Belarus. He served as a rabbi in Gateshead, England, and later moved to the Land of Israel, where he served as the *mashgiah* of the Ponevezh Yeshiva in Bnei Brak. His writings were collected in the work *Mikhtav MeEliyahu,* which deals with various topics in Jewish thought such as free will, the place of God in this world, and gratitude. His thinking was influenced by Hasidism and Kabbala.

From Rabbi Eliyahu Eliezer Dessler:

Every individual has free will at the point where his understanding of truth meets the apparent truth, which stems from falsehood. However, most of a person's actions occur in a place where truth and falsehood do not come into contact with one another. For there are many things on the side of truth that an individual has been educated to do, and it would never enter his mind to do the opposite. Likewise, there are many things that one does on the side of evil and falsehood, and he does not perceive that it is not fitting to do them.

(*Mikhtav MeEliyahu* 1, p. 113)

Rabbi Shlomo Wolbe

Rabbi Shlomo Wolbe (1914–2005) was born in Berlin, studied at the Mir Yeshiva, taught in Stockholm, Sweden, and helped the Jews of Stockholm to establish educational institutions after the Holocaust. He moved to the Land of Israel and was appointed as the *mashgiah* of the Be'er Yaakov Yeshiva. Subsequently, he settled in Jerusalem.

His book *Alei Shur* deals with the guidance and education of yeshiva students, and also discusses Torah study and mitzva observance. The book was published anonymously and is written in an unusual style, perhaps related to the fact that the author became religious at a young age. It emphasizes individual growth. Later in life, Rabbi Wolbe did not hold an official position, but gave talks in numerous places and was the address for questions on educational matters.

From Rabbi Shlomo Wolbe:

He is like an entire world; this is the one-of-a-kind nature of the human being. There was never another like him, and there will never be another like him until the end of days. [Every individual must know:] I, with my unique combination of strengths, the child of these particular parents, born at that time and in that place, certainly have a special task and a special portion of the Torah. All of creation is waiting for me to fix that which I must fix. For I cannot exchange tasks with any other person in the world.

(*Alei Shur* 1, p. 168)

Hasidism

Hasidism is a way of serving God that was founded by the Ba'al Shem Tov. It is a social movement that combines theory and practice.

Theory: Hasidism weaves earlier ideas together into a comprehensive philosophy. It deals with the classic dilemmas of Jewish thought, including the relationship between humankind and the Creator, the struggle between good and evil, divine providence, and the purpose of Torah and mitzvot. In this respect as well as others, hasidic literature resembles Musar writings. They both address what behaviors are proper and improper for a Jew, the individual's emotional connection to God, and the shaping of a person's character. And like kabbalistic teachings, Hasidism inquires into God's role in the world and the influence of Torah and mitzvot on the world and on an individual's soul. The innovation of Hasidism was that it bases all these complex ideas upon a simple and essential belief, namely, that God is everywhere, that He is constantly renewing the act of creation, and that one can serve Him in the physical world.

Practice: Hasidism emphasizes connection to God via every single action in this world, including religious acts, such as prayer and Torah study, and the thoughts, speech, and actions of daily life. Hasidism suggests practical ways in which to do this, such as through music and dancing, which bring a person joy; telling stories of saintly people, which teach us to believe with more complete faith; and focusing upon knowing God in all the ways that a human being can.

Hasidism as a movement: Groups of hasidim are organized around saintly leaders called rebbes, who are able to inspire the hearts and deeds of their followers, each follower in accordance with his particular character. Hasidism emphasizes the connection between the hasid and his rebbe. Likewise, it highlights the importance of concern and love for others.

The Ba'al Shem Tov and His Students

The Ba'al Shem Tov brought about a return to the most basic tenets of Judaism: faith in God, love of God, love of one's fellow Jews, and fear of Heaven. In doing so, he revolutionized the Jewish world. Many people, whether educated or ignorant, poor or rich, distinguished or simple, were drawn to his approach. His most outstanding students grew particularly close to him and formed the group with whom he would pray, speak about what it means to serve God, produce original Torah ideas, and travel throughout Europe helping Jews with both physical and spiritual matters. After his death, the members of this group disseminated the traditions that they had learned from him, some orally and some in writing. As a result, hasidic ideas spread throughout eastern Europe and the movement grew and was a powerful influence on subsequent generations.

Rabbi Yisrael, the Ba'al Shem Tov

The Ba'al Shem Tov (1698–1760) established the movement of Hasidism. He was born in Wallachia, Romania, and was orphaned at a young age. He lived in the towns of Tovste, Brody, and Kuty, and would seclude himself in the Carpathian Mountains. He earned his living as a ritual slaughterer, schoolteacher, caretaker of a synagogue, and mystical folk healer (this is the meaning of *baal shem*). The Ba'al Shem Tov became one of the community leaders of Medzhybizh, Ukraine, which is where he died, on the festival of *Shavuot*.

He did not leave behind any writings except for letters he wrote to his students. In one of his letters, he told his brother-in-law that his own soul had ascended to the hall of the messiah. The Ba'al Shem Tov asked the messiah when he will arrive in this world, and he replied, "when your ideas are revealed and become known...and your wellsprings flow outward." The Ba'al Shem Tov gained fame due to both his ideas and his character. His ideas constitute the foundation of Hasidism: God can be found in the physical reality of this world, and every single person is capable of serving Him, anytime and anywhere.

The Ba'al Shem Tov was revered by both Torah scholars and ordinary people because of his prayers and teachings, as well as the wonders he performed. His reputation spread rapidly throughout the Jewish world. He would travel to Jewish towns to inspire and reignite the people's connection to Torah and mitzvot. He would preach love of other people, wholehearted fulfillment of the mitzvot, and love and fear of God. The book *Shivḥei HaBesht* (*Besht* is an acronym for Ba'al Shem Tov) describes his life, deeds, and character. The books *Ba'al Shem Tov Al HaTorah*, *Keter Shem Tov*, and *Tzava'at HaRivash* contain his Torah discourses, which were recorded by his students.

From the Ba'al Shem Tov:

It is a great kindness from God that a person remains alive after prayer. According to the laws of nature, he should die, because he loses his strength, as he expends so much energy in prayer due to his mystical intentions.

(*Tzava'at HaRivash*)

Rabbi Dov Ber of Mezeritch

Rabbi Dov Ber (1710–1772), the *Maggid* of Mezeritch, was born in Lokachi, Poland, and studied with Rabbi Yaakov Yehoshua Falk, the author of *Penei Yehoshua*. He served as a *maggid*, one who gives sermons and admonishes the community, in several towns. Before meeting the Ba'al Shem Tov he had already studied both the revealed and mystical aspects of the Torah extensively, but the Ba'al Shem Tov made him see that his learning lacked soul; the Ba'al Shem Tov breathed new life into his Torah.

After the death of the Ba'al Shem Tov, Rabbi Dov Ber lived in the town of Mezeritch and became the unofficial leader of the hasidic movement. His mobility was limited due to a medical problem with his legs, so he could not travel and his students had to come to him. There are numerous historical accounts of encounters people had with the *Maggid*. His discourses appear in the books *Or Torah* and *Maggid Devarav LeYaakov*, as well as in the works of his students. He died in Mezeritch.

During his lifetime, a powerful movement of opponents to Hasidism and the changes that it stood for arose. These opponents of Hasidism came to be known as *mitnaggedim*, meaning "those who object." Rabbi Dov Ber worked assiduously to refute their objections.

From Rabbi Dov Ber of Mezeritch:

For God, the past and the future are equal, because He is beyond time. Before the Jewish people existed, every saintly person was revealed before Him, together with all their deeds and Torah discourses. As soon as the idea of Israel arose before Him, it was more delightful to Him than all the saintly people and their deeds.

(*Or Torah, Toledot* 31)

Biographies

Rabbi Yaakov Yosef of Polnoye

Rabbi Yaakov Yosef of Polnoye (1710–1782) was born in Sharhorod, Ukraine, and served as a rabbinical judge in Rascov and Polnoye, in Poland. His writings are *Toledot Yaakov Yosef*, on the Torah, and *Ben Porat Yosef*, a collection of sermons. As one of the closest disciples of the Ba'al Shem Tov, he expounds the Torah of his teacher in these works. He deals extensively with the role of the saintly individual, who elevates his surroundings, bringing about connection to God.

Before meeting the Ba'al Shem Tov, Rabbi Yaakov Yosef of Polnoye was mainly engaged in studying *halakha* and Kabbala, and would fast often, living the life of an ascetic. After he met the Ba'al Shem Tov, he learned to appreciate the simple Jew's connection to the mitzvot; to value humility and fear of Heaven over wisdom, which leads to pride; and to prefer the joy derived from the mitzvot over afflictions and fasting. The *mitnaggedim* banned his books, even burning them publicly and writing letters condemning him. The works of the Ba'al HaToledot, as Rabbi Yaakov Yosef of Polnoye was known, reflect the essence of early hasidic thought.

From Rabbi Yaakov Yosef of Polnoye:

A person is created from matter and form, and these are opposites. Matter is limited by the physical, the outer shell, whereas form desires that which is spiritual. Human beings were created in order to make form out of matter, merging them into one entity. Just as this is the purpose of the individual, the same is true with regard to the entire Jewish people.

(*Toledot Yaakov Yosef*, Introduction)

Rabbi Pinḥas of Koritz

Rabbi Pinḥas of Koritz (1726–1792) was born in Shklow, Belarus, to a distinguished family of rabbis. He lived in the towns of Koritz, Ostroh, and Shepetivka, which is where he died. He was one of the older students of the Ba'al Shem Tov, and was a good friend of Rabbi Yaakov Yosef of Polnoye and Rabbi Yeḥiel Mikhel of Zloczow.

Although his descendants owned a printing house in Slavita, they did not publish his works, because they had received a tradition that they should not do so. Notes from some of his Torah insights were compiled in the book *Midrash Pinḥas*, and his halakhic analyses were published in *Givat Pinḥas*. He also studied Hebrew grammar and philosophy, and was known for his sharp intelligence.

From Rabbi Pinḥas of Koritz:

There are some people whose thoughts and movements are very quick and who do not have a settled mind.... They burn whatever they are thinking, and therefore their thoughts are not realized.

(*Midrash Pinḥas*, p. 6)

The Students of the *Maggid* of Mezeritch

Rabbi Dov Ber of Mezeritch gathered together a group of talented students who possessed exceptional leadership qualities, and he instructed them to spread hasidic teachings everywhere. He told them to divide up the different geographical regions between them, matching the character of each place with the appropriate teacher. Some of the students served as the rabbis of towns, others became rebbes who established hasidic courts, and some traveled throughout eastern Europe giving public sermons to inspire the people. This changed the face of Judaism in eastern Europe, from Lithuania in the north to Romania in the south, and from Germany in the west to the Land of Israel in the east. The influence of Hasidism increased, and within a short time it became immensely popular.

Rabbi Elimelekh of Lizhensk

Rabbi Elimelekh of Lizhensk (1717–1787) was born in Tykocin, Poland. He studied both Talmud and Kabbala. Together with his brother, Rabbi Zusha of Hanipol, he wandered throughout Europe in self-imposed "exile" for many years, becoming students of Rabbi Dov Ber, the *Maggid* of Mezeritch. Subsequently, Rabbi Elimelekh established a hasidic court in the town of Lizhensk, which is where he died. Rabbi Elimelekh of Lizhensk was a role model for many subsequent generations of hasidim and saintly people.

His book *Noam Elimelekh* consists of lessons on the weekly *parasha* and the festivals, based on his weekly Shabbat sermons, which were written down by his son. The book was published after Rabbi Elimelekh's death. It discusses the nature of a saintly individual: his personality and how he should worship God, as well as his public image and role as a community leader. The book is considered one of the fundamental works of Hasidism, and in many communities there was a custom to study it each Shabbat.

From Rabbi Elimelekh of Lizhensk:

His words to other people should be gentle. If they praise him he must promptly denounce himself, saying, "Why are they praising me? I am nothing. If only they knew how contemptible and foolish I am, with all of my evil deeds. How will I hold my head up before the Creator, who knows and sees my deeds at every moment? Nevertheless, He has mercy on me in all matters."

(*Noam Elimelekh, Hanhagot HaAdam*)

Rabbi Shmelke of Nikolsburg

Rabbi Shmelke of Nikolsburg (1726–1778) was born in Chortkiv, Galicia, and served as the head of the yeshiva and the head of the rabbinic court in Sieniawa. He became the rabbi of Nikolsburg, Moravia, now in the Czech Republic, which is where he died. His works of Hasidism are *Divrei Shmuel* and *Imrei Shmuel*, and his works on the revealed aspects of the Torah are *Nezir Hashem* and *Semikhat Moshe* on *Shulḥan Arukh, Even HaEzer*.

His brother was Rabbi Pinḥas HaLevi Horowitz, the author of the book *Hafla'a* on tractate *Ketubot*, and the rabbi of Frankfurt. Initially, the brothers studied with the Vilna Gaon, who was opposed to Hasidism, but they subsequently became students of Rabbi Dov Ber, the *Maggid* of Mezeritch. Rabbi Shmelke and his brother became the foremost advocates for the hasidic movement among Torah scholars and the educated. Due to his halakhic expertise and eloquence, he inspired many Torah scholars and other distinguished individuals to embrace Hasidism.

From Rabbi Shmelke of Nikolsburg:

Everything that a person rectifies brings about the building of the Jerusalem that is in heaven, one stone at a time. Therefore, we say [the blessing], "who builds Jerusalem," because every day, it is slowly being built.

(*Divrei Shmuel, Behukotai*, p. 132)

Rabbi Menaḥem Naḥum of Chernobyl

Rabbi Menaḥem Naḥum of Chernobyl (1730–1797) was born in Norynsk, Ukraine. He would wander from town to town giving sermons. Later, he established a hasidic court in the city of Chernobyl, which is where he died.

His book *Me'or Einayim* consists of sermons on the weekly *parasha* and festivals. At the end of the book there is a short composition called *Yismaḥ Lev*, which consists of hasidic novellae on the Talmud. It is said that Rabbi Menaḥem Naḥum sought to include in the book only sermons that he had not remembered giving, and to remove the rest, because forgotten ideas reflect words that were said with divine inspiration.

Rabbi Menaḥem Naḥum was known to be an excellent scholar and preacher. One of his well-known ideas is that within each Jew there is a spark from the soul of the messiah. In his position as rebbe, he would dress in fine clothing, collect money for charity, and hold a Shabbat *tisch* (literally "table"), a gathering of hasidim around their rebbe, with singing and Torah discourses. His descendants, the subsequent leaders of the Chernobyl hasidic dynasty, continued in the same way.

From Rabbi Menaḥem Naḥum of Chernobyl:

It is certainly impossible to learn Torah all the time; one must also discuss worldly matters. "The righteous will walk in them" (Hosea 14:10), namely, in the ways of the Lord; even when they speak of worldly matters, saintly people are connected to God, and their words are truly words of Torah, for they elevate souls just as when they are engaged in Torah. For there are some souls that can be elevated higher through such talk than through Torah study, as they are not able to connect to Torah or to be elevated by Torah, but only through talk of worldly matters.

(*Me'or Einayim, Vayeshev*)

Rabbi Zusha of Hanipol

Rabbi Zusha of Hanipol (1730–1800) was born in Tykocin and was the rebbe of Hanipol. He wandered throughout Europe in self-imposed "exile" together with his brother, Rabbi Elimelekh of Lizhensk; they would never sleep in any one place for more than one night. His Torah discourses were collected in the books *Menorat Zahav* and *Botzina Kadisha*.

He was a paragon of righteousness, humility, and fear of Heaven. He was not arrogant, saw the good in everything, and did not take notice of the evil in the world. He would confess his sins, such as they were, publicly, inspiring repentance in his listeners. It is told that he would pray with such fervor that it actually caused him to change physically. Although he behaved as a simple Jew, his friends and students recognized the greatness of his purity, simplicity, and fear of Heaven, and they would request his letters of approbation for their published works.

From Rabbi Zusha of Hanipol:

When one makes a blessing...the body of an angel, without life, is created. But when one answers, "Amen," which constitutes the intention and the life force of the blessing, the soul of the angel, which is its essence, is created.... If one has full intention when making a blessing, this is considered like answering, "Amen," and the soul of the angel is created by means of this as well.

(*Botzina Kadisha* 31)

Rabbi Menaḥem Mendel of Vitebsk

Rabbi Menaḥem Mendel of Vitebsk (1730–1788) was born in Vitebsk, Belarus, and spread hasidic ideas in Belarus and Lithuania. He moved to Safed and then Tiberias, where he died. He was recognized from a young age for his brilliance. His father brought him to the Ba'al Shem Tov when he was nine, and he eventually became one of the devoted students of Rabbi Dov Ber, the *Maggid* of Mezeritch.

He is the author of *Peri HaAretz*, which contains sermons on the weekly *parasha* and the festivals. The book also contains letters that he wrote to his students concerning the importance of strengthening Jewish settlement in the Land of Israel, as well as his last will to his students.

He was a close friend of Rabbi Shneur Zalman of Liadi, and the two of them endeavored to meet with the Vilna Gaon in order to ease the concerns of the *mitnaggedim*, and to convince the Vilna Gaon to remove the ban that he had instituted against the hasidim. Their attempts were unsuccessful, and they did not meet with him.

Due to the persecution of hasidim and the attempts to excommunicate them, Rabbi Menaḥem Mendel decided to move to the Land of Israel with a group of his students. There, he suffered persecution at the hands of the Ottoman authorities. He spent all of his money supporting the Jewish community, becoming destitute himself. He established the hasidic community in the Land of Israel and cultivated its ties with the Sephardic community. His son married the daughter of Rabbi Avraham Abulafia of Tiberias.

From Rabbi Menaḥem Mendel of Vitebsk:

And so all the simple spiritual entities adjust themselves to the shape of the vessel in which they are manifest, as can be understood from the analogy of water that adjusts to the shape of its vessel, whether it is round or square. And so even the most simple spiritual entity, when it descends into a person, it changes into that which is a person.

(*Peri HaAretz, Shelah*)

Rabbi Yisrael of Kozhnitz

Rabbi Yisrael of Kozhnitz (1736–1814) was born in Opatow, Poland. He served as the *maggid*, preacher, in Kozhnitz, Poland, giving sermons and admonishing the community there, where he died. He wrote books on a wide range of Torah subjects: Bible, Talmud, Kabbala, and Jewish thought, and the title of each work contains his name, Yisrael. He encouraged the printing of the works of Maharal and emphasized the close link between Maharal's ideas and those of Hasidism. He even wrote a book, *Geulat Yisrael*, explaining the thought of Maharal.

Although he experienced illness and suffering, he always projected optimism and enthusiasm. He was the head of a hasidic study hall for many years, and attracted many students. During Napoleon's conquest of Russia he supported a Napoleonic victory because he believed that it would be good for the Jews of eastern Europe and would hasten the arrival of the messiah. He died shortly after Napoleon's defeat.

From Rabbi Yisrael of Kozhnitz:

Everything that the Holy One, blessed be He, created was for the sake of His honor, namely, for those who do His will.... All creatures are elevated through a human being's elevation, and all foods are elevated through being eaten by people who perform God's will. They rise from the level of animal, vegetable, or mineral, to the level of one who speaks: a human being. This occurs when a person who eats something uses the energy derived from it in order to serve God.

(*Avodat Yisrael, Aharei Mot*)

Rabbi Aharon of Karlin

Rabbi Aharon of Karlin (1736–1772) was the founder of Karlin Hasidism. He was born in Jonava, Lithuania, and spread the teachings of Hasidism in Karlin, Belarus, which is where he died. He was one of the preeminent students of Rabbi Dov Ber, the *Maggid* of Mezeritch. He did not write any books, but his ideas can be found in the works of his grandson, the second Rabbi Aharon of Karlin, who is known as the *Beit Aharon*.

While praying, Rabbi Aharon of Karlin would cry out and move from one side of the room to the other. Karlin hasidim maintain this tradition, praying fervently and loudly. In the writings of the *mitnaggedim*, this custom was viewed as offensive and lacking the proper respect for the Creator. Some opponents of Hasidism referred to all hasidim as "Karliners."

Rabbi Aharon possessed musical talent, and he wrote the words and tune to the well-known Shabbat hymn, *Yah Ekhsof*.

From Rabbi Aharon of Karlin:

Sadness is not a sin, but it confounds the heart more than all the sins in the world.

(*Beit Aharon*)

Rabbi Shlomo of Karlin

Rabbi Shlomo of Karlin (1738–1792) was born in Tulchyn, Ukraine, and was a student of Rabbi Dov Ber, the *Maggid* of Mezeritch, and of Rabbi Aharon of Karlin. His Torah novellae were collected in the book *Shema Shlomo*. He spread hasidic ideas in Lithuania and was known as a miracle worker. After the death of Rabbi Aharon of Karlin, he became the leader of Karlin Hasidism, consolidating its philosophy and building up its influence. Subsequently, he passed on the mantle of leadership to Rabbi Aharon's son, Rabbi Asher of Stolin. During a struggle between Russia and Poland, Cossacks carried out a pogrom in the city of Ludmir. Rabbi Shlomo was in the synagogue, in the midst of prayer, and did not notice the ensuing panic. A Cossack shot him through the window, and he lay on his deathbed for five days before passing away.

From Rabbi Shlomo of Karlin:

The greatest act of the evil inclination is to make a person forget that he is of royal lineage.

(*Shema Shlomo*)

Rabbi Zev Wolf of Zhitomir

Rabbi Zev Wolf of Zhitomir (died 1798) was probably born in Ukraine. He was a student of Rabbi Dov Ber, the *Maggid* of Mezeritch. He spread the ideas of Hasidism in Zhitomir, Ukraine, and died in nearby Ivyanetz. Rabbi Zev Wolf was a wine merchant and served as a *maggid*, traveling and preaching in synagogues on matters of Musar and Hasidism. His book *Or HaMeir* contains sermons on the weekly *parasha*, which were written down by his student, Rabbi Elazar. The book describes the study hall of the *Maggid* and quotes him, developing and expanding upon his thoughts. A major theme addressed in the book is the insignificance of life in the physical world, including all its pain and suffering. One can achieve an understanding of this through connecting to God. *Or HaMeir* is considered one of the fundamental works of Hasidism.

From Rabbi Zev Wolf of Zhitomir:

There are no words or sounds in the world through which an intelligent person cannot hear words of Torah and Musar, deriving from them allusions to wisdom just as well-known scholars would. With my own eyes, I have seen how wise scholars find allusions to wisdom in every word, even in the conversations that take place between two people.

(*Or HaMeir, Vayera*)

Rabbi Levi Yitzḥak of Berditchev

Rabbi Levi Yitzḥak of Berditchev (1740–1809) was born in Husakiv and served as the rabbi of Zelechow, Pinsk, and Berditchev, Ukraine, where he died. His book *Kedushat Levi* contains sermons on the weekly *parasha* and the festivals. He was known as "the defender of Israel," because he would speak in praise of every Jew, even those whose actions were on the surface sinful. He was passionate and energetic, and was described as being "like a blazing fire" in all that he did.

His family was strongly opposed to Hasidism, and when he joined the hasidic movement, his city ostracized him and he was removed from his rabbinical position. Later, he became the rabbi of Berditchev, which was more accepting of Hasidism. Rabbi Levi Yitzḥak would lead the prayer services in the synagogue. Some of the prayers he wrote are still recited today.

His surname, Derbaremdiker, means "the merciful One" in Yiddish. It is told that he received this name when a government official came to register him and asked for his surname; Rabbi Levi Yitzḥak was in the midst of his prayers, and was heard to be saying this term.

From Rabbi Levi Yitzḥak of Berditchev:

When one fathoms the greatness of the Creator, his heart is awakened, his soul yearns, and his passion burns like fire with true love, desiring to be close to God always, so that he will not be separated, or distanced, or disconnected from Him, but will always be connected to Him, seeing His greatness, loftiness, and glory. This love means that one will always be with the Creator; namely, he will not separate himself from Him even for one moment.

(*Kedushat Levi, Likutim*)

Rabbi Barukh of Medzhybizh

Rabbi Barukh of Medzhybizh (1757–1811) was born in Medzhybizh to Odel, the daughter of the Ba'al Shem Tov. He served as the rebbe of Tulchyn and Medzhybizh, where he died. His Torah discourses were collected in the book *Botzina deNehora*. He studied with Rabbi Dov Ber, the *Maggid* of Mezeritch, and with Rabbi Pinḥas of Koritz, and he disagreed with the views of Rabbi Shneur Zalman of Liadi and Rabbi Naḥman of Breslov, who was his nephew. He believed himself to be faithful to the Hasidism taught by his grandfather.

He was known to be intelligent and sharp-witted. He would speak forcefully, no matter whom he was talking to, and would criticize the saintly people of his generation. Nevertheless, his words are peppered with irony and self-deprecation. The legendary prankster Hershele of Ostropol was one of his followers, and would attempt to cheer him up, as Rabbi Barukh was known to suffer from melancholy. Like the rebbes of Ruzhin, Poland, he would display his wealth, and he even required his hasidim to contribute their own money to maintain his court. Additionally, he required them to give charity toward the settlement of the Land of Israel.

From Rabbi Barukh of Medzhybizh:

It is amusing that some people, when they eat a piece of fruit and a concern arises that there might be a worm in the fruit, immediately dispose of it so that they do not violate the prohibition against eating worms. Yet when such an individual becomes angry at another, he immediately sets upon that person with all manner of attacks against both his body and soul, essentially "devouring" him. This is the meaning of King David's words, "But I am a worm and not a man" (Psalms 22:7): You are careful not to swallow worms, yet you treat me like a worm; therefore, I will be saved from your mouth.

(*Botzina deNehora*)

Chabad Hasidism

Chabad Hasidism was established by Rabbi Shneur Zalman of Liadi in the third generation of the hasidic movement. The word "Chabad" is an acronym for *hokhma*, *bina*, and *da'at*, which are the intellectual powers of humankind: wisdom, understanding, and knowledge. Chabad Hasidism sees the intellect as the means through which an individual can effect change in his soul. If, for example, one wants to instill love of God in his heart, he must learn about God's greatness, eternity, and constant providence over all of creation. As a result of this learning, he will begin to experience love of God.

Chabad Hasidism developed the notion of *hitbonenut*, i.e., deep contemplation or meditation. Through *hitbonenut*, one internalizes ideas that he has learned and understood, and as a result, these ideas are able to influence his spiritual experience. Without *hitbonenut*, such concepts can remain theoretical and disconnected from real life. According to Chabad Hasidism, the assimilation of an idea and the connection to it is the most significant stage of the learning process.

The ideas of Chabad span hundreds of books. All are based on the *Tanya*, which was written by Rabbi Shneur Zalman. He, as well as his successors, then expanded on and deepened the ideas of Chabad, which now touch upon every aspect of Torah and Jewish life.

The Alter Rebbe – Rabbi Shneur Zalman of Liadi

Rabbi Shneur Zalman of Liadi (1745–1812) was the founder of Chabad Hasidism. He was born in Liozna, Belarus, was active in Belarus, and died in Liadi, Ukraine. He was part of the third generation of the hasidic movement. He wrote the *Tanya*, the first work that systematically presented the ideas of Hasidism. He was one of the prominent students of Rabbi Dov Ber, the *Maggid* of Mezeritch. Rabbi Shneur Zalman's associates called him "the Litvak," because he came from the scholarly region of Lithuania and Belarus.

He was considered a genius and extremely knowledgeable in all Torah subjects, and the *Maggid* charged him with writing a new version of the *Shulḥan Arukh*, which is known as *Shulḥan Arukh HaRav*. Rabbi Shneur Zalman's Torah discourses are found in a number of works, chiefly the *Tanya*, *Torah Or*, and *Likutei Torah*. According to the *Tanya*, not every individual can reach the level of a saintly person, but everyone has the potential to be a *beinoni*, his term for one who has full control over his actions, speech, and thoughts, although the evil inclination is still present within him, enticing him toward wrongdoing. Not long after the *Tanya* was printed, Rabbi

Biographies

Shneur Zalman's opponents accused him of treason against the czarist government, and he was imprisoned for almost two months. After his release he increased his dissemination of hasidic ideas.

From Rabbi Shneur Zalman of Liadi:

The brain rules over the heart by nature. This is how the human being is created from birth; every individual can, with his will, which is part of his brain, restrain himself and subdue the drive of lust in his heart so that it will not fulfill his desires through action, speech, or thought.

(*Tanya, Likutei Amarim* 12)

Rabbi Dovber Schneuri

Rabbi Dovber Schneuri (1773–1827), known as the Mitteler (middle) Rebbe, was the son of Rabbi Shneur Zalman of Liadi. He was born in Liozna, served as the rebbe of Lubavitch, Russia, and died in Nizhyn, Ukraine.

He wrote many hasidic works, including *Bi'urei HaZohar*, a hasidic commentary on the Zohar; *Torat Ḥayyim* on the Torah; *Ateret Rosh* on Rosh HaShana and Yom Kippur; *Sha'ar HaEmuna* on Passover; and *Shaarei Ora* on Hanukkah and Purim. His Torah discourses are based on the ideas of his father, and he explains and expands upon them at length. It may be said that Rabbi Dovber developed hasidic thought into a distinct field of study. He also wrote a tract called *Kuntres HaHitpaalut*, which describes how to reflect on hasidic concepts. It emphasizes the importance of *hitbonenut* as an essential method of serving God. *Hitbonenut* is when a person studies and focuses his thoughts on one matter until he has a spiritual experience in connection with that matter. The essential element of *hitbonenut* is the combination of intellectual study and inner passion.

Rabbi Dovber assigned his followers different books for different types of hasidim: Abstract analyses for the intellectuals and rousing sermons for more emotional individuals. Nevertheless, he required seriousness and depth of all his followers.

He worked to establish Jewish farming communities in Russia and to support the Jewish settlement in Hebron. He worked with the authorities on various matters. On one occasion he was suspected of planning a revolution and was imprisoned.

From Rabbi Dovber Schneuri:

It is clear that the masses become enthused due to an illusory experience in their souls and hearts during prayer, which is manifested in the external cry of their hearts of flesh....

Although this, too, is called connection to God, or inspiration, it is false connection.... It is the opposite of divine enthusiasm.

(*Kuntres HaHitpa'alut*, p. 3)

Tzemaḥ Tzedek – Rabbi Menaḥem Mendel Schneersohn

The Tzemaḥ Tzedek (1789–1866) was born in Liozna, Belarus. He was the grandson of Rabbi Shneur Zalman of Liadi and the son-in-law of Rabbi Dovber Schneuri. He served as the rebbe in Lubavitch, which is where he died. He wrote many works of *halakha* and Hasidism. His main halakhic work was the book of responsa *Tzemaḥ Tzedek*, which contains novellae on the Talmud, as well as halakhic rulings. His works of Hasidism include *Derekh Mitzvotekha* on the mitzvot; *Or HaTorah* on the Torah; and *Sefer HaḤakira*, a work of philosophy about Hasidism.

In his youth, he made his living as a carpenter and by making wax seals for letters, and later by making sacks. Only after many attempts to persuade him did he agree to be appointed as rebbe. He had contact with many great rabbis, and he organized gatherings and conventions to address contemporary issues. In particular, he resisted the attempts of the Russian authorities to make changes to the curricula of Jewish educational institutions. He was punished for this with house arrest.

He encouraged Jews to farm the land, and he worked to support the cantonists, Jewish youths who were kidnapped and forced to join the Russian army and who consequently became disconnected from Judaism. Eventually, the Tzemaḥ Tzedek was awarded the title "honored citizen for posterity" by the Russian government for his life's work. He would write down his Torah novellae and ideas on Hasidism every day, and it is told that these writings amounted to tens of thousands of pages, but most of them were lost in a great fire that broke out in Lubavitch.

From Rabbi Menaḥem Mendel Schneersohn:

All Jewish souls together constitute one complete entity, the soul of Adam the first man, which is their general, all-embracing identity. Although the soul contains 248 individual elements, they are interrelated, each containing the others. This is just like the human body; although it is divided into separate organs, e.g., the head, legs, arms, and fingernails, each one incorporates all the others. Within the arm, there is something of the leg's life force, due to the interconnecting veins. The same is true for all the other organs as well.

(*Derekh Mitzvotekha, Mitzvat Ahavat Yisrael*)

Rabbi Shmuel Schneersohn

Rabbi Shmuel Schneersohn (1834–1882) was the youngest son of the Tzemaḥ Tzedek. He was born in Lubavitch, served as the rebbe there, and died there. His hasidic discourses on the Torah, festivals, and various other subjects are collected in the series *Torat Shmuel*. His writings are concise, deep, and clear, and they can be grasped by all readers. He would divide up his long discourses into series so that his followers could study one topic over a period of time.

He suffered from poor health and engaged in exercise and woodwork on the advice of his doctors. He worked to support the Jews of Russia, and to this end he traveled all over Europe, learning many languages. He also acquired knowledge of the sciences. He fought to prevent the Russian pogroms that began in 1881, but was unable to do so.

From Rabbi Shmuel Schneersohn:

The world believes: When you cannot go under an obstacle, you must go over it. But I believe that from the outset, one must go over it. One should act with strength and not be deterred by anything; rather, one must do what needs to be done. When we begin in this way, the Holy One, blessed be He, assists us.

(*Likutei Diburim* 5, p. 1270)

Rabbi Shalom Dovber Schneersohn

Rabbi Shalom Dovber Schneersohn (1860–1920) was the son of Rabbi Shmuel Schneersohn. He was born in Lubavitch and served as the rebbe there, and died in Rostov, Russia. His writings consist in the main of discourses he gave over the years, as well as pamphlets on specific topics. Many of his discourses, such as *Yom Tov Shel Rosh HaShana 5666* and *BeSha'a Shehikdimu 5672*, are intended for the advanced scholar of Hasidism, but he also wrote discourses and tracts addressing the wider hasidic community: *Kuntres HaAvoda*, *Kuntres HaTefilla*, and *Kuntres Etz HaḤayyim*. In his discourses, he shaped theoretical hasidic thought into a complete, orderly, and comprehensive framework.

He established the Tomkhei Temimim Yeshiva in Lubavitch and the Torat Emet Yeshiva in Hebron (which later moved to Jerusalem). He instilled in the yeshiva students seriousness, depth, self-discipline, and self-sacrifice for the sake of Torah and mitzvot. Although this was not the practice in other yeshivas, he instituted set times in his yeshiva for studying Hasidism, reviewing hasidic discourses, and engaging in *farbrengens* (gatherings of

Chabad hasidim that may include the teaching of hasidic ideas, the telling of stories, and the singing of songs, as well as eating refreshments).

He worked hard for the sake of Russian Jewry, struggling both against Jews who sought to encourage secularization and against the Russian government, whose laws were designed to restrict religious education. He worked to help the Jewish soldiers who were conscripted into the army during the Russo-Japanese War. During the blood libel trial of Menaḥem Mendel Beilis, he came to the defense of the accused.

From Rabbi Shalom Dovber Schneersohn:

The excuse of uncontrollable passion is not a real one, for natural passion comes from the natural, animal soul, and this is why we were given the godly soul, in order to overcome the natural soul. This is why a person is created: To increase the power of the godly soul and to restrain the power of the natural soul. Were it not for this task of restraining the natural soul, the person would not have been created at all.

(*Kuntres UMa'ayan* 13:1)

Rabbi Yosef Yitzḥak Schneersohn

Rabbi Yosef Yitzḥak Schneersohn (1880–1950), Rabbi Shalom Dovber's only son, was born in Lubavitch, served as the rebbe in Rostov and Leningrad, was exiled to Riga, Latvia; Otwock, Poland; and Warsaw, and finally arrived in New York, which is where he died. He left behind collections of discourses explaining the ideas of Hasidism, talks on various topics, and records and stories that vividly and beautifully describe life in the court of Chabad. He instituted the daily study of portions of Torah, Psalms, and *Tanya*, according to a yearly cycle.

He strongly opposed the Communist Party's prohibition against living an actively religious life. He ensured the continuity of Jewish life in the Soviet Union by building *mikvaot* (ritual baths) and religious schools, printing religious books, and distributing ritual items. He required that his hasidim be prepared to sacrifice themselves for the sake of Jewish continuity.

He was saved from death twice: The first time, he was arrested by the Communist secret police and sentenced to death. His sentence was commuted due to immense pressure placed on the authorities. Eventually he was released but was compelled to leave Russia. The second time his life was saved was when he was rescued from Nazi-occupied Warsaw and managed to escape to New York.

Rabbi Yosef Yitzḥak led campaigns to strengthen Orthodox Judaism in communities throughout the United States, and opened a study hall and international center of Chabad Hasidism at 770 Eastern Parkway, in Brooklyn, which is known as "770." He founded many other Chabad institutions and supported the establishment of the Kfar Chabad village in the Land of Israel.

From Rabbi Yosef Yitzḥak Schneersohn:

We will not be saved with sighing alone. A sigh is merely the key that opens the heart and eyes so that one does not sit idle, but rather sets up endeavors and activity. Each individual must do what he can to strengthen Torah, spreading Torah and mitzva observance widely. One individual does this through writing, another through speaking, and another through his wealth.

(*HaYom Yom,* 23 Tevet)

The Lubavitcher Rebbe – Rabbi Menaḥem Mendel Schneerson

Rabbi Menaḥem Mendel Schneerson (1902–1994), son-in-law of Rabbi Yosef Yitzḥak, was born in Mykolaiv, Ukraine, studied Torah with his father, and studied mathematics and engineering at universities in Berlin and Paris. He escaped the Nazis and came to the United States. He served as rebbe for over forty years in New York, where he died. His Torah discourses encompass all fields of Torah, and are published in the form of talks, articles, and letters.

His fundamental message, which was also taught by his father-in-law, Yosef Yitzḥak, concerns the preparation of the world for the arrival of the messiah and the redemption. He believed that the messianic era was near, and that it was therefore essential to spread the ideas of the Ba'al Shem Tov and to prepare the people. He sent out emissaries to communities throughout the Jewish world and instructed them to increase Torah study, mitzva observance, and awareness of the redemption in these communities. He instituted mitzva campaigns to increase the observance of mitzvot, and in particular the mitzvot of *tefillin* (phylacteries), Torah study, family purity, Jewish education, loving one's fellow Jews, affixing a *mezuza* scroll to one's doorpost, giving charity, keeping the dietary *halakhot*, lighting Shabbat candles, and possessing Jewish books in the home. Additionally, he instituted the daily study of a portion of Rambam's *Mishneh Torah* according to a set cycle, giving every Jew the opportunity to study "the entire Torah." He was

fluent in many languages and devoted much time to advising politicians and leaders, both Jewish and non-Jewish, about contemporary issues.

From Rabbi Menaḥem Mendel Schneerson:

In our time especially, there are many infants and children who, for one reason or another, have "fallen from their cradle." They have been cut off from the true Jewish "cradle" (or they were never in it in the first place), and they are crying...because of the distress of their soul, which is truly a part of God above; it is hungry and thirsty for the word of God and for His Torah and mitzvot. But there is no one to care for them and fulfill their need with education about purity and holiness.... It is forbidden to ignore the cry of these Jewish children, whether they are children according to their age or children according to their knowledge of Torah and mitzvot. Every man and woman is commanded: Do not sin against the child. Stop all your other activities and care for the child. Return him to his Father, our Father, the compassionate Father. He will learn the Torah of our Father and fulfill the mitzvot, and he will thereby attain eternal life, a life that is full, complete, and good.

(*Igrot Kodesh* 22:8558)

Rabbi Hillel Paritcher

Rabbi Hillel Paritcher (1794–1864) was a kabbalist and *mashpia* (spiritual mentor and teacher of Hasidism). He was born in Khmilnyk, Ukraine, but grew up in Chemtz (in the vicinity of Minsk, Belarus), served as the rabbi of Paritch and Babruysk, and died in Kherson. His written works include *Pelaḥ HaRimon,* a hasidic commentary on the Torah and festivals, and *BeReish Hormanuta deMalka,* an essay on the *Zohar.* He was a follower of Rabbi Dovber Schneuri and the Tzemaḥ Tzedek, and even heard Rabbi Shneur Zalman of Liadi speak, although he did not meet him face-to-face. He devoted himself to spreading hasidic ideas, particularly in the remote rural areas of Ukraine. He endeavored to serve God by praying with all his heart, and he emphasized self-nullification before God like a slave before his owner.

From Rabbi Hillel Paritcher:

The Torah's powers were given to each and every Jew, who can evoke, through their words of Torah and their observance of mitzvot, the revelation of "I am who I am." This is, his nature and essence, which He imbues into a person's soul.... This is the meaning of "[God] spoke...saying...I am" (Exodus 20:1–2). He instilled these words into all Jewish souls so that through them, every Jew could say, "I am," and evoke the revelation of "I am who I am" that is in his soul.

(*Pelaḥ HaRimon, Exodus,* p. 240)

The Courts of Peshisẖa and Kotzk

As Hasidism became a popular movement, both the anxiety and the intensity that characterize a revolutionary movement in its early stages abated. In the fourth and fifth generations of the hasidic movement, the saintly leaders of the courts of Peshisẖa and Kotzk sought to restore the "edge" to Hasidism through a radical renewal of hasidic thought. They reestablished the focus on the individual hasid, his independence of thought, his aspiration to ascend in matters of holiness, and his obligation to seek out, and demand, the truth.

A group of outstanding followers gathered around these leaders. They were prepared to overturn all their prior assumptions and devote their lives to serving God. They would never accept any conceptual premise before scrutinizing and evaluating it fully. By the next generation, this approach, too, required a suitable framework in which there was a place for all the hasidim, but at the same time, where those on the highest spiritual levels could pursue their aspirations to ascend in their service of God.

Rabbi Simẖa Bunim of Peshisẖa

Rabbi Simẖa Bunim of Peshisẖa (1765–1827) was born in Wodzisław, Poland, studied Torah in Nikolsburg, now in the Czech Republic, and in Mattersdorf, Austria, and served as the rebbe in Przysucha (Peshisẖa), Poland, where he died. His Torah discourses were compiled by his students in the books *Kol Simẖa* and *Ramatayim Tzofim*. He was known to be sharp-witted and clear thinking.

He was an anomalous figure on the hasidic landscape, both with regard to his way of life and what he taught. He worked as a timber merchant for the estate of one of the richest Jewish women in Poland, Temerel Bergson, and later completed his studies to become a licensed pharmacist. He spoke several languages and would dress in modern clothing (a short coat, as opposed to the traditional hasidic long coat), and would even engage in discussions with members of the Jewish Enlightenment in Lviv, Ukraine.

His approach emphasizes intellectual openness and the pursuit of the truth without any self-deception. He valued the in-depth study of the Talmud, as well as the works of Maharal, which make kabbalistic ideas more accessible.

From Rabbi Simẖa Bunim of Peshisẖa:

All the miracles that God performed were done so that all people would know and recognize that He is the Creator of everything and that He extends His providence to all creatures in the upper and lower worlds, acting upon them in accordance with His will. He puts this faith into people's hearts, and that was the purpose of miracles. Nevertheless, such awareness was merely temporary; some time after a miracle was performed, people did not retain their understanding, but only a kind of memory.... But with regard to the Torah that God gave us, through it we grasp His godliness, His oneness, and the fact that He extends His providence to all creatures.

(*Kol Simḥa, Numbers*, p. 52)

Rabbi Menaḥem Mendel of Kotzk

Rabbi Menaḥem Mendel of Kotzk (1787–1859), known as the Kotzker Rebbe, was born in Goraj, Poland, studied in Zamosc, and later spent time with the Seer of Lublin (Rabbi Yaakov Yitzḥak HaLevi Horowitz, 1745–1815), and with Rabbi Simḥa Bunim of Peshisḥa. He established his hasidic court in Tomaszow and then in Kotzk, where he died. His Torah discourses were compiled in the books *Ohel Torah* and *Emet VeEmuna*. He did not write any works himself, but many incisive statements, some of which are quite radical, have been quoted in his name. Some of these are cited by Rabbi Shmuel Bornsztain in *Shem MiShmuel.*

Rabbi Menaḥem Mendel's behavior was extreme; despite being a hasidic leader, he secluded himself in his room for around twenty years, refusing to see anyone who came to him. Nevertheless, his closest followers remained in his court. He was known to be a fierce critic of self-deception and falsehood. He always demanded the truth, and sought to devote his life to it. His hasidim were also independent, individualistic, and demanding of the truth, each on his own level. Nevertheless, because of the dissolution of leadership in his court, some of his hasidim left and became followers of Rabbi Mordekhai Yosef of Izhbitze. After Rabbi Menaḥem Mendel's death, many of his hasidim became followers of Rabbi Yitzḥak Meir Alter of Ger. His own descendants led small courts.

From Rabbi Menaḥem Mendel of Kotzk:

"Beauty and eternity are the Eternal's."[3] Anything beautiful in the world is beautiful only for one, two, or three moments, and afterward it loses its beauty and charm. But that which is His who lives forever possesses eternal beauty.

(*Emet VeEmuna* 191)

3. A quote from the well-known hymn *HaAderet VehaEmuna* composed by Rabbi Meshulam ben Kalonymus.

Rabbi Yitzḥak Meir Alter

Rabbi Yitzḥak Meir Alter (1799–1866) was born in Magnuszew, Poland, and studied under the rebbe of Kozhnitz, Rabbi Simḥa Bunim of Peshisḥa, and Rabbi Menaḥem Mendel of Kotzk. Later, he established his court in the town of Ger (Góra Kalwaria), Poland, where he died. He was known to be sharp-witted and erudite, and wrote several books: *Ḥiddushei HaRim* (*Rim* is an acronym for Rabbi Yitzḥak Meir) on the Torah, Talmud, and *Shulḥan Arukh,* as well as a book of responsa. He earned his living as a book merchant. He was a student and close friend of Rabbi Menaḥem Mendel of Kotzk, and was the only one with whom the latter would agree to speak during his years of seclusion.

Rabbi Yitzḥak Meir was very involved in communal affairs. He represented the Jewish community before the Polish government in the face of anti-Semitic legislation, and managed charity funds in support of the Land of Israel. After the death of Rabbi Menaḥem Mendel of Kotzk, Rabbi Yitzḥak Meir led many of his hasidim, but he tempered the anarchic spirit of Kotzk, replacing it with the requirement that the individual study Torah with all his strength as the means of pursuing the truth. Ger Hasidism operates according to this principle until today.

From Rabbi Yitzḥak Meir Alter:

The main element of the performance of a mitzva is the command; this is higher than all intentions. Nadav and Avihu were people of greatness, and acted with intentions and unifications, but because God did not command them to act, they were punished. All the more so...when one performs a mitzva in order to fulfill the commandment of the Creator, even if he knows nothing, it is considered as though he has all the correct intentions.

(*Ḥidushei HaRim, Shemini,* p. 167)

Rabbi Mordekhai Yosef of Izhbitze

Rabbi Mordekhai Yosef of Izhbitze (Izbica) (1800–1854) was born in Tomaszow and was a student of Rabbi Simḥa Bunim of Peshisḥa and both a student and friend of Rabbi Menaḥem Mendel of Kotzk. He started a hasidic court in Izhbitze, where he died.

His book, *Mei HaShiloaḥ,* contains sermons on the weekly *parasha* and festivals. These were compiled and printed after his death. It is evident from the work that he was an independent thinker. One of the topics discussed in the book is the relationship between free will and divine foreknowledge. According to Rabbi Mordekhai Yosef, rather than relating to a person's actions, free will concerns the way in which one chooses to relate to life. This view influenced the thinking of Rabbi Mordekhai Yosef's student, Rabbi Tzadok HaKohen of Lublin, although many others rejected it.

Rabbi Mordekhai Yosef left Kotzk Hasidism after a disagreement with Rabbi Menaḥem Mendel concerning whether to embrace students or to push them away, and what can reasonably be demanded of them. He replaced the extremism of the Kotzk way of life with radical ideology.

From Rabbi Mordekhai Yosef of Izhbitze:

Look to God in everything, and do not act by rote. Although one may have performed the same action yesterday, nevertheless, today, a person should not rely on himself, but on God; namely, that God will illuminate His will for him once again.

(*Mei HaShiloaḥ, Vayeshev*)

Rabbi Tzadok HaKohen of Lublin

Rabbi Tzadok HaKohen (1823–1900) was born in Kreuzberg, Latvia to a non-hasidic family, and became a hasid of Rabbi Mordekhai Yosef of Izhbitze. Later, he became a rebbe in Lublin, where he died. He wrote many books across the range of Torah subjects: *Tzidkat HaTzaddik,* hasidic novellae; *Peri Tzaddik,* sermons on the Torah and festivals; *Tiferet Tzvi* on *Shulḥan Arukh, Yoreh De'a*; and *Resisei Layla* on dreams. In his books, his vast Torah knowledge is evident, as well as his depth, originality, and creativity.

He became a hasid when, in his youth, he was collecting the signatures of one hundred rabbis so that he would be halakhically permitted to divorce his wife even without her consent, though she ultimately did accept a divorce. Along the way, he met Rabbi Mordekhai Yosef, who persuaded him to become a hasid.

Rabbi Tzadok made a living from a clothing store belonging to his second wife, and became a rebbe in Lublin only toward the end of his life. Using funds from his hasidim, he established a Torah library and became an expert in identifying manuscripts. It is said that he had full command of every book in his possession.

From Rabbi Tzadok HaKohen:

The most essential part of repentance occurs when God illuminates one's eyes to see that willful sins are like good deeds; namely, one understands that every sin he performed was also in accordance with God's will.

(*Tzidkat HaTzaddik* 40)

Rabbi Avraham Bornsztain

Rabbi Avraham Bornsztain (1838–1910) was born in Bedzin, Poland, and served as the rabbi of Sochatchov (Sochaczew) and the rebbe of the local hasidim. He died in Sochatchov. His book *Eglei Tal* discusses the thirty-nine types of labor forbidden on Shabbat, and thoroughly analyzes their definitions according to the Talmud. His work *Avnei Nezer* is a book of responsa covering all areas of Torah.

Rabbi Avraham was married to the daughter of Rabbi Menaḥem Mendel of Kotzk, who provided for him financially but did not want Rabbi Avraham to adopt practices of Hasidism, so that he would dedicate all his time to Torah study. In the introduction to *Eglei Tal*, Rabbi Avraham writes that he learned from Rabbi Menaḥem Mendel how to truly learn Torah, rather than merely engage in scholastic debate.

Rabbi Avraham believed that the time had come to fulfill the mitzva of settling in the Land of Israel. To this end he sent his son and son-in-law there to redeem land, but their efforts were unsuccessful due to the Ottoman Empire's prohibition against selling land to citizens of other countries. Many of Rabbi Avraham's students became eminent rabbis and halakhic authorities in Poland.

From Rabbi Avraham Bornsztain:

The essence of the mitzva of Torah study is to be joyful, happy, and to take delight in one's learning. The words of Torah are then absorbed into one's blood. Because the individual has derived pleasure from words of Torah, he is connected to the Torah.

(*Eglei Tal*, Introduction)

Rabbi Shmuel Bornsztain

Rabbi Shmuel Bornsztain (1855–1926) was the son of Rabbi Avraham Bornsztain. He was born in Kotzk, served as rebbe and head of the yeshiva in Sochatchov, and died in Otwock. His main work was the comprehensive, multi-volume *Shem MiShmuel*, which comprises hasidic sermons on the Torah and festivals. In the work, he quotes his father and Rabbi Menaḥem Mendel of Kotzk, and consequently *Shem MiShmuel* is an invaluable historical source of their statements.

Like his father, Rabbi Shmuel encouraged immigration to the Land of Israel. Some members of his family did come to the Land of Israel, but most of his children remained in Poland and were murdered in the Holocaust.

From Rabbi Shmuel Bornsztain:

One's obstacles are not a disadvantage, God forbid; on the contrary, they are a great advantage, because when one casts his obstacles aside and disregards them, he reaches high levels of holiness.

(*Shem MiShmuel, Hayei Sarah* 5671)

Rabbi Yehuda Aryeh Leib Alter

Rabbi Yehuda Aryeh Leib Alter (1847–1905) was born in Warsaw and served as the rebbe in Ger, where he died. He wrote works under the title *Sefat Emet* on the Talmud and Bible, including hasidic sermons on the Torah. In his works, he returns to the same themes, such as the holiness of Shabbat and the holiness of the Jewish people, sharpening and varying his main ideas each year. His hasidic approach was in line with that of his grandfather, Rabbi Yitzḥak Meir Alter, emphasizing in-depth Talmud study. Many were drawn to this clear, orderly approach. Ger Hasidism grew during his time, and it was stated in jest that all the rabbis and wealthy men of Poland were hasidim of Rabbi Yehuda Aryeh Leib.

He became the rebbe at a very young age, but never desired any honor for himself. He would not sit at the head of the table, nor at a special place in the study hall. He lived in a simple apartment and wore ordinary clothes. His wife supported the family by running a store that sold tea, sugar, and cigarettes.

From Rabbi Yehuda Aryeh Leib Alter:

In accordance with how much a person yearns for completion and feels its absence, he is given abundance from Heaven.

(*Sefat Emet, Ekev* 5642)

Rabbi Avraham Mordekhai Alter

The eldest son of Rabbi Yehuda Aryeh Leib Alter, Rabbi Avraham Mordekhai Alter (1866–1948) was born in Ger and died in Jerusalem. His book, *Imrei Emet,* is a compilation of his notes on Torah, but most of his writings, as well as his immense library, were buried in Poland at the beginning of World War II and have not yet been found. He led the Ger hasidim for almost fifty years and helped to establish *Agudat Yisrael,* the ultra-Orthodox political party, as well as the *Beit Yaakov* school system for girls and the *Hamodia* newspaper.

He traveled to the Land of Israel five times in order to support Jewish settlement there. He purchased land in Jaffa and Tiberias, and encouraged his hasidim to give money toward the settlement of the land and to settle there themselves, although he did not support the secular Zionist movement. After the German invasion of Poland, his hasidim managed to smuggle him to the Land of Israel. There, he went on to lead the survivors and rebuild Ger Hasidism. He died during the War of Independence and was buried near the Mahane Yehuda market because it was impossible to access the cemetery on the Mount of Olives during the war.

From Rabbi Avraham Mordekhai Alter:

A true servant of God must constantly engage in renewal.... Even in matters of holiness and fear of Heaven, one must constantly be renewing; otherwise, the matter will become habit.... Nature is in opposition to holiness. This is why the world was called *olam*, a word derived from the term *he'elem*, concealment; for holiness is concealed there.

(*Imrei Emet,* Exodus, p. 58)

Breslov Hasidism

Breslov Hasidism is based on the ideas of Rabbi Naḥman of Breslov, which were written down by his student, Rabbi Natan. Breslov hasidim customarily seclude themselves in order to speak to God [*hitbodedut*]. They try to enhance joy and inspire excitement in one another for the worship of God, and to prevent one another from falling into despair. They aspire to have pure, complete faith in God, and they traditionally spend Rosh HaShana at the grave of Rabbi Naḥman in Uman, Ukraine.

After Rabbi Naḥman's death, Breslov Hasidism remained without a leader, as he had not appointed a successor and Rabbi Natan did not want to accept the role. Breslov hasidim continued to be faithful to the ideas of Rabbi Naḥman, even though over the years they have been attacked and treated with contempt for being "dead hasidim," hasidim without a leader. Until recently there were very few Breslov hasidim, but the Breslov movement has undergone a resurgence, becoming very popular due to the way that Rabbi Naḥman's ideas relate to the struggles of modern life.

Rabbi Naḥman of Breslov

Rabbi Naḥman of Breslov (1772–1810) was born in Medzhybizh and was the great-grandson of the Ba'al Shem Tov. He served as the rebbe of Breslov, Ukraine, and died in Uman. His student, Rabbi Natan, transcribed most of his works: *Likutei Moharan,* a book of hasidic discourses; *Sipurei Ma'asiyot,* folktales based on kabbalistic themes; *Siḥot HaRan,* Rabbi Naḥman's description of the service of God; and *Shivḥei HaRan,* a record of his journey to the Land of Israel.

His Torah statements address the tension between the opposing extremes that exist within an individual, such as wisdom and innocence, doubt and faith, aspiration and despair, and joy and sadness. Rabbi Naḥman proposes ways to diminish this existential tension: through *hitbodedut*, an intimate conversation with God just like one has with another person; through music, dancing, and clapping hands, and ensuring that one not become depressed; and through strengthening one's pure faith in God's providence. His journey to the Land of Israel and the various adventures he had along the way, such as being in Akko during Napoleon's siege of the city, and returning to Europe on an Ottoman battleship, contributed to the formation of his thinking.

Rabbi Naḥman did not have a joyful life. He was oppressed by other rebbes who opposed his ways, was forced to wander from place to place, had only a few students, and died at a young age of tuberculosis. He asked to be buried in Uman after hearing that thirty thousand Jews were martyred there and are buried in a mass grave.

From Rabbi Naḥman of Breslov:

To the world, faith is a small thing, but to me, faith is a very great thing.

(*Siḥot HaRan* 33)

Rabbi Natan of Breslov

Rabbi Natan of Breslov (1780–1844) was born in Nemyriv, Ukraine, was the foremost disciple of Rabbi Naḥman of Breslov, and died in Breslov. He was the unofficial leader of Breslov Hasidism after Rabbi Naḥman's death, although he did not accept the title of rebbe. In addition to writing down Rabbi Naḥman's ideas, he wrote a huge work, *Likutei Halakhot,* which contains hasidic discourses and comments on the *halakhot* in the *Shulḥan Arukh,* in accordance with Breslov thought. This work is unique in its integration of halakhic minutiae and the hasidic way of serving God.

Rabbi Natan established set times for the gathering of Breslov hasidim, erected a structure over Rabbi Naḥman's grave, and printed books in a printing press that he set up in his home. Rabbi Natan came from a wealthy family that opposed Hasidism. He became a student of Rabbi Naḥman at a young age, and attended him until the latter's death. His life story is reminiscent of Rabbi Naḥman's. He too was oppressed by rebbes of other hasidic groups, traveled to the Land of Israel during wartime, and endured a great deal of persecution.

From Rabbi Natan of Breslov:

One who aspires toward the truth and girds himself to go to war for the truth, always wins.

(*Etzot Yesharot*)

Other Hasidic Thinkers

After the founding and expansion of Hasidism, it became a popular movement. Many Jews in eastern Europe felt like part of the movement in some sense, whether because they observed some hasidic customs, were influenced in some way by hasidim, or visited hasidic courts to hear the ideas taught by the rebbes and to spend time among the hasidim. During this time, certain leaders and thinkers arose who continued to introduce new ideas connecting the hasidic themes to the rest of Torah, e.g., *halakha*, Kabbala, exegesis, and mysticism. In this way Hasidism has returned to its spiritual roots and consolidated its status as a genuine part of traditional Judaism.

Rabbi Ḥayyim Tyrer

Rabbi Ḥayyim Tyrer (1740–1817) was born near Buchach, Ukraine. He served as a rabbinical judge in Mogilev and Chisinau, and as the rabbi of Chernivtsi. Later in life, he moved to Safed, where he died. He wrote the book *Be'er Mayim Ḥayyim* on the weekly *parasha*, and *Sidduro Shel Shabbat* about the sanctity of Shabbat. He established synagogues and charitable institutions. He fought for the Jews of Vienna against the Austrian government, and for the Jews of Safed against the Ottoman government. He was known for his love of Shabbat. Although he was not wealthy, he was always willing to spend money on the Shabbat meals. He would remain awake for the entire Shabbat, devoting himself entirely to matters concerning the holy day.

From Rabbi Ḥayyim Tyrer:

The entirety of my intention is to honor Shabbat.... This is like an analogy that I heard, of a king who wrote to his subjects that they were to prepare a place of honor for him. His subjects could not understand what he wrote; it was like a closed book to them. Every day, they would give the king's letter to anyone who seemed like they might understand something of how to interpret it. Each of these individuals interpreted the command in his own way. The people, who worked hard so that the word of the king would be implemented and who yearned to fulfill his command, carried out all these plans, in order to fulfill all the different opinions. When the king saw this, he asked them, "Why did you exert yourselves so much?" They answered that they needed to fulfill their obligation in accordance with the opinion of every interpreter. When he saw that everything was done in order to honor him, he was pleased with them and considered it as though they had fulfilled everything that was written.

(*Sidduro Shel Shabbat* 1:9:1:14)

Rabbi Kalonymus Kalman Epstein

Rabbi Kalonymus Kalman Epstein (1751–1823) was born in Nowy Korczyn, Poland. He was a student of Rabbi Elimelekh of Lizhensk and taught in Krakow, where he died. His work *Ma'or VaShemesh,* a book of sermons on the festivals and the weekly *parasha,* contains kabbalistic insights and develops hasidic thought on various topics, and is considered a comprehensive work of hasidic doctrine. It was printed together with the text of the Torah, and consequently was widely distributed.

In Krakow, he was oppressed by *mitnaggedim,* who banned his works, and he was prevented from establishing a hasidic court there. Even at an advanced age, he was a student of the saintly men of Poland: Rabbi Yisrael of Kozhnitz; Rabbi Yaakov Yitzḥak HaLevi Horowitz, the Seer of Lublin; and Rabbi Menaḥem Mendel of Rimanov. He himself did not become a rebbe.

From Rabbi Kalonymus Kalman Epstein:

One who merely possesses a life force [*nefesh*] may not involve himself with the mystical aspects of the Torah. Once his life force has been purified by the revealed aspects of the Torah, he will receive a spirit [*ruah*] and will be able to attain the level of exegesis [*derash*]. Then, he will receive a soul [*neshama*] and will be able to attain the level of allusion [*remez*]. Subsequently, he will receive vitality [*haya*] and will be able to attain the mystical aspects of the Torah [*sod*].

(*Ma'or VaShemesh, Yitro*)

Rabbi Tzvi Elimelekh Shapira

Rabbi Tzvi Elimelekh Shapira (1783–1841) was born in Jawornik, Galicia. He was a relative of Rabbi Elimelekh of Lizhensk and a student of the Seer of Lublin. He served as the rabbi of Mukachevo and of Dinov, where he died. He wrote many books, on a range of Torah subjects, including *Derekh Pikudekha* on the mitzvot, and *Agra deKhala* on the Torah.

His most famous hasidic work is *Benei Yisaskhar,* a book of sermons on the months of the year and the festivals. It contains original, incisive kabbalistic explanations of the account of the months that is given in *Sefer Yetzira.* It also contains explanations of various *halakhot* and customs, such as playing with a bow and arrow on *Lag BaOmer,* and with a spinning top on Hanukkah. Likewise, it includes historical explanations of the battles of the Maccabees and the spreading of Kabbala as a result of the invention of the printing press, as well as an analysis of the reasons for the expulsion of the Jews from Spain. Rabbi Tzvi Elimelekh would make use of *gematriya,* the numerical values of letters, not merely to augment his claims, but as a significant element of his interpretations. He developed a complex system for calculating *gematriya*. It was said that he engaged in subjects that were related to the root of his soul: Hanukkah, because he was a descendant of the Hasmoneans; and the Jewish calendar and *gematriya*, because he was a descendent of the tribe of Issachar (see I Chronicles 12:33).

While serving as the rabbi of Mukachevo, he prohibited the force-feeding of geese before they are slaughtered. The leaders of the community quarreled with him about this matter and he was forced to leave his position.

From Rabbi Tzvi Elimelekh Shapira:

The customs of our patriarchs are Torah. On Hanukkah, the children play with a four-sided piece of wood, and carved into its sides are the letters *gimmel*, *shin*, *nun*, and *heh*, as these letters allude to the four different forces within a human being: physical [*gufani*], spiritual [*nafshi*], intellectual [*sikhli*], and the heavenly power, which contains everything [*hakol*].

(*Benei Yisaskhar,* Kislev 2:25)

Rabbi Ḥayyim Halberstam

Rabbi Ḥayyim Halberstam (1797–1876) was born in Tarnogrod, Galicia, and was a student of Rabbi Naftali of Ropshitz (1760–1827). He was the rabbi of Sanz for around fifty years, and died there. He was the founder of the Sanz hasidic dynasty.

All his works are published under the title *Divrei Ḥayyim*. He wrote on various subjects, including Talmud (a commentary on *Bava Metzia*), *halakha* (the *halakhot* of divorce and of the *mikve*, or ritual bath), and Hasidism (in a commentary on the Torah). His work of responsa is extensive and reveals his brilliance and his mastery of Talmud and *halakha*. He corresponded with all the halakhic giants of his generation. His work of responsa is unique in that it at times addresses specifically hasidic topics, such as how to position two pairs of *tefillin*, the recitation of *Kiddush* over liquor, the inheritance of the position of rebbe, and the kosher status of machine-made *matza* versus that of handmade *matza*.

He was known to give much charity, and he would pray fervently. He suffered from an ailment of the legs, and his father-in-law, Rabbi Yisrael Leipnik, said of him that "He has a crooked leg, yet his mind is straight."

From Rabbi Ḥayyim Halberstam:

If a sinner repents out of love, and he recalls that when he fell into temptation how strong was his desire for emptiness, then his desire and love for serving God may grow more and more. The result is that out of the sin that he committed, great love and desire for the worship of God have blossomed.

(*Ḥemda Genuza, Ki Tavo,* p. 25)

Rabbi Yisrael Shapira of Grodzisk

Rabbi Yisrael Shapira (1874–1942) was born in Grodzisk and was murdered at the Treblinka extermination camp. His works *Binat Yisrael* and *Emunat Yisrael* contain hasidic sermons on the festivals and the weekly *parasha*. He was a descendent of Rabbi Elimelekh of Lizhensk and of Rabbi Yisrael of Kozhnitz. He was exiled to Warsaw by the Russian army, and there, he re-established the hasidic court of Grodzisk. He was known to be musically talented.

From Rabbi Yisrael Shapira of Grodzisk:

The receiving of the Torah was two-sided. The children of Israel accepted upon themselves to observe the mitzvot of the Torah, and not to transgress, God forbid, any of the negative commandments; and the Holy One, blessed be He, accepted upon Himself to help the children of Israel to fulfill the positive commandments in the Torah.

(*Binat Yisrael, Likutim,* p. 172)

Rabbi Kalonymus Kalman Shapira

Rabbi Kalonymus Kalman Shapira (1889–1943) was born in Grodzisk, Poland, to a family of hasidic rebbes. He led his community in Piaseczno and then in the Warsaw Ghetto. He was murdered near Lublin by the Nazis.

He wrote several books on the subject of education: *Ḥovat HaTalmidim, Hakhsharat HaAvrekhim, Benei Maḥshava Tova,* and *Derekh HaMelekh.* In his books, he emphasizes the young person's responsibility for his own actions, the importance of having peers who help one another in their worship of God, and the possibility of achieving a visionary experience by quieting the mind and clearing it of thoughts, which is the way to achieve maximal concentration on one idea.

His book *Esh Kodesh* contains sermons on the Torah, and was written in the Warsaw Ghetto. These sermons were hidden in the ghetto and were discovered after the war. In them, Rabbi Kalonymus Kalman refers to the daily struggles with hunger, cold, and death, and states time and again that he has no answers to questions concerning divine providence during the Holocaust; yet he demands that his hasidim continue to believe that terrible suffering, too, comes from Heaven.

From Rabbi Kalonymus Kalman Shapira:

When one has been struck with terrible afflictions, it is difficult not to cry out at the pain.... Therefore, for people like us, especially amid bitter suffering such as this, it is impossible not to cry out and pray to God, even on Rosh HaShana and Yom Kippur, concerning our torment and pain. But our souls cry bitterly at this, too: about the fact that on these holy days we must pray, "Give us life; give us food," rather than lofty prayers for spiritual needs.

(*Esh Kodesh*, p. 125)

Rabbi Menaḥem Ekstein

Rabbi Menaḥem Ekstein (1890–1943) was born in Rzeszow, Galicia, to a family of Dzhikov hasidim. He lived in Vienna and was murdered in the Holocaust. His book *Tena'ei HaNefesh LeHasagat HaḤasidut* describes hasidic meditation techniques. The book was written in Hebrew, and according to the introduction, it was intended for the wider, educated community, and not necessarily for observant Jews. The book contains guided imagery exercises that intensify the individual's experiences and teach him how to use his spiritual strengths.

From Rabbi Menaḥem Ekstein:

In the beginning, we will explain visualization.... First, we will try to visualize the earth in our minds. We will imagine it as though we can see the entire earth from afar, with its landmasses and its oceans. Then, we will imagine all the nations, in all parts of the world, with their various languages and borders, as well as the number of people belonging to each nation.

(*Tena'ei HaNefesh LeHasagat HaḤasidut*, p. 21)

Rabbi Areleh Rabin

Rabbi Areleh Rabin was the rabbi of Lanivtsi, Ukraine. He was murdered in the Holocaust. Little is known about his life.

Rabbi Shalom Noah Berezovsky

Rabbi Shalom Noah Berezovsky (1911–2000) was born in Baranavichy, Belarus. He immigrated to Tiberias, moved to Tel Aviv, and then served as the head of Beit Avraham Yeshiva in Jerusalem for forty years. In Jerusalem, he was appointed as the rebbe of the hasidic dynasty of Slonim. His books are known as *Netivot Shalom,* and they contain discourses that he gave at his *tisch* on topics including the Torah, the festivals, Hasidism, and education. The books are written in a simple style, explaining deep ideas in a clear way such that they may be understood by all readers.

From Rabbi Shalom Noah Berezovsky:

What is one's obligation in this world? Each individual is a small world unto himself, comprising unique conditions in accordance with his particular mind and the root of his soul. This person is not like that person, and the world in which one is found constitutes his purpose and obligation.

(Netivot Shalom 1, p. 241)

Bibliography

Bibliography

A listing of many of the works mentioned in this volume, organized by genre.

Kabbala

***Zohar*:** Pritzker Edition vols. I–XII. Edited and translated by D. C. Matt. Stanford University Press.

Rav Yitzḥak Luria (Arizal): *Apples from the Orchard: Gleanings from the Mystical Teachings of Rabbi Yitzchak Luria (the Arizal) on the Weekly Torah Portion*. Translated and edited by M. Y. Wisnefsky. Malibu, CA: Thirty Seven Books, 2006.

Rav Yitzḥak Luria: *Sha'ar HaGilgulim*: *Gate of Reincarnations: An English Translation of the Arizal's Work on Reincarnation*. Translated by Pinchas Winston. Jerusalem: Thirtysix.org, 2014.

Rabbi Moshe Cordovero (Ramak): *Tomer Devora*: *The Palm Tree of Deborah*. Translated by S. Alfassa. New York: ISLC, 2009.

Rav Moshe Ḥayyim Luzzatto (Ramḥal, 1707–1747): *Mesilat Yesharim: The Path of the Just*. Translated by S. Silverstein. Jerusalem, New York: Feldheim Publishers, 1987.

Rav Moshe Ḥayyim Luzzatto: *Derekh Hashem*: *The Way of God and An Essay on Fundamentals*. Translated by A. Kaplan. Jerusalem, New York: Feldheim Publishers, 1997.

Rabbi Ḥayyim Vital: *Sha'arei Kedusha*: *Gates of Holiness*, Part IV. Brooklyn: Research Institute of Esoteric Literature, 1999.

Rabbi Ḥayyim Vital: *Ktavim Chadashim – New Writings: Brit Menuḥa – Covenant of Rest; Shaarei Kedusha – Gates of Holiness*. Translated by Hadani and Getz. Lightning Source Inc., 2007.

Rabbi Ḥayyim of Volozhin: *Nefesh HaḤayyim*: *The Soul of Life: The Complete Neffesh Ha-Chayyim*. Translated by E. L. Moskowitz. Teaneck, NJ: New Davar Publications, 2012.

Medieval Jewish Philosophy

Rabbi Yosef Albo: *Sefer HaIkkarim: Book of Principles: Sefer ha-'Ikkarim*. Translated by I. Husik. Jewish Publication Society of America, 1929.

Rav Yitzḥak Arama: *Akedat Yitzḥak: Akeydat Yitzchak: Commentary on the Torah*. Translated by E. Munk. Jerusalem: Lambda Publishers, 2001.

Rambam (Rav Moshe ben Maimon – Maimonides): *Commentary on the Mishnah, Tractate Sanhedrin*. Translated by F. Rosner. New York: Sepher-Hermon Press, 1981.

Rambam: *Commentary on Avot. Shemoneh Perakim of the Rambam: The Thirteen Principles of Faith*. Translated by E. Touger. New York: Moznaim Publishing Corp., 1994.

Rambam: *Guide of the Perplexed*. Translated by S. Pines. Chicago University Press, 1974.

Rambam: *Selected letters of Maimonides: Letter to Yemen: Discourse on Martyrdom*. Translated by A. Y. Finkel. Scranton, PA: Yeshivath Beth Moshe, 1994.

Ramban (Rav Moshe ben Naḥman – Naḥmanides): *Commentary on the Torah*. Translated by C. Chavel. Brooklyn: Shilo Publishing House, Inc., 1971–1976.

Ramban: *The Torah Commentary*. Translated by Y. Blinder. Brooklyn: Mesorah Publications, 2004–10.

Ramban: *Sha'ar HaGemul: The Gate of Reward*. Translated by C. Chavel. Brooklyn: Shilo Publishing House, Inc., 1983.

Ramban: *Writings of the Ramban*. Translated by C. Chavel. New York: Shilo Publishing House, 2009.

Rav Se'adya Gaon: *Emunot VeDe'ot*: The Book of Doctrines and Beliefs. Translated by A. Altmann. Indianapolis: Hackett, 2002.

Rav Yehuda HaLevi: *The Kuzari: In Defense of the Despised Faith*. Translated by Rabbi N. Daniel Korobkin. Feldheim Publishers, 2009.

***Sefer HaḤinnukh*:** *Selected Portions of Sefer Hachinuch*. Translated by A. Y. Finkel. Scranton, PA: Yeshivath Beth Moshe, 2011.

Maharal (Rabbi Yehuda Loew of Prague, c. 1515–1609): *Gevurot Hashem: The Book of Divine Power*. Translated by S. Mallin. New York: Ber-Aryeh International, 1979.

Maharal: *Pirkei Avot, Commentary Based on Selections from Derekh Hayyim.* Translated by T. Basser. Brooklyn: Mesorah Publications, 1997.

Maharal: *Tiferet Yisrael.* Translated by Ramon Widmonte. Jerusalem: Urim Publications, 2017.

Maharal: *Netivot Olam, Netiv HaTorah: An Appreciation of Torah Study.* Translated by E. Willner. Brooklyn: Mesorah Publications, 1994.

Rabbeinu Baḥya ibn Ḥalawa: *Kad HaKemah: Encyclopedia of Torah Thoughts.* Translated by C. Chavel. New York: Shilo Publishing House, 1980.

Rabbi Ḥayyim ben Atar, *Or HaḤayyim*: *The Light of Life: The Ohr Hachaim on the Torah.* Translated by Chaim Richman. Brooklyn: Rachav Communications, 1995.

Modern Jewish Philosophy

Rabbi Samson Raphael Hirsch: *Commentary on the Torah.* Translated by I. Levy. Brooklyn: Judaica Press, 2005.

Rabbi Samson Raphael Hirsch: *The Collected Writings I–IX.* Jerusalem, New York: Feldheim Publishers, 1984–2012.

Rabbi Samson Raphael Hirsch: *The Nineteen Letters about Judaism.* Jerusalem, New York: Feldheim Publishers, 1996.

Rabbi Yosef Dov Soloveitchik: Rabbi Joseph B. Soloveitchik. *Kol Dodi Dofek: Listen – My Beloved Knocks.* Jersey City, NJ: KTAV Publishing House, 2006.

Rabbi Yosef Dov Soloveitchik: Rabbi Joseph B. Soloveitchik. *On Repentance: The Thought and Oral Discourses of Rabbi Joseph Dov Soloveitchik.* Edited by Pinchas Peli. Lanham, MD: Rowman & Littlefield, 2004.

Halakha

Rambam (Rav Moshe ben Maimon – Maimonides): *Mishneh Torah.* Translated by E. Touger. New York: Moznaim Publishing Corp., 1989–2001. Can also be found on Sefaria website.

Rabbi Yeḥiel Michel Tukachinsky: *Gesher HaḤayyim*: Rabbi Tucazinsky. *Gesher Hachaim: The Bridge of Life.* Jerusalem: Etz Hayim, 1983.

Musar

Rabbeinu Baḥya ibn Pakuda (1050–1120): *Ḥovot HaLevavot: Duties of the Heart.* Translated by Y. Feldman. Northvale, NJ: Jason Aronson, Inc, 1996.

Rabbeinu Yona Gerondi (1210–1263): *Commentary on Pirkei Avot: Rabbeinu Yonah on Pirkei Avos.* Brooklyn: Judaica Press, 2008.

Rabbeinu Yona Gerondi: *Sha'arei Teshuva: The Gates of Repentance.* Translated by Y. Feldman. Northvale, NJ: Jason Aronson, Inc., 1999.

Rav Yehuda HaḤasid (d. 1217): *Sefer Ḥasidim*: Rabbi Yehudah HeChasid. *Sefer Chasidim: The Book of the Pious.* Translated by A. Y. Finkel. Northvale, NJ: Jason Aronson, Inc., 1997.

***Sefer HaYashar* (thirteenth century):** *The Book of the Righteous.* Translated by N. Y. Kornfeld. Scranton, PA: Divrei Emes, Yeshiva Beth Moshe, 2016.

***Orḥot Tzaddikim* (fifteenth century):** *The Ways of the Righteous.* Translated by S. Cohen. Jerusalem, New York: Phillip Feldheim, Inc., 1969.

Rabbi Yeshaya HaLevi Horowitz (Shelah, 1558–1630): *Shenei Luḥot HaBerit: Shney Luchot Habrit on the Written Torah.* Translated by E. Munk. Jerusalem: Lambda Publishers, Inc., 1992–1999.

Rav Moshe Ḥayyim Luzzatto (Ramḥal, 1707–1747): *Mesilat Yesharim: The Path of the Just.* Translated by S. Silverstein. Jerusalem, New York: Feldheim Publishers, 1987.

Rav Moshe Ḥayyim Luzzatto: *Derekh Hashem: The Way of God and An Essay on Fundamentals.* Translated by A. Kaplan. Jerusalem, New York: Feldheim Publishers, 1997.

Rabbi Eliezer Papo (1786–1827): *Peleh Yo'etz: Pele Yoetz: Profound Advice for a Successful Jewish Life.* Translated by S. Kurtz. Jerusalem: Noam Eliezer, 2011.

Rabbi Yisrael Salanter (1810–1883): *Or Yisrael: Ohr Yisrael: The Classic Writings of Rav Yisrael Salanter and His Disciple Rav Yitzchak Blazer.* Translated by Z. Miller. Southfield, MI: Targum Press, 2004.

Rabbi Elḥanan Wasserman (1874–1941): *Ikveta deMeshiḥa: The Era Preceding Mashiach.* Translated by A. Y. Finkel. Brooklyn: Mesorah Publications, 1994.

Rabbi Eliyahu Eliezer Dessler (1892–1953): *Mikhtav MeEliyahu: Strive for Truth*. Edited by A. Carmell. Jerusalem: Feldheim Publishers, 1978-1999.

Hasidism

Rabbi Levi Yitzḥak of Berditchev: *Kedushat Levi: Torah Commentary*. Translated by E. Munk. Jerusalem: Urim Publications, 2009.

Rabbi Shalom Noaḥ Berezovsky: *Gems from the Sefer Netivot Shalom*. Edited by S. B. Ginsberg. Lakewood, NJ: Israel Bookshop Publications, 2014–2018.

Rabbi Shmuel Bornsztain: *Shem MiShmuel: Selections on the Weekly Parashah and Festivals*. Edited by Zvi Belovski. Southfield, MI: Targum Press, 1998.

Rabbi Naḥman of Breslov: *Likutei Moharan* (15 vols.). Jerusalem, New York: Breslov Research Institute, 1999.

Elimelekh of Lizhensk (1717–1787): *Mipeninei Noam Elimelech: A Selection of Teachings, Stories, and Parables of Rebbe Elimelech of Lizhensk*. Edited by T. Zwecker. Southfield, MI: Targum Press, 2008.

Rabbi Kalonymus Kalman Epstein: *Ma'or VaShemesh: Letters of Light: Passages from Ma'or va-shemesh*. Translated by A. Wineman. Eugene, OR: Pickwick Publications, 2015.

Ger

Rabbi Yehuda Aryeh Leib Alter: *Sefat Emet: Days of Awe: Ideas and Insights of the Sfas Emes on the High Holydays*. Translated by Y. Stern. Brooklyn: Mesorah Publications, 2001.

Rabbi Yehuda Aryeh Leib Alter: *Sefat Emet: Insights on Chanukah and Purim Based on the Sefas Emes*. Translated by Z. Schlifstein. Jerusalem: 1987.

Rabbi Yehuda Aryeh Leib Alter: *Sefat Emet: The Language of Truth: The Torah Commentary of the Sefat Emet*. Translated by A. Green. Philadelphia: Jewish Publication Society, 1998.

Chabad

Rabbi Shmuel Bornsztain (1855-1926): *Shem MiShmuel: Selections on the Weekly Parashah and Festivals*. Edited by Zvi Belovski. Southfield, MI: Targum Press, 1998.

Shneur Zalman of Liadi: *Tanya* vols. I–V. Translated by N. Mindel. Brooklyn: Kehot Publications, 1965–1972.

Rabbi Menaḥem Mendel Schneersohn (Tzemaḥ Tzedek, 1789–1866): *Sefer HaMa'amarim Melukat: Holiday Maamarim.* Edited by David Rothschild. Tzfat: Collel Tzemach Tzedek, 2008.

Rabbi Menaḥem Mendel Schneersohn (Tzemaḥ Tzedek): *Derekh Mitzvotekha: Selections from Derech Mitzvosecha.* Translated by E. Touger. Brooklyn: 2004-2007.

Rabbi Shalom Dovber Schneersohn: *Kuntres Etz HaḤayyim: The Tree of Life – Kuntres Eitz HaChayim: A Classic Chassidic Treatise on the Mystic Core of Spiritual Vitality.* Translated by E. Touger. Brooklyn: 1998.

Rabbi Shalom Dovber Schneersohn: *Kuntres UMaayan: Overcoming Folly.* Translated by Z. I. Posner. Brooklyn: Kehot Publications, 2006.

Rabbi Yosef Yitzḥak Schneersohn and Rabbi Menaḥem Mendel Schneersohn: *Sefer HaMa'amarim* and *Sefer HaMa'amarim Melukat: Wedding Ma'amarim.* Brooklyn: Kehot Publications, 2017.

Rabbi Yosef Yitzḥak Schneersohn: *Sefer Hayom Yom: Tackling Life's Tasks.* Brooklyn: 2009.

Rabbi Yosef Yitzḥak Schneersohn: *The Principles of Education and Guidance.* Translated by Y. E. Danzinger. Brooklyn: Kehot Publications, 1995.

Rabbi Kalonymus Kalman Shapira: *Esh Kodesh: Sacred Fire: Torah from the Years of Fury 1939–1942.* Translated by Hershy J. Worch and edited by Deborah Miller. Lanham, MD: Jason Aronson, Inc., 2004.

Rabbi Kalonymus Kalman Shapira: *Ḥovat HaTalmidim: A Student's Obligation: Advice from the Rebbe of the Warsaw Ghetto.* Lanham, MD: Jason Aronson, Inc., 2004.

Rabbi Menaḥem Mendel Schneerson (1902–1994): Rabbi Menachem Mendel Schneerson. *Letters from the Rebbe.* New York, Jerusalem: Otsar Sifrei Lubavitch, Inc., 2001.

Rabbi Menaḥem Mendel Schneerson: *Torah Studies: Discourses by the Lubavitcher Rebbe.* Adapted by Jonathan Sacks. Brooklyn: Kehot Publications, 1996.

Glossary

Glossary

Adar – Month of the Jewish calendar, occurring during February/March.

afikoman – Part of the middle matza at the Passover Seder, which is set aside during *Yahatz* and eaten at *Tzafun*, after the meal.

aggada (pl. aggadot) – Rabbinic story meant to impart an educational lesson.

Al HaNisim – Lit. "for the miracles"; a paragraph added to the *Amida* and the Grace after Meals on Purim and Hanukkah, thanking God for the miracles He wrought on behalf of the Jewish people.

aliya – Subdivision of the weekly Torah portion; the honor of being called up to the Torah for the reading of such a subdivision.

Amen – A response to a blessing indicating agreement with it and belief in its content..

Amida – A prayer comprising nineteen blessings that forms the central part of the prayer service. Also known as *Shemoneh Esreh* (lit. eighteen), because its original formulation had eighteen blessings.

arava (pl. aravot) – Willow branch, one of the four species taken on *Sukkot.*

ark – Repository in the prayer hall for Torah scrolls.

Ashkenazim (adj. Ashkenazic) – Segment of the Jewish population; broadly, Jews of European descent.

aufruf – Yiddish for "calling up." In Ashkenazic custom, a groom is called up to the Torah on the Shabbat before his wedding. This is observed as a celebratory event.

Av – Month of the Jewish calendar, occurring during July/August.

bar mitzva, bat mitzva – When a Jewish child reaches maturity and becomes formally obligated in mitzva observance. For a boy this occurs at the age of thirteen, for a girl at twelve.

baraita – A tannaitic statement that does not appear in the Mishna.

Barekhu – An invitation by the prayer leader to the congregation to recite a blessing. This marks the beginning of the blessings before *Shema* and of the blessings recited when one is called up to the Torah.

bima – The table in the synagogue upon which the Torah scroll is placed for Torah reading.

Birkot HaShahar – Morning Blessings.

Blessings over the Torah – Blessings said as part of the Morning Blessings, thanking God for the Torah and requesting His assistance to cleave to it.

brit – Circumcision ritual in which the baby is given his name.

dreidel – A four-sided spinning top played with on Hanukkah.

Edot HaMizrah – A general term for Sephardic congregations or the version of liturgy they use in their prayer services.

eiruv – A solution instituted by the Sages with regard to Shabbat prohibitions against carrying between domains and against walking far out of one's town; commonly used to refer to one type of *eiruv*, *eiruv hatzerot*.

eiruv hatzerot – The symbolic joining of private domains belonging to different people, thereby allowing them to carry from one place to another on Shabbat. This is accomplished when food belonging to the different residents is placed in one location.

eiruv tavshilin – When Shabbat falls on the day after a festival day, one must set aside bread and a cooked dish for a Shabbat meal before the festival begins. This allows him to cook or to carry out other preparations for Shabbat on the festival.

eiruv tehumin – The placement of food in a particular location, which establishes that location as a person's Shabbat residence. This allows him to travel two thousand cubits, the maximum distance one may travel on Shabbat (see *tehum Shabbat*), from that new location, rather than from his home.

Elul – Month of the Jewish calendar, occurring during August/September.

etrog – Citron, one of the four species taken on *Sukkot*.

farbrengen – Gathering of Chabad hasidim that may include the teaching of hasidic ideas, the telling of stories, and the singing of songs, as well as refreshments.

Full Kaddish – An Aramaic prayer of praise of God that is recited in the synagogue service, often by mourners.

gabbai – The synagogue sexton, who oversees the services.

gebrokts – Yiddish term for matza that has come into contact with liquid. Many Jews of hasidic descent have a custom not to eat *gebrokts* on Passover.

gematriya – A system in which each Hebrew letter is given a numerical value. It often highlights connections, sometimes mystical ones, between words.

geniza – Storeroom or repository in a synagogue used for discarded, damaged, or defective sacred books, papers, and objects.

Grace after Meals – Blessings recited after eating bread. Known in Hebrew as *Birkat HaMazon* and in Yiddish as *Bentching*.

hadas – Myrtle branch, one of the four species taken on *Sukkot*.

haftara – A portion from the Prophets read after the Torah reading on Shabbat, festivals, and public fasts.

haggada (pl. *haggadot*) – The text that presents the order of the Passover Seder. It contains instructions for the different parts of the Seder, and includes the text traditionally recited as fulfillment of the mitzva to retell the story of the redemption from Egypt.

HaGomel – Blessing said by one who is saved from a dangerous situation.

hakafot sheniyot – The seven rotations taken with the Torah, accompanied by music and dancing, on the night following *Simhat Torah*. This is customary in some communities.

halaka – Ceremonial first haircut, given to boys at age three; means haircut in Arabic. The Yiddish term is *upsherin*.

halakha (pl. halakhot) – Jewish law.

halakhic hour – One-twelfth of the period of daylight, may be longer or shorter than ordinary hours.

Half Kaddish – A shortened version of the Kaddish prayer (see Full Kaddish) that is recited by the prayer leader at certain points in the synagogue prayer service.

halla (pl. hallot) – Braided bread eaten on Shabbat and festivals. The name derives from the mitzva of *halla,* which is to separate a piece of dough and give it to a priest. Nowadays, however, the dough is destroyed.

Hallel – A series of psalms of praise recited on festivals.

hametz – Leavened grain products, which are prohibited for consumption on Passover.

HaMotzi – The blessing before eating bread.

Hanukkah – Eight-day holiday in the winter commemorating the victory of the Hasmoneans over the Seleucid Empire and the rededication of the Temple. On each day candles are lit.

hanukkiya – Hanukkah menora, the eight- or nine-branched candelabrum on which Hanukkah candles are lit.

hasid – Literally, a pious person. A member of the hasidic movement founded by the Baal Shem Tov in the eighteenth century.

hasidic – Having to do with Hasidism.

Hasidism – Pietist, anti-elitist movement founded by Rabbi Yisrael Baal Shem Tov in the eighteenth century. Hasidism emphasizes the service of God in all of one's actions, especially through ecstatic prayer and celebration, and the connection to God through the intervention of a *tzaddik,* a saintly person. Within a generation, Hasidism also became an intellectual movement, applying kabbalistic thought to an individual's religious life.

hatan me'ona – The name given in Sephardic communities to the penultimate *aliya* to the Torah before concluding the Torah on *Simhat Torah.*

hatan Torah – Literally, bridegroom of the Torah. The person who receives the *aliya* for the reading of the last section of the Torah on *Simhat Torah.*

Havdala – The ceremony for concluding the Sabbath. The blessing is said over a cup of wine, and with a candle and sweet-smelling spices.

hazan – Prayer leader in the synagogue, cantor.

hevra kadisha – Burial society, responsible for both preparing the deceased for burial and the actual interment.

hitbodedut – Seclusion practiced by Breslov hasidim for personal communication with God.

hitbonenut – Deep contemplation or meditation on one matter until the person has a spiritual experience regarding that matter. *Hitbonenut* combines intellectual study and spiritual passion.

Hol HaMoed – Intermediate days of *Sukkot* and Passover. On these days certain activities are prohibited, but there is no general prohibition of performing labor.

Hoshana Rabba – The seventh day of *Sukkot*, called *Hoshana Rabba* due to the custom of circling the *bima* seven times in a procession while reciting prayers that begin with the word *hoshana*.

huppa – Literally wedding canopy; *huppa* also refers to the wedding ceremony as a whole.

Isru Hag – The day after Passover, *Shavuot*, and *Sukkot*.

Iyar – Month of the Jewish calendar, occurring during April/May.

Kabbala – The Jewish tradition of mystical theory and practice.

Kabbalat Shabbat – The prayer service said at the onset of Shabbat on Friday night, as instituted by the Sages of Safed in the sixteenth century.

kabbalists – Thinkers who make use of the traditions of Kabbala

Kaddish – Prayer praising God that is said at particular intervals during the prayer service. See Mourner's Kaddish, Half Kaddish, and Rabbis' Kaddish.

kasher – To render a pot or a utensil kosher, usually by immersing it in boiling water or by heating it directly.

kashrut – The theory and practice of ritually kosher food.

Kedusha – Literally, sanctification. In this prayer, said during the repetition of the *Amida*, Israel joins forces with the angels in sanctifying God.

keli rishon – Primary vessel (lit. "first vessel"). The vessel in which something is cooked, even after it has been removed from a heat source.

kelipa (pl. kelipot) – Literally, husk. The kabbalistic term for those elements of existence that are forces of evil that need to be removed.

ketuba – A marriage contract that guarantees the wife a certain sum of money in the event of divorce or her husband's death.

kezayit – Olive-bulk, a halakhic measure of volume that generally corresponds to the amount of food one needs to consume in order to fulfill a mitzva or be liable to punishment for a transgression. According to the most prevalent halakhic opinion, an olive-bulk is about 27 ml.

Kiddush – The blessing made over wine at the beginning of Shabbat and festival meals. The *Kiddush* said on Friday night includes a blessing consecrating Shabbat.

kiddush – Light meal at which *Kiddush* is said on Shabbat morning.

Kiddush Levana – The blessing said once a month at the appearance of the new moon. Usually said on Saturday night at the close of Shabbat.

kiddushin – The part of the wedding ceremony involving the groom giving the ring to the bride. Once *kiddushin* has been performed they are formally married.

kimha depis'ha – Aramaic for "Passover flour," also known as *ma'ot hittin* (lit. "money for wheat"). Charity given before Passover to enable the poor to buy food for the holiday.

kinnot – The liturgical poems that lament the destruction of the Temple and other tragedies, recited on *Tisha BeAv*.

Kislev – Month of the Jewish calendar, occurring during November/December.

kitniyot – Foods derived from edible seeds such as rice, beans, and lentils. These are not *hametz,* but are prohibited on Passover in the Ashkenazic tradition.

kittel – A white robe worn by many married men on Yom Kippur, Seder night and other occasions.

kohen (pl. kohanim) – A person of priestly lineage, a descendant of Aaron.

kol hane'arim – The *aliya* on *Simhat Torah* in which all the children of the community are called to the Torah. An adult recites the blessing.

Kol Nidrei – The prayer said at the onset of Yom Kippur in which the prayer leader asks to nullify all the vows made in the community that year.

Lag BaOmer – The thirty-third day of the *omer,* the eighteenth of the month of Iyar. *Lag BaOmer* is the day of the passing of Rabbi Shimon bar Yohai and also, in many customs, the end of the mourning period of the *omer*.

Various customs of *Lag BaOmer* include lighting bonfires and visiting Rabbi Shimon's grave at Meron.

lehem mishneh – Two whole loaves of bread that are used for the blessing at the beginning of a Shabbat meal.

Lekha Dodi – Liturgical poem composed by Rabbi Shlomo Alkabetz that is traditionally sung on Friday evening during *Kabbalat Shabbat.*

lulav – Palm branch, one of the four species that are taken together on *Sukkot.* Often, *lulav* is used to refer to all four species.

Ma'ariv – The evening prayer.

maftir – The additional reading at the conclusion of the Torah reading on Shabbat, festivals, and fast days. The person who receives the *maftir aliya* also reads the *haftara.*

maggid – In Eastern Europe before the Holocaust, a *maggid* was a person who gave sermons and admonished the community, e.g., the Maggid of Koznitz.

mahzor – Prayer book for festivals, Rosh HaShana, or Yom Kippur.

Marheshvan – Month of the Jewish calendar, occurring during October/November.

mashgiah – (1) *Kashrut* supervisor; (2) In many yeshivot, the person in charge of the spiritual development of the students.

matanot la'evyonim – Literally, gifts to the poor. Giving a gift to at least two poor people is one of the obligations of Purim.

matza (pl. matzot) – Unleavened bread that is eaten on Passover.

matza sheruya – See *gebrokts.*

megilla – Literally, scroll; often refers to the book of Esther.

melakha – Productive, creative activity (lit. "labor"), which is prohibited on Shabbat.

melaveh malka – Literally, "accompanying the queen." The meal customarily served on Saturday night to acknowledge the end of Shabbat.

messiah – Literally, "the anointed one." The anointed king from the house of David who will appear at the end of days and rule Israel righteously.

mezuza (pl. mezuzot) – The scroll affixed to the doorposts of a Jewish home containing the verses beginning *Shema Yisrael.*

mikva – Ritual bath. Food utensils acquired from gentiles must be immersed in a *mikva* before being used. A woman immerses herself in a *mikva* a week after her menstrual period before she resumes relations with her husband. Some men have the practice of immersing themselves in a *mikva* either every morning or every week.

Minha – The afternoon prayer service.

minyan – The quorum of ten men required for public prayer and Torah reading.

mishlo'ah manot – Gifts of food given on Purim.

mishnayot – Plural of mishna.

mishteh – Feast, one of the mitzvot on Purim.

mitnagged (pl. mitnaggedim) – Opponents of Hasidism. The original *mitnaggedim* fiercely opposed the innovations of the Baal Shem Tov and his followers. Once Hasidism became established, the *mitnaggedim* became a competing ideological movement that was centered in the great yeshivot of Eastern Europe.

mitzva (pl. mitzvot) – Literally, commandment. Traditionally there are 613 commandments in the Torah. Mitzva is often also used more loosely to refer to any religious obligation.

mohel – One who performs a ritual circumcision.

molad – The moment when the new moon becomes visible. See *Kiddush Levana.*

Morning Blessings – Blessings said upon rising in the morning celebrating the beginning of a new day.

Mourner's Kaddish – Kaddish said by mourners, usually by children for a parent, commemorating and elevating the soul of the deceased. See Kaddish.

muktze – An item that may not be handled on Shabbat or festivals. An item is *muktze* either because it serves no purpose (e.g., sticks and stones) or because its purpose involves a prohibited action on Shabbat or a festival (e.g., a pen).

Musaf – The additional prayer service said after the morning service on Shabbat and holidays.

Musar – (1) A type of Jewish literature devoted to moral development and spiritual and psychological growth; (2) A movement begun in the second half of the nineteenth century by Rabbi Yisrael Salanter that emphasized moral reflection and self-improvement, often through the study of Musar literature.

Ne'ila – The closing prayer service on Yom Kippur.

Nisan – Month of the Jewish calendar, occurring during March/April.

nisu'in – The second part of the Jewish marriage ceremony, in which blessings are recited under the wedding canopy.

nolad – An item that has just come into being. This concept is used in various *halakhot*, including those of festivals.

nusah – Version of a prayer used by a particular community.

Nusah Sefarad – Version of the prayer service used by those of hasidic heritage.

Old Yishuv – Ultra-Orthodox communities that were present in the Land of Israel prior to the various waves of Zionist immigration in the nineteenth and early twentieth centuries.

omer – An offering brought from the new crop of barley on the sixteenth of Nisan; the period from the sixteenth of Nisan until *Shavuot*.

onen – An acute mourner, one whose close relative has died but has not yet been buried. An *onen* does not perform any positive mitzvot.

panim hadashot – Literally, a new face. In order to recite the seven blessings celebrating the bride and groom during the week following the wedding, there must be *panim hadashot*, a person who was not present at the wedding.

parasha – The weekly Torah portion.

pareve – Food containing neither dairy nor meat ingredients.

pe'ot – Sideburns. Jewish men are forbidden to remove their sideburns above about half the ear. Some hasidic groups have the custom of growing their *pe'ot* long.

pesik reisha – Performing an action that will unintentionally bring about the performance of labor on Shabbat or a holiday is permitted. However, if such an unintentional result will necessarily occur, the action is called a *pesik reisha* and is prohibited. For example, it is prohibited to open a refrigerator on Shabbat if that action will necessarily cause an incandescent light bulb to be lit in the refrigerator, even if one opened the refrigerator with no intention of turning on the light.

Pesukei DeZimra – The psalms said at the beginning of the morning service.

pidyon haben – Redemption of the firstborn, performed on firstborn sons of Israelite lineage on the thirtieth day of life.

pikuah nefesh – Saving a life. Saving a life overrides all mitzvot in the Torah except for the prohibitions against murder, illicit sexual relations, and idolatry.

prozbol – Legal transfer of the responsibility for the collection of one's debts to the court. *Prozbol* is performed during the Sabbatical Year in order to avoid the cancellation of those debts.

Rabbis' Kaddish – The Kaddish prayer that is said after studying Torah. It includes a passage praying for the welfare of Torah scholars and their students.

Retzeh – (1) The third-to-last blessing of the *Amida,* in which we pray for the renewal of the Temple service; (2) The addition to Grace after Meals for Shabbat.

Rosh Hodesh – The first of the month, which is a minor holiday. Jewish months have either 29 or 30 days. When the preceding month had 30 days, *Rosh Hodesh* is celebrated on the 30th day of the preceding month and the first of the new month. When the preceding month had 29 days, *Rosh Hodesh* is celebrated only on the first of the new month.

sandak – The person at a circumcision ceremony who holds the baby during the actual circumcision. To be *sandak* is regarded as an honor, often given to one of the newborn's grandfathers.

Sanhedrin – The High Court of the Jewish people, composed of 71 members. The Sanhedrin continued to exist after the destruction of the Second Temple for about 350 years.

seder – Literally, order; one of the six sections of the Mishna.

Seder – Ceremonial Passover meal in which four cups of wine are drunk, matza and bitter herbs are eaten, and those present read the haggada.

sefer Torah – Torah scroll, in which the entire Pentateuch is written by hand, using special calligraphy.

Sefira (pl. Sefirot) – The ten different manifestations of the Divine according to Kabbala. The *Sefirot* bear structured relationships with one another, and the relationships between them serve to explain every aspect of Being.

Sefirat HaOmer – The counting of the *omer,* the mitzva to count the days and weeks beginning on the second day of Passover and concluding on the day before *Shavuot.*

segula – An object or practice that serves as a favorable omen or a talisman for receiving some benefit.

sekhakh – Sukka roofing. Sekhakh must be made from a plant that is no longer attached to the earth and is not edible or any sort of utensil (and therefore is not subject to ritual impurity).

Selihot – Prayers, mostly composed as liturgical poems, that petition God for mercy and forgiveness. *Selihot* are said on fast days, during the days before and between Rosh HaShana and Yom Kippur, and on Yom Kippur itself.

Sephardim (adj. Sephardic) – Jews who trace their traditions and liturgy back to medieval Spain and Portugal. Today, most Sephardic families trace their more recent origins to Middle Eastern countries, from Morocco in the west to Iran in the east.

seuda shelishit – The third Shabbat meal.

seudat havra'a – The meal prepared for mourners upon their return from the funeral, by their friends and neighbors.

seudat mitzva – A celebratory meal held in honor of the performance of a mitzva, including a wedding, bar mitzva, circumcision, and *siyum.*

Shabbat (pl. Shabbatot) – Saturday. Shabbat is the day of rest and the *halakha* proscribes thirty-nine specific labors on that day.

Shabbat Hatan – Literally, groom's Shabbat. On the Shabbat either immediately before or after a wedding the groom's family and friends gather to celebrate. The groom usually receives an *aliya* to the Torah.

Shaharit – The morning prayer service.

Shalom Zakhar – Traditional Ashkenazic ceremony in which family and friends gather on the Friday evening after the birth of a baby boy to sing, share words of Torah, and celebrate the birth.

Sheheḥeyanu – The blessing recited on the occasion of a new experience: when one makes a significant purchase, upon eating a fruit or vegetable that was previously out of season, the first time one performs a mitzva, and at the beginning of holidays.

Shekhina – The Divine Presence, the manifestation of God in the world. In Kabbalistic thought, the *Shekhina* is identified with the *Sefira* of *Malkhut*.

sheloshim – The thirty-day period of mourning after the death of a close relative.

Shema – The verse "Hear, Israel: the Lord is our God, the Lord is one" (Deut. 6:4). It is a mitzva to recite the *Shema* (along with other verses) every morning and evening. The *Shema* is a declaration of one's acceptance of the yoke of Heaven and is the ultimate expression of a Jew's loyalty to and faith in God. As such it has often been recited by martyrs at their deaths.

Shemini Atzeret – The eighth day of the festival of *Sukkot*, which is in many ways a separate holiday, as the mitzvot of *Sukkot* such as *lulav* and *sukka* do not apply to it.

sheva berakhot – The seven blessings recited at a wedding and at subsequent meals made for the couple in celebration of their wedding in the following week.

Shevat – Month of the Jewish calendar, occurring during January/February.

shevut – Actions on Shabbat that the Sages prohibited beyond those prohibited by Torah law.

shiva – The seven-day mourning period observed after the death of a close relative.

shofar – A hollowed-out ram's horn that is sounded on Rosh HaShana.

siddur – Jewish prayer book.

Simhat Beit HaSho'eva – The celebration of the drawing of the water, a celebration that took place in the Temple on *Sukkot* in honor of the water libation that was brought on that festival. *Simhat Beit HaSho'eva* has become a general term for a celebration held on the festival of *Sukkot*.

Simhat Torah – The last day of the festival of *Sukkot*. In Israel, *Simhat Torah* is celebrated on *Shemini Atzeret*, while in the diaspora it is celebrated on the following day. On this day the yearly cycle of Torah reading is completed and begun again.

sitra ahra – Literally, the other side. In kabbalistic thought, the *sitra ahra* is the metaphysical locus of the forces of evil.

Sivan – Month of the Jewish calendar, occurring during May/June.

siyum – A celebration marking the completion of the study of a talmudic tractate or some other significant work of Torah literature.

sukka – A covered booth (see *sekhakh*). On *Sukkot*, it is a mitzva to dwell in a *sukka* rather than in one's house.

Sukkot – The festival beginning on the fifteenth of Tishrei, in which we are commanded to dwell in *Sukkot* and to take up the four species. *Sukkot* lasts seven days, concluding on the eighth day with *Shemini Atzeret* and in the diaspora extending a ninth day with *Simhat Torah*.

Tahanun – A petitionary prayer recited on weekdays following the *Amida* in both the morning and afternoon services. It is the custom in Ashkenazic (and some Sephardic) synagogues to lean over and cover one's face with one's arm during this prayer.

tallit – A prayer shawl, a four-cornered garment with *tzitzit* that is worn by men during the morning service.

Tamuz – Month of the Jewish calendar, occurring during June/July.

tanna – A Sage of the period of the Mishna.

tefillin – Phylacteries, leather boxes containing scrolls upon which are written passages from the Torah. The boxes are attached to one's forehead and one's upper arm with leather straps. *Tefillin* are worn by Jewish men during weekday morning prayers.

tehum Shabbat – The Shabbat limit, the maximum distance one may travel on Shabbat: two thousand cubits beyond one's place of dwelling, or in a city, from the city limit.

tena'im – Literally, conditions. The contract explicating the monetary commitments of both sides in a marriage and the consequences for each side if they do not go through with the marriage. In many communites today, this is not done at all or if it is, it is merely a ritualized formality.

tereifa – An animal that has a certain type of physical defect that renders it non-kosher. The most common type of defect is a hole in the lung.

Tevet – Month of the Jewish calendar, occurring during December/January.

Three Weeks – The three-week period between the Seventeenth of Tammuz and Tisha BeAv, a period of mourning for the destruction of the two Temples.

tikkun – A set text of prayers and readings from the Bible and from rabbinic and kabbalistic works, read on evenings when it is customary to study Torah at night. These occasions include *Shavuot, Hoshana Rabba,* and the eve of the seventh day of Passover. Each day has its own *tikkun.*

tisch – Literally, table. A gathering of hasidim around their rebbe, with singing and Torah discourses.

Tisha BeAv – The ninth day of the month of Av, which is the anniversary of the destruction of both the first and second Temples. as well as of other disasters that befell the Jewish people. *Tisha BeAv* is a day of mourning and a fast day.

Tishrei – Month of the Jewish calendar, occurring during September/October.

Tu BeAv – The fifteenth of the month of Av. It is a minor holiday in commemoration of an ancient practice recorded in the Mishna (*Ta'anit* 4:8) whereby young women would dance in the vineyards in search of a bridegroom.

Tu BeShvat – The fifteenth of the month of Shevat, known as the New Year for the trees. This date has halakhic significance in terms of the calculation of the year for the purpose of tithes. Many have the custom to hold special celebrations on this day.

tza'ar ba'alei hayim – Causing unnecessary pain to animals. Not only is this forbidden, but one is also obligated to alleviate the pain of animals in one's possession.

tzadik (pl. tzadikim) – In general, a *tzadik* is a righteous person. In Hasidism, a *tzadik* is an extraordinary individual who has a special connection to God. Ordinary people can connect to God through a *tzadik*, either by becoming his hasidim, his followers, or by his acting as an intermediary for them.

tzedaka – Charity, or more generally, righteousness. *Tzedaka* is used specifically to denote monetary gifts to the poor.

tzedaka box – A small box into which people put small amounts of money for charity.

tzimtzum – Literally, contraction. The kabbalistic/theological principle that God "contracted" Himself in order to create a "space" for the universe to exist.

tzitzit – Ritual fringes that one is commanded to place at the corners of a four-cornered garment.

Wayfarer's Prayer – A prayer one recites when he travels between cities, to request divine protection.

Ya'aleh VeYavo – The prayer inserted into the *Amida* and Grace after Meals on Rosh Hodesh and festivals.

yad soledet bo – The temperature at which one's hand spontaneously recoils from an item's heat. Used for *halakhot* of Shabbat and *kashrut*.

yahrzeit – The anniversary of someone's death. On that day Kaddish is recited by his or her children.

Yedid Nefesh – A liturgical hymn composed by Rabbi Elazar Azikri in the sixteenth century. In many communities it is sung at the beginning of Friday night prayers. It is also often sung at the third meal on Shabbat.

yeshiva – A traditional institution for Torah study. The focus of the curriculum is usually the Talmud.

yetzer hara – The evil inclination, the aspect of the human personality that desires to sin. In some contexts the *yetzer hara* is conceived of as a metaphysical force.

yihud room – The room in which the bride and groom briefly seclude themselves following their wedding ceremony.

Yizkor – A prayer said in memory of the deceased. Usually said by his or her children on the last day of each festival and on Yom Kippur.

Zeved HaBat – Celebration for the birth of a girl.

zimmun – The invitation to recite Grace after Meals, added when three men (or three women) eat together.

A Concise Guide to Mahshava

Rabbi Adin Even-Israel Steinsaltz

English Edition

Executive Director, Steinsaltz Center
Rabbi Meni Even-Israel

Editor in Chief
Rabbi Jason Rappoport

Translators
Eliezer Kwass
Oritt Sinclair

Editors
Rabbi Yehoshua Duker
Rabbi Anthony Manning
Rabbi Michael Siev

Copy Editors
Caryn Meltz, Manager
Rachelle Emanuel
Dvora Rhein
Ilana Sobel
Avi Steinhart

Technical Staff
Adena Frazer
Adina Mann

Hebrew Edition

Senior Editors
Menachem Brod
Amechaye Even-Israel

Editor
Shaul Yonatan Weingort
Uriel Segal – Biographies

Research
Yehuda Hershkovitz
Avichai Gamdani

Designer
Eliyahu Misgav

Typesetters
Rina Ben-Gal
Estie Dishon